SHAKESPEARE AND SOCIAL THEORY

This book provides a bridge between Shakespeare studies and classical social theory, opening up readings of Shakespeare to a new audience outside of literary studies and the humanities. Shakespeare has long been known as a "great thinker" and this book reads his plays through the lens of an anthropologist, revealing new connections between Shakespeare's plays and the lives we now lead.

Close readings of a selection of frequently studied plays—*Hamlet, The Winter's Tale, Romeo and Juliet, A Midsummer Night's Dream, Julius Caesar*, and *King Lear*—engage with the texts in detail while connecting them with some of the biggest questions we all ask ourselves, about love, friendship, ritual, language, human interactions, and the world around us. The plays are examined through various social theories including performance theory, cognitive theory, semiotics, exchange theory, and structuralism. The book concludes with a consideration of how "the new astronomy" of his day and developments in optics changed the very idea of "perspective," and shaped Shakespeare's approach to embedding social theory in his dramatic texts.

This accessible and engaging book will appeal to those approaching Shakespeare from outside literary studies but will also be valuable to literature students approaching Shakespeare for the first time, or looking for a new angle on the plays.

Bradd Shore is Goodrich C. White Professor Emeritus of Anthropology at Emory University, USA. A psychological and cognitive anthropologist, he has authored some 65 scholarly papers and three books.

SHAKESPEARE AND SOCIAL THEORY

The Play of Great Ideas

Bradd Shore

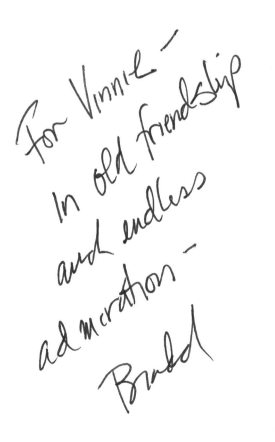

For Vinnie —
In old friendship
and endless
admiration —

Bradd

Routledge
Taylor & Francis Group

LONDON AND NEW YORK

First published 2022
by Routledge
2 Park Square, Milton Park, Abingdon, Oxon OX14 4RN

and by Routledge
605 Third Avenue, New York, NY 10158

Routledge is an imprint of the Taylor & Francis Group, an informa business

British Library Cataloguing-in-Publication Data
A catalogue record for this book is available from the British Library

Library of Congress Cataloging-in-Publication Data
Names: Shore, Bradd, 1945- author.
Title: Shakespeare and social theory : the play of great ideas / Bradd
Shore.
Description: Abingdon, Oxon ; New York, NY : Routledge, 2022. | Includes
bibliographical references and index.
Identifiers: LCCN 2021009179 | ISBN 9781032017174 (hardback) | ISBN
9781032017167 (paperback) | ISBN 9781003179771 (ebook)
Subjects: LCSH: Shakespeare, William, 1564–1616--Criticism and
interpretation. | Sociology in literature. | LCGFT: Literary criticism.
Classification: LCC PR3024 .S59 2022 | DDC 822.3/3--dc23
LC record available at https://lccn.loc.gov/2021009179

ISBN: 978-1-032-01717-4 (hbk)
ISBN: 978-1-032-01716-7 (pbk)
ISBN: 978-1-003-17977-1 (ebk)

DOI: 10.4324/9781003179771

Typeset in Bembo
by SPi Technologies India Pvt Ltd (Straive)

To the beloved memory of Frank Manley

CONTENTS

ILLUSTRATIONS

ACKNOWLEDGEMENTS

This book has been on my mind for over 50 years, since writing my honors thesis on *The Winter's Tale* as an English major at Berkeley in 1967. My mentor back then, Prof. John Anson, first introduced me to the pleasures and the thrill of close readings of the plays. His seminar bypassed the usual play-a-week reading schedule for such courses, and we were treated to a chance to spend almost a month reading and discussing each of just four plays. The deal was, however, that we would agree to read each play many times, and let the text sink in. This pace with these texts and this brilliant teacher made for a life-changing experience.

The honors tutorial on *The Winter's Tale* came on the heels of the seminar, and I confronted that text pretty much on my own. I must have read the play a dozen times. Each reading moved me deeper into the puzzling text, affording new insights and questions that earlier readings had not uncovered. To broaden my intellectual scope, I also had a chance to take Stephen Orgel's graduate course on Elizabethan literature.

At the same time as my work in Renaissance English literature, I was also studying political science from Shelden Wolen, Michael Rogin, and John Schaar, focusing my attention on classic works in political theory. Gradually, the issues we were dealing with in works by Plato, Aristotle, Machiavelli, Hobbes, Locke, and other political theorists began to find their way into my reading of Shakespeare.

The boundaries between the genres of theory and literature began to blur, and I began to think of Shakespeare as a great social theorist as well as a playwright. One day, I decided, I would bring these two worlds together. But that day would be half-a century and a long career as a cultural anthropologist away. My earliest debt is to these scholars and teachers at Berkeley, especially John Anson.

Frank Manley, to whom this book is dedicated, co-taught a course with me on Ritual in Shakespeare at Emory for over 25 years, and the fingerprints of our discussions in class and over frequent lunches are everywhere in this book.

I have been actively writing this book for almost a decade. Along the way, a lot of friends, family members, students, and colleagues have read and commented on early drafts of these chapters. For detailed comments and advice, I would like to thank Stephen Lehmann, Michael Davis, Robert Shore, Ken Shore, Stephen Orgel, Robert Paul, Stephen Greenblatt, William Dillingham, Gary Hauk, Rima Shore, Bill Chace, JoAn Chace, Don Saliers, Brooks Holifield, and Josh Zlatkus. Thanks also to Mel Konner, Leslee Nadelson, Vincent Murphy, Gretchen Schultz, Jerome Bruner, Mark Auslander, Ellen Schattschneider, Barbara Shore, Emily Shore, and my wife Linda Shore for advice and support along the way. The final version of the book has benefitted considerably from the editorial skills of my acquisitions editor from Routledge, Polly Dodson, and my helpful editorial assistants Zoe Meyer, Victoria Parrin, and Krishanu Maiti.

INTRODUCTION

Reading Shakespeare through anthropology

Between 1977 and 1981, Steve Allen, the original host of *The Tonight Show*, brought to Public Television a remarkable dramatized series called *Meeting of Minds*. In two dozen hour-long episodes, Allen hosted small gatherings of actors portraying famous historical figures in conversation with one another. With well-researched scripts and a talented cast, the series was honored with numerous awards, including a Peabody, an Emmy, and a TV Critics Circle Award. Unusual TV fare in its time, a show like *Meeting of Minds* would be almost unimaginable today.

Wherever possible, Allen allowed his characters to speak words that they had actually written. When he had to invent words for them, Allen took great pains to make sure the characters were historically accurate. A mix of quotes and credible invented dialogue was skillfully woven into a semblance of spontaneous conversation focusing on great ideas. The format was simple and compelling. Allen assembled an entertaining mismatch of celebrity guests around the table from different historical periods and different walks of life and hosted a brilliantly scripted tea party. The first chat brought together Theodore Roosevelt, Cleopatra, Thomas Aquinas, and Thomas Paine. Later conversations produced another 23 unlikely but tantalizing combinations.

Season three featured a pair of back-to-back conversations with Shakespeare. Rather than inviting other historical figures to the table to exchange ideas with William Shakespeare, Allen chose a novel format. The playwright is reunited with famous characters from his plays in a kind of *tête-á-tête* with himself. The theme is love. Allen welcomes Shakespeare and introduces him to the audience. The first of his characters to arrive is uninvited. She is "The Dark Lady" of Shakespeare's Sonnets, who introduces herself simply as Woman. Woman crashes the party defiantly, apparently viewing the gathering as a men's club with delusions of expertise on love.

DOI: 10.4324/9781003179771-1

Shakespeare is surprised and irritated to see her. Woman loses no time in letting the audience know that, in her view, Shakespeare is no genius on the subject of love.

WOMAN
Ah, there you are, sweet William.

SHAKESPEARE
Now see here. I wasn't told you were going to be here!

WOMAN
And what if you had been told? Your vanity would still have brought you here! So you're going to talk about love, are you?

SHAKESPEARE
And why not? Our Lord himself tells us it's the greatest of the virtues.

WOMAN
It's certainly the only one we repent.

SHAKESPEARE (*To Steve*)
Sir I did not agree to this and I'm not going to submit to it (*He exits.*)

(Allen 1989: 123)

By the time the invited characters (Hamlet, Othello, Romeo, and Iago) arrive, Shakespeare is nowhere to be found. For the rest of the hour, we are left with the characters performing eloquent speeches from their plays on the theme of love. Allen acknowledges this unexpected turn of events at the end of the episode: "Well, this has been a strange experience, I'm sure you'll agree," he remarks.

> I've been looking for Shakespeare himself, but without success. In any event, we've seen, this evening, some of the ways in which Shakespeare dealt with the theme of love. It's been interesting enough, needless to say, but I had hoped to put questions to the playwright himself directly rather than just make inferences about his views on love from the fates and the lines he devised for his characters.
>
> (Allen 1989: 143–144)

Shakespeare's characters are left onstage to speak for themselves. The audience, lacking any direct access to Shakespeare, is forced to infer Shakespeare's vision of love from his characters. But is this a realistic expectation? What conclusions can we draw about Shakespeare's view of love from the lines and fates he devises for his characters?

Viewed through a pastiche of quoted fragments, images of love proliferate, but they never converge into a coherent vision. We are treated to memorable moments of love. But love itself, that "ever fixèd mark," is, like the playwright, nowhere to be found. The more love poetry we hear, the more elusive love becomes. Dramatically, that's probably as it should be. Love has many faces, and no patchwork quilt of love's moments could be expected to cover love in its entirety. The integrity of any one play is going to be lost in this gorgeous bouquet of excerpts plucked from here and there in Shakespeare's work.

But the bigger question is whether we should expect Shakespeare to have a more general view of love. The primary aim of theater, we might well conclude, is not to showcase the essence of love or, for that matter, the essence of anything. The playwright's first obligation is to bring engaging stories to life on the stage. While these stories will often reflect on great themes of philosophy, in plays, ideas are generally embedded in characters, places, and events. On the stage, ideas are presented in living color rather than in the gray shades of philosophical abstraction. This means that their characters and stories will often upstage successful playwrights. We will inevitably feel that we have come to know Juliet and Romeo in a way we can never know Shakespeare. This is, in part, why it was so much easier for Steve Allen to bring Shakespeare's lovers to life than Shakespeare himself. His characters speak eloquently about their experience of love. But after watching his plays, it is far more difficult to know with any confidence what Shakespeare himself believed about love.

A virtuoso storyteller, Shakespeare writes his plays in a narrative voice rather than a philosophical one. Strictly speaking, his plays go a step further than narrative, from commentary about life into enactments of life itself. Most playwrights give their characters voices of their own and then seemingly disappear from the scene. More didactic writers might remain on stage speaking through the mask of one or another character. But Shakespeare seems to leave us alone with his characters, trusting them to entertain us by themselves. Which of Shakespeare's characters could be said to speak for him about love? Romeo? Juliet? Viola? Antony? Hermione? Hermia? Othello? Cleopatra? Desdemona? Perhaps Iago? The question doesn't make much sense. One could as easily say that none of them speak for Shakespeare as claim that all of them do.

Shakespeare's lovers are too real and particular to stand in for any general portrait of love. Shakespeare's own voice intruding on the scene might well be greeted as a distraction rather than a welcome addition to the play. It would seem to make more sense to just perform his plays and sustain the immediacy and complexity of his vision. This might suggest that there is nothing much to be gained by inviting Shakespeare into the conversation to ask what he means about anything.

This seems to be an appealing argument since it invites us to approach Shakespeare in a full-bodied way. The argument essentially frees us from any serious interpretive obligation. If there is no privileged point of view, we can stop looking for one. Released from the burdens of insight, we can accept the pleasures of the play at face value. Abandoning the quest for Shakespeare in favor of his plots and characters allows us to leave the text alone, enjoying it "as you like it."

However attractive this argument may seem initially, I believe that this view of Shakespeare underestimates his virtuosity. Assuming that Shakespeare speaks only through his characters deprives him of a voice of his own. It leaves the plays with no general point of view but that of the story, pulsing with a full heart but half a head. Is there no "theoretical voice" to be found in Shakespeare? Is there no role on Shakespeare's stage for Shakespeare himself, the author as participant-observer and commentator on the action taking place on stage?

Philosophy in the interrogative mood

Let me propose another possibility. What if we acknowledge that we have drawn too rigid a line between sensuous performance and commentary? Shakespeare's plays could be understood not just as the unfolding of events and characters but also as enacted ideas. In addition to the familiar playwright of the Shakespearean stage, I think that there was another Shakespeare concealed between the lines of his texts, a thinker of the first order, with philosophical insights and intriguing questions as consequential as any in the works of, say, Plato, Sigmund Freud, or the sociologist Emile Durkheim.

Shakespeare lived in a rapidly changing England, straddling the Elizabethan and Jacobean periods, on the early edge of modernity. This was a period of fundamental demographic, political, religious, and cultural transformation. Shakespeare's perspective on the world spanned a receding medieval past—famously (if misleadingly) sketched by E.M.W. Tillyard in *The Elizabethan World Picture*—and an emerging modern world with a radically different aspect. If Tillyard's medieval vision suggests the conviction of theologically grounded dogma, the perspective that Shakespeare revealed, one that I am calling "theoretical," might be said to be framed more in the interrogative mood. Shakespeare's genius was to interrogate—playfully and dramatically—almost every certainty on which the older world picture rested, while carefully skirting the official court censors who had to approve all theatrical productions.

While there is nothing unusual about philosophically nuanced literature, Shakespeare appears to have developed a particularly brilliant approach to combining theatre and theory, a literary technique that I like to think of as "holographic." Viewed straight on, we find in Shakespeare's works magnificent poetry, unforgettable stories, and complex characters. This is a Shakespeare to be watched and heard. But viewed more obliquely, we find in his plays something else: deeply theoretical commentary. This is a Shakespeare to be read and studied. By deftly embedding theoretically motivated subtexts into the heart of his stories, Shakespeare was able to bridge the formidable gap between telling a story and exploring a conceptual problem. Through masterful control of language and dramatic form, I believe that Shakespeare had found a way to present a story dramatically and interrogate this story theoretically *at the same time*.

As a thinker, Shakespeare's insights were not limited to particular characters or speeches. They often speak to us through ironic relations among speeches and characters that create an ongoing commentary paralleling the play's action. These relations are not normally obvious to a casual audience but emerge only with a second look or a careful *reading* of the play. Thus, each play has a kind of double life, a sensuous life of character and action as watched and heard on stage, and a more contemplative life of ideas emerging from a thoughtful study of the text. Such ideas, planted in playful turns of language and action, cohabit comfortably with and never intrude upon the play's more immediately accessible stage life. I see this reflexive layer of theoretical commentary as the brains at the heart of Shakespearean drama.

This stratified vision of Shakespearean texts suggests an archeological character to the plays. It returns Shakespeare's voice to his stage, not as a character but as a philosophically sophisticated dramaturge. We could think of this as the voice of a prompter positioned just beneath the floorboards. Shakespeare's prompts, mere whispers between the lines, would not generally be aimed at any specific character or any particular speech. A master voice among the play's voices, the prompts would be directed at a discerning audience and point to unexpected layers of meaning in the plays.

The anthropologist's Shakespeare

This archeological path through the texts is the one I will follow in these pages. It affords Shakespeare's plays another look and some unexpected vistas, approaching his work not only through the play of poetry, action, feeling, and character but also through the play of great ideas. In advocating this kind of oblique reading of Shakespeare's plays, I have no interest in analyzing away Shakespeare's stories by reducing him to a social theorist. Who would want to reduce Shakespeare to anything?

There are numerous Shakespeares to be discovered in his work, a fact that has allowed both Shakespeare scholarship and Shakespeare productions to thrive in seemingly endless variations for over four hundred years. The "other Shakespeare" I explore in these pages is surely not the only one worth our attention. But it is an often-overlooked writer of extraordinary intellectual vitality and subtlety who has many surprises in store for us. This Shakespeare, the participant-observer of his own creations, the social critic and commentator, is what I like to think of as "the anthropologist's Shakespeare." Like an anthropologist, Shakespeare was a participant-observer of the world he knew. He was an ethnographer of this world and an interrogator of its grand ideas and persistent dilemmas. Shakespeare tacks between story-telling (what anthropologists call "ethnography") and theoretical commentary, straddling both the participant's and the observer's points of view. In his text, the "position" of Shakespeare, like that of the anthropologist, is neither exclusively in the story itself nor the analysis of the story, but rather in their relationship. Anthropologists call this perspective "participant-observation," and, yes, it is a kind of paradox.

This recognition of the anthropologist in Shakespeare allows us to invite Shakespeare to the table and engage him in a set of conversations on a wide range of topics that anthropologists call "social thought." As a student of both anthropology and Shakespeare, I learned long ago that many of his plays work well as commentaries on a wide range of social and philosophical issues familiar to anthropologists. Having studied Shakespeare as an undergraduate, I decided four decades ago to throw my lot in with the anthropologists rather than enter graduate school in English literature. But my interest in Shakespeare never abated. I hoped to find a way to continue learning from Shakespeare, not as a break from anthropology, but as an integral part of my anthropology education.

As things turned out, finding a place for Shakespeare in anthropology was fairly easy. Early on in my teaching, I began incorporating Shakespeare into my anthropology courses: *Romeo and Juliet* in a course on Language and Human Nature, *Hamlet* in a class on ritual, and *Julius Caesar* in a course on social theory. I treated the plays as lively theoretical texts fully equivalent to classic texts in social thought, pairing them with classic theoretical works in social thought. In the mid-1980s, I started co-teaching with Frank Manley, a colleague and friend in the English Department, a course entitled "Ritual in Shakespeare," which was cross-listed in the English and Anthropology Departments. Manley was a distinguished Latinist, a John Donne and Thomas More scholar, and a gifted playwright and novelist. He was a keen reader and lively thinker. We didn't always agree on our readings of the plays and must have made an odd couple in the classroom. But the chemistry somehow worked. Manley was a closet anthropologist; I was a closet literary scholar, and we both loved Shakespeare.

Using texts in ritual studies and performance theory as commentary along with relevant Shakespeare criticism, we slowly read through a small number of Shakespeare's plays in which Shakespeare treated ritual and related performances in provocative and problematical ways. In the process, we managed to establish a productive conversation between anthropology and Shakespeare. The plays informed the anthropology; the anthropology informed the plays.

Manley retired at the dawn of the 21st century, and in 2009 he passed away. Partly to honor Frank's memory and our long friendship, I continued to teach this class as an anthropology course at Emory until my retirement in 2020. The enrolment remained a more-or-less even mix of anthropology students and literature students. Through Shakespeare, students of the two disciplines talked to each other, learning about ritual and Shakespeare and the connections between the two. Anthropology opened windows with unfamiliar vistas onto the plays; the plays brought the ideas of social theory to life. This course was taught for over 25 years. It was always among my most popular and successful courses. Our success in getting students to view Shakespeare's plays as theoretical texts (in addition to dramatic and poetic texts) was gratifying. My students' enthusiastic response over the years to the course and my years of stimulating conversation about Shakespeare and anthropology with Frank Manley in and out of the classroom have both served as major encouragements in my decision to write this book. The book is dedicated to Frank's memory.

The organization of the book

Shakespeare scholarship is a universe unto itself. One might assume that no stone had been left unturned in exploring the landscape of Shakespeare's plays over the last four centuries. But the plays can still yield some surprises. Many of the issues that captured Shakespeare's imagination have also been the principal fare of classic social theory. But rather than dealing with them in the abstract language of social theory, Shakespeare brings ideas to the stage through the interplay of theatrical form, character, event, and word. By staging great ideas in this way, Shakespeare brings them, literally, to life. The book argues for including Shakespeare among history's great social theorists. Shakespeare's way with ideas was the product of his intellectual genius and the times he wrote. And so, Part II of the book takes a tour through the Elizabethan world, a world in flux, poised between an older medieval world framed by a Church Universal and an emerging modern world dominated by a fractured Church, expanding commerce, exploration, and scientific rationality. This early modern world was fertile soil for Shakespeare's challenging of old certainties about the order of things. It is this world that shaped his radical intellectual disposition.

Part I of the book examines Shakespeare's world. Chapter 1 begins with a guided tour *inside* Shakespeare's world, through the maze of *Hamlet's* Denmark. In its radical questioning of the world and its meaning, *Hamlet* is a perfect introduction to Shakespeare's interrogative frame of mind and the world that produced it. The chapter presents a picture of Shakespeare's mind at its most intense, reflected, and refracted in Denmark's hall of mirrors.

Chapter 2 begins our look at the world in which Shakespeare lived and wrote by examining the foundations of Shakespeare's training as a thinker. The chapter outlines the rhetorical traditions which were part of the Elizabethan grammar school curriculum. Inspired by the Ciceronian technique of *disputatio in ultramque partem* (arguing from both sides of a question), students learned to broadly interrogate philosophical questions from many angles rather than arguing dogmatically from first principles. The theatrical analog to this rhetorical tradition was the Elizabethan tradition of "explorative theatre" to which Shakespeare subscribed, an approach to playwriting that subjected accepted ideas and values to question rather than to the reductive certitudes of didactic theatre.

Chapter 3 focuses on the changing understandings of the heavens and the effects that discoveries in astronomy and optics were having on the older beliefs in astrology and supernatural agency. The chapter looks at how the emergence of the New Cosmology challenged important Christian assumptions about the cosmos world and its connections with the human world. These issues are then examined within Shakespeare's work.

Part II comprises four chapters examining how Shakespeare's radical interrogation of the world shaped four of his plays. Chapter 4 is devoted to *The Winter's Tale*. The other plays treated in this section are *Romeo and Juliet, A Midsummer Night's Dream* and *Julius Caesar*. Close readings of the plays open a window onto some of Shakespeare's great ideas as seen through the eyes of an anthropologist. For example, in addition to one of the world's most famous and tragic love stories, *Romeo and Juliet* is also a powerful set of reflections on the relation between love and language. It explores the power of poetry, not just to evoke love but to take its place. Romeo is not just any lover. He is the model Petrarchan sonneteer, the frustrated lover-as-poet who seeks to replace elusive flesh with effusive words. These chapters on *Romeo and Juliet* demonstrate how this play may be understood as Shakespeare's romp through what I call "the kingdom of Cratylus" transplanted to Verona. We see how the play evokes echoes of Plato's *Cratylus*, his dialogue on the relation of language to reality. *Cratylus* proposes a world where language can directly produce reality through the power of naming. By reading Shakespeare through this focus on ideas, we get a new understanding of what Shakespeare was doing in his plays and how he was doing it. The analyses in this book ask that we turn from *watching* to *reading* the plays, attending to the wonders of Shakespeare's literary craftsmanship.

In Part III (Chapters 8–9), the book turns from questions of *what* the plays mean to *how* they mean. This final part of the book is called "Shakespeare's craft" and considers some of Shakespeare's literary techniques to reconcile the narrative demands of compelling storytelling with the competing demands of theoretical analysis. These chapters suggest how Shakespeare was able to reconcile staged entertainment and theoretical reflection. Chapter 8, *Just nothing: How King Lear means,* explores how Shakespeare used a sophisticated understanding of metaphor to enable the audience to *experience* the tragic emptying out of Lear's world. Using a close reading of *King Lear,* the chapter reveals, in Shakespeare's brilliant use of metaphor, a literary device for embedding the terrifying evacuation of meaning experienced by Lear into the contours of a text. As we read, we unravel with Lear. Shakespeare's understanding of tropes, especially his remarkable play with metaphor, suggests a nascent theory of language that anticipates modern metaphor theory and cognitive linguistics.

Chapter 9 explores Shakespeare's play with perspective, focusing on how he adapted to language and theater techniques of perspective manipulation from the great painters of his day. Shakespeare's language play is shown to be a literary analog of anamorphic painting.[1] Anamorphism is a perspective technique first used by Leonardo Da Vinci but made popular in the 16th century by Hans Holbein the Younger and others. Using distorted anamorphic projection of images onto flat canvasses, artists were able to show one picture when viewed straight on and another, more radical vision, when the canvass was viewed obliquely. Shakespeare was aware of this painting technique, making numerous references to anamorphic art in his plays. But to credibly demonstrate how Shakespeare adapted anamorphism as a literary technique, we have to pay careful attention to Shakespeare's texts and how the complex relations between sound and sense in poetry can be used for the same purposes as anamorphic image distortion. Shakespeare's extraordinary powers of wordplay allowed him to create straightforward stories that reveal a surprising parallel landscape of great ideas embedded in the stories when viewed from an oblique angle.

Anamorphic painting is explored in the context of Elizabethan interests in optics, perspective, and conceptual relativity. What eventually became known as anamorphism was an Elizabethan precursor to holographic representation and afforded artists a way of building a double representation into a single work of art. By adapting anamorphism to language rather than visual imagery, Shakespeare found a way to construct his plays so that his elaborated reflections on questions of social thought could live within the text viewed from another angle, without impeding the immediacy of the flow of action and character.

Note

1 The term anamorphic was first coined in the 19th century, though the techniques had been in use for the previous four centuries.

PART I

Shakespeare's world

1

TO SEE AND NOT TO SEE

Hamlet's undiscovered country

Hamlet, Shakespeare's celebrated revenge tragedy, has been called "a meta-theatrical play," a four-hour rumination on the complex relationship between theater and life. In its treatment of plot and character as well as in its masterful anticipation and manipulation of its audience's responses, *Hamlet* raises basic questions about the human attempt to perform life into meaning in a world that does not easily yield coherent insight. In his fascinating study of *Hamlet*, *To Be and Not to Be*, James Calderwood develops this reading of *Hamlet* as meta-theatrical theater by focusing on the paradox of acting: the enactment of absence as presence in the borderland of the stage where "to be" is also "not to be" (Calderwood 1983). And so, the drama turns out to be as much about *Hamlet* the play as it is about Hamlet the Prince.

In his plays, Shakespeare repeatedly stages the complex relations between being and acting. *A Midsummer Night's Dream* treats the rehearsal of a play by a set of amateur actors as a powerful analog to the making of a marriage (see Chapter 6). Act II of *Henry IV, Part I* has Falstaff taking on Prince Hal's father's role as the Prince rehearses for his impending interview with the old king. In *As You Like It*, Jaques famously proclaims that "All the world's a stage, And all the men and women merely players," a histrionic vision of living that many theorists like Erving Goffman (1959, 1982), Victor Turner (1969, 1974, 2001), Kenneth Burke (1945, 1950), and Judith Butler (1990) have sought to develop theoretically.

We shall shortly return to the place of performing in *Hamlet* since the play treats acting as a significant way in which people attempt to make sense of things. But first, we face the most basic question about *Hamlet*: what on earth (or not on earth!) is this play about? There have been many conventional answers to the question. The play's proposed themes are all great ones: revenge, succession, fratricide, regicide, agency, incest, guilt, procrastination, love, and adultery. The play is also about the troubled relations between seeming (acting) and authentic being. All of these themes can be found in *Hamlet*. True enough, and yet…not enough.

DOI: 10.4324/9781003179771-3

Hamlet might credibly be accused of spinning out both too many meanings and not enough meaning. Confronting this paradox of too-much-too-little meaning in *Hamlet* brought back many memories of my earliest fieldwork as a newly minted anthropologist. I had gone to Samoa in 1972 as a graduate student to study law and social control in a Samoan village noted for its history of social conflict. I lived for a year as the "son" in the family of one of the two senior chiefs of the village and found myself caught up in a real-life murder mystery close to home when my Samoan father was shot dead by the other chief's son following an argument over a card game. My dissertation and, later, my first book became an ethnography of Samoan village politics framed as a murder mystery (Shore 1982). Starting with the raw events surrounding the murder, I sought to unpack the layers of cultural meaning that illuminated my father's death so that the murder mystery might be revealed as a cultural mystery. However, the deeper I dug into the murder, the more layers of interpretation emerged. There seemed to be no bottom, no end to interpreting.

Then, there was the problem of how to "act" in the midst of this tragedy and its aftermath. I was playing several parts at once. In this drama, I was a family member, a kind of adopted "son" to the murdered man, but also an anthropologist studying conflict and trying to collect data for my dissertation objectively. Do I give the victim's son a ride on my motorcycle out of the village as he flees the scene where he had just assaulted his father's murderer with a bush knife, or do I stand back and take notes on the chaos around me? I chose the former path. But my shock and despair at the murder were mixed with an emerging awareness that I had hit the motherload in the search for good data on conflict. Caught up in a tangle of confused roles, I was unsure of how to act and think and feel about what was going on. I didn't know how to perform the role of the anthropologist-as-adopted-son in the face of this sort of tragedy.

And now, returning to *Hamlet* years later as a seasoned anthropologist vividly brought back the humbling dilemma that faces any anthropologist trying to unravel the mysteries of cultural worlds: the ethnographer's Hamlet-esque stance as "participant-observer," attempting to participate in this alien world while professionally disappearing into the background. By entering the world of *Hamlet*, I understood in a new way the impossibility of producing a final account of any cultural mystery given the fragile relations between what we can see, what we can know, and what actually is. I had come upon an anthropologist's dreamwork: a play about the proliferating possibilities that lie just beyond our horizon of knowing, and why arriving at a coherent and stable interpretation of things is such a challenge. As a play about its own interpretation, *Hamlet* runs for over four hours, theatrically encompassing the full circumference of the hermeneutic circle.

The human struggle to wrest meaning out of the events and people in our lives is of great interest to cultural anthropology. Some of us call it the problem of "meaning-construction." What exactly does it mean to "make meaning" of our lives? How do people do it? Is there "meaning" in the world or just in our minds? Having spent many years exploring meaning-construction in relation to culture and cognition, I turn at this late date in my career back to literature to see what insights into meaning-making Shakespeare's *Hamlet* can provide. We begin our Shakespearean odyssey by entering the disquieting hall of mirrors that Shakespeare constructed in his vision of a troubled Denmark. More than any other play, *Hamlet* conveys the radical interrogative mood that characterizes the Shakespearean play of ideas as he choreographs for Hamlet as well as his audience, the human attempt to find meaning in a world both unsteady and unyielding.

In seeking "the meaning" of Shakespeare's Danish tragedy, we face a problem: *Hamlet* is impenetrable. Interpretations keep unfolding and then unraveling so that there seems to be no end to what the play is about. This problem makes any discussion of *Hamlet* especially challenging. Shakespeare's longest and most celebrated work is also his least accessible. However, *Hamlet* is also oddly affecting. Despite all that has been written and said about *Hamlet*, its curiosity is that we can be so deeply absorbed by a play whose point remains elusive. *Hamlet* is not entirely unintelligible. We almost get it. It is just meaningful enough to keep us watching and guessing, at once in conclusion and inconclusion.

The play thrusts the audience into the midst of trouble from the opening scene, and we struggle to find our footing. Part of the problem with *Hamlet* is that its action is dis-placed. From the start, it is not clear from where *Hamlet*—both the play and the dead King—is speaking to us. Reading or watching *Hamlet*, I have often felt I was not encountering the real play. Self-consciously theatrical, *Hamlet* tempts us to contemplate the possibility that we are watching a replacement, a rehearsal perhaps, of a parallel *Hamlet* set just out of view in the wings. *Hamlet* seems to be more off-staged than staged. Though set in Denmark, the play's real home is somewhere else (which turns out to be true). The play opens on the parapets of Elsinore Castle at the changing of the guard. Its opening words ("Who's there?/Nay, Answer me. Stand and unfold yourself") allude to an unseen world that refuses full disclosure. Even as performance, the play's action is impelled by forces beyond the stage's temporal and spatial frames rather than by the characters or events at hand. From his first words, Hamlet is an enigma. Even as we get to know Hamlet better as the play unfolds, the full scope of his problem remains clear neither to the audience nor to the King and Queen, nor to Hamlet himself. By the play's end, the butchered corpses of its central figures scattered about the stage and a new order unexpectedly breaking in from the outside, the meaning of it all still seems to be left only half-disclosed.

T.S. Eliot warned us about *Hamlet*. In his 1921 essay "Hamlet and His Problems," Eliot called the play "intractable," a failed work rather than the masterpiece it has been proclaimed.

> Of the intractability there can be no doubt. So far from being Shakespeare's masterpiece, the play is most certainly an artistic failure. In several ways the play is puzzling, and disquieting as is none of the others. Of all the plays it is the longest and possibly the one on which Shakespeare spent most pains; and yet he has left in it superfluous and inconsistent scenes which even hasty revision should have noticed.
>
> (Eliot 1921: 90)

Eliot brilliantly noted that *Hamlet* was Shakespeare's attempt to represent "an experience which exceeded the facts" (p. 94). In this view, the crux of Shakespeare's problem was his inability to provide a believable basis for the emotions of the play's main characters, particularly the Prince. Eliot termed this elusive motive for excessive feeling an

> objective correlative…a set of objects, a situation, a chain of events which shall be the formula for that particular emotion; such that when the external facts, which must terminate in sensory experience, are given, the emotion is immediately evoked.
>
> (*ibid.*: 93)

In Eliot's view, *Hamlet* tries too hard to know something which is inherently unknowable.

In one sense, the charge that *Hamlet* lacks an objective correlative to make sense of the Prince's emotional state seems unfair. The play proposes many sources for Hamlet's discontent, perhaps too many. The murder of fathers, the stifled compulsion for revenge, the adultery of mothers, a brother's treachery, an uncle's usurpation of a throne, love confounded and misdirected—these are enough to justify rage and madness many times over. But what is so troubling about *Hamlet* is that the play assures us that even this tide of misery does not sufficiently disclose Denmark's rot. Whatever we come to know, we never know enough. However much trouble we see in the words and actions of Hamlet, *père* and *fils*, Laertes and Ophelia, Claudius and Gertrude, the source of Denmark's corruption points to a further world into which we are not allowed to glimpse.

Ultimately, Eliot's famous denunciation of *Hamlet* goes too far in seeing this absence of motive as a literary failure. Time and the play's enduring popularity have shown Eliot's judgment of *Hamlet* to be shortsighted. Nevertheless, his criticism is not completely without merit. In fact, Eliot does not go far enough in his account of what is missing. The trouble with *Hamlet* is not just the absence of an *objective* correlative for its characters' emotional states. *Hamlet* also lacks a clear "subjective correlative"—a coherent model of feeling—for an absent situation upon which the play's credibility rests. We can agree with Eliot that the play lacks a credible model for linking a state of affairs with a state of mind. But this gap lies at the heart of its greatness and motivates the seemingly endless impulse to re-stage and re-watch the play.

Clifford Geertz (1973) once pointed out that without some sort of public "template"—a cultural model for feeling through which we can experience and perform our emotions—even our deepest feelings remain largely inaccessible to us. This emotional cueing is what a film's musical score does to help viewers know how to feel about what they are seeing. But the cues for knowing and feeling in *Hamlet* are never clear. The problem of correlatives, objective and subjective, is tied to the problem of action-as-performance in *Hamlet*. We can grasp neither Hamlet's state of mind nor his precise feelings because he cannot grasp his own feelings, let alone his frame of mind. We therefore scan the play for someone who knows what is going on. What both Hamlet and his audience seek is the clarifying moment of a performance that will reveal both his state of mind and its cause unambiguously. However, every attempt to perform such a revelation proves incomplete. Something is not only rotten in Denmark: something is rotten and missing. Lacking a coherent musical track, the play's interpretation must rest on improvisation.

The challenge of playing the role of Hamlet is tied to this absence. An actor must somehow embody in a powerful presence an absent attitude toward an even more absent situation. Front and center as a performer, Hamlet must also show himself to be offstage. In the play's opening scene, we learn of Hamlet's dead father's mysterious appearance on the ramparts of Elsinore Castle, where he hovers as a ghostly apparition, at once on stage and off, both present and past. In parallel fashion, the younger Hamlet appears in the play's second scene in a grand castle hall. Like his father, the Prince shows himself to be both here and away, presenting himself in full theatrical mode to Gertrude and Claudius, but then retreating into his "away mode" once they are gone and accessible to us only through the "offstage" device of the soliloquy. The challenge for the actor playing Hamlet is to find a way to be and not to be at the same time. Hamlet's simultaneous presence and absence on stage are paralleled by the dislocation of young Hamlet's motives, partly residing in his inchoate suspicions and partly in the yet-to-be-revealed story soon to be told by the elder Hamlet's shade, patrolling the wings offstage.

A conventional reading of *Hamlet* proposes that Hamlet's problem is procrastination: whether, how, and when to act out the joint revenge of Hamlet—father and son—against Claudius. But Hamlet's problem is how to act in both senses of the word: how to link his resolve for revenge with his sensibility for staging performance. However, this nexus linking action and performance is blocked by the play's "undiscover'd country"—a domain of forbidden knowing and feeling, of unspeakable thoughts and desires that spill beyond the bounds of the play's speakable crimes. At stake is not just the meaning of the particular acts and speeches of the play, but the possibility of any final understanding.

Hamlet's true subject matter remains undiscovered, ever-present and never-present on stage. As with any inchoate presentation, this absence both provokes perplexity and incites troubling imaginings. This gap between what we know and what we need to know but can never know about the play is the key to the greatness of *Hamlet,* not its failure. In its attempt to express the problem of representing too much meaning, *Hamlet* is a kind of inversion of the tragedy of Lear, whose fate was to discover a vast emptiness that lay just beyond the walls of his castle (see Chapter 8). Both plays are about the struggle to make meaning of life, to make sense of things. If *King Lear* is the tragedy of discovering too little meaning at the culmination of a life, a stripping down and evacuation of signification, *Hamlet* is the tragedy of too many meanings, staging the struggle to bring something into view where the ultimate ground of meaning has spilled out of sight. The theatrical challenge for *Hamlet* is to perform this absent heart of the play. This means that *Hamlet* is inevitably about its own representation, the possibilities, and limits of theater to bring into view the missing center that will render its characters' actions credible.

Three ways of meaning-making

With his life so intimately involved with theater, Shakespeare's view of meaning-making naturally gravitated to the affordances of the stage for making sense of things. *Hamlet* proposes three ways that humans extract and make sense of experience: (1) *performance,* (2) *observation,* and (3) *classification.* In the following pages, it can be shown how each of these sense-making strategies is in play in Hamlet's world and how each is seriously hobbled. *Hamlet* leads its audience through a kingdom in which the basic meaning-making processes have been dislocated, twisted out of joint. *Hamlet* invites its audiences to join the troubled Prince in experiencing what it is like to simultaneously understand and not understand, to try and make sense of a world whose meaning eludes full disclosure.

Performing meaning

The fact that meaning can be pursued through *performing* suggests the histrionic dimension of human life. We talk about "performing" our duties. Our behavior is said to be how we "act." To perform something is to raise action beyond the ordinary. All humans have ways of distinguishing certain spaces, persons, objects, or actions from the ordinary. Such marked action *beyond* the ordinary is the domain of the sacred. Jerome Bruner called this human capacity for reframing behavior or thought by shifting up a level, "going meta" (Bruner 1996: 62; Shore 1997: 34). In the same way as we can reframe certain things as "sacred," humans possess the capacity to mark certain sequences of behavior as self-conscious "performances," above and beyond everyday actions, allowing for heightened awareness. Such reflexive forms of behavior have been called "meta-performative frames." I prefer the simpler phrase "scripted behavior." Scripted behavior creates a distinction between ordinary action (the real) and performance (the pretend). However, the boundary between the real and the pretend is often not so clear, and so we confront the problem of the "performative" nature of human life. Is all human behavior a performance? What would "authentic" behavior be? How would we know the difference?

One of the best-known theoretical discussions of this human capacity to specially frame behavior as "metacommunication" is Gregory Bateson's essay "A Theory of Play and Fantasy" from his book *Steps to an Ecology of Mind* (Bateson 1972). For Bateson, the capacity to frame certain communications as special in their degree of awareness and intentionality is a hallmark of mammalian evolution. Bateson uses the term "metacommunication" for self-referential messages about the communication itself rather than about the communication's obvious content. While recognizing the roots of this framing capacity in animals other than humans (such as in the dog's "nip" or its bared teeth, both of which communicate a meta-message about the deliberate withholding of its capacity to bite), Bateson acknowledges the special significance of the elaboration of metacommunication for human evolution. Bateson calls the most basic act of metacommunicative framing "play." Bateson argues that play behavior is intrinsically paradoxical in that it is both "not real" and "not not real." Play affords humans the capacity to reflect on their acts and the important human capacity for the simulation or rehearsal of behavior. Play holds the reality of action in temporary limbo. As a form of behavior that is also a simulation of behavior, play both *is* and *is not* real behavior. Stage acting is one particularly refined kind of play behavior, which is why theatrical dramas are called "plays." The paradoxical character of play as both not real and not not real affords humans the capacity "to be and not to be" simultaneously.

Metacommunicative frames include a spectrum of performance genres such as rituals, spectacles, rehearsals, lies, simulations, games, and theatrical performances (MacAloon 1984). Because they are related to each other on a spectrum, these frames produce inevitable ambiguities about how to interpret observed behavior, specifically about the degree to which any action can be considered as "real" or "pretend." In the shadow of performance, the very notion of "truth" becomes problematic. The human capacities for deceit (below the real) and an apprehension of the sacred (beyond the real) are born from play. As we all learn from experience, the contingencies of interpretation, and the possibility of error and miscommunication, enter into any evaluation of human behavior.

As a play, *Hamlet* is itself a performance piece. But it is also composed of a chain of performances. Claudius, Hamlet, and Polonius are all continually staging "performances" and assembling audiences, though often by engaging unwitting players. *Hamlet* unfolds as a string of rituals, ceremonies, soliloquies, rehearsals, dumb-shows, theatrical performances, and staged "encounters." The problem is that every one of these performances is "maimed:" interrupted, unfinished, upstaged, colonized, or otherwise broken. Broken performance becomes a master leitmotif of the play. "Who's there?" (I, i, 1), asks Bernardo as the play opens. *Hamlet* begins in a double disruption. The changing of the palace guard at the stroke of midnight is broken by the intrusion of what appears to be the ghost of old Hamlet. An ordinary disruption (the changing of the guard) is upstaged by an extraordinary one (the intrusion of old Hamlet's ghost). The ghostly presence is both within the play and "away," momentarily breaking through to the visible world from another place that cannot be described. This intrusion echoes that other interrupted "changing of the guard," the succession to Denmark's throne where Prince Hamlet's uncle Claudius serves as the interloper, interrupting Hamlet's succession to the throne.

When the ghost of the old King finally speaks to Hamlet (in the fifth scene of the opening act), still another interrupted transition is evoked. The ghost reveals that his passage to Heaven has been blocked. Trapped in Purgatory, the ghost of Hamlet-the-elder is doomed to endure the incomplete passage of a sinner who had not properly confessed his sins:

> I am thy father's spirit,
> Doomed for a certain term to walk the night,
> And for the day confin'd to fast in fires
> Till the foul crimes done in my days of nature
> Are burnt and purg'd away.
>
> (I, v, 14–18)[1]

Young Hamlet cannot complete his mourning; the elder Hamlet cannot complete the transition from the living to the dead. For both father and son, death has become perpetual dying, eluding both closure and disclosure.

Interrupted performance continues when the scene shifts to the Court at Elsinore, and we see the royal Court ritual broken by Hamlet's refusal to acknowledge it. Young Hamlet remains within the court but also outside, transforming ritual into theater through the force of his soliloquies. Hamlet speaks, but to whom? This confusion of space is mimicked by a conflation of rituals which should be distinct. Hamlet accuses the King and Queen of upstaging his father's funeral right with their wedding celebration, as Gertrude has married her brother-in-law Claudius soon after old Hamlet's untimely death. "The funeral bak'd meats," Hamlet laments to Horatio, "Did coldly furnish forth the marriage tables" (I, ii, 187–188). As a result, Hamlet occupies a social world where he can lay claim to an "uncle-father" and "aunt-mother" (II, ii, 389). Claudius, clearly sensing the root of Hamlet's discomfort, uses elevated courtly language in an attempt to ritually re-order the distorted relationships and create a sense of fake normalcy. Yet the mischief afoot in Denmark cannot be so easily masked. In his attempt to reaffirm a sacred order, Claudius' true state of mind is betrayed by a flood of self-negating images and by his long rhetorical delay in producing the offending punch-line:

> Therefore our sometime sister, now our queen,
> Th'imperial jointress of this warlike state,
> Have we, as 'twere with a defeated joy,
> With one auspicious and drooping eye,
> With mirth in funeral and with dirge in marriage,
> In equal scale weighing delight and dole,
> Taken to wife
>
> (I, ii, 8–14)

Described as a union of self-canceling opposites, the power of conventional rites has been undermined by the collapse of the distinctions they are supposed to enforce. Funeral rites have been cut short by impetuous nuptials. Marriage has been wed to death.

In the bedroom scene between Hamlet and his mother (III, iv), the confrontation between mother and son is twice disrupted, once by the discovery and murder of Polonius, and again by the reappearance of the ghost of Hamlet's father warning Hamlet to keep steadfast to his promise to avenge his father's murder. When Claudius and Gertrude fail to provide Polonius with an adequate funeral, they inform Laertes of his father's death at Hamlet's hands. Laertes bemoans not just his father's murder but also his "obscure funeral."

> No trophy, sword, nor hatchment o'er his bones,
> No noble rite, nor formal ostentation—

Cry to be heard, as 'twere from heaven to earth,
That I must call't in question.

(IV, vi, 39–42)

Just as Polonius is denied a full funeral, his daughter's burial rites are also left incomplete. Noting the truncated rites for his sister, Laertes asks the priest, "What ceremony else?" (V, i, 216), and is informed that Ophelia's death, a suspected suicide, cannot be ritually acknowledged in full:

Her obsequies have been as far enlarg'd
As we have warranty. Her death was doubtful;
And but that the great command o'ersways the order,
She should in ground unsanctified be lodged
Till the last trumpet: for charitable prayers
Shards, flints, and pebbles should be thrown on her.

(V, i, 233–239)

Laertes implores, "Must no more be done?" But rather than ritually expanding the rites, he adds to the disruption by jumping into the grave and proclaiming:

Hold off the earth awhile,
Till I have caught her once more in my arms.
Now pile your dust upon the quick and dead,
Till of this flat a mountain you have made
T'o'ertop old Pelion or the skyish head
Of blue Olympus.

(V, i, 261–266)

Spurred by Laertes' performance of grief, Hamlet emerges from hiding to join Laertes in the grave and, in a parody of an oratorical contest, attempts to out-grieve Laertes: "I loved Ophelia. Forty thousand brothers/Could not with all their quantity of love, make up my sum. What wilt thou do for her?" (V, i, 285–287). The solemn tones of ritual give way to a performance that is pure theater.

LAERTES
O, treble woe
Fall ten times treble on that cursèd head
Whose wicked deed thy most ingenious sense
Deprived thee of!—Hold off the earth awhile,
Till I have caught her once more in mine arms.
Leaps in the grave.
Now pile your dust upon the quick and dead,
Till of this flat a mountain you have made

> T' o'ertop old Pelion or the skyish head
> Of blue Olympus.
>
> **HAMLET,** *advancing*
> What is he whose grief
> Bears such an emphasis, whose phrase of sorrow
> Conjures the wand'ring stars and makes them stand
> Like wonder-wounded hearers? This is I,
> Hamlet the Dane.

(V, I, 258–271)

The contest degenerates into a brawl, and the scene concludes. But Ophelia's burial rite does not. The repeated interruptions of the funeral rite have buried, not Ophelia, but her funeral. The truncated ritual has been further interrupted and effectively overtaken by Laertes' and Hamlet's theatrics.

Of all the instances of interrupted or incomplete performance in *Hamlet*, two stand out as particularly salient. At the center of the play, Hamlet mounts a performance by the visiting troupe of actors, a play purported to be based on a true Italian story, "The Murder of Gonzago." Hamlet calls his stage version *The Mousetrap* because he hopes to trap Claudius by staging a theatrical murder that closely mimics his uncle's killing of the elder Hamlet. By watching his uncle's reaction to the play, Hamlet hopes to confirm Claudius' role in his father's murder, as well as letting Claudius know that the secret is out and that Hamlet knows perfectly well how his father died.

However, the theatrical performance is twice interrupted. The first interruption is by Hamlet himself, who breaks into the dialogue to announce that the murderer who has entered the stage is one Lucianus, nephew to the king. Following this announcement is the second interruption, this time by Claudius, who, clearly disturbed by what he has witnessed (but what exactly *has* he witnessed?), stops the performance and, calling for light, leaves the theater in a rage. This remarkable *Mousetrap* scene is central to understanding *Hamlet*. We shall return to it below.

The other key break in *Hamlet* takes place in the play's final scene, just at the point when all of the main characters have killed one another. The focus is now on Horatio, who is the only central character left alive on the stage, and whom Hamlet has, in his dying words, instructed to tell his story. Exactly at this climactic moment, young Fortinbras of Norway, who all along has been plotting to avenge for the death of his own father, breaks into the scene from the wings to claim the throne of Denmark. Fortinbras' succession to the Danish throne effectively completes both the play's succession plot and the revenge scenario. However, it does so from the wings. Moreover, these unexpected endings are from a different story: an off-staged conclusion. These are surely not the resolutions to the succession story that we had been expecting.[2]

As if to underscore how the fabric of *Hamlet* is woven from too many threads, Fortinbras' unanticipated late entrance in the play is followed by an even more marginal disclosure. In the closing minutes of the play, the English Ambassadors suddenly arrive. Surveying the bloody scene, the first Ambassador announces:

> The sight is dismal
> And our affair from England come too late.
> The ears are senseless that should give us hearing
> To Tell him his commandment is fulfill'd,
> That Rosencrantz and Guildenstern are dead.
> Where should we have our thanks?
>
> (V. ii, 407–412)

Horatio answers, "Not from his mouth/Had it the ability of life to thank you. He never gave commandment for their death." And so, the play sputters to a conclusion with an afterthought, a forgotten thread in the tangled web of relations in *Hamlet*'s Denmark, a final instance of the offstage business at the heart of *Hamlet*.

As a meditation on theater and interpretation, *Hamlet* was conceived as a patchwork of performances: rituals, rehearsals, and theatrical performances. Their successes and failures, their distinctions and confusions make up much of the play's subject matter as well as shape its dramatic structure. Besides his professional engagement with theater, there are many theoretical reasons why Shakespeare chose to construct *Hamlet* around the idiom of performance. Rituals and theatrical performances are both forms of scripted behavior where human action is transmuted into a more-or-less fixed form, stripped of its status as events-in-time and rendered repeatable as a generalized *form of action*. As performance, behavior can be edited, rearranged, and re-used, independent of whatever brought it into existence. As ritual, mutable acts and transient figures are transformed into repeatable and durable forms and made accessible as forms of collective memory. Lucien Levy-Bruhl long ago described ritual as memory re-presented (Levy-Bruhl 1973). If rites are a form of social memory, then failures of ritual performance amount to a kind of public forgetting, as well as a primal sign of social disorder. Unlike theater, ritual does not generally have an author but is accepted as simply existing or having a sacred origin. Ritual is the most common medium of sacred reenactment, a bringing-into-presence of holy acts and actors. This link between ritual and the sacred is hardly fortuitous since ritual embodies the experience of transcendence.

The experience of ritual performance reverses our normal understanding of the relationship between actor and action. Strictly speaking, people do not perform rituals, but rites perform themselves in devotees' bodies, proclaiming and reinforcing the primal religious experience of a transcendent agency. The experience of "agency reversal," where the body is experienced as being performed by a transcendent force, is central to the connection between ritual and religious experience. While the gradual changes in ritual practice serve to transform rituals in the long run, rituals are most commonly experienced as signs of continuity and stability.

Victor Turner's classic studies of ritual symbols clarify the power of ritual to restore memory and make visible what is otherwise hidden from view. In his studies of ritual form among the Ndembu people of Zambia, Turner explains how ritual symbols work by using the Ndembu conception of a ritual symbol as "a blaze," a light to make what is hidden come into view (Turner 1970). For Turner, ritual symbols work through a combination of *condensation* and *reification*. Rituals often exploit their symbols' polyvalent character, whereby a range of referents, both conventional and personal, are collapsed into a single complex symbol. A symbol like the Ndembu's *mudyi* tree, by virtue of its milky white sap, represents for Ndembu a range of potential referents associated with motherhood, health, and the value of the matrilineage. One ritual symbol can thus condense both social referents (e.g., matrilineal descent) and personal bodily experiences (e.g., milk production, semen), engaging individuals' deepest experiences of themselves.

But these Ndembu ritual symbols bring together aspects of Ndembu experience which are ultimately coherent. Here condensation brings together disparate aspects of Ndembu life to expand the coherence and meaningfulness of Ndembu experience. Because of this power of ritual symbols to bring the hidden into view and to bridge disparate dimensions of experience, failures of ritual performance are equally powerful expressions of disorder. Such failures of ritual have a special place in *Hamlet*. The multivalent symbols which come together in *Hamlet*'s performances often involve things that are best kept apart: brotherly love and erotic love, marriage and death, filial love and murderous rage, mother and aunt, uncle and father, mother and lover, killer and victim. These are things that cannot be condensed without engaging deeply disturbing feelings and evoking a primal intuition of disorder. And in *Hamlet*'s Denmark, such ambivalent symbols are the coin of the realm.

Another important characteristic of ritual that anthropologists have stressed is their "non-propositional" character. In Susanne Langer's terms, a ritual code is a kind of "presentational" symbolism distinct from discursive communication forms like natural language. Discursive codes discourse about or around phenomena (Langer 1957). They are used to propose "propositions" about the world, statements subject to acceptance, challenge, or denial. By contrast, non-discursive communication, such as ritual acts, brings unquestioned truths into view. In an influential essay, "The Obvious Aspects of Ritual" (1979), Roy Rappaport stresses the conservative character of what he calls "liturgical orders," such as ritual. Rappaport claims that liturgical orders convey sanctified messages, messages accepted without question, and not subject to disconfirmation or question. Ritual statements or acts do not "propose" questionable truths as ordinary language does. Rituals enact truths by reifying presupposed truths as palpable action. A ritual is not a claim but an accomplished act. Only failed or otherwise distorted ritual can throw its credibility as experience into question, which is why "maimed rites" figure so prominently in *Hamlet*. Failed ritual often takes on the desacralized character of theater.

In *Hamlet*, ritual vies with theater as the dominant performance genre. The play's plot strings together a series of conventional rites such as the changing of the guard, court ritual, wedding feasts, funerals, duels and alternates them with a series of self-consciously theatrical performances mainly directed by Hamlet. Some of the theatrical events are soliloquies staged by Hamlet to himself, while others are rehearsals as in the visiting actors' spontaneous command performance of Aeneas' speech recounting Priam's slaughter to Dido (II, ii, 470–522). With Hamlet's staging of *The Mousetrap*, the dramatic centerpiece of the play, we are offered a full-blown play-within-a-play performed simultaneously to the fictional Elsinore audience within the play and the actual audience in the theater. More ambiguously performed is Polonius' staging of the encounter between Hamlet and his mother in her bedchamber. While Polonius observes from behind an arras, the encounter between Hamlet and Gertrude is understood as an observed performance only to the witting participants (i.e., Gertrude, Polonius, and, problematically, old Hamlet's ghost). However, until he discovers Polonius behind the arras, Hamlet remains unaware that his conversation with his mother was a staged bit of spy-theater.

The line between theater and ritual in *Hamlet* is easily blurred. To the extent that a performance sheds its character as sacred reenactment and becomes self-conscious "acting," ritual can become theater.[3] Performance genres differ importantly along an arc defined by the two poles that Richard Schechner calls *flow* and *reflexivity*. Flow is the actor's capacity to lose herself in her performance, decreasing distance between actor and role. Reflexivity refers to the opposite capacity of acting to enforce a kind of self-critical distancing for actor and/or audience who come to see themselves and their situation in a new way. Flow decreases self-consciousness and encourages transformation; reflexivity increases self-consciousness and encourages evaluation (Schechner 1985: 118). Transformation of failed ritual into theater is central to *Hamlet* where failed rites start to look more like theater than ritual, disrupting one of the fundamental ways humans make and reinforce conventional meaning. Sacred certitude becomes perpetual questioning. Hamlet's unstable boundary between ritual and drama underwrites the tension between the flow of conventional action and the paralyzing hyper-reflexivity that haunts the play.

For much of the play, Hamlet is caught in this performative limbo between the reflexivity of thought and the flow of action. While ritual and theatrical performances both produce reflexivity and flow, the two genres have distinct emphases. Most discussions of ritual emphasize its participatory character, and its transformative power through the loss of distance between actor and role. Theatrical performances generally have an audience while rites have only participants. Theatrical performances self-conscientiously "pretend," enforcing reflective awareness and distancing in a way quite different from ritual. When ritual loses its aura of sacredness and authenticity, it is experienced as theater, as in *Hamlet* where rites like funerals and court rituals take on the character of pure theater. The perpetual failure of conventional rituals in Hamlet's Denmark subverts one of the key resources for meaning-making.

Ritual is the public revelation of assumed truth. Disrupted ritual represents a failure of disclosure and a lapse of social memory. With its ritual components so frequently interrupted, *Hamlet* is an unfinished story. And it is not the story to which our attention has been drawn. Just as key performances in the play are left incomplete, so are the backstories that fully illuminate the play's main characters' hearts and minds. Take, for instance, the seminal disclosure that the ghost of old King

Hamlet makes to his son early on in the play. Even as the father unburdens himself to his son and to the audience, another unrevealed thread is glimpsed.

> I am thy father's spirit,
> Doomed for a certain term to walk the night,
> And for the day confined to fast in fires,
> Till the foul crimes done in my days of nature
> Are burnt and purged away. But that I am forbid
> To tell the secrets of my prison house.
> I could a tale unfold whose lightest word
> Would harrow up they soul, freeze thy young blood.
> Make thy two eyes like stars start from their spheres,
> Thy knotty and combinéd locks to part,
> And each particular hair stand on end,
> Like quills upon the fretful porcupine.
> But this eternal blazon must not be
> To ears of flesh and blood. List, Hamlet, O list!
> If thou dids't ever thy dear father love-

(I, v, 14–29)

"List, Hamlet, O list!"—to what? Just whose "foul crimes" does the ghost have in mind? Which crimes? What are the "secrets of [his] prison house?" However closely young Hamlet listens, those secrets are not for his (or our) ears. This remarkable passage initiates a conversation between the two Hamlets, father and son, which both discloses and forecloses a sinister story beyond what we can know. In effect, the ghost is telling Hamlet to listen to a tale that cannot be told. Though the old King eventually reveals the circumstances of his death, we are assured that this story is *not* the appalling tale he wants to tell. In *that* story, old Hamlet is the victimizer and not the victim. And *that* story is blocked, and the one we get is merely a stand-in, a place-holder for the real *Hamlet*.

Old Hamlet's disclosure/closure of meaning is repeated by his son at the play's end. In his last speech, young Hamlet cannot find the words to express what he has within him. In his dying breath, the younger Hamlet can only recapitulate his father's lament:

> I am dead, Horatio. Wretched Queen adieu!
> You that look pale and tremble at this chance,
> That are but mutes or audience to this act,
> Had I but time, as this fell sergeant Death
> Is strict in his arrest—O, I could tell you—
> But let it be, Horatio, I am dead:
> But thou liv'st; report me and my cause aright
> To the unsatisfied.

(V, ii, 365–372)

"O, I could tell you"—what? What is Hamlet's untold story that Horatio is supposed to report? By the end of this long play, we might reasonably expect full disclosure. But that is not to be. Like his father, Hamlet both reveals and conceals his story, withholding an unspeakable narrative in favor of an incomplete surrogate report which Horatio is authorized to give. The story that has occupied our four hours is not the genuine article but merely a stand-in for another story that has yet to be told. Having told Horatio that his tale could not be fully told, Hamlet announces, "But let it be, Horatio, I am dead." Hamlet now speaks as Hamlet's character, the theatrical incarnation of himself, destined endlessly to rehearse an unfinished story. The *passage* of his life has been transmuted from time into a script.

Meaning-making through observation

A performance implies an audience. Observation is the flip side of performance and is the second dimension of meaning-making that *Hamlet* explores. Observation generally implies visual knowledge, vision always suggesting a special relation to truth. It is from sight that we derive insight. While there are other ways of knowing, it is seeing, we are assured, that is believing. Indeed, in English, the primary metaphor governing our everyday understanding of knowledge is "knowing is seeing" and "I see" taken to mean "I know" or "I understand."[4]

The seen and the unseen play a central but equivocal role in how events are construed in *Hamlet's* world. The play opens on the palace watch, as the sentinels Francisco and Barnardo report to Horatio a sighting of Old Hamlet's ghost. Amazed, the guards do not know whether to trust what they have seen.

BARNARDO
Welcome, Horatio. Welcome, good Marcellus.

HORATIO
What, has this thing appeared again tonight?

BARNARDO
I have seen nothing.

MARCELLUS
Horatio says 'tis but our fantasy
And will not let belief take hold of him
Touching this dreaded sight twice seen of us.
Therefore I have entreated him along
With us to watch the minutes of this night,
That, if again this apparition come,
He may approve our eyes and speak to it.

(I, i, 25–34)

When the ghost reappears, they see it but do not hear it. It refuses to speak, so the meaning of this apparition must be inferred from sight alone.

MARCELLUS
Peace, break thee off! Look where it comes again.

BARNARDO
In the same figure like the King that's dead.

MARCELLUS, *to Horatio*
Thou art a scholar. Speak to it, Horatio.

BARNARDO
Looks he not like the King? Mark it, Horatio.

HORATIO
Most like. It harrows me with fear and wonder.

BARNARDO
It would be spoke to.

MARCELLUS
Speak to it, Horatio.

HORATIO
What art thou that usurp'st this time of night,
Together with that fair and warlike form
In which the majesty of buried Denmark
Did sometimes march? By heaven, I charge thee,
speak.

MARCELLUS
It is offended.

BARNARDO
See, it stalks away.

HORATIO
Stay! speak! speak! I charge thee, speak!

Ghost exits.

MARCELLUS
'Tis gone and will not answer.

BARNARDO

How now, Horatio, you tremble and look pale.
Is not this something more than fantasy?
What think you on 't?

HORATIO

Before my God, I might not this believe
Without the sensible and true avouch
Of mine own eyes.

MARCELLUS

Is it not like the King?

HORATIO

As thou art to thyself.
Such was the very armor he had on
When he the ambitious Norway combated.
So frowned he once when, in an angry parle,
He smote the sledded Polacks on the ice.

(I, i, 47–74)

In scenes four and five, with Hamlet now present, the ghost returns and silently beckons Hamlet to follow it. Hamlet commands the ghost to speak. With Hamlet present, it finally speaks, revealing to Hamlet the story of how Claudius murdered him and married his wife. Thus, the ghost reveals itself in a double movement, at first seen but not heard, and subsequently speaking its story to Hamlet. This double revelation will be recapitulated later in the play by the theatrical revelation of this same story in Hamlet's *Mousetrap*: the story first unfolding silently in the dumb show, followed by its spoken analog. In both cases, seeing turns out to be an unreliable basis of knowledge. Rather than confirming one another, the relation of the seen to the said leads to mystery rather than clarity.

In the third act, Hamlet advises the visiting players on the purpose of theatre. He famously invokes the mirror metaphor to illustrate how good acting should work:

Suit the action to the word, the
word to the action, with this special
observance, that you o'erstep not the modesty of
nature. For anything so o'erdone is from the purpose
of playing, whose end, both at the first and
now, was and is to hold, as 'twere, the mirror up to
nature, to show virtue her own feature, scorn her
own image, and the very age and body of the time
his form and pressure.

(III, ii, 18–26)

However, something is wrong with Hamlet's use of the mirror image here. For if a mirror reflects the world, it does so through reversal, inverting what it reflects. Mirrors in Shakespeare's day distorted as well as reflected those who gazed into them.[5] This irony was not lost on Shakespeare, as we will see when we look at what gets reflected in the several performances that make up Hamlet's *Mousetrap*. The mirror reappears later in Act II as Hamlet, having observed his uncle and mother watching *The Mousetrap*, confronts his mother in her closet. He is desperate to get the Queen to see herself and her sins more clearly.

> Come, come, and sit you down, you shall not budge
> You go not till I set you up a glass
> Where you may see the inmost part of you.
>
> (III, iv, 23–25)

Ironically, at exactly this point in the scene, Hamlet hears a sound behind the arras. Unable to see who the intruder is, Hamlet wrongly assumes the intruder is Claudius, and he stabs the unseen intruder behind the arras and kills Polonius. Turning from the corpse of Polonius back to his mother, Hamlet demands that she compares the pictures of her dead husband and her current spouse:

> Look here upon this picture and on this,
> The counterfeit presentment of two brothers.
> See what a grace was seated on this brow,
> Hyperion's curls, the front of Jove himself,
> An eye like Mars' to threaten and command,
> A station like the herald Mercury
> New-lighted on a heaven-kissing hill,
> A combination and a form indeed
> Where every god did seem to set his seal
> To give the world assurance of a man.
> This was your husband. Look you now what follows.
> Here is your husband, like a mildewed ear
> Blasting his wholesome brother. Have you eyes?
> Could you on this fair mountain leave to feed
> And batten on this moor? Ha! Have you eyes?
>
> (III, iv, 63–77)

To which the Queen responds:

> O Hamlet, speak no more!
> Thou turn'st my eyes into my very soul,
> And there I see such black and grainèd spots
> As will not leave their tinct.
>
> (III, iv, 99–102)

Again, confidence in the reliability of visual knowledge is undercut as the ghost of Old Hamlet appears. More precisely, the ghost appears to Hamlet. The Queen sees nothing and attributes the vision to Hamlet's madness.

QUEEN
Alas, how is 't with you,
That you do bend your eye on vacancy
And with th' incorporal air do hold discourse?
Forth at your eyes your spirits wildly peep,
And, as the sleeping soldiers in th' alarm,
Your bedded hair, like life in excrements,
Start up and stand an end. O gentle son,
Upon the heat and flame of thy distemper
Sprinkle cool patience! Whereon do you look?

HAMLET
On him, on him! Look you how pale he glares.
His form and cause conjoined, preaching to stones,
Would make them capable. *To the Ghost.* Do not
look upon me,
Lest with this piteous action you convert
My stern effects. Then what I have to do
Will want true color—tears perchance for blood.

QUEEN
To whom do you speak this?

HAMLET
Do you see nothing there?

QUEEN
Nothing at all; yet all that is I see.

HAMLET
Nor did you nothing hear?

QUEEN
No, nothing but ourselves.

HAMLET
Why, look you there, look how it steals away!
My father, in his habit as he lived!
Look where he goes even now out at the portal!
Ghost exits.

QUEEN
This is the very coinage of your brain.
This bodiless creation ecstasy
Is very cunning in.

(III, iv, 133–159)

In *Discipline and Punish*, Michel Foucault demonstrates how observation becomes a powerful tool of social control when tied to state power (1977). For Foucault, the seminal model for observation as a form of power was Jeremy Bentham's conception of a Panopticon, which Bentham imagined as a benevolent kind of control for inmates of social institutions such as schools, mental asylums, and prisons. The Panopticon, an all-seeing central observation tower, was the prescient precursor of the ubiquitous security cameras that now record every move high above our streets and buildings.

In *Hamlet*, Denmark's Panopticon is the network of spies dispatched by Claudius and Polonius to surreptitiously observe Hamlet, Ophelia, and Laertes in an attempt to uncover buried motives, hidden feelings, and thoughts. Shakespeare's Denmark anticipates Bentham's world of totalizing observation. Unbeknownst to Hamlet, Claudius and Polonius secrete themselves to observe Hamlet's meeting with Ophelia in an attempt to understand Hamlet's strange behavior regarding Polonius' daughter. Later in the play, Polonius spies on Hamlet behind the arras in the Queen's chamber to observe Hamlet's relation to his mother, with fatal consequences for the old man and ultimately for Hamlet as well. Hamlet spies on Claudius in prayer and contemplates killing him. Polonius dispatches Voltemand to Paris to spy on Laertes. In Act II, ii, anxious to understand what is troubling the young Prince, Claudius engages Rosencrantz and Guildenstern to closely observe their friend "Sith nor th' exterior nor the inward man/ Resembles that it was" (II, ii, 6–7). Just offstage we have the Ghost of Old Hamlet watching everything. And finally, there is the audience, the ultimate unobserved observers of *Hamlet*.

But in *Hamlet,* spying does not work. How accurate is vision in figuring out the characters that populate *Hamlet*? The audience observes this play for over four hours, and by the end, what do they know? What does Hamlet feel for Ophelia? What is Hamlet's real problem? What secrets lie within Ophelia's head and heart? Who is Laertes really, and what or whom does he desire? What did Gertrude know, and when? Does Old Hamlet's ghost really appear to Hamlet as he accuses his mother of incestuous relations, or is it merely a hallucination? Even those closest to these characters do not seem to know. In matters of character, it would seem, seeing is not to be believed.

In the ultimate reflexive move, characters are also urged to spy on themselves. Before he leaves for France, Laertes warns his sister to beware of her own desires, fearing that she does not know herself.

For Hamlet, and the trifling of his favour,
Hold it a fashion and a toy in blood,

A violet in the youth of primy nature,
Forward, not permanent, sweet, not lasting,
The perfume and suppliance of a minute,
No more.

OPHELIA
No more but so?

LAERTES
Think it no more.
For nature, crescent, does not grow alone
In thews and bulk, but, as this temple waxes,
The inward service of the mind and soul
Grows wide withal. Perhaps he loves you now,
And now no soil nor cautel doth besmirch
The virtue of his will; but you must fear,
His greatness weighed, his will is not his own,
For he himself is subject to his birth.
He may not, as unvalued persons do,
Carve for himself, for on his choice depends
The safety and the health of this whole state.
And therefore must his choice be circumscribed
Unto the voice and yielding of that body
Whereof he is the head. Then, if he says he loves you,
It fits your wisdom so far to believe it
As he in his particular act and place
May give his saying deed, which is no further
Than the main voice of Denmark goes withal.
Then weigh what loss your honour may sustain
If with too credent ear you list his songs
Or lose your heart or your chaste treasure open
To his unmastered importunity.
Fear it, Ophelia; fear it, my dear sister,
And keep you in the rear of your affection,
Out of the shot and danger of desire.

                                                            (I, iii, 6–39)

To this, Ophelia responds with her admonition to her brother that he also may not know himself:

OPHELIA
I shall the effect of this good lesson keep
As watchman to my heart. But, good my brother,
Do not, as some ungracious pastors do,

Show me the steep and thorny way to heaven,
Whiles, like a puffed and reckless libertine,
Himself the primrose path of dalliance treads
And recks not his own rede.

LAERTES
O, fear me not.

(I, v, 49–56)

Both Laertes and Ophelia warn each other about hidden desire, aspects of themselves that are not only invisible to the rest of the world but may be hidden from
themselves. Polonius also mistrusts his understanding of his son and in Act II dispatches Reynaldo to Paris to spy on Laertes "to make inquire/ Of his behaviour"
(II, I, 4–5). Polonius fears that his son may have a secret life of vice in Paris, a life
that is not evident in the Laertes that we see in Denmark.

Inquire me first what Danskers are in Paris;
And how, and who, what means, and where they keep,
What company, at what expense; and finding
By this encompassment and drift of question
That they do know my son, come you more nearer
Than your particular demands will touch it.
Take you, as 'twere, some distant knowledge of him,
As thus: "I know his father and his friends
And, in part, him." Do you mark this, Reynaldo?

REYNALDO
Ay, very well, my lord.

POLONIUS
"And, in part, him, but," you may say, "not well.
But if 't be he I mean, he's very wild,
Addicted so and so." And there put on him
What forgeries you please—marry, none so rank
As may dishonor him, take heed of that,
But, sir, such wanton, wild, and usual slips
As are companions noted and most known
To youth and liberty.

REYNALDO
As gaming, my lord.

POLONIUS
Ay, or drinking, fencing, swearing,
Quarreling, drabbing—you may go so far.

REYNALDO

My lord, that would dishonor him.

POLONIUS

Faith, no, as you may season it in the charge.
You must not put another scandal on him
That he is open to incontinency;
That's not my meaning. But breathe his faults so quaintly
That they may seem the taints of liberty,
The flash and outbreak of a fiery mind,
A savageness in unreclaimèd blood,
Of general assault.

(II, i, 8–39)

Our confidence in what we have observed of Laertes and Ophelia (and by implication every other character in the play) is undercut by a suspicion that there is more to each of them than meets the eye. Observation in the play turns out to be a perilous path to knowledge of others and knowledge of oneself.[6]

Meaning through classification

Classification, the interplay of contrast and analogy is a third strategy of meaning-making that Shakespeare puts to the test in *Hamlet*. In my book *Culture in Mind* (1996), I proposed that meaning-making for humans involves categorization (opposition) and analogy (parallelism)—the interplay of difference and similarity. Scholars have long stressed the importance of categories and stable distinctions as a basic foundation for human cognition and meaning-making.[7] The importance of analogical thinking and similarity-mapping for meaning-construction has been less frequently emphasized but has emerged as a central issue in metaphor theory.[8] Numerous forms of structural and sensory replication ranging from synesthesia (the cross-modal mapping of sensory qualities between domains such as the perception of light and dark sounds) to metaphor to structural parallelism are central to how humans construct and extend meaning.

In *Culture in Mind*, I coined the phrase *analogical schematization* for the fundamental process of constructing analogies in the quest for meaning. This process includes but goes well beyond linguistic mappings. Thus, the power of metaphor in human meaning-making, so thoroughly elaborated and illustrated by metaphor theorists like George Lakoff (1987), Max Black (1962), Andrew Ortony (1993), Zoltan Kövecses (1986), Giles Fauconnier (1997), Mark Turner (1996), and Raymond Gibbs (1994), is the most obvious instance of the power of analogical thinking in human experience applied to the domain of words.[9] Support for the importance of analogy in meaning construction can be found in anthropology, cognitive psychology, and linguistics. It is also implied in Plato's dialogue on learning, *The Meno*, where Plato suggests that all learning is a kind of remembering such that new knowledge is always a replication of things already known. Novel knowledge always has an analog in what we already know. Plato called this kind of learning, *anamnesis*, a deliberate recalling of buried knowledge.

Less well documented is the importance for meaning-making of the dialectical interplay of difference (as in categorization or metonymy—part-to-whole relations) and similarity (as in analogical reasoning or metaphor). As Lévi-Strauss famously proposes in *The Savage Mind* (1966), traditional societies often express sophisticated philosophical ideas through categorical oppositions (like nature/culture, sacred/profane, raw/cooked, or good/evil), mapping the abstract distinctions analogically onto a vast array of particular phenomena, thereby creating powerful cultural models using the language of concrete phenomena. For structuralists like Lévi-Strauss, constructing a meaningful cultural world requires both the stability of key conceptual categories and the ability to project these categories analogically onto a large variety of disparate phenomena. Meaning-making requires complex categorization exploiting the interplay of difference and similarity.

With an obvious grasp of the significance of difference and similarity in making-meaning, Shakespeare constructed *Hamlet* around a great variety of oppositions and mappings at every level of the play, presumably aware that they would trigger a natural effort towards meaning-making for the audience. Making sense of Hamlet's world requires comprehending distinctions between father/son, brother/brother, Hamlet Sr./Hamlet Jr., mother/wife, mother/aunt, uncle/father, Hamlet/Hamlet, victim/murderer, innocent/guilty, Hamlet/Fortinbras, performance/reality, living/dead, funeral/wedding, among many others. Equally important as these distinctions are the play's many structural parallels of plot, character, action, and performance, which lend the play the feeling of ritual performance.

Francis Fergusson has called Shakespeare's theatre a form of "ritual drama," reflecting what he calls its "ancient roots." The narrative technique in such ritual theatre is "argument by emblem rather than by propositional means" (Fergusson 1949: 120). Fergusson cites Caroline Spurgeon's claim that Shakespeare was possessed of a "pictorial imagination" through which he developed his ideas. This kind of ritual drama is especially effective in communicating ideas through its constituting forms. J.A. Bryant Jr. goes even further in examining Shakespeare's attraction to analogical structures, proposing that Shakespeare's work, particularly in his later plays, depended on Christian allegory for their ultimate meaning:

> Profitable as it is to consider Shakespeare's plays as studies in human relations or as reflections of the Elizabethan world picture, we are lingering on the periphery when we limit our attention to such matters. Fundamentally Shakespeare's plays are explorations of mythic fragments, whereby the movement of the fable at hand, whether from English history, Roman history, Italian novella, or English fabliau, is revealed as participating by analogy in an action which, from the poet's point of view, is Christian, divine, and eternal.
>
> (Bryant 1955: 211)

Shakespeare uses both categorical difference and analogical parallelism throughout *Hamlet*. Because *Hamlet* is constructed on a foundation of repeated plot structures, the play would seem to provide strong support for Shakespeare's reliance on analogical structures in constructing his plays. Denmark is filled with echoes. The revenge plot, most saliently manifested in Hamlet's struggle to avenge his father's murder, is repeated by the Fortinbras revenge story and eventually by Laertes' revenge of his father's murder and more obliquely by the almost-lost revenge story of the Polish soldiers who burst into the story at its very end.

The revenge theme replicates itself more fundamentally, producing an endless loop in which the victim becomes the victimizer, the murderer becomes the murdered. The elder Hamlet is the victim in relation to Claudius, but the killer in relation to Old Fortinbras. This loop is built into the heart of the revenge scenario. By killing Claudius, Hamlet mimics the very act that led to his revenge. The replications proliferate when Hamlet unwittingly kills Polonius and becomes the murderer in Laertes' revenge story. This is the paradox at the heart of revenge and why revenge so easily moves from event to ritual. The revenge plot's repetitive character is a kind of grotesque transformation of the royal succession theme in which one Hamlet (the father) dies so that another Hamlet (the son) can take his place. In his first encounter with Hamlet in Act I, Claudius effectively parodies this endless reiteration in the chain of death and succession that underlies the revenge scenario in urging Hamlet to bring his perpetual mourning to an end:

> 'Tis sweet and commendable in your nature, Hamlet,
> To give these mourning duties to your father.
> But you must know your father lost a father,
> That father lost, lost his, and the survivor bound
> In filial obligation for some term
> To do obsequious sorrow.

(I, ii, 90–96)

But for Hamlet, his father's perpetual dying is transformed into perpetual mourning, which is itself transformed into perpetual cycles of revenge.

"Unalogy" and *The Mousetrap*

Hamlet seems to overflow with what Francis Fergusson (1949) calls "analogies of action." However, a closer look at how they are developed in the play suggests a more complex use of analogy in the form of self-canceling pseudo-parallelisms, tropes which might be better called "unalogies." The intent to reveal hidden truth through the power of analogy makes possible *Hamlet's* central act, the staging of *The Mousetrap*. Hamlet's play-within-a-play might be thought of as a kind of divination rite. Its intended purpose is to enforce reflective self-knowledge by staging a powerful theatrical analog to the unrevealed murder story, forcing Claudius to see himself and thus betray himself.[10]

However, in *Hamlet*, the emergence of meaning through generative analogical projection is fatally disrupted.[11] Consider the fate of conventional categorical differences in *Hamlet*. We have seen how in the unseemly overlapping of rituals at Elsinore Castle, marriage and funeral rites were conflated, their distinction blurred. Hamlet's father-as-ghost is neither living nor fully dead. Ophelia cannot keep her love for her father and that for Hamlet apart, while Hamlet comes close to confusing Ophelia's country matters with his mater's undiscoverable "country." The quest for clear contrasts is repeatedly disrupted by emergent and uninvited similarities as distinctions blur and oppositions run together.

Moreover, Hamlet's attempt at evoking meaning by analogy in his staging of *The Mousetrap* is disrupted by the unexpected intrusion of difference. The staging of old Hamlet's murder as a play at Court produces an unanticipated result. Hamlet mounts not one but three dramatic versions of the revenge scenario. The first, the Player's rehearsal of the Pyrrhus-Priam scene, is just words. The second, a dumb show, is just gesture. The third, the play itself, is both word and gesture. However, rather than repeating one another, each enactment seems to reveal a supplementary reading, a repetition that is at once the same and different, an echo and a counter. Each enactment spills beyond its expected message, showing us more than is intended, more, one suspects, than even Hamlet wishes to see. Where we crave the comforts of similarity, we encounter disconcerting difference. Where we crave distinction, we get disarming similarity. The effort after meaning is fundamentally impaired.

Hamlet's own words prove ironically prophetic. The purpose of playing, he lectures the players, "was and is to hold, as 'twere, a mirror up to nature" (III, ii, 19–21). Yet as we have noted, if a mirror can reflect nature, it does so only by inversion. Where replication marries inversion, art is not simply mimetic but radically transformative. The mirror image proves not so much an exact copy as an alteration, at once illuminating and dissembling. Each version of *The Mousetrap* provides just such a transformation. Where we had sought a reassuring repetition, we experience a troubling dislocation. The theatrical mirror has become a kaleidoscope.

The initial performance is a kind of audition for the actors that Hamlet orders up, a spontaneous recitation of a scene enacting Pyrrhus' revenge against Priam for his father Achilles' death by the hand of Priam's son Paris. While not a direct recounting of old Hamlet's murder, the scene stages an initial reading of the revenge motif. However, rather than a clear picture of the revenge scenario, the scene enacts an equivocal view of revenge in which the victim and the victimizer are conflated. In terms of the revenge scenario at the heart of *Hamlet*, Old Priam "the unnervéd father," is both "the victimized son" and "the father of Pyrrhus' father's killer." For his part, Pyrrhus triggers two quite different emblems: "the avenging son" (avenging his father's death) and the "killer son" (slaying Priam "the father"). The revenge scenario implodes in a dizzying set of reversals. Of what mental state and of what state of affairs does this reading represent an objective correlative? How are we supposed to feel about what we are seeing?

The second staging of the murder story by Hamlet is the dumb show preceding the play. It is straightforward enough: a king is poisoned surreptitiously by an intruder, who then marries the King's widow. But because there are only actions and no names, we do not know who this intruder is. The audience assumes that this version is a clear enactment of Claudius' treachery, as the ghost has revealed to Hamlet. After all, that is Hamlet's explicit intent on staging the play for the king and queen. However, when the prologue gives way to the third staging, the spoken version of the play (presumably a repeat of the dumb show) Hamlet breaks into the action to assure us that the poisoner is not the King's brother, but one Lucianus, "nephew to the King." In Hamlet's account, it is the nephew rather than the uncle who kills the king and marries the widow. The revelation afforded by *The Mousetrap* is not the one we had expected. And in conflating uncle and nephew, we have an incoherent hybrid of two very different stories. The multiple retellings of the story do not add up. Uncle and nephew, killer and (indirect) victim have changed places. At the expected moment of its central revelation, the revenge scenario falls apart.[12] The attempt at theatrical illumination collapses in the face of unanticipated revelation.

Instead of the uncle/brother's expected revelation as murderer/adulterer, what is revealed is the unanticipated guilt of the nephew/son who kills his uncle and marries the uncle's wife. Revenge and fratricide fuse in a disconcerting pastiche. When Claudius calls for light (ironically at the entrance of "Lucianus") and flees the theater, is he reacting to recognizing himself as the murderer (of the old Hamlet) or as the victim (of his nephew's revenge)? The introduction of Lucianus (a name derived from light) into the performance has brought him only darkness. Taken together, the distinction between murderer and victim, central to the moral force of revenge, collapses on itself. To put these three accounts of the initial situation together is to look at the world through a prism in which images split and recombine in powerfully suggestive but fundamentally uninterpretable ways.

By confounding the work of similarity and difference, *The Mousetrap* reveals not just one hidden truth but a tangle of conflicting meaning, both more and less than we wanted to know. Whose conscience is caught in Hamlet's Mousetrap? The performance traps Claudius as surely as it was intended to do, but it has also snared Hamlet himself, and both the internal and external audiences watching the play. In the unexplained and unexpected images they disclose (Hamlet-as-victim, Hamlet-as-murderer, Hamlet-as-incestuous-adulterer), the expanded "Mousetrap" (i.e., the audition plus the dumb show plus the play) becomes as much a reflection of Hamlet's own undiscovered country as it of his uncle's hidden misdeeds.

The play's three repetitions do not achieve Hamlet's aim of focusing the viewer on a single guilty act or a principal culprit, but work to spread the guilt beyond its original habitation. As a vehicle of clarification, *The Mousetrap* backfires. Instead of providing a clear resolution of Denmark's problem, these performances increase the possibilities of interpretation in a particularly disturbing way. *The Mousetrap* propagates a succession of conflicting images, a tangled chain of guilt which threatens to encompass all of Denmark. Claudius, craving light, flees the theater and momentarily stops the expanding chain of signification set into motion by the performances.

Just as the expected analogs (the three stagings of *The Mousetrap*) have exploded into a cacophony of unexpected differences, a key distinction (victim and murderer) has imploded, producing an unanticipated and unwelcome analog. Like that indistinguishable pair, Rosencrantz and Guildenstern, a difference is at once proposed and erased. Presumed opposites have become interchangeable and reversible.[13] This movement anticipates the play's final scene when the two swords (one, a real weapon, envenomed with poison, the other just a prop) are unexpectedly exchanged for each other so that Hamlet and Laertes become at the same moment both murderers and victims of each other. In their deaths, Hamlet and Laertes are at once opposed and conjoined.

Hamlet engages us simultaneously as both a series of particular events and as general forms. Its particular characters and events unfold for us within historical time and space. However, they also represent a series of emblems rippling like repeated echoes throughout the play. These emblems, analogies of action and character, appeal not so much to our sense of the dramatic as to our ritual sensibilities. The play's forms spill over its local inhabitants, providing both a sense of the particular "instance" and an intuition of the abstract "type." The first reading of *Hamlet* is as theater, the second as a ritual form.

There are many Hamlets, each an echo of the other, each at once a repetition and a difference. The analogies proliferate. There is the avenger emblem: young-Hamlet-as-young-Fortinbras, old-Hamlet-as-old Fortinbras, and Hamlet-as-Laertes. Most surprising is Hamlet-as-Claudius, a reading revealed in *The Mousetrap*, which suggests that for Hamlet to avenge a regicide, he must repeat the regicide. Through the proliferation of maimed analogies, *Hamlet* produces a failure of both distinction and similarity in making meaning. Where we need a difference, we get unwelcome replication; where we need an analogy, we get unwelcome distinction. Distinction and analogy have collapsed into unalogy, leaving us, like Claudius, in the dark.

The pervasive compulsion to repetition in Hamlet points to the play's characteristic problem: negotiating identity and difference. Conflating compulsive repetition and authentic action, the play works on its characters and its audience to disrupt the ability to distinguish acting from being. This problem is the source of the notorious and much misunderstood theme of incest that inhabits the play like a shadowy presence rummaging around in the basement. Incest is a particular kind of repetition compulsion, a self-canceling conflation of love objects. In Western thought, at least, it is the mother of all such compulsions, the foundational emblem of all "unalogy." Here, desire fails to make distinctions that both are and are not called for between two people, people who are both different and not.

What is the matter with Hamlet? That matter is closely linked with Hamlet's mater. The "matter/mater" link is repeated obsessively throughout *Hamlet*, most often concerning Gertrude. So much hinges on what (or who) we take to be Hamlet's "matter." As he plays the role of a madman in his uncle's Court, the Prince speaks of "country matters" to Ophelia, but nearly falls into the wrong lap. "Country matters," it turns out, fall perilously close to the "mater's country," an "undiscovered country" that both reveals and conceals its presence in the play's basement.

Yet incest is not *the* theme of Hamlet, not its ultimate meaning. To reduce Hamlet to Oedipus is to misread the play. This is true not just because Hamlet is not Oedipus, but because the play is inherently irreducible and cannot be accounted for by a single meaning. *Hamlet* is constructed to proliferate a chain of incomplete readings rather than to suggest a final, primal ground for its action. Incest is a significant link in this chain, another (but not *just* another) analogy for something with no clear source. It acts as a disturbing reminder of the impossibility of uniting objective and subjecting correlatives for the play's action. Incest remains another image of the "offstage" (here, the unconscious), in relation to which we seek to make sense of what we can know of the play.

Hamlet is about a chain of interrupted successions and confused relationships. In seeking to become his father, Hamlet must not take the identification too literally, as the nephew does in *The Mousetrap*, both avenging the father, and marrying his wife. For her part, Ophelia's passions do not always distinguish between her feelings for Laertes, for Hamlet, and her dead father. We never directly witness any indication of the erotic nexus in which Ophelia and Hamlet are reportedly bound. Its reality in the play is as reported speech, and through dramatic indirection, as are Hamlet's attachment to Gertrude and Ophelia's to her father. As for Gertrude, her passions conflate brother and brother, husband and son.

Feelings run amok, as the play unsuccessfully seeks a coherent and workable pattern for its emotional content. Structurally primed for meaning by the proliferation of analogical forms and conventional categories, we perceive clusters of incompatible acts and feelings instead. Ophelia's lyrical mad scenes are mad not because she has succumbed to grief over the loss of her father, but because she cannot distinguish her loss of Polonius from that of Hamlet, his murderer. Thus, her lament is out of joint, erotically charged just where it should be filially devout. In *Hamlet*, many things are out of joint. What should be separated is fused; what should be joined is severed. It is hardly surprising that within *Hamlet*'s Denmark the conventional ritual forms are perilously muddled and fail to maintain their distinctness. In his book, *How Societies Remember*, Paul Connerton (1989) discusses the privileged role of ritual as a collective embodiment of social memory, exploited by all human communities. What sort of social memory is made possible by ritual forms that fail to articulate in this way? The world of *Hamlet* is one in which life-affirming distinctions and meaning affirming analogies fail to hold.

One analogy would seem to illuminate a path to a final understanding of *Hamlet* and a legitimate alternative as the play's authentic setting. In this view, the offstage center of *Hamlet* is Norway. The play's conclusion suggests that perhaps the real plot of *Hamlet* is the Fortinbras revenge and succession story. One of the great ironies of the play is that, as an enactment of the succession scenario, the play is ultimately not Hamlet's story. In terms of its dramatic structure, the play does not turn on the problem of Hamlet's succession to his father's throne, but on another succession tale, the one so many productions omit. At once the play's past, and its future, the Fortinbras succession story encapsulates *Hamlet* and transcends it. It precedes the events on stage, following Hamlet's prophesy of young Fortinbras' succession to Denmark's throne, and moves us beyond the play's action at its end.

Though central to *Hamlet*, the Norway plot is notable mainly for its absence.[14] The Fortinbras story adds a strange undercurrent of unease for us as if we have been watching a story whose center is displaced. Relying on observation to make sense of our world always risks the possibility that we are attending to the wrong thing. We pay attention to the Hamlet revenge story only if we forget the Fortinbras story. In his first encounter with Hamlet, after recounting the story of his murder to his son, the ghost departs, but not before warning Hamlet not to forget him. Hamlet's response says it all, though ironically, the audience may well miss the point:

> Adieu, adieu, adieu. Remember me.
> *He exits.*

HAMLET
O all you host of heaven! O Earth! What else?
And shall I couple hell? O fie! Hold, hold, my heart,
And you, my sinews, grow not instant old,
But bear me stiffly up. Remember thee?
Ay, thou poor ghost, whiles memory holds a seat
In this distracted globe. Remember thee?
Yea, from the table of my memory
I'll wipe away all trivial, fond records,
All saws of books, all forms, all pressures past,
That youth and observation copied there,
And thy commandment all alone shall live
Within the book and volume of my brain,
Unmixed with baser matter.

(I, v, 99–111)

Hamlet vows to wipe all other concerns from his memory, focusing only on his father's story. And in so doing, his attention is diverted from what turns out to be the real point. In his speech, the key phrase is "this distracted globe," a piece of ironic wordplay that carries more meaning than Hamlet intends. The distracted globe simultaneously refers to Hamlet's distracted state of mind, a distracted world, and a distracted audience (of the Globe Theater) whose attention is at that very moment being focused by Shakespeare on the wrong murder and the wrong revenge story to make sense of the actual succession story that (we will all learn) is in play.

But then again, this is not really Denmark, not really Elsinore: it is a theater. What naturally claims our attention is not always what we need to be observing. As every director of *Hamlet* has concluded, if the play is to work at all, whatever the ultimate truth of the matter, Norway cannot take Denmark's place as the play's real home. For some directors, the Fortinbras story begs to be cut from the production in the interest of achieving an acceptable focus for the play.[15] The play's emotional structure will not support both Hamlet and Fortinbras: one of them needs to go. Inevitably it is Fortinbras, though he will eventually return. Even when the story is left intact, the audience generally forgets that story until forced to remember at the play's end. If Hamlet is "away," I doubt that he has gone to Norway.

If Norway is to be understood as the play's undiscovered country, the objective correlative for Denmark's troubles is woefully out of sync with Hamlet's emotional state. The split makes effective theater impossible, though it paradoxically contributes to the play's greatness. This correlative proves inadequate to make a case for the play. We need something else to make the play whole. The symbolizing impulse runs wild, generating empty analogs and failed distinctions.

Inconclusion

Funeral rites simultaneously acknowledge mortality and deny it by an affirmation of social memory and the life-giving powers of public commemoration. Through ritual, as in art, death takes on an articulate form, becomes momentarily conceivable. Funeral rites both acknowledge death and seek to subdue its power. But without coherent rituals, a society has no power over death, no way to bring it safely into view while moving the departed safely out of view. There is no template to construct an appropriate feeling. Death remains unthinkable in such a world, perhaps even unfeelable, an undiscovered country, ever absent, yet always present. As Connerton has suggested, the crippling of conventional templates for social memory is closely linked to what psychoanalysts call "acting out" and its characteristic compulsive repetition:

> It is as a result of this compulsion to repeat that analysands deliberately place themselves in distressing situations: in this way repeating an old experience. But in compulsive repetition the agents fail to remember the prototype of their present actions. . . . The compulsion to repeat has replaced the capacity to remember.
>
> (Connerton 1989: 25)

For *Hamlet*, the linked notions of *acting out* and of *repetition compulsion* suggest the troubled nexus in the play between theatrical performance and ritual. No death in *Hamlet* is successfully resolved through conventional rites. Failed rite becomes brilliant theater. For his part, Old Hamlet, already dead, refuses to go away. What is memorialized, however, is not the old King's life, but merely his interminable dying. "Too much in the sun/son," young Hamlet will not cease his mourning, refusing to complete and thereby to affirm the ritual work by which contemporaries are translated into ancestors. He cannot succeed his father if he will not let go. He cannot let go until he can remember.

By the play's end, at Horatio's direction, Hamlet is carried up to the ramparts of the castle where the play began, his dying interrupted, transmuted into a theatrical passage. The play ends where it had begun, on the castle's parapets, with a dead

Hamlet unable to complete his story, and a surrogate asked to tell it for him. This final act does not serve to resolve Hamlet's death ritually. It fails to find a form by which to bring appropriate closure to the play. Instead, Horatio's commemoration serves only to fold the play back upon itself.[16] In *Hamlet,* ritual cannot complete its work until the memory which it is repeatedly compelled to represent can be uncovered, and a coherent set of correlatives—objective and subjective—for the play's action can be brought to light. But memory can only do its work when we have a workable strategy for interpreting what has transpired. By the play's conclusion, the attempt to stage this buried memory sputters out, ending but not concluding. Instead of a satisfying conclusion, we get another telling of the play, a desperate repetition which becomes both the intended means of finding meaning, and the impediment to its emergence.

In conclusion, we get inconclusion. *Hamlet* is transformed from living theater into compulsive rite and then back again into theater. The play ends up as an endless rehearsal of an incomplete script. Thus, it is not without irony that *Hamlet* finds its place as the ultimate repeatable piece of theater, endlessly spawning new versions of itself. One last time, the play strives and fails to bring forth its absent center, reveal its ultimate meaning, and thereby to complete itself. In the end, doomed to recapitulation without end and recall without memory, *Hamlet* fails to stage its own funeral.

Notes

1 For ease of access and consistency, all quotes from Shakespeare's plays are based on the Folger library online texts of Shakespeare plays which can be accessed at https://shakespeare.folger.edu/.

2 The surprise at the end of *Hamlet* is not simply that young Fortinbras avenges the death of his own father, but that the "Polack" armies who fight for him are at last wreaking their own revenge for their earlier defeat by old King Hamlet, revealed in a seemingly irrelevant anecdote at the very beginning of the play when Horatio says that the ghost of Old Hamlet was wearing

> …the very armor he had on
> When he the ambitious Norway combated.
> So frowned he once when, in an angry parle,
> He smote the sledded Polacks on the ice.

(I, i, 71–74)

3 Schechner 1985. On the complex relations between theatre and ritual, see also Geertz, 1980 and Mullaney 1991.

4 Lakoff 1994: 200.

5 In her book *Shakespearean Neuroplay* (Cook 2010), Amy Cook closely examines the use of mirrors in Shakespeare's plays in light of the historical development of mirrors, emphasizing its place in *Hamlet.*

6 On a historical note, it is telling that Shakespeare's image of universal spying was more than a literary device. Spying was a ubiquitous fact of life in Elizabethan England. From

1573 until he died in 1590, Elizabeth's principal secretary, Sir Frances Walsingham, acted as Elizabeth's spymaster, engaging a vast network of spies throughout England and beyond on the Continent to ferret out plotting Papists and supporters of Spain's King Phillip, who were a constant threat to Elizabeth's reign and life. Elizabeth's fears were well-founded, and Walsingham successfully prevented several plots against Elizabeth's life. *Hamlet*, however, suggests not the power of spying but the fallibility of the observing eye.

7 Lévi-Strauss (1966); Lévi-Strauss (1967); Hertz (2004); Douglas (2002); Rosche and Lloyd (1978); Lakoff (1987); Frank Keil (1987); Keil and Kelly (1987); Medin and Barsalou (1987).

8 Lakoff and Johnson (1980); Marks and Bornstein (1987); Robert Haskell, ed., *Cognition and Symbolic Structures, The Psychology of Metaphoric Transformation*, Norwood, NJ: Ablex 1987.

9 Immanuel Kant also recognized intuitive analogy, which he called s*ymbolization,* as an essential component of human aesthetic judgment (Kant 2000: 227). See also Makkreel (2015, 71).

10 On the alternation between "flow" and "reflexivity" in ritual performance, see Kapferer 1989.

11 In his analysis of the language of gender in *The Winter's Tale*, Maurice Hunt proposes that Shakespeare's language often betrays an impulse to undercut the conventional binaries of what we now call modernist thought, anticipating Baudrillard's recognition of the fundamental disruption of categories characteristic of Postmodern thinking:

> The implosion of binary opposites, especially the traditional antitheses of modernist thought, characterizes a recurrent postmodern action. Postmodern "hyperreality ... brings with it the collapse of all real antagonisms or dichotomies of value. . . ."
>
> (Hunt 1993–1994: 83–94)

12 *The Mousetrap's* disconcerting inversion of victim and culprit parallels Shakespeare's handling of the original true story of the "Murder of Gonzago" on which Hamlet's play is based. In 1538, the Duke of Urbino, Francesco Maria I della Rovere, died under mysterious circumstances. Under torture, the barber-surgeon attending the Duke confessed to having killed the Duke by pouring a vial of poison in the Duke's ear at the behest of a kinsman of the Duke's wife. That kinsman was named Luigi Gonzaga. While the barber was executed for the act, the rumored guilt of Gonzaga was never proved. In his version of the story, Shakespeare named *the victim* of the murder Gonzaga. The indirect agent of the murder becomes its victim, just as in *The Mousetrap*, the indirect victim switches place with the murderer.

13

KING
Thanks, Rosencrantz and gentle Guildenstern.

QUEEN
Thanks, Guildenstern and gentle Rosencrantz.

(II, ii, 35–36)

14 In an unpublished paper, Robert Paul has convincingly argued that *Hamlet* represents one version of the inter-generational succession scenario that dominated Shakespeare's thinking. Paul suggests that the Hamlet story represents a peculiar diversion in the play from its authentic problematic—the succession to the throne of Norway (Paul n.d.).

15 More than four hours in its uncut form, *Hamlet* begs to be heavily edited by a director and is almost always staged with many cuts to the original text. Clearly, Shakespeare
knew that this play would demand heavy editing by any director. He appears to have
constructed *Hamlet* so that directors would likely cut scenes and speeches (such as the
dumb show or Horatio's long speech in Act I detailing the Norway backstory) that would
appear extraneous to an effective production, but would actually eliminate key information from the play, rendering ultimate interpretation all the more difficult even as it made
the play more palatable to watch.

16 This interpretation of the play is most evident in Olivier's 1948 film version, which has
the play ending on the castle's parapet, just where it began.

2
SHAKESPEARE, IN THEORY

Few would deny Shakespeare's talents as a poet and dramatic storyteller. In this book, I focus on another side of Shakespeare's genius: his gifts as a thinker, a master of what social scientists call "social thought." With a few qualifications, I would call Shakespeare a major social theorist. Identifying Shakespeare as a theorist might seem to diminish his achievements as a playwright/poet, threatening to wring the life out of his work and turn his plays into something aridly abstract. While Shakespeare might not fit the standard image of a theorist, when viewed as great ideas wrapped in great stories, his plays conform very well to the classical idea of theory. "Theory," derived from the Greek term *theoria* ($\theta\epsilon\omega\rho\iota\alpha$), originally meant "viewing" or "observing." It came to have a more limited meaning as knowledge derived through contemplation. Theoretical knowledge is often contrasted with pragmatic knowledge, which is assumed to derive more from doing rather than speculation. Theory is sometimes used ironically in the sense of "just theory" to characterize an erroneous belief contradicted by experience.

"Grey…is all theory, And green the golden tree of life," wrote Goethe in Part I of *Faust* (Goethe 2003: 83). However, it is worth recalling that Goethe chose to give these words to Mephistopheles, in his attempt to lure a student away from his studies. Nonetheless, the student was easily seduced by the contrast between the ashen hues of theory and life's green fields. The very idea of staged theory can easily sound like a leaden alternative to the more engaging business of life. Unrelieved by the here-and-now of direct experience, the theoretical frame of mind might seem too austere and intimidating. Just as many fans of literature resist the rigors of literary theory, it is easy to argue for banishing theory from Shakespeare's stage. Yet this skeptical dismissal of the power of theory misses the excitement of discovering great ideas sequestered within great stories. It also misses the link between our immediate experience and the sometimes complex concepts we depend on to make sense of that experience. The psychologist Kurt Lewin once suggested in a paper on Field

DOI: 10.4324/9781003179771-4

Theory, "There is nothing more practical than a good theory" (Lewin 1952: 169). "Or less useful than a bad one," he might have added. Theory may energize, bore, confuse, or enlighten us, but it is an inevitable part of the human effort to figure things out. In writing his dramas, Shakespeare had figured out a good deal, more than we usually recognize.

Great literature will always have two contradictory effects on the reader. The centripetal force of fiction produces imaginative engagement, suspending disbelief and pulling the audience into the story. At the same time, a great text also exerts a contrary centrifugal force that provokes reflective disengagement. This centrifugal distancing is the famous "defamiliarization" of experience that Russian formalist critic Victor Shklovsky (1917) identified as the primary work of poetic art when it uses language to defamiliarize ordinary things, counteracting the dulling effects of habituated thought. Defamiliarization is literature's theoretical impulse. In writing plays that were meant both to engage the audience and cultivate philosophical speculation, Shakespeare faced a complex rhetorical dilemma that he resolved through a variety of literary techniques to be explored in Part III.

For some, Shakespeare's play with ideas may not appear systematic or explicit enough to count as genuine theory. This is not the place to debate which ideas count or do not count as genuine theory. What is certain is that Shakespeare's plays can be profitably read as serious reflections on many great ideas, many of which have been taken up by famous social theorists, but which tend to go unnoticed by his audiences, whose attentions are taken up with character and action. In these pages I hope to remedy that problem. One thing this book is *not* about is how theory has treated Shakespeare. Whereas literary theory often mines texts for exemplary passages illustrating a particular literary theory, my interest in theory is concerned with Shakespeare as a self-conscious theoretical mind. The aim is to treat the plays as creations of a sophisticated imagination enamored both with the pulse of life as lived and the more rarified plane of big ideas. In the rest of this chapter and the following chapter, we will examine some key influences from Shakespeare's own time that shaped his theoretical imagination. Getting our footing in Shakespeare's work means understanding his complex relationship to his society and culture. For example, Elizabethan literary traditions and Tudor education encouraged the creation of philosophically informed theater. Popular drama and philosophical exploration were understood as compatible modes of writing. In important ways, Shakespeare's grammar school education prepared him for the kind of theater he was to create.

Though he was relentlessly open to questioning conventional understandings of his day, it is nevertheless important to understand the worldview that shaped popular thought of Shakespeare's time. Our take on Elizabethan and Jacobean worldviews has changed over the last half-century. In the 1960s, when I first encountered Shakespeare as an undergraduate, it was common to assume that his plays reflected a late medieval worldview that shaped the thoughts and actions of Shakespeare's contemporaries. Students of Shakespeare were often introduced to Shakespeare's world by reading E.M.W. Tillyard's *The Elizabethan World Picture* (Tillyard 1955).

Though Tillyard's conservative vision of Shakespeare's England has not held up well among many contemporary historians and literary scholars, his book is still popular in classrooms to set the stage for an understanding of the cultural context of Shakespeare's plays.[1]

Tillyard's slim book was offered as a corrective to what Tillyard understood as a misleading secular vision of Elizabethan society current in his day:

> People still think of the Age of Elizabeth as a secular period between two outbreaks of Protestantism: a period in which religious enthusiasm was sufficiently dormant to allow the new humanism to shape our literature. They admit indeed that the quiet was precarious and that the Puritans were ever on the alert. But they allow the emphasis to be on the Queen's political intuitions, the voyages of discovery, and the brilliant externals of Elizabethan life.
>
> (p. 3)

For Tillyard, secular interpretations of Elizabethan culture too often overlooked the medieval, religiously grounded framework of ideas and values that shaped the Elizabethan "world picture." That picture included a general scheme for cosmic order governing the operation of the universe at every level. A great analogical chain linked the divinely ordained organization of the cosmos to hierarchical political and social arrangements, the normative relations among men, women, and children in a household, and even the natural organic relations governing the physical and moral constitution of a person. God's creation operated on the dual principles of hierarchy and analogy. The proper functioning of the universe depended on each constituent playing its divinely ordained part.

Tillyard cites as evidence for this worldview numerous passages from Milton, Spenser, and Shakespeare. His most frequently cited literary example of this great chain notion is a long but somewhat abridged excerpt from Ulysses' speech on "degree" from *Troilus and Cressida*'s first act. Here is part of the long the passage Tillyard offers.

> The heavens themselves, the planets, and this centre
> Observe degree, priority and place
> Insisture course proportion season form
> Office and custom, in all line of order
> And therefore is the glorious planet Sol
> In noble eminence enthron'd and spher'd
> Amidst the other whose med'cinable eye
> Corrects the ill aspects of planets evil
> And posts like the commandments of a king,
> Sans check, to good and bad.
>
> (I, iii, 89–98)

In her essay "The Ambiguity of *Troilus and Cressida*," [2] Joyce Carol Oates (1966) specifically discusses the ironic implications of this speech:

> Ulysses on degree is much quoted. His imagery is vivid in its power to create a sense of impending anarchy… But the faith in hierarchy is intended to support a military power. Ulysses' philosophy, though evoking universal imagery, is earthbound, and perhaps not so representative of the Elizabethan era as it is usually considered. Degree, *per se*, is idolized and, once reason has established this hierarchy reason is no longer free to question it. Questioning of the order is idolatry and repels Ulysses. There is not suggested here a chain of being which reaches from man to God but rather a chain of command which controls the individual. Moreover, it must be remembered that the intention of these philosophical remarks is simply to devise a means—it turns out to be rather simple, of enticing Achilles into battle. Ulysses speech at once transcends its context and is bound by it. If it is to be taken as the philosophical center of the play, then the play, on an ideological level, moves to complete tragedy; appetite "the universal wolf" will indeed eat himself up at last.
>
> (pp. 143–144)

Significantly, Oates' reference to appetite as "the universal wolf" is a reference to one of the lines from Ulysses' speech omitted by Tillyard.[3] Tillyard's practice of supporting his claims by assembling text fragments from early modern literature tends to isolate the quotes from their literary context. This decontextualization sometimes creates a misleading impression of what the authors had in mind. For example, in Ulysses' speech quoted above, Tillyard assumes that Shakespeare was putting an eloquent statement of Shakespeare's own view of the world in Ulysses' mouth and that this view might be used to make sense of his plays. The bombastic language of this declamation is itself a hint that the speech is intended ironically and is in no sense a simple statement of Shakespeare's view of how the world is organized. Irony, it would seem, was not included in Tillyard's picture of the Elizabethan world. Ulysses' appeal to an absolute order governing human life occurs in a famously problematical play that is structurally and thematically anything but a literary model for a finely tuned universe. *Troilus and Cressida* has been frequently criticized for its troublesome moral ambiguity and its stylistic incoherence. In its very structure, *Troilus and Cressida* is an odd play to use to justify Shakespeare's traditional view of world order since it fails to conform to any recognizable dramatic genre, its tone alternating repeatedly and unaccountably between comedy and tragedy.

Tillyard's Great Chain of Being is perpetually threatened by its evil twin, an impulse for disorder and chaos. Violations of this order and its restoration were understood in terms of sin and redemption. A kind of entropy (in human terms, an ever-present temptation to sin) competes relentlessly with God's mandate for order. Sin is both opposed and fused to order. This tension and its contingencies underwrite for Tillyard historical variations in literary representation and account for the distinctive character of Elizabethan literature in its relationship with the Christian sin-redemption narrative. So even Tillyard's tightly ordered picture does not depict a neatly ordered human world. The central link on that chain was the monarch who sat at the apex of the English social hierarchy and was understood to derive all power and legitimacy from God. In Tudor England, the office of king was supported by an elaborate set of practices, beliefs, and legal doctrines that underwrote the legitimation of the office and its occupants. Medieval theology figured prominently in justifications of the divine right of kings. Tillyard's Great Chain of Being was an ideology framing a politically and theologically conservative understanding of the nature of human society and its relation to an encompassing divinely ordained order.

An important legacy of medieval political theory still influential in Elizabethan England is the idea that the monarch comprised two bodies, a physical "body natural," and a spiritual or conceptual "body politic." This doctrine of "the king's two bodies" helped legitimate the institution of kingship and the doctrine of The Divine Right of Kings that emerged in the later years of Elizabeth's reign and was fully articulated by her successor, James I. In *The King's Two Bodies*, Ernst Kantorowicz (1957) traces the origins of the two-bodies notion as it emerged in legal and political disputes in the Elizabethan court. While the theoretical issues at stake in the court reports Kantorowicz cites were couched in obscure legal and theological abstraction that bordered on the mystical, the source of the controversy during the fourth year of Elizabeth's reign that produced the documents was the disposition of vast tracts of land. The case was recorded in detail by Edmund Plowden, an Elizabethan court reporter who was eventually appointed by Elizabeth as Counsel to the Duchy of Lancaster.[4] The matter at issue was the legal right of the Queen to control certain lands of the Duchy of Lancaster, lands that had once been owned as private property by the Lancastrian kings. These lands had been leased to an individual by Elizabeth's father, Henry VIII, for a period of 21 years. That individual had died before the expiration of the lease, and the land was leased again by Henry's successor Edward VI to a second individual for another 21-year period. Elizabeth sought to invalidate this second lease and reclaim the land, claiming that the lease was not legally binding since Edward VII was not of age when the lease was made. The justices denied Elizabeth's petition because the second lease performed by Edward VI was still the King's act, despite the nonage of the Edward at the time the lease was drawn up. Here, quoted at length by Kantorowicz, was the court's somewhat tortuous reasoning:

> although he [the King] has, or takes, the land in his natural Body, yet to this natural Body is conjoined his body Politic, which contains his royal Estate and Dignity; and the Body politic includes the Body natural, but the Body natural is the lesser, and with this the Body politic is consolidated. So that he has a Body natural, adorned and invested with the Estate and Dignity royal; and he has not a Body natural distinct and divided by itself from the Office and Dignity royal, but a Body natural and a Body politic together indivisible; and these two Bodies are incorporated in one Person and make one body and

not divers, and that is the Body corporate in the Body natural, *et e contra* the Body natural in the body corporate. So that the Body natural by this conjunction of the Body politic to it, (which Body politic contains the Office, Government, and the Majesty royal) is magnified, and by the said consolidation hath in it the body Politic.

(p. 9)

The idea of the king's two bodies entailed a doctrine of the transmission of the soul of the body politic at the officeholder's death to the physical body of the monarch's legitimate successor. It provides the theological justification for the continuity of the State beyond any given ruler's life and the re-embodiment of that state in the person of each succeeding monarch. The reasoning employed by the justices in the case of the Duchy of Lancaster had roots in the notion of the twinned nature of Christ, who, as God-made-flesh, was both human and divine. Kantorowicz notes this elaboration of traditional medieval political theology in the Elizabethan court's reasoning about kingship:

The jurists styled by Roman law so suggestively "Priests of Justice," developed in England not only a "Theology of Kingship"—this had become customary everywhere on the continent in the course of the twelfth and thirteenth centuries—but worked out a genuine "Royal Christology."

(p. 16)

While the idea of the two bodies surfaced explicitly in the legal writings of the Elizabethan court, Kantorowicz is at pains to show that this concept was a legacy of medieval political thought. In Chapter 3 of *The King's Two Bodies*, entitled "A Christ-Centered Kingship," Kantorowicz traces the two bodies concept to an anonymous medieval text dated around 1100 AD, written by a Norman author and found in the library of a prominent Elizabethan, Archbishop Matthew Parker. The text was a set of reflections on the king's dual nature and explicitly linked the notion of twinned kinship to the mysteries inherent in Christ's double identity.

Kantorowicz finds ample support within Shakespeare's plays for the influence of medieval theological and political conceptions in Elizabethan thought. Chapter 2 of *The King's Two Bodies* is a detailed analysis of *Richard II*, which Kantorowicz interprets as an exploration of the two bodies idea:

The legal concept of the King's Two Bodies cannot…be separated from Shakespeare. For if that curious image, which from modern constitutional thought has vanished all but completely, still has a very real and human meaning today, this is largely due to Shakespeare. It is he who has externalized that metaphor. He has made it not only the symbol, but indeed the very substance and essence of one of his greatest plays: *The Tragedy of King Richard II* is a tragedy of the Kings Two Bodies.

(p. 26)

Kantorowicz is right to highlight Shakespeare's interest in the idea of the king's two bodies. The paradoxes and dilemmas of kingship are not only recurrent themes in the history plays but are central issues in Shakespeare's tragedies of kingship such as *Hamlet, King Lear, Richard II, Henry IV Pts. 1 and II,* and *Julius Caesar.* The notion of plural selfhood implicit in the two bodies concept is a theme to which Shakespeare returns repeatedly in his work. It shaped Shakespeare's sense of the performative nature of self and the complex relations between the actor and his stage persona that were discussed in Chapter 1 in relation to *Hamlet.*[5]

Theory in the interrogative mood

As Tillyard and Kantorowicz suggest, Shakespeare's worldview was influenced by medieval theological and political beliefs central to Elizabethan political discourse. However, citing passages from the plays that allude to these older beliefs without recognition of their often-ironic rhetorical status in the plays does not demonstrate that Shakespeare held a monolithic medieval view of the cosmos and its relation to the state. The Great Chain of Being might be an accurate description of an idealized Elizabethan world picture, but, by itself, was not a picture that could make sense of the often-untidy realities of life and thought in Tudor England. While they may have overstated the case for the medieval foundation of Shakespeare's worldview, Tillyard and Kantorowicz both illuminate Shakespeare's keen interest in political theory and the nature of power.

Shakespeare's interest in ideas, however, was not limited to political theory. Like his dramatic sensibilities, Shakespeare's theoretical vision was broad and varied. His work encompasses a vast tableau of ideas spanning a wide range of philosophical issues: human nature, the relations between individual and society, the bonds that unite and divide people from one another, gender and sexuality, politics and power, the rocky road connecting love and marriage, the performativity of human life, moral dilemmas, the power and the danger of language, and, always, the slippery relations between art and life. Shakespeare went beyond developing his stories and plays around grand themes. In his plays, ideas do not always sit on the sidelines of the action. A close reading of his plays reveals a fearless theoretical sensibility at work, an analytical acuity often more reminiscent of a philosopher than a storyteller. In many of his plays, he develops what can only be called theoretical treatises that unfold just behind the stories. How Shakespeare carried out this sort of philosophical analysis without disrupting the story's narrative flow is something of a literary miracle, which will be the subject of Chapter 9.

In using Shakespeare to support his conservative picture of the Elizabethan worldview, Tillyard seems to assume that Shakespeare was an ideologist, planting his own views in the words of his characters. But Shakespeare was more daring and more equivocal than this suggests. He was not attracted to conventional solutions to philosophical questions. The notion that Shakespeare's plays present monolithic theoretical positions on major philosophical issues or clean resolutions to venerable theoretical debates is misleading. Shakespeare's theoretical inclinations were not those of an ideologue. He was neither a reductionist nor a systematizer. Shakespeare was a philosophical trouble-maker, writing in the interrogative mood and approaching the world as a set of intractable dilemmas. As a dramatist, he explored ideas by portraying people trapped by life's dilemmas. Shakespeare's genius was not in his ability to resolve dissonance but to crystallize great conundrums and their implications. While his characters represent humanity's full spectrum and speak in many voices, Shakespeare's own voice was characteristically ironic. The irony that often runs through his texts is what most often produces his work's distinctive theoretical mood. It is one thing to suggest that Shakespeare's plays offer incidental reflection on significant political, social, and philosophical issues. But it is something else altogether to propose that the plays were written explicitly as theatrically framed explorations of significant philosophical questions. The aim of this book is not to set the theatrical or poetic virtues of Shakespeare's work in competition with his interest in ideas but to explore how he was able to deftly fuse the disparate genres of theater and social thought so that the plays speak seamlessly to us in a voice that is at once great storytelling and great philosophy.

Along with Plato, Shakespeare was perhaps the most accomplished practitioner of an art of philosophical discourse framed as storytelling. This was hardly a form of philosophy unique to Shakespeare. It was an approach to rhetoric taught to all schoolboys in 16th-century England as an essential component of their grammar-school education. While to the modern ear, theoretical debate and dramatic narrative are incompatible literary genres, this is not the case in Tudor England. In his wonderful book, *The Tudor Play of Mind: Rhetorical Inquiry and the Development of Elizabethan Drama*, Joel Altman explores the development of Tudor literature by (among others) Henry Medwall, Thomas More, Erasmus, John Lyly, Thomas Kyd, Christopher Marlowe, and Shakespeare to trace the emergence of two contrasting traditions of Elizabethan theater, a homiletic or didactic tradition of morality plays and what he calls "explorative theater" which had a very different flavor (Altman 1978). He argues that explorative theater has not been commonly recognized as such, although it encompasses the period's most famous dramas.

Altman provides an account of the roots of explorative theater in Elizabethan England by examining the grammar-school curriculum in rhetoric for clues about how 16th-century schoolboys were taught to use dramatic dialogue as a frame for philosophical argument.[6] Humanists had established a curriculum for Tudor grammar school students which stressed skills of argumentation suitable for effective public service. Altman shows how, in his outline of aims and methods for the curriculum at St. Paul's School (where Milton studied), Erasmus emphasized two important rhetorical skills:

> [T]he student is to see in historical or fictional events the "underlying sentiments" or universal principles that inform them, and he is encouraged to regard these as controversial issues – rashness versus caution, profligacy versus cupidity. These emphases lay the foundation for a mimetic fiction of

explorative character, one that teaches and delights by examining through exempla which engage the emotions the diverse existential claims that govern human life. The concern to link the universal principle with the with the particular example – which lies at the heart of Renaissance poetic theory – and the interest in developing the ability to see both sides of the question remain constants throughout the program.

(Altman 1978: 44)

The 16th-century rhetoric curriculum training program in rhetoric was based on a 4th-century text, *The Progymnasmata* by the grammarian Aphthorius. *The Progymnasmata* outlines 14 distinct forms of written argumentation to be mastered by the young pupils. These fourteen genres differ in their rhetorical goals and formal characteristics. The *destructio* taught students to counter an argument based on probability with another argument using a different probability. The *confirmatio* demonstrated the way to counter the *destructio* by evoking an equivalent probability of exemplary stories.[7] Aphthonius distinguishes practical theses (e.g., "Should a person take a wife?") from speculative ones (e.g., "Are there many universes?"). *The Progymnasmata* provides examples of arguments based on these theses. Typically, Aphthonius offers an example of a thesis supporting a general position along with its counter-thesis. This emphasis on framing questions from opposed points of view reflects Cicero's preference for arguing *in utramque partem*—from both sides of the question. It privileges what rhetoricians called *inventio* (invention), the capacity to approach a problem from as many angles as possible.[8]

The other important feature of this early schooling in rhetoric that left its mark on Renaissance theater was the distinction made by Quintilian, Cicero, and Aphthonius between arguing by *thesis* and *hypothesis*. For Aphthonius, the difference between *thesis* and *hypothesis* is that the latter introduces into an argument "complicating circumstances."[9] Hypothetical argument employs particular instances or cases to reason through a general problem. Arguing from *hypothesis* is equivalent to basing legal decisions on considerations of equity rather than law. While the application of law attempts to judge cases using abstract, general principles, the application of equity acknowledges the qualifying relevance of particular circumstances to the adjudication of a case. In modern terms, hypothetical arguments are a form of "case-based reasoning," where concrete narrative replaces general principles as the essential component of problem-solving.[10]

Through detailed analyses of a wide variety of Tudor literature, Altman argues persuasively that this training in rhetoric cultivated "mimetic fiction—transforming *thesis* to *hypothesis*—by supposing certain persons, in a certain place, at a certain time, under certain circumstances, to be confronting a general question *in their own terms*" (p. 65). Philosophical at its core but grounded in the case-based logic of legal argument, mimetic fiction puts ideas into play with particular characters and circumstances, transcending the constraints of philosophical orthodoxy while embracing its goal of interrogating the world. Altman characterizes the interrogative mood of this literary genre as "aesthetic skepticism."

> Literature not only offered...edifying precepts vividly set forth, but also induced a play of mind that overran the boundaries traditionally set by the orthodoxy of the outside world and allowed them to enjoy what might best be described as an experience of aesthetic skepticism-an interlude of extended quest, free from the constraints of political choice, that enriched their vision of reality and return them to the actual with a deeper sense of its complexity.
>
> (p. 30)

Altman proposes that Elizabethan theater's explorative tradition comes directly from this rhetorical training in argument by hypothesis. Deeply theoretical in its grounding in exploring ideas, explorative drama also evades the impulse common to social theory of systematizing answers to great questions. Instead, the ideas are put into play with life's contingencies. The effect of this training is not evident just within Shakespeare's works or even just Renaissance drama but is apparent in early modern attitudes to philosophical issues. In his volume on Shakespeare's language, Russ McDonald discusses the powerful effect of this training in *disputatio in ultramque partem*:

> Learning to promote opposing positions in equally convincing terms appears to have generated in the apt pupil a kind of perspectival understanding of the world, a consciousness of the provisional nature of all philosophical positions and of the contribution of rhetoric to the validity of all ideas. Recent students of rhetoric in early modern Europe have identified 'its connection to skepticism, its sense of the contingency of the world of experience, its recognition of the gap between language and reality, and its reassuring commitment to dialogue and debate rather than dogmatic assertion.'
>
> (McDonald 2001: 49)

This suggests a non-reductive approach to the meaning of Shakespeare's plays. As proposed in the analysis of *Hamlet* in Chapter 1, the intractability of the world to final human understanding sits at the center of Shakespeare's most famous play. If interpretive closure is antithetical to the way humans actually live or how they understand their world, then reductive accounts of meaning become a misunderstanding of Shakespeare's vision. Shakespeare's reflections on ultimate matters may be sketched out in the contingent language of character and action rather than in theological or scientific abstraction. But this does not make the reflections any less philosophical. Shakespeare's mind may have frequented the intellectual stratosphere, but his feet were firmly planted in the realities of people's lives. Like the modern ethnographer, he was a participant-observer of his world.

Shakespeare invites us to reflect on the meaning human life offers. However, he offers little comfort to those seeking interpretive closure, which is why his plays have continued to fascinate us 450 years after they were written. No interpretation can exhaust the meaning of a Shakespeare play. This open view of meaning is captured by Charles Sanders Peirce's notion of "semiosis." For Peirce, interpretation of texts or of life itself always involves an ongoing active encounter between a sign, its referent, and the sign's effect upon an interpreter, which he called "the interpretant" (Peirce 1998: 478). This encounter is what Peirce meant by semiosis, and it is what makes humans special. For our purposes, the key aspect of Peirce's notion is that semiosis involves an active and ongoing process of interpretation. It has the character of infinite extension, at once exhilarating and unsettling.

> [P]art and parcel of Peirce's early account of signs is that an infinity of further signs both proceed and precede from any given sign. This is a consequence of the way Peirce thinks of the elements of signs at this early stage and seems to stem from his idea that interpretants are to count as further signs, and signs are interpretants of earlier signs. Since any sign must determine an interpretant in order to count as a sign, and interpretants are themselves signs, infinite chains of signs seem to become conceptually necessary.[11]

This infinite extension does not make understanding Shakespeare impossible, but it certainly affects what it means to understand the texts. It also renders any single interpretation inevitably partial and tentative. Shakespeare's plays are written in such a way as to both invite interpretation and resist interpretive closure.

In *Shakespeare and the Problem of Meaning*, Norman Rabkin argues that Shakespeare's embrace of this lack of finality in our understanding of things is perhaps his greatest virtue as a playwright:

> The essence of our experience is our haunting sense of what does not fit the thesis we are tempted at every moment to derive. If one hallmark of an authentic work of art and a central source of its power is its ability to drive us to search out its central mystery, another way may be its ultimate irreducibility to a schema. Both of these qualities are present in Shakespeare's plays. They are there because Shakespeare put them there. If we are going to call the distillation of our experience of one of the plays its meaning, we must acknowledge that it includes both the paradigm to which the controlling patterns of the play tempt us to reduce our experience and elements of that experience which resist or weaken or complicate the paradigm.
>
> (Rabkin 1981: 23)

Shakespeare's genius was to lead his audience into powerful insights and significant possible understandings of the world without ultimately shutting down the inquiry by offering up a final interpretation. This is one of the ways in which Shakespeare successfully reconciled his theoretical and narrative inclinations. His plays are so engaging and brimming with insight that they provoke our deepest impulses to keep digging into the mysteries of our lives even without the prospect of reaching bottom. They lead us from the complexities of life to contemplating great ideas and, ultimately, back again to life.

Paradox

Perhaps the best indication of Shakespeare's "play" with philosophical questions is his attraction to paradox. Paradox is a self-negating proposition. In formal logic, paradox involves two or more statements that cannot logically co-occur but nevertheless appear to be true. Though paradox always involves logical contradiction, a paradox is distinct from the ordinary sense of contradiction. Whereas a contradiction begs to be straightened out, a real paradox begs to be accepted as true despite its illogical status.

In his essay "The Ways of Paradox," the logician Willard Quine distinguished among three different kinds of paradox (Quine 1966; Platt 2009). *Veridical paradoxes* are statements that are internally contradictory but nevertheless true. *Falsidical paradoxes* are absurd statements that base their claim to truth on false reasoning that careful analysis shows to be false. To these he adds a third type of paradox, which he calls *antinomies*. Antinomies are intrinsically self-canceling statements that are beyond the logic of truth and falsehood. Antinomies are what I am calling "genuine paradoxes." To accept a genuine paradox is to force a reframing of one's understanding. Genuine paradoxes, in other words, encourage us to change our minds.

The best-known paradox, an instance of Quine's antimony, is The Liar's Paradox, proposed by Epimenides the Cretan when he said, ironically, "All Cretans are liars." (Quine 1966: 4). Other versions of this paradox are "This statement is false" or, most simply, the ancient Greek *pseudomenon* "I am lying." Antinomies are the most radical form of paradox, engaging the mind in a logical loop that both frustrates and provokes thought. Quine recognized the radical potential of antinomies to transcend conventional thinking by forcing the mind to, literally, think outside the box. He credits antinomies with being the seeds of Thomas Kuhn's "paradigm shifts" (Kuhn 1962).

> A veridical paradox packs a surprise, but the surprise quickly dissipates itself as we ponder the truth. A falsidical paradox packs a surprise, but it is seen as a false alarm when we solve the underlying fallacy. *However, an antinomy packs a surprise that can be accommodated by nothing less than a repudiation of part of our conceptual heritage.*
> The revision of a conceptual scheme is not unprecedented. It happens in a small way with each advance in science, and it happens in a big way with the big advances, such as the Copernican revolution and the shift from Newtonian mechanics to Einstein's theory of relativity. We can hope to get used even to the biggest of such changes and find the new schemes natural. There was a time when the doctrine that the earth revolves around the sun was called the Copernican paradox, even by the men who accepted it. And perhaps the time will come when even truth locutions without implicit subscripts, or like safeguards, will really sound as nonsensical as the antinomies show them to be.
> (Quine 1966: 6, emphasis added)

Paradox is not simply a logical issue, but in the hands of a great artist, it becomes a powerful defamiliarization tool, compelling an audience to question their ordinary assumptions about the order of things. Inherently radical and intrinsically dangerous, paradoxy dislocates orthodoxy and undermines the acceptance of canonical truth.

Not surprisingly, Shakespeare was attracted to paradox. He was especially attracted to paradoxical language. Consider, for example, the speech by Romeo in the opening scene of *Romeo and Juliet*, where he laments being out of favor with the current object of his desire, Rosalyn:

ROMEO
Alas, that love, whose view is muffled still,
Should, without eyes, see pathways to his will!
Where shall we dine? O me! What fray was here?
Yet tell me not, for I have heard it all.
Here's much to do with hate, but more with love.
Why, then, O brawling love! O loving hate!
O any thing, of nothing first create!
O heavy lightness! serious vanity!
Mis-shapen chaos of well-seeming forms!
Feather of lead, bright smoke, cold fire, sick health!
Still-waking sleep, that is not what it is!
This love feel I, that feel no love in this.
Dost thou not laugh?

(II, i, 174–188)

The oxymoron serves here as the linguistic analog to Romeo's state of mind, giving a linguistic shape to the self-canceling experience ("that is not what it is") of the Petrarchan lover. The paradoxical spirit is extended to more complex and self-nullifying phrases ("Still-waking sleep, that is not what it is/This love feel I that feel no love in this"). The tropes foreshadow the tragic paradox to come in the play, when the young couple's love will simultaneously unite them (as Romeo and Juliet) and divide them (as Montague and Capulet), suggesting a disturbing answer to Juliet's famous question: "What's in a name?"

As we saw in Chapter 1, *Hamlet* is riddled with paradox. To avenge his father's murder, the avenger must become the murderer, both annulling and repeating the murderous act. *Hamlet* opens in the middle of the changing-of-the-guard at Elsinore castle, as one day passes into another. We learn that old King Hamlet has recently died, succeeded by his brother. But the dead king keeps reappearing on the parapets, unable to fully die and pass from the scene. In a perverse twist on idea of "the king's two bodies," old Hamlet's refusal to pass on parodies the paradox embodied in "The King is Dead, long live the King," through which succession is both announced and produced. As a result, the Danish throne now has two kingly bodies: old King Hamlet and new King Claudius. When we encounter Claudius in the court in Scene 2, his first words, filled with self-canceling contradictions, announce that the new King's quick marriage to his brother's widow has hopelessly tangled the royal family: "With mirth in funeral and with dirge in marriage" (I. ii. 12). Claudius' uncomfortable announcement, betraying the incestuous character of his new marriage, has left the family in a liminal state. Circumstances, Claudius announces, have impelled him and his new wife into an over-hasty marriage, forcing "our whole kingdom/To be contracted in one brow of woe." "Contracted" bears the paradoxically twin senses of expansion (as in a marriage alliance) and reduction (as in a brow saddened by mourning). And this is just Act I. Another illustration of Shakespeare's keen feeling for paradox is the division of the kingdom scene that opens *King Lear*. Here, paradox is built into the odd structure of the play. Lear has decided to stage the reading of his will, and so the play begins with a man directing his own funeral. Ritually, Lear has buried himself alive. Having begun the play with what amounts to the funeral of the leading man, where are the remaining four acts to take us? Lear's paradoxical opening act promises that this play is going to be no ordinary journey.

Shakespeare's attraction to paradox has been long noted by poets and scholars, though it has been subject to many interpretations.[12] In 1817, Keats, in a letter to his brothers Thomas and George, characterized the paradoxical frame of mind as Negative Capability, an openness to the mysteries and possibilities of a world that could not be finally explained by any closed system of knowledge. For Keats, Shakespeare is the epitome of an artist whose genius directly emerges from this Negative Capability: "when a man is capable of being in uncertainties, mysteries, doubts, without any irritable reaching after fact and reason..." (Keats 1900: 277).

In his 1947 essay "The Language of Paradox," Cleanth Brooks proposed that paradox was intrinsic to poetic language. This affinity of poetry to paradox, Brooks argued, distinguishes poetic language from the language of science:

> The tendency of science is necessarily to stabilize terms to freeze them into strict denotations; the poet's tendency is by contrast disruptive. The terms are continually modifying each other, and thus violating their dictionary meanings.
>
> (Brooks 1947: 6)

Brooks considers the role of paradox in several famous poems but chooses to conclude his essay with a close analysis of Shakespeare's 1601 love poem, "The Phoenix and the Turtle." This cryptic poem celebrates the paradox of a platonic love affair in which the lovers are at once two and one. Noting the long tradition in literary studies of trying to guess whose relationship the poem allegorized, Brooks proposes that the poem celebrates something different from a love affair, something quite surprising. Quoting three stanzas from the heart of the poem, Brooks proposes that the poem might actually celebrate paradox itself.

> So they loved as love in twaine,
> Had the essence but in one,
> Two distincts, Division none,
> Number there in love was slaine.
> Hearts remote, yet not asunder;

Distance and no space was seene
Twixt this Turtle and his Queene;
But in them it were a wonder....
Propertie was thus appalled,
That the selfe was not the same;
Single Natures double name,
Neither two nor one was called.

(25–40)

Although the nature is single, the name is double. The poet can call it neither two nor one and so the only option is paradox. Brooks concludes that "The Phoenix and the Turtle" celebrates the paradoxical character of the human imagination, which he sees as the fount of all poetry.

Not all scholars or audiences have applauded or even acknowledged Shakespeare's deft way with paradox. In Shakespeare's use of paradox, some have seen obfuscation. Others who accept paradox as a positive aspect of Shakespeare's art nonetheless insist that Shakespeare deployed paradox in his plays in order to resolve it. King Lear must somehow find wisdom in suffering and reconcile himself to an unjust world. Hamlet must finally hit bottom and understand at long last Denmark's woe. In *Shakespeare and the Culture of Paradox,* Peter Platt takes on these critics directly, asserting that in seeking clean resolution to the problems Shakespeare offers up in his plays, they have missed the point:

> Critics of Shakespeare have not sufficiently recognized the power of paradox—the ways in which Shakespeare uses paradox not only to play with contradictions, but also to expand, challenge, or even dismantle the personal and social belief systems that help to constitute his plays. This neglect, I would argue, is the result of the critical tendency to conceive of paradox as paralyzing and ineffectual. Shakespeare's plays, on the contrary, in "paradoxing the orthodox," often reveal paradox as an agent of action and change. This is in no small part because of the paradoxical nature of theater itself: something on the stage always provokes a "natural perspective that is and is not."
>
> (Platt 2009: 4)

Platt distinguishes between a dialectical approach to paradox, which always views paradoxical arguments as moving through internal contradiction on the way to inevitable resolution, and a view of paradox closer to the kind of interpretation that Jacques Derrida sought, "that argues for a technique that resists and disorganizes 'without ever reaching for a solution'" (Platt 2009: 5). Platt urges that we resist the temptation to rationalize Shakespeare's art by insisting on framing his dilemmas as resolvable contradictions rather than recognizing the more disquieting but ultimately greater gift that Shakespeare's art has to offer.

The question can always be raised, whether one can attribute a genuine theoretical impulse to a writer who resolutely resists the comforts of closure. What could such a writer's theoretical position be on any significant issue? Taking a monolithic theoretical stand is not the same thing as engaging in theoretical reflection. Politics requires the articulation of clear positions. Great art and good philosophy only require fidelity to the complexity of things and coherence only to the extent that the world affords it. In not proposing closure on any issue, Shakespeare may be elusive, but he is never vague. He remains faithful to the complexity of the human condition. Shakespeare traffics in some of the most profound paradoxes of human life, and, better than any other writer, crystallizes these irreducible dilemmas in unforgettable stories and memorable characters.

While some take pleasure in experiencing well-orchestrated paradox, paradox is not universally appealing. In the hands of pedants, philosophical paradox can come off as maddeningly obscure and indecisive. In the interest of coming to a clean conclusion, many readers or viewers of Shakespeare will ignore or overlook Shakespeare's attraction to paradox. But Shakespeare's flirtation with the paradoxical comes from his appreciation of how competing aspirations so often become tangled up when they are played out in real life. Shakespeare chose playwriting rather than philosophy as his career. He was interested in great ideas but not in pure ideas. His dramas are the meeting ground where great ideas tangle with the play of life. This is not evasion, but rather intellectual courage and honesty. We can revel in the paradoxes and the lack of resolution in much of Shakespeare's work and still recognize the great insight and wisdom they reflect.

Coda: putting Shakespeare to music

One of Shakespeare's greatest admirers not only recognized the wisdom of Shakespeare's love of paradox—he set it to music. Giuseppe Verdi had a special affinity for Shakespeare, recognizing how life-affirming paradox was in Shakespeare's hands. In Verdi's final opera, *Falstaff*, an adaptation of Shakespeare's *The Merry Wives of Windsor* (with a little help from *Henry IV*), Verdi celebrates the comic face of Shakespeare's sense of the inevitability and irresolvability of human dilemma. The opera is famous for its complex and often ironic dialogue between plot and music in which the orchestral score assumes a crucial choric role.

Falstaff traces an intricate and ultimately ludicrous chain of deceptions and their consequences. It opens with the doubly duplicitous Falstaff swearing his love in identical letters to both Mistresses Alice Ford and Margaret Page, two wealthy Windsor wives. The wives are twice duped, since the actual object of Falstaff's lust appears to be their husbands' money. Comparing their letters, Mistresses Ford and Page discover Falstaff's deceit. Falstaff's scheme begets a counter-scheme as the wives, in league with their friend Mistress Quickly, seek revenge on Falstaff. They concoct an intricate trap to expose and humiliate him.

Throughout the opera's three acts, the plot piles deception upon deception. By the final act, nearly every character has assumed some sort of disguise, and universal duplicity has produced a crescendo of chaos. Just in time to end the play, the schemes are all finally uncovered, and all the Jacks (except, of course, Jack Falstaff) manage to claim their Jills. However, rather than ending the opera by celebrating reconciliation and harmony, Verdi chooses to celebrate the cacophonous laughter the opera has brought forth from singers and audience alike. In most productions, the opera concludes with the cast suddenly stepping out of character and lining up on stage to directly face the audience. Falstaff exclaims, *"Tutto nel mondo è burla"* ("Everything in the world is a jest"), setting in motion the opera's musical finale. One by one, the lead characters repeat the phrase until it takes hold as a fugue. Falstaff has the final say, and the words come slowly and heavily from his lips: *"Tutti gabbati"* ("Everyone is duped!"). The rest of the cast again picks up the phrase and this time is propelled at a furious pace into a final fugue that ends the opera.

While the words appear to celebrate a world worthy only of laughter, the musical fugue on which the lyrics float celebrates the power of art to provide a transcendent sense of order and meaning. And on this brilliant musical crystallization of the paradoxical marriage of chaos and order, the ludicrous and the serious, the curtain falls both on Verdi's opera and on his career as a composer. At the very end of Verdi's career, he brilliantly translated Shakespeare's love of paradox and irony into music. Rather than obscuring the contradictions and costs entailed by human dilemmas, Shakespeare forces us to confront them. Irresolvable paradox is part of the human condition. Any theory involving the human that evades contradiction and paradox in the interest of a tidy clarity will turn out to be a bad theory. Shakespeare looks humanity squarely in the eye and asks us to take the world as it comes.

This raises the question of just how the world came in Shakespeare's day? Shakespeare's plays may have a universal appeal, but they were equally the product of a particular time and place. What kind of society produces a Shakespeare, and what historical and cultural factors contributed to the theoretical mood that runs through Shakespearean drama? Shakespeare played with ideas but not in the sense of an ideologue. Shakespeare was a brilliant observer of his world, but his observations took place in a predominantly interrogative rather than a declarative mood. Little evaded Shakespeare's skeptical eye. While it is possible to force Shakespeare's thought into a traditional medieval worldview, I have suggested that this older, conservative view of Shakespeare is misleading and misses Shakespeare's more radical appraisal of his society.

Shakespeare was especially gifted in the imaginative staging of his world. His interrogation of Elizabethan conventions suggests a society in flux. The Elizabethan world view may have rested on a medieval foundation, but there were significant cracks in that foundation. Shakespeare wrote in a world that was beginning to understand itself in radically non-traditional terms. Today we do not characterize Tudor and Elizabethan England as late medieval societies but are more likely to call Shakespeare's England pre-modern. The next chapter traces some of the key themes that defined these transformations, transformations that underwrite the subjunctive and interrogative moods of Shakespeare's drama.

Notes

1 Tillyard, E.M.W. *The Elizabethan World Picture*, New York: The Macmillan Company 1944.
2 For another ironic reading of this speech, see Harris (2010: 29–40).
3 Shakespeare's line is likely derived from a famous Latin saying *Homo homini lupus* (Man is a wolf to man) attributed to *Asinaria,* a comedy by the Roman playwright Plautus (195 BC) where a character says: *Lupus est homo homini, non homo, non quom qualis sit novit* (One man is a wolf to another, not a man, as long as he doesn't know what he is like). Thomas Hobbes included the saying in the dedication to his 1651 book *De Cive.*
4 On Plowden, see Bryan 2009.
5 For an influential study of Elizabethan and Jacobean notions of selfhood, see Greenblatt 1980.
6 For studies of the Tudor grammar school curriculum, see Whitaker 1953 and Baldwin 1949.
7 Altman 1978, pp. 46–47.
8 According to Cicero, invention was the most important of a trained speaker's five basic skills, the other four being memory, elocution, arrangement, and delivery.
9 Nadeau 1952, p. 281.
10 The claim is sometimes made that all reasoning is in fact case based, employing past experiences as the basis of solving new problems. See Aamodt and Plaza 1994.
11 Atkin, Albert 2010.
12 See Colie 1966; Rabkin 1981; Platt 2009; Crockett 1995; Malloch 1956.

3

REVOLUTIONS

Through clever metaphor, Shakespeare's *Henry V* proclaims a new vision of the world. The play opens with a tense exchange between the Archbishop of Canterbury and the Bishop of Ely, discussing the threatened resurrection of an old law passed initially under Henry IV but long unenforced. Stripping the Church of all the "temporal lands" willed by private donors, the law threatens to deprive the Church of what Canterbury calls "the better half of our possessions." The prelates anticipate young King Henry's support, who, they believe, has mended his ways since his days of youthful excess. The Bishops reflect on the dramatic change in young Henry's character:

CANTERBURY
The king is full of grace and fair regard.

ELY
And a true lover of the holy church.

CANTERBURY
The courses of his youth promised it not.
The breath no sooner left his father's body,
But that his wildness, mortified in him,
Seem'd to die too; yea, at that very moment
Consideration, like an angel, came
And whipp'd the offending Adam out of him,
Leaving his body as a paradise,
To envelop and contain celestial spirits.
Never was such a sudden scholar made;
Never came Reformation in a flood,

DOI: 10.4324/9781003179771-5

With such a heady currance, scouring faults
Nor never Hydra-headed wilfulness
So soon did lose his seat and all at once
As in this king.

(I, i, 24–39)

Marveling that such a wise and devout monarch had emerged from such an unpromising prince, Ely finds a parallel for this fortunate turn of events, not in the biblical idiom of miracles, but the natural history of plants:

ELY
The strawberry grows underneath the nettle
And wholesome berries thrive and ripen best
Neighbour'd by fruit of baser quality:
And so the prince obscured his contemplation
Under the veil of wildness; which, no doubt,
Grew like the summer grass, fastest by night,
Unseen, yet crescive in his faculty.

(I, i, 63–69)

To which Canterbury replies:

It must be so; for miracles are ceased;
And therefore we must needs admit the means
How things are perfected.

(70–72)

Stripped of its miracles (as well as many of its earthy holdings), the Church in Shakespeare's day was increasingly challenged to explain "how things are perfected" by recourse, not to biblical history, but natural law. What was true for the natural history of plants might serve just as well as a model for human affairs. The Reformation and the rapid spread of Puritanism in England signaled more than an ecclesiastical revolution. They ushered in a radical shift in the understanding of how the world worked. Both the physical world and human society were being reimagined, troubling, and eventually shattering the older vision of the order of things. At stake was a whole way of thinking and seeing. Ultimately these changes, along with developments in science and optics, would radically change not just the Elizabethan perspective on the world, but the very idea of perspective itself.

For a long time, these new understandings shared the stage with the more traditional worldview. This mix of old and new ways of thinking was particularly evident in the status of "magical thinking." The middle ages had left in its wake a wide range of occult beliefs tied to popular religion. While not official Church doctrine, many of these beliefs and practices were tacitly tolerated by the Catholic Church. Keith Thomas has documented the impressive hold that magic and other forms of supernatural causation had on the English mind (Thomas 1971). He sees the widespread beliefs in the malevolent influences of ghosts and witches in everyday life as a legacy of magical elements of medieval Catholicism. These notions survived in England long after the Reformation and the disestablishment of the Catholic Church. Some saw these forces as the handiwork of God operating in mysterious ways. "That which we call fortune," wrote the Elizabethan Bishop Thomas Cooper, "is nothing but the hand of God working by clauses and causes that we know not. Chance or fortune are gods devised by man made by our ignorance of the true, Almighty and everlasting God" (Thomas 1971: 80). The Church of England was anxious to purge itself of superstitious beliefs and practices associated with Rome. For the Roman Church, the line was not always clear between superstition and divine agency.

Shakespeare makes effective use of these archaic forms of supernatural agency in plays like *Hamlet, Julius Caesar, Midsummer Night's Dream, The Winter's Tale, King Lear,* and *Macbeth.* Whether he believed in the reality of witches, ghosts, fairies, omens, oracles, prophecies, dreams, and the like is a matter of speculation. It is certainly not clear from the plays themselves. What is clear is that Shakespeare knew that his audiences were prepared to grant an important role to the supernatural forces that haunt his plays. Widespread belief in the intervention of natural and supernatural powers in human life may have been commonplace in Elizabethan England, but they were also widely contested. The "magical thinking" associated with witchcraft, sorcery, geomancy, necromancy, alchemy, and astrology was increasingly coming under attack from within the Church and undermined by natural science.

Judicial and natural astrology

The emergence of astronomy as a science distinct from astrology was gradually turning Shakespeare's world topsy-turvy. A new understanding of the heavens began to take its toll on what was known as "judicial astrology" in 16th and 17th-century England. During the Italian Renaissance, judicial astrology—beliefs in the influence of planetary positions and movements on human affairs—had developed into a sophisticated explanatory system that had the feel of a scientific theory. It is difficult for the modern mind to grasp how pervasive (and persuasive) astrological thinking was in Renaissance Europe. Judicial astrology had intuitive appeal, confirmed by the natural astrology of farmers' almanacs that explained the sun's observable effects and the moon on weather, crops, and tides.[1] Faith in the celestial influence on human affairs was not merely a folk belief. Elizabeth I employed a personal astrologer, John Dees, a scientist who exemplified the odd mix of scientific rationality and occult belief common in early modern England. In addition to his encyclopedic knowledge of science and mathematics, Dees was notorious for arranging séances with spirit mediums in the hope of contacting spirits, which would reveal to him the secrets of the philosopher's stone (Kocher 1952: 112). Elizabeth had initially engaged Dees to work out her horoscope to decide on a propitious day for her coronation. The Queen would have occasion to consult him again about the appearance of the comet of 1577.

Reliance on astrological prediction became fashionable at Court, though it is not clear that the Queen herself was convinced of the stars' role in human affairs. Still, in a letter she wrote to Mary Stuart in 1658, chastising her for her changeableness, Elizabeth attributes at least some influence of heavenly bodies over human dispositions:

> If it were not that I consider that by nature we are composed of earthly elements and governed by heavenly, that I am not ignorant that our dispositions are caused in part by supernatural signs, which change every day, I could not believe that in so short a time such a change could take place.
>
> (Rouse 1971: 260–261)

Astrologers were consulted in everyday life, in matters relating to agriculture, political decisions, and the timing of medical interventions. The personal physician to Henry VIII believed in the influence of the moon and the stars on human organs, and in 1598 a French physician–astrologer, Claude Dariot, published a volume on the medical uses of astrology called *Astrologicall Judgement of the Starres* (Overholser 1959: 337). Elizabethans believed that the moon's phases had a significant impact on behavior. The moon was held accountable for certain forms of madness ("lunacy").

Heavenly bodies were also said to affect psychological dispositions through their interaction with the body's four humors, the essential chemical elements determining an individual's "temperament." Humoral medicine is generally associated with Hippocrates and Galen, but for Elizabethans, the mapping of the bodily humors onto a celestial template of astrological influences had been laid out in detail in 1652 by Nicholas Culpeper (Culpepper 1652/2009). A predominance of blood produced the sanguine temperament associated with a happy disposition, personal charm, and energy. It also predisposed the sanguine personality to lust and passion. An individual dominated by phlegm (associated with the lungs and the brain) possessed a phlegmatic temperament: calm, passive, and unemotional but inclined to luxury. Changes in sky-body links produced subtle psychological variations. Thus, a phlegmatic individual born under the influence of the moon might well be cowardly and foolish as well. A choleric individual whose temperament was dominated by yellow bile produced in the spleen was associated with the planet Mars and was ill-tempered, easily angered, and prone to violence. The melancholy individual, dominated by the black bile from the gall bladder, was given to bouts of sleeplessness and despondency or "melancholia," what we now call depression (Overholser 1959: 242–243). Like humoral medicine, astrology had the look of a highly rational system of explanation. Both were systematic theories that derived human affairs from the regularities of natural phenomena. As great a thinker as Auguste Compte saw astrology as a laudable attempt at a genuine proto-scientific system of historical explanation (Lecky 1919: 277; Thomas 1971: 326–327). Since it was grounded in mathematical calculation, astrology had a particular appeal to intellectuals since it shared many of the characteristics of what we now recognize as scientific empiricism.

While many Elizabethans believed in some degree of astral influence over human affairs, they were also keenly aware of the potential abuse of astrological prognostication by charlatans or those seeking to exploit judicial astrology for political

gain. Recognizing the potential threat of ill-intentioned astrological prognostication, Elizabeth's second Parliament passed a bill punishing astrological prophecy in
1653. Astrology also ran into trouble with churchmen. The compatibility of astrological explanation with Christian thought was a highly contentious question in
Shakespeare's day. Astrology provoked passionate disagreement in a Church whose
beliefs and practices were subject to constant challenge. While no clear distinction
had yet emerged in Shakespeare's England between astrology and astronomy, people
generally distinguished between natural and judicial astrology. Natural astrology, the
study of the motion of stars and planets and their effects on natural phenomena like
tides and weather, was widely accepted. But judicial astrology, the analysis of the
impact of planets and stars on human fortune, health, and the formation of personal
temperaments (what today we call astrology), was more contentious. By the end
of the 16th century, a debate erupted about judicial astrology's validity in a series
of books attacking and defending it. In 1601 John Chambers published his *Treatise
against Judicial Astrology*, where he noted growing skepticism about judicial astrology.
Chambers produced a litany of conventional objections against judicial astrology,
citing problems with astrological predictions due to the great number of stars, the
evidence that twins born at the same time frequently diverge in their fortunes,
and the disagreements over whether a horoscope should be based on the hour of
one's conception or of one's birth. Claiming that there were 71,209,600 stars in
the heavens, Chambers wondered at astrologers' reference to just 1028 of them
and their actual reliance on only seven celestial objects in their forecasts (Camden
1933: 31). Astrology's defenders had argued that the different fates of twins could
be accounted for by rapid changes in planetary alignment between the two births.
Chambers pointed out that celestial bodies reconfigured themselves too fast for
anyone to observe accurately from the Earth, rendering astrology impossible. Armed
with considerable learning in astronomy, Chambers affirmed the value of knowledge of the heavens in furthering the legitimate science of astronomy, reserving his
skepticism for the use of astrological information in predicting human affairs. He
called on Parliament to outlaw judicial astrology altogether.

Chambers' vigorous attack on judicial astrology inspired an equally impassioned defense. In his 1603 book, *A Defence of Judicial Astrology*, Sir Christopher
Heydon sought to refute Chamber's objections to judicial astrology, point by point.
He aimed to clarify astrology's scientific grounding and demonstrate the essential compatibility of astrology with Christianity. Well-schooled in mathematics and
the astronomy of his day, having read Copernicus, Tycho Brahe, and the math-
ematicians Edward Wright and Regiomontanus, Heydon was a close friend of the
astronomer John Bainbridge and the mathematician Henry Briggs (Rouse 1971:
272). Heydon's defense of astrology was answered in turn by a volume dyspepti-
cally titled *Astronotomania: The Madness of Astrologers* by George Carleton, a strongly
anti-Catholic Calvinist. Dismissing astrological predictions as a form of intuitionism
masquerading as science (Rouse 1971: 273), Carleton saw in astrological forecasting
the hand of Satan. He called judicial astrology "the Devil's university." He was wary
of the mathematical calculations that astrologers used to support their predictions,
viewing them as a black art and a form of Popish conjuring (Thomas 1971: 362).

Some saw in astrology Satan luring unsuspecting men into the black arts. In his 1624 book, *The Madness of Astrologers*, George Carleton sees judicial astrology as equivalent to black magic. He suggests that

> the cause why the Astrologer sometimes speaketh true, is not because he seeth it in the Starres, as in natural causes of that Euent…but because either by plaine compact, or else by secret illusion of Satan, he cometh to the knowledge thereof: which illusion may bee so great that the Astrologer may belieue that he readeth it in the Starres.
>
> (Carleton 1624: 38)

Evidence could not be trusted to resolve the debate. Both sides could always come up with convincing examples to prove their point. The Bible provided no conclusive word on astrology. In fact, it offered too many conflicting words on the subject. Astrology's friends and foes both resorted to Scriptural support for their beliefs. Those supporting judicial astrology could point to Moses' claim that God intended the stars to serve humanity as signs. Opponents of astrology could turn to passages from Isaiah and Jeremiah, suggesting that astrologers were charlatans (Camden 1933: 35).

In the long run, the cards were stacked against reliance on astrological prediction in human affairs. Astrology simply could not withstand the loss of confidence that followed from its empirical failures. At the same time, a new cosmological science was reshaping how people understood the heavens. By the end of the 17th century, astrology had been largely discredited. The most important reason for its loss of standing as a science was the emergence of an astronomical science based on the work of (among others) Copernicus, Tycho Brahe, Galileo, and Newton.

Celestial anomalies

The cosmology that had sustained belief in astrology assumed a fixed and known cosmos. This assumption was shattered by the arrival of previously unknown stars in 1572 and 1604. The Milky Way Supernova that appeared in 1572 was viewed by many notable astronomers of the day, including Thomas Digges and John Dee. But the new star was most carefully studied by the Danish astronomer Tycho Brahe, who described it extensively in his publication *De Nova et Nullius Aevi Memoria Prius Visa Stella* (Concerning the Star, New and Never Before Seen in Anyone's Life or Memory). It soon became known as Tycho's Star. The second supernova appeared in 1604 in the constellation Ophiuchus, bursting forth three degrees from the ecliptic, near the spot where Mars and Jupiter had just converged, following a once-in-a-century third meeting of Jupiter and Saturn.[2] Observers speculated whether this new star's birth was linked to these planetary convergences. The supernova of 1604 had been observed by Galileo, at the time a young mathematics professor in Padua. Galileo gave three public lectures on this new star, speaking in Latin to a packed lecture hall. These observations of the birth of new stars completely disrupted the assumptions of astrology, which depended on the distinction between celestial (eternal) and terrestrial (mutable) bodies central to Aristotelian physics. This distinction between superlunary and sublunary bodies could not survive scientific scrutiny in the face of an emerging cosmology that would fundamentally change the understanding of the heavens and their relations with things terrestrial.[3]

Astrology never completely disappeared in England and survives today as part of New Age culture.[4] But by the late 16th century, judicial astrology was coming under increasing critical scrutiny. The most crucial challenge to astrology and other forms of magical thinking came from advances in scientific knowledge and method. Astrology was challenged in two different ways by the astronomy of the time. First was the discovery of new stars—supernovas—by European astrologers, which was inconsistent with the astrologer's assumption that celestial bodies like stars and planets were fixed and eternal. But an emerging scientific skepticism also challenged the credibility of judicial astrology on other grounds as well. Science called for empirical validation for the sorts of claims astrologers were making. Faith in beliefs simply because they were traditional or venerable was no longer enough. Astrology could not withstand the scrutiny of the new science, and the numerous failures of astrological predictions could no longer be rationalized away. Scientific doubt had begun to replace religious faith as the basis of conviction. The Elizabethan passion for exploration was not only an economic and political priority for England; hand-in-hand with scientific inquiry, the desire for exploration signaled a change in outlook and mood, a change inconsistent with the static worldview suggested by the Great Chain model of the world. Exploration implies a fundamental openness to discovery and a reminder of all the things, both wondrous and terrifying, that lie beyond our current horizon of understanding.

The Copernican revolution

The Aristotelian universe had divided all matter between terrestrial and celestial bodies. Terrestrial or "sublunary" bodies were composed of the four elements (fire, air, earth, and water). Celestial bodies comprised the moon, the seven wandering stars (planets), and a vast number of fixed stars located beyond the planets. The seven planets all circulated about Earth. The medieval science of alchemy assumed that each planet had dominion over a specific metal: the Sun over gold, the Moon over silver, Mercury over quicksilver or mercury, Venus over copper, Mars over iron, Jupiter over tin, and Saturn over lead. Sublunary matter on Earth had variable weight or *gravitas* and was believed to move with horizontal motion. In contrast, celestial bodies, composed of a fifth element ("quintessence"), were assumed to move in perfect circular orbits of invariable speed around Earth. Renaissance scientists had already begun to peek behind the curtains of conventional wisdom about the order of the universe. What they saw had begun to upend the taken-for-granted world. The upheaval in religious thought and practice accompanying the Reformation was matched by the challenges that the New Astronomy presented to the understanding of the cosmos. Shakespeare wrote at a time when the world was experiencing, in Beverly Ridgely's words, "the most thorough and difficult change on record in man's outlook on the nature of the physical universe and his own position in the scale of creation" (Ridgely 1958: 26).

Sometime between 1510 and 1514, Nicolaus Copernicus, a Pole who had moved to Italy to pursue a doctorate in Canon Law as well as medical training, turned his attention to astronomy. Copernicus may be the most famous scientist to propose a heliocentric universe, but he was hardly the first. Early Greek observers had hypothesized two distinct kinds of stars: wandering stars (i.e., planets) and fixed stars, which remained in place. In the 4th century B.C., a Greek mathematician and astronomer, Aristarchus of Samos, used geometric calculation to propose that the sun was many times bigger than any of the planets and that therefore it was unlikely that it would orbit around a body as small as the Earth. He proposed that the sun rather than the Earth was the center of the universe and that the stars' apparent motion must mean that the Earth rotated about its axis (Heath 1913; Stahl 1970). Unfortunately for the history of science, Aristotle discounted Aristarchus' theory, arguing that if the earth rotated about its own axis, it would generate a great wind on the Earth's surface. Moreover, he objected that if the Earth rotated, we would be unable to drop an object and have it land just below the point from where it was dropped. And so, the heliocentric theory of the universe went underground for 17 generations.

What eventually revived the heliocentric theory in the European Renaissance were the inconsistencies and anomalies that observers had long noted in the geocentric model of the cosmos. Observations of planetary motion suggested that the movement of planets was far from uniform. In fact, the outer planets seemed to stop temporarily at a point in their rotation and reverse direction, what was called retrograde motion, before resuming their forward movement. The Earth moreover did not appear to be precisely at the center of the planets' orbits. In the 2nd century, the Greek astronomer Ptolemy published a revision of Aristotelian cosmology, a refinement of an earlier proposal by the Greek astronomer Apollonius of Perga. Ptolemy intended to account for the observed anomalies in his book *Almagest*. In the revised theory, planets had several kinds of simultaneous movement. First, they moved eastward in what was called "epicycles," or small orbits like the moon's orbit around the Earth. At the same time, each planet was said to move eastward in a larger orbit around the Earth called the "deferent." Combining these two rotations was hypothesized to produce a somewhat irregular orbit of the planet around the Earth, approximating a circle with three evenly distributed bulges, a path defined by the mathematical form epitrochoid.

Dissatisfied with this Ptolemaic attempt to save the geocentric cosmology of Aristotle, Copernicus proposed a much more radical revision: a heliocentric model that displaced the Earth as the center of the universe and placed the sun as the rotational center. Contrary to the accepted cosmology of his time, Copernicus hypothesized that the Earth was a center of gravity and that the moon circled it in a regular orbit. The other planets, he believed, orbited around the sun and not the Earth. The sun, Copernicus believed, was close to the center of the universe. His full report, a six-volume work titled *De Revolutionibus Orbium Coelestium* (On the Revolution of the Heavenly Spheres), was completed in 1539, first appearing in print in Nuremberg in 1543, two decades before Shakespeare's birth. In this work, Copernicus proposed a model of the universe comprising eight spheres, with a motionless sun at the center and a sphere of fixed stars at the outermost periphery. Six planets (Mercury, Venus, Earth, Mars, Jupiter, and Saturn) orbited the sun, each in its own sphere, at an increasing distance from the sun, while the moon orbited the Earth. *De Revolutionibus* is a specialist text. Even for educated non-specialists, it is far from an easy read and is far too technical to attract a large readership. Only 400 copies were printed, and even this modest edition failed to sell out. While few actually read the book, news of the revolutionary cosmology it proposed spread quickly in Europe. It did not take long to catch the attention of theologians, triggering intense debates about whether this new heliocentric vision of the universe was compatible with Scripture. Copernicus, trained in Canon Law and employed as a Church administrator, was hardly predisposed to theologically radical views. But in the end, his scientific judgment won out over his theological commitments. Fully aware that he was entering theologically murky waters with the publication of his book, Copernicus had tried to soften the impact of his findings by dedicating the volume to Pope Paul III.

The most explicit contradiction between Copernicus' cosmology and Scripture is with the story of the Battle of Gibeon recounted in the Book of Joshua. Joshua, fearing that the enemy would use the coming nightfall to evade defeat, prays for victory, causing the sun and the moon to stand still. This inconsistency was noted by Martin Luther, whose objections were shared by his close collaborator, the theologian Philipp Melanchthon, who in 1547 advocated that Copernicus and his followers be severely restrained from promulgating theories that clearly contradicted scripture.[5] By the 17th century, the Church of Rome had come to no official conclusion about Copernicus' views. Espousing the new heliocentric cosmology was initially not considered a heresy, but Church leaders were uncomfortable with this new cosmology. By 1616, the Sacred Congregation at the Vatican placed *De Revolutionibus Orbium Coelestium* on the Church's "*Index Liborum Prohibitorum,*" the list of officially forbidden books. It was banned along with another work, *Commentary on Job*, by Spanish philosopher Diego de Zúñiga that defended Copernicus'' views as compatible with Catholic belief. The Sacred Congregation's official ban concluded that "in order that [Copernicus''] opinion may not creep any further to the prejudice of Catholic truth, the Congregation has decided that the books by Nicolaus Copernicus [De revolutionibus] and Diego de Zúñiga [On Job] be suspended until corrected" (Shea and Artigas 2004: 84–85). The Church's reaction fell short of a full ban on the book. It merely asked that the offending books be withdrawn from circulation pending certain corrections to the text that clarified that this proposed cosmology was only a hypothesis and was as yet unproven. Copernicus complied with these requested changes, and the revised version of the book was eventually withdrawn from the Index. But *De Revolutionibus* never appeared in its approved form. Copernicus' book remained officially off-limits for Catholics until 1758 for all but specially approved scholars in its published form.[6] Copernicus'' book was the opening gambit in a full-blown scientific and cosmological revolution in the

16th and 17th centuries. It is important to remember that the acceptance of the Copernican model of the cosmos was slow in coming, and it was disconcerting for those living in the 16th and early 17th centuries.

In the late 16th century, the Danish astronomer Tycho Brahe attempted to reconcile the Copernican model of the universe with the older Ptolemaic cosmology in what became known as the Tychonian system.[7] Tycho's compromise cosmology had five planets revolving about the sun, while the stars and the moon revolved about the Earth. Tycho adopted the Aristotelian distinction between celestial and terrestrial bodies. Celestial bodies, thought to be composed of the quintessence ether, were by nature lightweight, moving with constant and eternal motion in perfect circles. By contrast, terrestrial bodies had mass and weight and were subject to decay. Their natural state was stasis rather than eternal motion. From these assumptions, Tycho reasoned that the Earth was simply too sluggish to be in constant motion around the sun (Blair 1990). Tycho's alternative cosmology was intuitively appealing and remained a formidable competitor to the Copernican model of the universe until the early 18th century when English Astronomer Royal James Bradley proved conclusively that the Earth orbited the sun. In addition to proposing this compromise cosmology, Tycho Brahe used the observations of the great comet of 1577 passing through the solar system to demonstrate that Copernicus' "spheres" were merely mathematical and not physical entities. The atmosphere of the universe was recognized to be continuous and not physically segmented.

The new picture of the universe outlined in this chapter presented significant challenges, not just to Christian orthodoxy, but to the everyday understanding of the necessary order of things during Shakespeare's time. The certainties that had sustained medieval political theology were increasingly subject to question and doubt. The new world was coming into view both geographically and culturally just beyond the old world's horizon. The declarative mood of medieval thinking had begun to yield to more interrogative frames of mind. We see the subversive side of this new frame of mind in the opening act of *Hamlet* when Hamlet assures his friend: "There are more things in heaven and earth, Horatio/Than are dreamt of in your philosophy." Hamlet's later chilling reference to this unknown world conflates it with the afterlife, which he calls "The undiscovered country from whose bourn/ No traveler returns." Here he makes a direct connection between the risks inherent in exploring the New World and the dangers inherent in seeking to peek behind the curtains of conventional understanding that frame the stage on which we play out our lives. Not only did the Copernican revolution work to decenter the traditional geocentric cosmos, but it threw into question the place of humankind and their institutions in that cosmos. The threads anchoring people to their world had begun to unravel.

The challenge of the new astronomy

The Copernican universe presented significant challenges for the theology of Shakespeare's day. Thomas Kuhn nicely summarizes the revolutionary implications of a heliocentric cosmos for Elizabethan thought, laying out a host of contradictions produced by the new cosmology.

> When it was taken seriously, Copernicus' proposal raised many gigantic prob-
> lems for the believing Christian. If, for example, the Earth were merely one
> of six planets, how were the stories of the Fall and the Salvation, with their
> immense bearing on Christian life, to be preserved? If there were other bodies
> essentially like the Earth, God's goodness would surely necessitate that they,
> too, be inhabited. But if there were men on other planets, how could they be
> descendants of Adam and Eve, and how could they have inherited the origi-
> nal sin, which explains man's otherwise incomprehensible travail on an earth
> made for him by a good and omnipotent deity.
>
> (Kuhn 1957: 193)

Such contradictions were disturbing not just to theologians and scientists but also to writers like Shakespeare and his near-contemporary John Donne. By the end of the 17th century, the heliocentric universe imagined by Copernicus and his fellow astronomers would become accepted knowledge. But in Shakespeare's day, the New Astronomy was widely contested and deeply disturbing. The new science's most far-reaching effect was to gradually replace traditional religious authority with a fundamental skepticism and empiricism that are the hallmarks of modern science. The fabric of assumptions by which Shakespeare's contemporaries understood the universe was unraveling under the new astronomers' gaze. The New Astronomy not only displaced Earth as the center of the universe, but it also undermined the fundamental distinction between the sublunary domain of human life, governed by growth and decay, and the eternal realm of the heavens.

One of Shakespeare's near-contemporaries to reference New Astronomy in a satirical way was John Donne. In 1611, five years before Shakespeare's death, Donne featured Copernicus, Kepler, Tycho Brahe, and Galileo in a satire directed at Catholics, and especially Jesuits. Titled "Ignatius His Conclave," the piece has been the subject of conflicting interpretations. Older critics often identified the sympathetic narrator with Donne himself, while more recent critics have tended to see Donne as far more critical of the new learning in its misplaced reliance on reason rather than faith:

> Donne's gullible, impressionable narrator, in his awe toward and exuberance
> over the discoveries of the new astronomers, certainly represents the equally
> naive contemporary of Donne's, who might so thoroughly confuse scientia
> and sapientia as to believe that the very heavens were being reshaped and
> governed by these new titans. His confusion is in part that of his age.
>
> (Hassel Jr 1971: 334)

Whatever Donne's actual opinion about the truth of the new learning, the radically revised astronomy came to represent to him a terrifying vision of chaos, a view which he famously proclaims in his 1621 poem "Anatomie of the World" excerpted below.

> Then, as mankinde, so is the world's whole frame
> Quite out of joint, almost created lame...
> And new Philosophy calls all in doubt,
> The Element of fire is quite put out;
> The Sun is lost, and th'earth, and no mans wit
> Can well direct him where to looke for it.
> And freely men confesse that this world's spent,
> When in the Planets, and the Firmament
> They seeke so many new; they see that this
> Is crumbled out againe to his Atomis.
> 'Tis all in pieces, all coherence gone;
> All just supply, and all Relation:
> Prince, Subject, Father, Sonne, are things forgot,
> [F]or every man alone thinkes he hath got
> To be a Phoenix, and that then can be
> None of that kinde, of which he is, but he.
> This is the worlds condition now...

It is impossible to read Donne's words without realizing the profound disruption and shock the New Astronomy represented to the traditional Elizabethan world view.

In 1624, in his *Devotions Upon Emergent Occasions and Seuerall Steps in My Sicknes,* Donne alludes again to the Copernican vision in Meditation 21. He uses the "new philosophy's" idea of a rotating earth as a metaphor to describe the vertigo he experienced when standing up following a severe episode in his long illness.

> I am up, and I seem to stand, and I go round, and I am a new argument of the new philosophy, that the Earth moves round; why may I not believe that the whole Earth moves, in a round motion, though that seem to me to stand, when as I seem to stand to my company, and yet am carried in a giddy and circular motion as I stand? Man hath no centre but misery; there, and only there, he is fixed, and sure to find himself.
>
> (Donne 1959: 140).[8]

For Donne, Copernican theory represents the disorientation of a man who has lost the sense of having any center other than misery. Despite his discomfort, however, Donne remained equivocal on the truth of Copernican theory. The universe was revealing itself as a vast mechanism. Where they had once radiated divinely inspired meaning and moral certainty, the disenchanted heavens now offered humans only the cold comfort of mathematical precision. God's laws were giving way to the flat Newtonian predictability of a world governed by mechanics. This new vision of the heavens reshaped how people saw humanity's terrestrial existence. It was not just the observations and discoveries of the New Astronomy that were beginning to dislocate the traditional Christian universe, but the very methods and attitudes of the founders of modern empirical science.

By the middle of the 17th century, just 35 years after Shakespeare's death, the implications of a mechanistic vision of the universe were vividly laid out by Hobbes in the introduction to his 1651 treatise on government, *The Leviathan*:

> Nature (the art whereby God hath made and governes the world) is by the art of man, as in many other things, so in this also imitated, that it can make an Artificial Animal. For seeing life is but a motion of Limbs, the begining whereof is in some principall part within; why may we not say, that all Automata (Engines that move themselves by springs and wheeles as doth a watch) have an artificiall life? For what is the Heart, but a Spring; and the Nerves, but so many Strings; and the Joynts, but so many Wheeles, giving motion to the whole Body, such as was intended by the Artificer?
>
> (Hobbes 1651/2011: vii)

Viewed as a vast, artificial mechanism governed by laws of physics rather than by divine inspiration, Hobbes' universe bears little resemblance to the world of Shakespeare and Donne. Little wonder that the Roman Church was so reluctant to accept the new astronomy.

Shakespearean heavens

Shakespeare was born some two decades after Copernicus death, the same year as Galileo. By the start of Shakespeare's career, Copernicus' major work had been in print for half a century. Copernican ideas circulated widely in England and were the topic of lively debate in intellectual circles. In the summer of 1583, the Italian philosopher Giordano Bruno gave a series of lectures at Oxford University on Copernican theory. Finding his Oxford audience contentious, Bruno returned to London where his talk was far better received at Elizabeth's court and he found favor with the Queen and her advisors. While the New Astronomy was not universally accepted during Shakespeare's lifetime, neither was it "new." Aristotelian and Ptolemaic cosmologies were still widely accepted, but the revolutionary discoveries of Renaissance astronomy were beginning to cast a long shadow over the practice of judicial astrology. Shakespeare's use of astrology reflects its contested status. The plays make numerous references to astrology that Shakespeare's audience would have been quick to understand. However, Shakespeare's use of astrological prediction reveals a skeptic's questioning of the meaning of the cosmos and its relation to human affairs.

Take, for instance, the famous description in the Prologue to *Romeo and Juliet* of the doomed couple as "star-crossed lovers." The phrase suggests the influence of misaligned stars in the couple's tragic end. Rhetorically, the prologue serves as a literary analog to this astral determination since, like the stars, the opening sonnet "pre-dicts" (fore-tells) the play's tragic end. One might imagine that the prologue would serve as a spoiler for the audience, who, assured of the play's bleak outcome, would give up on *Romeo and Juliet* and lose interest. But it never does. Shakespeare understood that, whatever the ultimate sway that transcendent powers claim on us, the human world is powered by hope, not by resignation. Neither the Prologue nor the stars govern our apprehension of the play. We temporarily suspend our fore-knowledge of the promised end to enter into the play's contingencies as if they were life rather than a completed script. In *Romeo and Juliet*, astral influence is upstaged by an intense interest in the power of human agency.

Julius Caesar prominently features the unexpected appearance of heavenly bod-ies portending Caesar's death and its tragic aftermath. Caesar's impending death is foreshadowed in the play by a variety of omens and predictions by the Soothsayer, including this famous description by Casca in Act I of the heavens' power to forecast human events. Addressing Cicero, Casca inquires:

> Are not you moved, when all the sway of Earth
> Shakes like a thing unfirm? O Cicero,
> I have seen tempests, when the scolding winds
> Have rived the knotty oaks, and I have seen
> The ambitious ocean swell and rage and foam,
> To be exalted with the threatening clouds:
> But never till to-night, never till now,
> Did I go through a tempest dropping fire.
> Either there is a civil strife in heaven,
> Or else the world, too saucy with the gods,
> Incenses them to send destruction.

(I, iii, 3–13)

Cicero answers:

> Indeed, it is a strange-disposed time:
> But men may construe things after their fashion,
> Clean from the purpose of the things themselves.
> Come Caesar to the Capitol to-morrow?

(I, iii, 33–36)

Casca's account would seem to describe astrological signs of impending tragedy. But Cicero's response, rather than confirming Casca's interpretation, throws the whole notion of astrological prediction into question. What starts as a reference to the work of the heavens concludes with a reflection on the work of the mind. Astrology recedes in the face of an emerging psychology. As Cicero leaves the stage, Cassius enters. Again Casca addresses the portentous upheavals in the heavens.

> Who ever knew the heavens menace so?

(I, iii, 47)

Cassius, however, claims to be unafraid of the heavens,

> Those that have known the Earth so full of faults.
> For my part, I have walk'd about the streets,
> Submitting me unto the perilous night,
> And, thus unbraced, Casca, as you see,
> Have bared my bosom to the thunder-stone;
> And when the cross blue lightning seem'd to open
> The breast of heaven, I did present myself
> Even in the aim and very flash of it.

(I, iii, 48–55)

Casca responds with a conventional understanding of astrological portents, claiming that it is the role of men to defer to the superior knowledge of the heavens:

> But wherefore did you so much tempt the heavens?
> It is the part of men to fear and tremble,
> When the most mighty gods by tokens send
> Such dreadful heralds to astonish us.

(I, iii, 56–59)

Cassius, however, asserts his will against the power of the heavens and provides his own interpretation of disrupted nature, an understanding in line with his intentions to assassinate Caesar:

> But if you would consider the true cause
> Why all these fires, why all these gliding ghosts,
> Why birds and beasts from quality and kind,
> Why old men fool and children calculate,
> Why all these things change from their ordinance
> Their natures and preformed faculties
> To monstrous quality,—why, you shall find
> That heaven hath infused them with these spirits,
> To make them instruments of fear and warning
> Unto some monstrous state.

(I, iii, 65–74)

Not only is Cassius asserting his lack of fear of the celestial rumblings, but he is also deliberately interpreting the astrological signs in line with his intentions to assassinate Caesar. Far from maintaining the astral control over human affairs, he is implicitly demonstrating the power of political will, setting the power of the human mind directly against that of the heavens.

Act II of *Julius Caesar* opens in Brutus" orchard. Brutus has just awakened and addresses his sleeping servant Lucius.

What, Lucius, ho!
I cannot, by the progress of the stars,
Give guess how near to day. Lucius, I say!
I would it were my fault to sleep so soundly.
When, Lucius, when? awake, I say! what, Lucius!

(II, i, 1–5)

Unable to read the stars and infer the correct time, Brutus is baffled by Cassius' attempts to turn him against Caesar. Brutus can read neither the heavens nor the mind of man. He struggles to assess Caesar's character to see if it matches Cassius' dark account of him. Lucius brings Brutus an anonymous letter drafted by Cassius, who has instructed Cinna to throw it into Brutus' window. Brutus again struggles to do a correct reading:

The exhalations whizzing in the air
Give so much light that I may read by them.
[Opens the letter and reads]
'Brutus, thou sleep'st: awake, and see thyself.
Shall Rome, &c. Speak, strike, redress!
Brutus, thou sleep'st: awake!'
Such instigations have been often dropp'd
Where I have took them up.
'Shall Rome, &c.' Thus must I piece it out:
Shall Rome stand under one man's awe? What, Rome?
My ancestors did from the streets of Rome
The Tarquin drive, when he was call'd a king.
'Speak, strike, redress!' Am I entreated
To speak and strike? O Rome, I make thee promise:
If the redress will follow, thou receivest
Thy full petition at the hand of Brutus!

(II, i, 46–61)

Brutus can only read the letter by the light of the heavenly exhalations, and he doesn't quite understand what he reads. Ironically, it is not the celestial fireworks shaping Brutus' destiny but Cassius' political machinations. The astrological signs have become a stand-in for the power of Cassius' words to shape Brutus' loyalties. Instead of asserting the supremacy of heavenly bodies over human affairs, Shakespeare focuses on the workings of the political mind. Once again, a cosmological reading is upstaged by a psychological one. As for the heavens' ultimate role in determining Rome's fate, the audience can only wonder.

This shift from astrological signs to psychological symptoms is evident within Shakespeare's sonnets and is not just restricted to the plays. Sonnet XIV, where the swing in attention from the reading of the heaven's stars to a scanning of a lover's eyes is clear:

Not from the stars do I my judgement pluck;
And yet methinks I have Astronomy,
But not to tell of good or evil luck,
Of plagues, of dearths, or seasons' quality;
Nor can I fortune to brief minutes tell,
Pointing to each his thunder, rain and wind,
Or say with princes if it shall go well
By oft predict that I in heaven find:
But from thine eyes my knowledge I derive,
And, constant stars, in them I read such art
As truth and beauty shall together thrive,
If from thyself, to store thou wouldst convert;
Or else of thee this I prognosticate:
Thy end is truth's and beauty's doom and date.

This shift in attention from the stars to the eyes vividly reflects Shakespeare's interest in the mysteries of the human mind and human motivation, which fascinated him even more than the heavens' mysteries.

The same shift in attention is evident in King Lear. Probably, the best-known Shakespearean allusions to astrological prediction are in the debate between Gloucester and his son Edmund about the meaning of recent eclipses in Act I, scene 2 of the play.

GLOUCESTER

These late eclipses in the sun and
moon portend no good to us: though the wisdom of
nature can reason it thus and thus, yet nature finds
itself scourged by the sequent effects: love cools,
friendship falls off, brothers divide: in cities, mutinies;
in countries, discord; in palaces, treason; and the bond
cracked 'twixt son and father. This villain of mine
comes under the prediction; there's son against father:
the king falls from bias of nature; there's father against
child. We have seen the best of our time: machinations, hollowness, treachery,
and all ruinous disorders,
follow us disquietly to our graves. Find out this
villain, Edmund; it shall lose thee nothing; do it
carefully. And the noble and true-hearted Kent
banished! his offence, honesty! 'Tis strange.
[Exit.]

EDMUND

This is the excellent foppery of the world,
that, when we are sick in fortune,--often the surfeit

of our own behavior,--we make guilty of our disasters
the sun, the moon, and the stars: as if we were villains
by necessity; fools by heavenly compulsion; knaves,
thieves, and treachers, by spherical predominance;
drunkards, liars, and adulterers, by an enforced obedience of planetary influence; and all that we are evil in,
by a divine thrusting on: an admirable evasion of
whoremaster man, to lay his goatish disposition to
the charge of a star! My father compounded with my
mother under the dragon's tail; and my nativity
was under Ursa major; so that it follows, I am rough
and lecherous. Tut, I should have been that I am,
had the maidenliest star in the firmament twinkled
on my bastardizing. Edgar--
Enter EDGAR.
and pat he comes like the catastrophe of the old
comedy: my cue is villanous melancholy, with a sigh
like Tom o' Bedlam. O, these eclipses do portend
these divisions! fa, sol, la, mi

(I, ii, 109–144)

Edmund is Gloucester's eldest son. Having been conceived out of wedlock, he remains Gloucester's "natural" son rather than his legitimate heir, a child by nature rather than by law. The Gloucester subplot of *King Lear* hinges on Edmund's revenge: his designs on his father's title and his determination to turn his father against his younger brother Edgar, Gloucester's legal heir. Gloucester sees signs of impending civil discord in the recent eclipses, setting brother against brother, father against son, and subject against King. By the play's conclusion, Gloucester's reading of the heavens seems prescient. His predictions appear to have come to pass.[9] Once Gloucester exits the stage, however, Edmund mocks his father's faith in astrological prediction. He belittles the human tendency to hold the gods accountable ("a divine thrusting on") for the sins and follies of humans, calling it "an admirable evasion of whoremaster man."

Like Cassius in *Julius Caesar*, Edmund would seem to be asserting the decisive role of raw will against the forces of providence, custom, and law. Consistent with his standing as a natural son, Edmund sees astrological signs as evasive rationalizations of the real forces that govern human life: will and desire. Yet, in this play which, more than any other work of Shakespeare, throws into question the ultimate meaning of human life, something is wrong with Edmund's argument. Note how Edmund concludes his diatribe against astrology:

My father compounded with my
mother under the dragon's tail; and my nativity
was under Ursa major; so that it follows, I am rough
and lecherous. Tut, I should have been that I am,

had the maidenliest star in the firmament twinkled
on my bastardizing.

(I, ii, 135–140)

Rather than affirm his freedom to make his way in the world, Edmund attacks astrological prediction as *insufficiently deterministic*. Edmund sees himself as a bastard to
the core. "Tut," Edmund assures us, "I should have been that I am/ had the maidenliest star in the in the firmament twinkled/ on my bastardizing." Edmund views his
fate as fixed beyond even the pull of any planetary influences to change his nature.
Claiming for himself essential and irredeemable bastardy, Edmund concludes by
denying even the heavens any agency in shaping human life.

What sense are we to make of this unexpected turn in Edmund's argument?
The neat opposition between cosmic determinism and free will has turned on
itself, consuming its own logic. In the course of a single line, an apparently coherent
debate implodes, leaving us bereft of any intellectual footing. What is so disturbing
about Edmund is not just his rejection of social convention. Most troubling is his
utter rejection of the logical basis of all argument. "No cause, no cause" (IV, vii, 86),
Cordelia will comfort Lear at the end of the play. It turns out that her words are no
cause for comfort for those of us seeking explanatory closure in this most disconcerting of plays.

"Out of joint"

It is unclear how much contact Shakespeare had with the details of Copernican
thought, though his writing suggests that he was very aware of the New Astronomy.
The numerous references to astronomy in his plays often reflect a pre-Copernican
universe where the planets have clear mythological connections, and the movements in the heavens are signs directed at earthbound actors. Just how much of
the New Astronomy Shakespeare accepted has been much debated by scholars. In
a careful paper reviewing the evidence for Shakespeare's awareness of Copernican
thought, Alan Weber comes to the following conclusion:

> Copernicanism did not sweep Europe by storm after the publication of
> *De revolutionibus orbium coelestium* in 1543; knowledge of it was restricted to a
> few academics, and it did not come into the spotlight until near the end of
> Shakespeare's life when Galileo refuted several tenets of Aristotelian physics,
> such as the natural place of the elements. Ironically, non-Copernicans such as
> Tycho Brahe had further demonstrated that related Ptolemaic-Aristotelian
> concepts such as the crystalline spheres were physically impossible. But tech-
> nical astronomy aside, Shakespeare's later plays are certainly permeated with
> the philosophical ideas that were indirectly generated by newly emergent
> theories of cosmology: void, nothingness, infinity, new worlds, and most
> importantly, man's relationship to the cosmos.

(Weber 2012: 365)

Shakespeare's view of the Copernican model of the universe was likely not settled in his lifetime. Nevertheless, by the start of the new century, the conventional
understanding of the order of things had become unsettled. In 1621, John Donne
would write, with direct reference to Copernicus: "[S]o is the whole world's frame/
Quite out of joint." But Donne's words echo those penned by Shakespeare two
decades earlier, words by which young Hamlet ends the first act of the play bearing
his name:

> The time is out of joint: O cursed spite,
> That ever I was born to set it right.

(I, v, 10–11)

Hamlet is replete with astronomical references, but the universe to which
they point is more of an "undiscover'd country" than the world known to most
Elizabethans.

The shape of the world, like everything else in *Hamlet*, is in question. In the play's
first Act, the Prince confronts his father's ghost, who reveals to him the chilling story
of his murder at the hands of his brother. But at least as interesting is what the spirit
does not reveal: "I could a tale unfold whose lightest word/ Would harrow up thy
soul, freeze thy young blood" (I, v, 20–21). Old Hamlet is forbidden to reveal to the
living the ultimate terror of his situation. It is, he assures his son, sufficiently terrifying to "Make thy two eyes, like stars, start from their spheres" (I, v, 22). His reference
is to classical Ptolemaic cosmology. The apparent motion of what was assumed to
be fixed stars was accounted for by conceiving the universe as a series of rotating
concentric spheres or orbs, each studded with fixed stars. The spirit can conceive of
nothing more terrifying than the idea of the fixed stars jumping free of their spheres.

Another reference to disrupted cosmology can be seen in Hamlet's love letter to
Ophelia, a seemingly simple expression of his affection that, on reflection, becomes
an enigma.

> *Doubt thou the stars are fire;*
> *Doubt that the sun doth move;*
> *Doubt truth to be a liar;*
> *But never doubt I love.*
> O dear Ophelia, I am ill at these numbers;
> I have not art to reckon my groans: but that
> I love thee best, O most best, believe it. Adieu.
> Thine evermore most dear lady,
> whilst this machine is to him, Hamlet."

(II, ii, 124–132)[10]

On rereading Hamlet's poem, our initial certainty as to what Hamlet means falls
apart. The logic of Hamlet's argument in the opening lines is unfathomable. Are
these lines intended as questions (Do you doubt), possibilities (You might doubt),
or commands (You must doubt)? The poem is composed to be uninterpretable. As

if this complexity is not confusing enough, there are also linguistic problems with the passage. "Doubt," repeated four times, can mean both "to deny" and "to suspect." Maddeningly self-contradictory, Hamlet's poem both asserts and denies Hamlet's love for Ophelia. And, in its trope, this paradox of love carries with it the heliocentric universe. Like a verbal Mobius strip, the seemingly innocent love quatrain turns on itself endlessly without affording a final interpretation. The cosmic dislocation implied by the impossibility of knowing whether the metaphor affirms or denies the traditional view of the universe becomes the perfect metaphor for the impossibility of arriving at a coherent reading of Hamlet's feelings about Ophelia. Little wonder that Hamlet complains of being "ill at these numbers."

Hamlet repeats this sense of total dislocation later in the scene, complaining to Rosencrantz and Guildenstern that "The goodly frame the earth seems to me a sterile promontory" and that it's "majestical roof fretted with golden fire" now "appears no other thing to me than a foul and pestilent congregation of vapours" (II, ii, 324–326). Finally, he turns his lament on his disillusionment with man, who once had seemed "infinite in faculties, in form and moving how express and admirable, in action how like an angel, in apprehension, how like a god" (ll. 328–330). Not affirming the glory of Earth or man, Hamlet's famous lines express disenchantment with both. "And yet to me," Hamlet concludes, "what is this quintessence of dust?" What does Hamlet mean by this phrase? Aristotelian cosmology had claimed that the sublunary world comprised four essences (fire, air, earth, and water) and was by nature subject to growth and decay (to dust). Beyond the moon's orbit, the celestial world comprised the "quintessence" or fifth element, ether. Heavenly bodies were eternal, subject to neither growth nor decay. By referring to humanity as "this quintessence of dust," Hamlet characterizes the human as a paradoxical combination of the eternal celestial elements (quintessence) and the earthly mortal elements (dust), incompatible features that naturally belong to opposite realms. His simple phrase "quintessence of dust" is a self-consuming image of perpetual dissolution. Moreover, "quintessence of dust" parallels Hamlet's earlier paradoxical depiction of Earth (the site of growth and decay) as a "sterile promontory." However, the implied parallel only works if the eternal is understood as the analog of the sterile, rather than with divinity. The metaphoric parallelism creates an illusory similarity that actually works by inversion. To imagine a world out of joint, Shakespeare has brilliantly exploited cosmic metaphors in a set of self-canceling parallels. The distinctions that once gave the universe its meaning have been twisted beyond interpretation.

This description of man might be understood as a reference to the dual Christian conception of man as a mortal being possessed of an eternal soul. Yet in Hamlet, the reference is intended as unwholesome, a disturbing conflation of elements that by nature should be separate. In this setting, Hamlet's "quintessence of dust" recalls his reference to Claudius and Gertrude as his "uncle-father" and "aunt-mother," an unseemly conjoining of things that naturally belong to distinct domains, another example of "unalogy," Shakespeare's self-consuming metaphor, as discussed in Chapter 1. Hamlet's speech is pointing toward both the hidden rot he senses within Denmark and the more general dislocation attending the collapse of the old Aristotelian/Ptolemaic cosmology in the face of Copernicus' theory.

In recent years, this reading of Shakespeare through Copernicus has been a serious project for retired astrophysicist from Penn State University, Peter Usher. In a series of papers and two monographs, Usher has argued that Shakespeare was not only well aware of the Copernican revolution but that a number of his plays reflect his awareness of and his sympathy for the New Astronomy. His older work focuses on *Hamlet*, understood as a commentary on the struggle for hegemony between the old and new astronomy (Usher 1999 2005, 2007). His more recent book, *Shakespeare and the Dawn of Modern Science*, finds many allusions to Copernican thought hidden in *The Winter's Tale, Cymbeline, The Merchant of Venice, and Love's Labours Lost* in addition to *Hamlet* (Usher 2010).

Usher's reading of *Hamlet* is fascinating, as it involves more than just references to Copernican cosmology. Usher is convinced that Shakespeare conceived *Hamlet* as an allegory about the battle to overcome the old Ptolemaic view of the universe and the new Copernican vision. On the face of it, this claim seems exaggerated, given the conventional understanding of *Hamlet*. But some of Usher's discoveries are provocative and suggest that Shakespeare indeed wrote *Hamlet* with the Copernican revolution very much on his mind. Usher's main claims can be summarized as a series of intriguing parallels between the world of Hamlet and that of Copernicus.

- Claudius stands in allegorically for Claudius Ptolemy, the father of Ptolemaic astronomy.
- Tycho Brahe, who attempted to rescue Ptolemaic theory by devising a modified hybrid geocentric cosmology, was a Dane.
- A famous copper portrait of Tycho that Shakespeare might have viewed shows the Danish astronomer framed by a stone arch with columns on either side supporting heraldic shields inscribed with the names of Tycho's ancestors Sophie Gyldenstierne and Erik Rosenkrantz.
- The University of Wittenberg, where Hamlet is a student, was the first center of heliocentric thought.
- Fortinbras, who eventually defeats the Danes and assumes the Danish throne at the end of *Hamlet,* passes through Poland en route to Denmark. Poland was the birthplace of Nicolaus Copernicus.

Usher also notes Shakespeare's use of astronomical terms in unexpected ways in the play. Gertrude calls Hamlet's desire to return to Wittenberg "retrograde to our desire," where retrograde derives from an astronomical term for a reversal of planetary motion when the planet was directly opposite to the sun. Similarly, Claudius uses the term "conjunctive" to describe his relation to Gertrude, a word derived from planetary (as well as sexual) relations:

> She is so conjunctive to my life and soul,
> That as the star moves not but in his sphere,
> I could not but by her.

(IV, vii, 14–16)

While intriguing, this patchwork of associations does not make a convincing case for *Hamlet* as a strict allegory. The story of *Hamlet* can be traced back to ancient Icelandic and Scandinavian tales. A parallel story Amleth or Amlóði was recorded in 1200AD by Saxo Grammaticus in the *Gesta Danorum*. There is also the famous missing "Ur *Hamlet*" by Thomas Kyd, which was rumored to have been Shakespeare's primary source. In other words, Shakespeare already had a complicated story to tell that could never be reduced to the struggle for the New Astronomy. The astronomical drama that was reshaping the heavens and Earth in Shakespeare's world is unlikely to have been Shakespeare's main interest in writing *Hamlet*. However, Usher convincingly demonstrates that the Copernican drama is clearly a fascinating sideshow in *Hamlet*. The emerging Copernican revolution serves Shakespeare as a powerful idiom for exploring the idea of a radically dislocated world.

Usher makes a compelling case that Shakespeare was aware of the New Astronomy. He is likely right that Shakespeare wrote *Hamlet* with the dislocations implied by the Copernican revolution very much in mind. But in his attempt to colonize *Hamlet* with Copernicus, Usher wants to transform *Hamlet* into an allegory, something that it is not. This claim threatens to deflect attention from the many extraordinary things that *Hamlet* actually is. Usher's attempt to show that *Hamlet* is a Copernican morality tale in disguise raises methodological questions of how Shakespeare reconciled storytelling with the exploration of great ideas. These are questions of literary technique and craftsmanship. Considering Shakespeare as a literary craftsman, I would say that his bag of literary tools did not include allegory. Allegory, the stuff of morality tales, just doesn't *feel* Shakespearean. It's simply too flat. To try and turn any play of Shakespeare into a this-for-that allegory is to make Shakespeare speak in a foreign tongue.

But if Shakespeare did not produce theory through allegory, how did he do it? In Part III of the book, we will examine how the idea of the displaced center inherent in the New Astronomy conspired with innovations in optics and mirrors to contribute to Shakespeare's ability to use perspective to reconcile the conflicting requirements of narrative storytelling and philosophical commentary. The theme of shifting perspective central to the Copernican revolution explored in these pages shaped Shakespeare's approach to controlling his audience's perspective in experiencing his plays and poetry, allowing him to produce works that afford simultaneous multiple perspectives. But before we examine how Shakespeare embedded theory into narrative, we need to turn to a selection of the plays for a detailed look at Shakespeare's theory muse at work. In the following four chapters, we will rediscover Shakespeare as a social theorist by entering Shakespeare's glittering "globe" (the world of his theater) and wandering among some of the great ideas he explored. In addition to *Hamlet*, with which we began our journey, I have selected four other plays for discussion that illustrate Shakespeare's genius in staging social theory and let Shakespeare make his case for a vision of drama grounded in great ideas.

Notes

1 On the distinction between natural and judicial astrology, see Sondheim 1939; Smith 1958.
2 Jupiter and Saturn normally converge only twice every 20 years.
3 This old Aristotelian distinction between celestial and terrestrial bodies also derived Biblical support from Corinthians: "There are also celestial bodies, and bodies terrestrial: but the glory of the celestial is one, and the glory of the terrestrial is another" (1 Corinthians 15,40).
4 For an interesting study of the status of New Age "neopagan" religious practices in modern England that rely on traditional astrology, see Luhrman 1989.
5 Melanchthon eventually came to accept Copernicus' theory and even approved its inclusion in the curriculum of the University of Wittenberg (Kuhn 1957; Kobe 1998; 190).
6 According to the *Catholic Encyclopedia*, the original text of *De Revolutionibus* was only withdrawn from the Church's "Index of Forbidden Books" by Pope Benedict XVII in 1758.
7 Tycho's compromise model was very similar to an early cosmology proposed a century earlier in Kerala by the Indian mathematician and astronomer Nilakantha Somayaji. See Ramasubramanian 1994.
8 See also Shiff 2012: 20.
9 It is interesting to note that Gloucester's predictions do omit one breach that turns out to be the play's central social rupture: that between father and daughter.
10 Peter Usher subjects these lines to intense scrutiny. While his reading strikes me as a bit forced, he is certainly correct that the text's meaning is far from clear. See Usher 2005: 93–109.

PART II
Four plays

4

THE LONG WAY HOME

The Winter's Tale and the triumph of time

The Winter's Tale is one of Shakespeare's later works, most likely written in 1610 or 1611. Not as well-known as the other plays discussed in this book, the play is nonetheless remarkable. Beginning as tragedy and ending as comedy, the play is eccentrically structured, provoking critics while charming audiences. Though its miraculous conclusion challenges credibility, it makes for great theater. The First Folio of 1623 included the play among the Comedies, but it has always resisted classification. In 1875, Edward Dowden first used the term "Romances" for Shakespeare's later plays marked by elements of fantasy. The term has stuck, and, together with *The Tempest, Cymbeline, Pericles*, and *Two Noble Kinsmen, The Winter's Tale* is still generally grouped among Shakespeare's "Late Romances." Noting the play's ambiguous genre, its odd structure, its occasionally overwrought language, as well as the lack of clear motivation for Leontes' jealousy, some critics have included *The Winter's Tale* among Shakespeare's so-called "problem plays." But that label is of little value, serving more to alienate than inspire audiences while shedding little light on the virtues and complexities of this masterpiece. There is indeed a problem or two to be solved in making sense of this play, but these problems contribute to its greatness as well as its difficulty.

Early critics were not always kind to *The Winter's Tale*. Acknowledging its charm, they also found the play structurally awkward, thematically incoherent, intellectually shallow, and psychologically impenetrable. In 1875, D.J. Snider summed up the confusions that *The Winter's Tale* produced for readers and audiences of his day:

> This play is characterized by its frequent and direct defiance of the senses. Time and Space, which constitute the basis of the great world of sensation, seem to be entirely given over to the capricious play of the Poet's imagination. Even the so-called truths of the Understanding are laughed at in wanton mockery. History, Chronology, and also Geography, are violated with

DOI: 10.4324/9781003179771-7

an audacity which has often called forth the sneers and the ire of pedantic erudition.

(Snider 1875: 80)

A half-century later, the influential English novelist-critic Arthur Quiller-Couch wrote that *The Winter's Tale* "abounds in careless workmanship" (Quiller-Couch 1916: 754), concluding that, because of its structural flaws: "[W]e must admit that the play never lodges in our minds as a whole, is never compact . . . . It leaves no single impression" (*ibid.*: 759). Later 20th-century critics were more generous, acknowledging the play's effectiveness as theater but admitting to harboring doubts that this late fantasy contained any profound ideas. Instead of seeking some profound meaning in the play, they urged audiences to attend to the play's compelling theatrical qualities. They attributed the greatness of *The Winter's Tale* to its surfaces, the play's immediate emotional impact on the audience, rather than to any treasures to be mined from its depths (see Frey 1978).

In his 1963 book *Shakespeare: The Last Plays*, Frank Kermode wrote, somewhat defensively, "The greatness of the play is self-evident; it does not need the prestige of covert meanings" (p. 39). Kermode repeated this objection to approaching the play through its ideas rather than its dramatic impact in his *Introduction* to an edition of *The Winter's Tale* published in the same year:

> But we value [the play] not for some hidden truth, but for its power to realize experience, to show something of life that could only be shown by the intense activity of intellect and imagination in the medium of a theatrical form. It is not a great allegory or a great argument, but a great play.
>
> (Kermode 1963: xxxv)

In fact, there is much about *The Winter's Tale* that lies beneath its fairytale surface, contributing to its greatness. Fortunately, later commentators—particularly psycho-analytically inclined critics and the numerous feminist and gender theorists who emerged in Shakespeare studies in the late 20th century—discovered a much more complex play, exposing hidden streams of thought running through the text and underwriting much of the evocative power of the play's conclusion.

The play begins as a jealousy tragedy, much like *Othello*. It relates the calamitous undoing of a royal marriage and family brought on by a husband's unfounded suspicions about his wife's infidelity with his best friend. While *Othello* plays out Othello's jealousy to its dark conclusion, *The Winter's Tale* performs a series of unexpected twists on the jealousy plot. The consequences of Leontes' rage against Hermione and Polixenes unfold within the play's first half. Fully prepared by the first two acts for a tragic conclusion, the audience is unexpectedly transported at the start of Act III over wide spans of time (16 years), space (overseas to Bohemia), social setting (court to countryside), and genre (tragedy to comedy). By Act IV we are amidst preparations for a bucolic sheep-shearing festival. The rustic scenes that make up the long span of Act IV are set (at least initially) in a comic mood. Poised uneasily on the fulcrum defined by its contending halves, only a rapid turn of events in the final act manages to bring the play to a satisfying, if complex, resolution.

The triumph of time

The Winter's Tale closely tracks the plot of its source, Robert Greene's 1588 prose romance *Pandosto: The Triumph of Time*. Yet, the two stories have numerous differences. Shakespeare gives his own names for the characters, some with symbolic significance such as Leontes ("lion-like"), Perdita ("the lost one"), Florizel ("flowering"), and Mamillius (linked to the maternal breast). The kingdoms of Sicilia and Bohemia are retained, but reversed. Shakespeare adds a few characters to his version of the tale, including Paulina, Antigonus, and most notably, Autolycus. Shakespeare also adds the personification of Time, who is given a mere 32 lines as an introduction to Act IV. This "swift passage" of Time belies the essential role Time plays in *The Winter's Tale*. Although this chapter's sub-title "The Triumph of Time" was borrowed from Greene's work, it is more appropriate for Shakespeare's version of the tale. *The Winter's Tale* stretches the play over a gap of 16 years between the initial tragedy of Sicilia and the quasi-comedy in Bohemia. Time is a good candidate for the play's unsung hero. It is not simply that Shakespeare emphasizes what Leontes calls "the wide gap of time" over which the play unfolds. Time is powerfully transformative in *The Winter's Tale*. The metaphor of seasonal change runs throughout the play, suggesting the generative course of moral and psychological development, repentance, forgiveness, maturation, and understanding. But time does not quite operate in the same way in *Pandosto*. The prose style of *Pandosto* allows for a smooth and unremarkable narrative transition from the Shepherd's initial discovery of the baby to the introduction of 16-year-old Fawnia (Perdita) in the space of a single paragraph. *The Winter's Tale* highlights the double meaning of the "swift passage" of time, presenting time as a generative synthesis of art and nature. Here Shakespeare attempts to reconcile two contending versions of the immortality theme of his early sonnets: (a) the power of poetry to immortalize a lover and (b) the imperative of biological reproduction to guarantee immortality. This synthesis also unites the natural passage of seasons and the literary passage of theatrical time. [1] Metaphors of natural growth and decay work together with an artistically mediated gap in the play's action achieved by changes of act, genre, mood, and setting in an artistic refashioning of time. This dialectical interaction of art and nature is the promise of Time's meditation introducing Act IV.

> I, that please some, try all, both joy and terror
> Of good and bad, that makes and unfolds error,
> Now take upon me, in the name of Time,
> To use my wings. Impute it not a crime
> To me or my swift passage, that I slide
> O'er sixteen years and leave the growth untried
> Of that wide gap, since it is in my power.

> To o'erthrow law and in one self-born hour
> To plant and o'erwhelm custom.

(IV, i, 1–9)

Time controls both the seasonal cycle and theatrical artifice, presiding over the play both on the wing and in the wings. Time does not exercise the transformative power in Greene's story that it does in Shakespeare's. If Time triumphs in *Pandosto,* that triumph is more in its capacity to unfold the tragic consequences of sin and error than in any genuine redemption. It is in *The Winter's Tale,* and with the help of Shakespeare's art, that Time works its real magic.

The Winter's Tale unfolds in an arc of action: from the fatal ruptures of family and friendship in Leontes' Sicilian court, through the healing rustic notes of Bohemia's sheep-shearing festival, and finally back to a Sicilian finale marked by regeneration and reconciliation. This circle of action seems to mimic the seasonal cycle which shadows the play. But a look at the path the play takes back to its beginning suggests something different from a simple return. *The Winter's Tale* does not end where it began. Something is lost, something is added, and something is transformed. Time always leaves its mark. The seasons may flow in a cycle, evoking what Mircea Eliade called "The Myth of the Eternal Return," but human time is linear, marked by birth, growth, aging, and death (Eliade 1954). The attempt to cheat death by mapping the regenerative periodicity of seasonal change onto the linear trajectory of biographical time has been a perennial goal of both religion and of those institutions underwriting social and political reproduction. All cyclical ritual aims to evade the effects of time, inevitably failing.

In *The Winter's Tale,* this attempt to overcome the inevitable getting-older of biographical time by evoking the regenerative power of the seasons proves illusory. In a miracle of regeneration, both Hermione and Perdita are eventually restored to Leontes, but Prince Mamillius is not. He dies and, unlike his mother, he stays dead. Similarly, Paulina may win a new husband in her betrothal to Camillo, but only at the cost of the life of her old husband, Antigonus, who ends up as dinner for a hungry bear. Even as Hermione is miraculously resurrected for Leontes at the end of the play, time betrays its inexorable handiwork on the wrinkled face of the newly reborn Queen:

> Chide me, dear stone, that I may say indeed
> Thou art Hermione; or rather thou art she
> In thy not chiding; for she was as tender
> As infancy and grace. But yet Paulina,
> Hermione was not so much wrinkled, nothing
> So aged as this seems.

(V, iii, 28–33)

Hermione is restored to Leontes, but only through the power of art ("Thou *art* Hermione"), jointly guaranteed by Julio Romano's hand, Paulina's scheming, and Shakespeare's pen. Notwithstanding the power of art to preserve life and beauty, the

16-year "wide gap of time" will have the final say. The succession issue in the play is Leontes' attempt to avoid dying without an heir, another Leontes. As Shakespeare suggests in his early sonnets, institutional regeneration through marriage, inheritance, and succession are the political arts by which humans attempt to cheat death by replicating themselves. For a monarch, this concern is significant. But any regenerative cycle must contend against the forces of change and decay, and the unintended effects of history. Social reproduction will always bear the marks of this struggle since it necessarily rests on human artifice. In the end, the work of social organization in assuring social reproduction remains a staged illusion. Children may be their parents' heirs, their hopes to extend themselves beyond their own lives, but heirs can never actually replicate their parents.

Time, history, and the biological vagaries of genetics take their toll: the production of difference is inherent in the very process of reproduction. This is a truth that Leontes has yet to learn at the outset of the play. In Act I, Leontes confronts his son and muses aloud on his resemblance to Mamillius, apparently failing to understand that human reproduction is not mimesis:

LEONTES
How now, you wanton calf.
Art thou my calf?

MAMMILIUS
Yes, if you will my lord.

LEONTES
Thou want'st a rough pash and the shoots that I have
To be full like me: yet they say we are
Almost as like as eggs; women say so,
(That will say anything): But were they false
As o'er-dyed blacks, as wind, as waters; false
As dice are to be wish'd by one that fixes
No bourn 'twixt his and mine, yet were it true
To say this boy were like me.

(I, ii, 160–171)

Human attempts at regeneration can never successfully mimic the circularity of the seasonal cycle. Human reproduction will always move with a twist: replication by transformation. This is why Eliade's "eternal return" can only take place in the domain of myth.

Immortality and "the gift"

Among the arrangements humans have established as bulwarks against social dissolution, none has been more significant than "the gift." As anthropologists have long known, gift–giving is more than an act of giving something away. Rather than assuring loss, all gifts are really about guaranteeing a return of what's given. The economic and social implications of gift exchange were the subject of an early 20th-century classic treatise in comparative sociology, Marcel Mauss' *An Essay on the Gift: Form and Reason of Exchange in Archaic Societies.* Originally published in 1925 in the French journal *Année Sociologique*, and republished in English editions as *The Gift*, Mauss' essay has had a profound impact on social theory and moral philosophy. Reviewing gift exchange practices in a wide variety of human societies, Mauss proposed that traditional forms of exchange subordinated an interest in things to an interest in relationships. The key to gift exchange is not the accumulation of wealth, but the obligation to reciprocate. Gift exchange generates a network of mutual indebtedness that approximates what political philosophers have called "the social contract:"

> In the systems of the past, we do not find simple exchange of goods, wealth and produce through markets established among individuals. For it is groups, and not individuals, which carry on exchange, make contracts, and are bound by obligations; the personals represented in the contracts are moral persons-clans, tribes, and families; the groups or the chiefs as intermediaries for the groups, confront and oppose each other.
>
> (Mauss 1967: 3)

In Mauss' vision, the give-and-take inherent in gift exchange is the foundation of social morality, transforming the war of all against all (under the sway of self-interest) into relations of mutual dependence and common interest. Out of the anti-social impulses of greed and self-interest, a society is born. The philosopher's social contract is understood as an ongoing social process of this life-giving conversion implicit in the everyday give-and-take of social exchange.

Early on, *The Winter's Tale* emphasizes the darker side of exchange, the negative reciprocity inherent in revenge, and retribution. Falsely suspecting his betrayal by Hermione and Polixenes, Leontes initiates a chain of destruction, intended as payback. Leontes condemns both his wife and his best friend to death. His innocent newborn child, whom he refuses to acknowledge as his own, is made to pay for her mother's presumed sins. In exacting vengeance, Leontes appears to lose his wife, both of his children, his best friend, and his loyal servant Camillo. Yet *The Winter's Tale* also presents a more conventional vision of gift exchange. The brief opening scene features a pair of servants of the kings discussing the obligations entailed by the kings' history of gift exchange. Archidamus, the servant of Polixenes, proposes to Camillo a return visit of Leontes to Bohemia to reciprocate Leontes' hospitality in hosting Polixenes for the last nine months:

ARCHIDAMUS
If you shall chance, Camillo, to visit Bohemia, on the like occasion
whereon my services are now on foot, you shall see, as I have said, great
difference betwixt our Bohemia and your Sicilia.

CAMILLO

I think, this coming summer, the King of Sicilia means to pay Bohemia the visitation which he justly owes him.

ARCHIDAMUS

Wherein our entertainment shall shame us we will be justified in our loves, for indeed—

CAMILLO

Beseech you—

ARCHIDAMUS

Verily, I speak it in the freedom of my knowledge: we cannot with such magnificence—in so rare—I know not what to say. We will give you sleepy drinks, that your senses, unintelligent of our insufficience, may, though they cannot praise us, as little accuse us.

CAMILLO

You pay a great deal too dear for what's given freely.

ARCHIDAMUS

Believe me, I speak as my understanding instructs me and as mine honesty puts it to utterance.

(I, i, 1–21)

There is a hint of a dark side in this history of gift exchange between the two kings. While the kings' continuing friendship is the apparent subject of their reciprocal visits, the text is far more equivocal.[2] For critic Joseph Roach, this scene is portentous in an interesting way:

> Shakespeare forecasts . . . catastrophe in the straightforwardly expositional prose of the opening scene between Archidamus, a lord of Bohemia, and Camillo, a lord of Sicilia and adviser to Leontes, when Archidamus points out the "great difference betwixt our Bohemia and your Sicilia" (I.1.3–4). This difference is deep enough to construct the state visit of Polixenes as an embassy of encounter and exchange between alien potentates, which necessitates reciprocity in the manner of the gift-trading "archaic societies" described by Marcel Mauss.
>
> (Roach 2009: 123)

The mutual affection implicit in this ongoing exchange of hospitality rests on an undercurrent of competition. The language of the discussion suggests mercantile and legal ties rather than friendship. Camillo phrases Leontes' planned return visit to Polixenes as a payment "he justly owes him." When Archidamus expresses his fear that Polixenes will never be able to adequately repay Leontes' hospitality, Camillo protests: "You pay a great deal too dear for what's given freely." But, as Mauss has argued, gifts are never freely given. Every transaction places the recipient under an obligation of reciprocity. Even as Archidamus protests, "I speak as my understanding instructs me and as mine honesty puts it to utterance," the term "utterance"—which in Elizabethan English meant both "speech" and "selling"—suggests that the two servants and their masters are inevitably entangled in a web of delicate economic transactions. Gift-exchange always masks an undercurrent of calculation. At its fiercest, the gift is a stand-in for war.

Camillo's next words clarify just how the reciprocal hospitality between the kings has become "royally attorneyed" commerce. Revealing a bit of the play's backstory, Camillo relates a story suggesting that the relationship expressed by these visits is not quite the same relationship that had linked the two kings as boys.

CAMILLO
Sicilia cannot show himself over-kind to Bohemia. They were trained
together in their childhoods and there rooted betwixt them then such an affection which cannot choose but branch now. Since their more mature dignities and royal necessities made separation of their society, their encounters, though not personal, have been royally attorneyed with interchange of gifts, letters, loving embassies, that they have seemed to be together, though absent, shook hands, as over a vast, and embraced, as it were, from the ends of opposed winds. The heavens continue their loves!

(I, i, 22–33)

Camillo's claim that Leontes "cannot show himself *over-kind* to Bohemia" (I, i, 20) is a piece of Shakespearean irony, proposing two contrary ideas. On the face of it, Camillo suggests that Leontes' affection for his friend knows no limits. But "kind" also means "kindred" (as in Hamlet's famous "Less than kin and more than kind"). Camillo's claim that Leontes "cannot show himself over-kind" to his friend also suggests estrangement. Leontes and Polixenes can no longer be viewed as related by primal kin-like ties, the brotherly connection that transcends the logic of reciprocity. "Rooted together" like branches of the same tree in their youth, the friends' relationship suffered a rift as the boys matured into men and were forced to go their own ways, assuming adult roles and responsibilities. The friends are no longer linked organically by ties of mutual affection and identification, as when they were as "twinn'd lambs that did frisk i' the sun" (I, ii, 67). As adults, the two friends have entered Mauss' universe where relationships rest on mutual exchange, competitive transactions mediated by the calculating logic of reciprocity.[3] The old friends' encounters, Camillo explains, being no longer "personal," must, by necessity span a gulf mediated by gifts.

The *kula* ring: ritual circulation

In light of exchange theory, *The Winter's Tale* takes on a new look. The sheer scope of the ethnographic literature on exchange underscores the remarkable reach of *The Gift*. From the easily overlooked economy of reciprocal favors among friends and family, to the most elaborately ritualized exchanges, Mauss' vision of the centrality of the gift in creating and reinforcing moral relationships has been amply demonstrated. Cross-cutting economic life, religion, kinship, and politics, the gift is nothing less than "a total social fact." Maurice Merleau-Ponty underscored the crucial importance of exchange when he wrote, "exchange is not an effect of society, but society itself in act." (cited in Moore 2011: 41). As any child learns on the first day of school, once outside the security of family, each of us confronts "the other." We have no choice but to forge new relations with strangers. If Mauss is right, we accomplish this miracle largely through exchanges which are inevitably tinged with ambivalence. Given these complexities, how does exchange work to produce moral relations and mutuality of interest? To understand *The Winter's Tale* is to understand how Shakespeare answers this question in the play.

Ethnographic accounts of exchange provide some insight. The best-known ethnographic treatment of ritual gift exchange is Bronislaw Malinowski's *Argonauts of the Western Pacific* (1922). Malinowski's famous monograph describes in vivid detail the elaborate *kula* system of ritual trade that still circulates among the islands of the Massim region off the southeastern coast of Papua-New Guinea. Before the creation of the modern state of Papua-New Guinea in 1975, the islands making up the *kula* chain in the Milne Bay region were not regularly linked by ties of politics, kinship, or language. Like many of the tribes in pre-colonial New Guinea, they were largely autonomous societies and potential enemies. Trade was one of the few positive avenues for connection. While specific islands of the region possess useful resources and commodities in demand by their neighbors, the *kula* valuables, known collectively as *vaygu'a*, are exclusively of decorative rather than practical value. *Gimwali* or *self-interested* barter for practical goods goes on behind the scenes during *kula* visits, but it is never the focus of public attention and is looked down upon. *Kula* is seen as a ceremonious exchange, carried out through ritually mediated encounters between important men. Success in *kula* is tied to the quality of the valuables a trader receives and gives as well as the number and importance of his trading partners. Lifelong trade partnerships are valuable commodities in the region and important partnerships become a form of inheritance. Below I have included a number of the original photographs from Malinowski's 1922 book to give readers a more vivid sense of the *kula*.

Kula valuables feature two kinds of ornament: *Soulava*, red spondylus shell necklaces, circulate clockwise from island to island while *mwali*, white shell armbands, move counter-clockwise (see Figures 4.1 and 4.2).

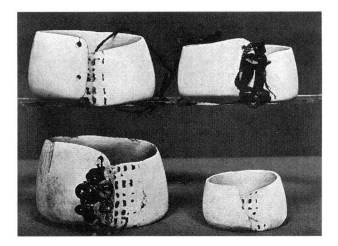

FIGURE 4.1 *Mwali*, shell armbands that circulate counterclockwise in the *kula* exchange circuit

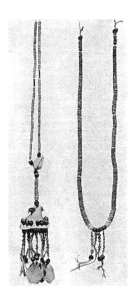

FIGURE 4.2 *Soulava*, red shell necklaces that circulate clockwise in the *kula* exchange circuit

Figures 4.3 and 4.4 show how these decorative items are worn.

FIGURE 4.3 Armbands (*mwali*) worn by men

FIGURE 4.4 Women wearing *soulava* necklaces

The two circuits are kept distinct, so *kula* traders have two sets of trading partners: (1) those partners to whom they travel by canoe to receive *soulava* and (2)
partners in the opposite direction to whom they travel to receive *mwali*. One never
handles *soulava* and *mwali* on the same voyage. This guarantees that each transaction will have the appearance of a pure gift, rather than a swap. As a total exchange
circuit, *kula* comprises two rings moving in opposite directions, as illustrated in
Figure 4.5 below.

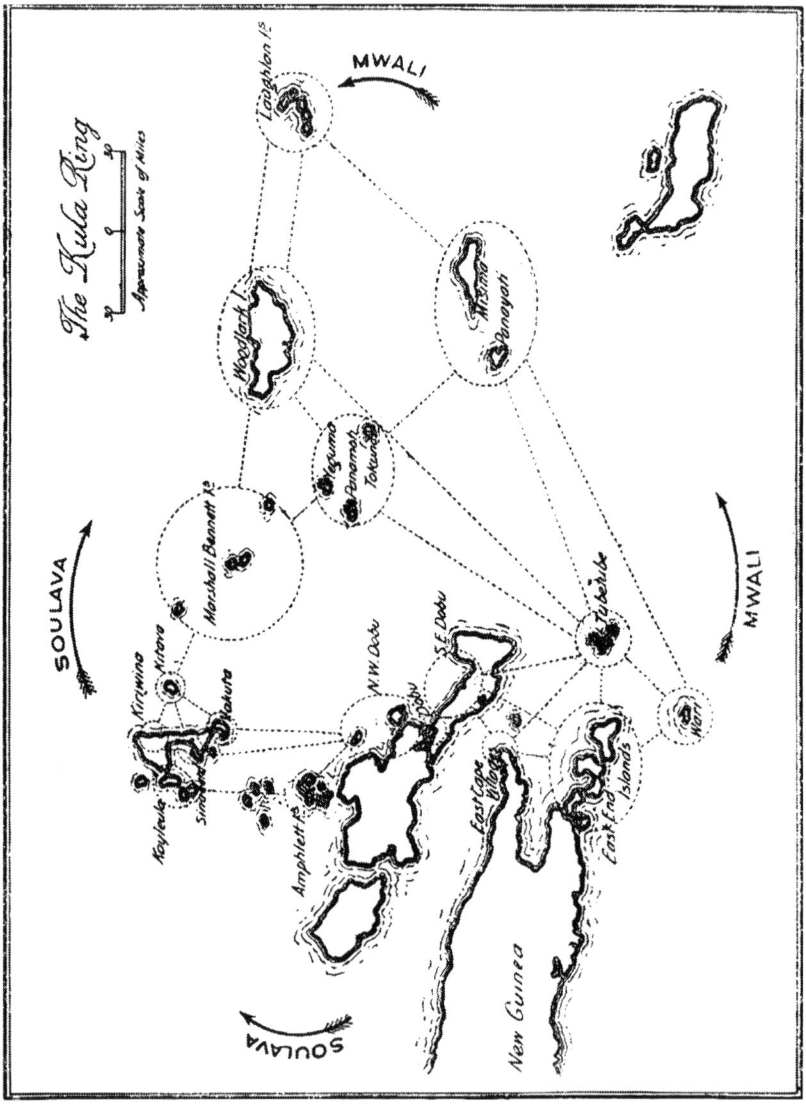

FIGURE 4.5 The *kula* ring and the circulation of *kula* valuables

Men, usually high-ranking leaders, embark on dangerous overseas journeys in their large sailing vessels, carrying exchange goods for their trading partners on other islands. But rather than practical goods, the focus is always on the *vaigu'a*, the decorative valuables. Men always sail to collect these valuables from their partners (Figures 4.6, 4.7).

FIGURE 4.6 A Trobriand sailing vessel at full sail filled with men heading for another island

FIGURE 4.7 A boat loaded with trade goods

Over time, status relations between partner islands remain more-or-less equal. *Mwali* transactions cancel out any status imbalance produced by *soulava*. Rather than relying on immediate reciprocity to guarantee equality (where a recipient of a valuable returns the same treasure to the original donor), a recipient of a *kula* treasure has to pass the object along in the opposite direction from which it came. The donor of a valuable can never get an immediate return from his partner. This arrangement produces a directional gift-chain from island to island. Eventually, the original treasure comes full circle around the ring, in rare cases, back to its original giver. Literal repayment for a given object must await the full circulation of that object (or its equivalent). The repayment for a valuable gift will have to come from a different partner than the one to whom it was originally given. Furthermore, there is no guarantee that the replacement will be exactly the same treasure that was originally given away. The "return" of the alienated object might well involve its replacement by a surrogate, a stand-in for a lost treasure.

What matters to traders is their personal prestige and trading success in relation to their neighbors. Success is a local, rather than global, matter. The big picture of *kula* as a giant ring connecting up a broad chain of islands is largely the anthropologist's creation. Before the publication of Malinowski's book, the *kula* as a social system was an emergent and unrecognized property of many individual transactions, not any kind of conscious global model. Through the ritual coordination of a chain of locally self-interested transactions, a regional system of interdependence transcending any individual trader or any individual community's interest was born.

Marriage exchange

In *The Winter's Tale*, despite the initial stress on the exchange of visits and gifts between the kings, it is ultimately Leontes' wife and daughter who figure as the most significant mediators between the kings. Both link and divide Leontes and Polixenes. Though the earliest anthropological studies of ritual gift circuits focused on exchanges of ceremonial items such as pigs, yams, shell necklaces, or woven mats, it was ultimately the exchange of women as wives that would play the leading role in the development of exchange theory in anthropology. The most influential single work on marriage exchange is Claude Lévi-Strauss' seminal book *The Elementary Structures of Kinship*. The book focuses on what the author calls "elementary marriage," arrangements governed by negative and positive marriage rules. Inspired by Mauss' ideas about gift exchange, Lévi-Strauss views each marriage system as an exchange system between groups. Different forms of cousin marriage are treated as alternative strategies for forming group alliances.[4] Scouring the ethnographic literature, Lévi-Strauss identifies numerous kinds of elementary marriage systems, but he is most interested in the many systems prescribing marriage with a cousin. Among these, the most common form of cousin marriage is the union of the children of a brother and sister, whom anthropologists call "cross-cousins."

In many societies, cross-cousins (mother's brother's or father's sister's children) are one's closest kin just outside the boundary of the "official" descent group. Parallel cousins, children of same-sex siblings (i.e., mother's sister's or father's brother's children) will potentially belong to the same descent group and are often considered lineage "siblings" and commonly prohibited as spouses.[5] Though obliged by incest prohibitions to marry outside one's own primary kin group, people often prefer not to stray too far from home in choosing their in-laws. Combining the prohibition of incestuous in-group marriage with the desire to marry close to home, marriage with a cross-cousin represents a perfect compromise. Cross-cousins as spouses neatly straddle the safety of "in-marriage" (endogamy) and the alliance benefits of "out-marriage" (exogamy).

The most common form of cousin marriage is "matrilateral cross-cousin marriage," where a man is encouraged to marry a cross-cousin on his mother's side (a "mother's brother's daughter") but is prohibited from marrying his cross-cousins on his father's side (his "father's sister's daughters"). Why make such an apparently arbitrary distinction? The answer is the exchange dynamic matrilateral-cross-cousin marriage produces, moving women from group to group in one direction, leading to "marriage chains" requiring at least three groups but usually more.[6] The marriage rings produced by matrilateral cross-cousin marriage mimic the basic exchange patterns in the *kula*. In the *kula* version, armbands circulate in one direction around the chain, while necklaces circulate in the opposite direction. In the marriage version of the chain, imported women as potential wives for a group move in one direction while their sisters and daughters are "exported" to a different group. Bride-wealth flows in a countercurrent to the flow of women. The strong resemblance between the exchange patterns in the *kula* and those in matrilateral cross-cousin marriage is a testament to the power of Marcel Mauss' original vision of gifting as an exchange and to Lévi-Strauss' insight in recognizing the principles of exchange inherent in the rules of elementary marriage systems.

A gap of time is a common feature of reciprocal exchange. Return a cup of sugar to your generous neighbor right away and the return becomes an insult. But wait too long before reciprocating a gift or a favor and you are equally guilty. The key to successful exchange is finding the right gap of time. A critical delay in reciprocity has been noted in the ethnographic literature on exchange. In *Argonauts of the Western Pacific*, Malinowski emphasizes that the *kula* is so organized that no direct exchanges of *kula* valuables can ever occur on a major *kula* expedition. Gift and counter-gift must be separated by a considerable gap in time. Marshall Sahlins highlights the functional aspects of delays in reciprocity in many traditional trade networks:

> Perhaps just as important are circumstances that put premiums on delayed exchange and so on tokens that store value in the interim. The outputs of interdependent communities, for example, may be unavoidably unbalanced in time-as between coastal and inland peoples, where an exchangeable catch of fish cannot always be met by complementary inland products. Here a currency acceptable on all sides very much facilitates interdependence-so that shell beads, say, taken for fish at one time can be converted for acorns at

> another .... Big-man leadership systems, it would seem from Melanesia, may likewise render delayed balanced exchange functional.
>
> (Sahlins 1972: 229–230)

Delays in reciprocity represent trust, but they also have practical functions. A delay can allow for the proliferation of relationships in creating and maintaining social networks. The spatial extension of alliances is obvious in the circular chains of connection that are engaged in both the *kula* ring and in cousin marriage systems. Long delays in reciprocation suggest that the ritual process plays a significant part in producing the changes that occur in exchange relationships.

The extended process of exchange is more than a simple return on a gift. An extended process of reciprocation can involve a crucial transformation of motive, what Freud and his followers called the "sublimation" (or lifting up) of a problematical desire into a socially acceptable form.[7] The potential hostility in exchange relations, where exchange implies a kind of competition or even warfare, can be crucially muted or transformed over time. Retaliation or feelings of shame gradually become experienced as reciprocation, so that a kind of "profit" or "interest" is generated by the gap separating the start and the conclusion of the exchange. Psychoanalytic theory uses the term "compromise formation" for this sublimation process. A primary, unacceptable impulse is replicated, but in a ritually altered form that renders it acceptable. The compromise simultaneously expresses and replaces the original desire. Understanding the work of exchange ritual in producing compromise formations is central to understanding the meaning of the wide gap of time operating in *The Winter's Tale*.

Implicit in Malinowski's account of *kula* is the role of the gift in transforming self-interest into collective interest. Malinowski is clear that the men engaging in *kula* are deeply motivated by a desire to accumulate possessions and renown. Yet, the etiquette of *kula* transactions forces participants to abide by a social code stressing *generosity* and *giving* as the path to renown. Self-interest is effectively harnessed in the service of sociality:

> Although, like every human being, the Kula native loves to possess and therefore desires to acquire and dreads to lose, the social code of rules, with regard to give and take by far overrides his natural acquisitive tendency.
>
> This social code, such as we find it among the natives of the Kula is, however, far from weakening the natural desirability of possession; on the contrary, it lays down that to possess is to be great, and that wealth is the indispensable appendage of social rank and attribute of personal virtue. But the important point is that with them to possess is to give and here the natives differ from us notably. A man who owns a thing is naturally expected to share it, to distribute it, to be its trustee and dispenser. And the higher the rank, the greater the obligation.
>
> (Malinowski 1922: 58)

In *kula* exchange, there is evidently a double transformation, both psychological and sociological. *Psychologically*, self-interest is channeled into generosity by a social and ritual code that emphasizes giving and not acquisition as the legitimate path to personal renown. *Sociologically,* chains of individual transactions are converted into a regional system of social interdependence. Through ritual, potential enemies become exchange partners.

The same sort of transformation is evident in cross-cousin marriage. If cross-cousin marriage is a compromise formation, what is the desire that is both evoked and denied? For Lévi-Strauss the answer is incest, an issue with which *The Elementary Structures of Kinship* both begins and ends. Lévi-Strauss sees the incest prohibition, universal in its general existence and local in the particularity of its rules in different societies, as a key marker of the boundary between nature and culture.

> The prohibition of incest is where nature transcends itself. It sparks the formation of a new and more complex type of structure and is superimposed upon the simpler structures of physical life through integration, just as these themselves are superimposed upon the simpler structures of animal life. It brings about and is in itself the advent of a new order.
>
> (Lévi-Strauss 1969: 26)

In the final chapter of *The Elementary Structures of Kinship*, Lévi-Strauss returns to the issue of incest and what it means for the human psyche. He turns to Freud's *Totem and Taboo* for insight:

> The desire for the mother or the sister, the murder of the father and the sons' repentance, undoubtedly do not correspond to any fact or group of facts occupying a given place in history. But perhaps they symbolically express an ancient and lasting dream. The magic of this dream, its power to mould men's thoughts unbeknown to them, arises precisely from the fact that the acts it evokes have never been committed, because culture has opposed them at all times and in all places. Symbolic gratifications in which the incest urge finds its expression, according to Freud, do not therefore commemorate an actual event. They are something else, and more, the permanent expression of a desire for disorder, or rather counter-order—.
>
> (*ibid*.: 491)

It is to this regressive desire for counter-order that Lévi-Strauss turns in seeking to understand the pervasiveness of cross-cousin marriage. While he has been accounting for these marriage systems in terms of their exchange properties and the benefits of the political alliances they afford, the surprising twist in his argument is that the real significance of cross-cousin marriage lies in its capacity to produce compromise. Marriages between cross-cousins manage to enable exchange and simultaneously evade it—almost. Cousin marriage thrives on ambivalence. Shadowing the permitted cross-cousin-as-spouse is inevitably the specter of the forbidden sibling-as-spouse.

Incest represents the ultimate form of a family's keeping something, or someone for itself. *Kula* ritual both harnesses the desire for possession and tames it through strong cultural norms enforcing the virtues of giving, rather than keeping. Cross-cousin marriage is Lévi-Strauss' version of the *kula*, a kind of primal alliance strategy turning a group outward toward the world of transactions, and it is at the same time an echo of incest. Marriage is prohibited between a brother and a sister *but prescribed for their children*. The universe of biological kin turns outward in one generation, only to turn back on itself in the following generation. In this sense, cross-cousin marriage is an "almost-incest system," an "in-again-out-again" marriage strategy, separating siblings in one generation only to reunite them (through the marriage of their children) in the next. The extension in the time required for full reciprocity in matrilateral cross-cousin marriage (i.e., the completion of a full circle of exchanges) is also the proliferation of the marriage's "profit," extended alliance networks through chains of marriage. The wide gap of time becomes equally a wide gap of space and a life-enhancing field of social alliance.

We can see how the gap of time in the ritual exchange process affords a space for compromise formation, a surrogate solution to an unrecognized or unspeakable problem. In *The Winter's Tale*, this gap, the 16 years between Acts III and IV, is linked intimately to the reconciliations that conclude the play. Yet, if the resolution of *The Winter's Tale* is really a compromise formation, what exactly is the compromise about? The union of Florizel and Perdita is not a union of cross-cousins. Nor is it an incestuous match, even though Perdita ends up marrying a kind of surrogate son for Leontes. But a close look at the play will suggest that the Florizel-Perdita union is but a step away from both and comes remarkably close to the anthropologist's vision of the work of cross-cousin marriage. Which brings us to the hidden problem of the play.

The hidden problem

Exchange theory suggests that the long-delayed union of Leontes' and Polixenes' children might involve a compromise resolving an undisclosed problem. *The Winter's Tale* is a story of troubled relationships that eventually harmonized through compromises, exchange, and transformations made possible by a 16-year delay. The 16-year gap both divides and reunites the two halves of *The Winter's Tale*. But this interpretation only makes sense if we can find the hidden problem resolved by the marriage of Perdita and Florizel. This account of the buried heart of *The Winter's Tale* involves the puzzling source of Leontes' jealous rage in Act I. If earlier critics were right, and *The Winter's Tale* was all surface drama, there would be nothing hidden to discover. But a close look at the play suggests just the opposite: a remarkable number of important people and events in the play are buried out of sight, left to reported speech and viewers' imagination. These hidden elements draw attention away from the story's surfaces, creating a sense of depth and mystery, pointing to something else. Consider the following things that are never presented on stage:

- Leontes' and Polixenes' childhood together.
- Polixenes' wife.
- Leontes' life during the 16-year gap.
- Hermione's life during the 16-year gap.
- Autolycus' service to Florizel.
- Perdita's childhood.
- Mamillius' death.
- Antigonus' grisly death.
- Hermione's (purported) death.
- Leontes' reunion with Perdita and Polixenes.

Significant parts of *The Winter's Tale* are not just unspeakable: they are invisible. Many of Leontes' closest friends and family members are banished from his sight. Of all the undisclosed aspects of the play, the most troubling is the source of Leontes' jealousy. If this essay were about Robert Greene's *Pandosto* rather than about Shakespeare's reworking of that story, we might reasonably claim that Leontes' jealousy is motivated by incestuous desire for Perdita. In *Pandosto*, the King sets his erotic sights on his daughter Fawnia. The resolution offered in that story involves Pandosto's suicide, paving the way for Fawnia's marriage to Dorastus. But there is no obvious suggestion in *The Winter's Tale* that Leontes is concealing incestuous feelings for his daughter, though we will have occasion to question this. If incest is not exactly the play's missing motive, then some other buried impulse drives Leontes' jealousy.

The play opens with Leontes and Hermione trying to convince Polixenes to extend his visit to Sicilia. When Leontes' arguments prove futile, he asks Hermione to convince Polixenes to delay his departure. It is only when Polixenes accedes to Hermione's invitation that Leontes turns to the audience to vent his repressed fury:

> [Aside] Too hot, too hot!
> To mingle friendship far is mingling bloods.
> I have tremor cordis on me: my heart dances;
> But not for joy; not joy.

> (I, ii, 139–142)

Leontes' anger is conventionally read as a husband's jealousy over his wife's suspected infidelity. This garden-variety jealousy, what Shakespeare in *Othello* calls "the green-eyed monster which doth mock/The meat it feeds on" is no stranger to Shakespeare's plays. It consumes Othello and is also at work in *Cymbeline*, *Twelfth Night*, and *A Midsummer Night's Dream*. But in *The Winter's Tale*, there are compelling reasons to look beyond conventional expectations. The audience would normally not find the behavior of Hermione and Polixenes suspicious. Leontes' rage takes the audience by surprise. While Othello's and Leontes' jealousy both lack a basis in fact, Shakespeare is at pains to provide a credible explanation for Othello's suspicions. Iago, harboring corrosive ill-will against Othello for his favoring of Casio as his lieutenant, plants a web of false evidence of Desdemona's alleged infidelity, intended to provoke Othello's suspicions. Though deeply irrational in its consequences, jealousy is a logical response to the available evidence in *Othello*. But *The Winter's Tale* gives us no Iago and no handkerchief to serve as a "smoking gun." Leontes' jealousy seems to erupt from nowhere.

Yet, the play does provide some clues. In the opening act of *The Winter's Tale*, Shakespeare hints at the basis of Leontes' rage by proposing an unexpected twist on the conventional jealousy theme. It comes in the brief exchange between the kings' attendants Camillo and Archidamus that opens the play:

CAMILLO
Sicilia cannot show himself over-kind to Bohemia.
They were trained together in their childhoods; and
there rooted betwixt them then such an affection,
which cannot choose but branch now.

(I, i, 22–25)

The exchange turns to a discussion about Leontes' heir, Mamillius and the "unspeakable comfort" (ll. 33–34) he brings. But what kind of comfort is "unspeakable?" Mamillius seems to be implicated oddly in Leontes' tirade. In the middle of his impassioned outburst, Leontes turns to his son and asks, "Mamillius, /Art thou my boy?" (I, ii, 150–151). A strange dialogue follows:

MAMILLIUS
Ay, my good lord.

LEONTES
I' fecks!
Why, that's my bawcock. What, hast
smutch'd thy nose?
They say it is a copy out of mine. Come, captain,
We must be neat; not neat, but cleanly, captain:
And yet the steer, the heifer and the calf
Are all call'd neat.--Still virginalling
Upon his palm!--How now, you wanton calf!
Art thou my calf?

MAMILLIUS
Yes, if you will, my lord.

LEONTES
Thou want'st a rough pash and the shoots that I have,
To be full like me: yet they say we are
Almost as like as eggs;

(I, ii, 152–166)

Mark Van Doren has called Leontes' outburst "the obscurest passage in Shakespeare" (Van Doren 1939: 316). The language is undoubtedly obscure, a chaotic pastiche of associations that run together helter-skelter. This passage is the best example of an "unspeakable" utterance in a play full of the unsaid and the unseen[8]. Whatever else Leontes reveals here about his disordered state of mind, his outrage at his wife and Polixenes is somehow linked in his mind with his son Mamillius, and, more than that, with his conception of Mamillius as his double. When Leontes asks Mamillius, "Art thou mine?" and says, "With what's unreal thou coactive art," "art" does double duty, as it often does in Shakespeare, underscoring the question of whether the son is a fair copy of the father. Though Leontes' suspicions about whether Polixenes could have fathered his child eventually shift to the infant Perdita, here Leontes conflates his anger at Hermione and Polixenes with doubts about his son's resemblance to him.

Some light on the fraught nexus linking Leontes, Polixenes, Hermione, and Mamillius is provided by the play's backstory that unfolds in an exchange between Hermione and Polixenes, as she tries to convince him to extend his visit. "Come," Hermione urges Polixenes, "I'll question you/Of my lord's tricks and yours when you were boys:/You were pretty lordings then?"

POLIXENES
We were, fair queen,
Two lads that thought there was no more behind
But such a day to-morrow as to-day,
And to be boy eternal.

HERMIONE
Was not my lord
The verier wag o' the two?

POLIXENES
We were as twinn'd lambs that did frisk i' the sun,
And bleat the one at the other: what we changed
Was innocence for innocence; we knew not
The doctrine of ill-doing, nor dream'd
That any did. Had we pursued that life,
And our weak spirits ne'er been higher rear'd
With stronger blood, we should have answer'd heaven

Boldly 'not guilty;' the imposition clear'd
Hereditary ours.

HERMIONE
By this we gather
You have tripp'd since.

POLIXENES
O my most sacred lady!
Temptations have since then been born to's; for
In those unfledged days was my wife a girl;
Your precious self had then not cross'd the eyes
Of my young play-fellow.

HERMIONE
Grace to boot!
Of this make no conclusion, lest you say
Your queen and I are devils: yet go on;
The offences we have made you do we'll answer,
If you first sinn'd with us and that with us
You did continue fault and that you slipp'd not
With any but with us.

(I, ii, 76–108)

The exchange reveals a picture of the original intimacy that linked Leontes and Polixenes as boys. Polixenes refers to the two friends as innocent "twinn'd lambs." In Polixenes' account, this pre-sexual, homoerotic phase comes to an end when the boys turn from their relations with one another to encounter their future wives and assume adult responsibilities. This loss of the boys' primal connection is viewed as a fall from innocence due to the temptations of heterosexual love. "By this," Hermione taunts Polixenes, "we gather you have tripp'd since." In this context, Leontes' jealousy is directed as much against Hermione for having come between him and Polixenes as for her unfaithfulness to him.

Stephen Orgel proposed this view of the origins of Leontes' jealousy in *Impersonations*. According to Orgel, the account of the disruption of Polixenes' and Leontes' childhood rests on a profoundly ambivalent male fantasy about adult sexual relations and the sexuality of women.

It is a fantasy that is crucial to the play, a determining feature of the subsequent tragic action. Critics for two hundred years have declared Leontes' paranoid jealousy inexplicable, but in the context of that dream of what it means to be a child, Leontes' behavior is not only understandable, it is in a way inevitable. No particular word or gesture is required to trigger Leontes' paranoid jealousy; the translation of the inseparable friend into the dangerous rival, and of the chaste wife into a whore, is implicit in the fantasy, its worst-case scenario, so to speak, replicating the situation Shakespeare has imagined with such detailed intensity in the Dark Lady sonnets. This is the consequence of women entering the world of male friendship.

(Orgel 1996b: 16–17)

Leontes' jealousy is a more complicated matter than the conventional sexual jealousy that drives *Othello*. This unanticipated misogynistic and homoerotic twist on the jealousy theme reveals the buried problem that will seek resolution at the end of the play. Gender theorists and psychoanalytically inclined critics have seized upon these early scenes in *The Winter's Tale* as landmarks pointing to the hidden heart of the play, and the source of Leontes' fury at Hermione.

Shakespeare's insights into the hidden recesses of jealousy anticipate those of Freud. In a 1922 paper, "Some Neurotic Mechanisms in Jealousy Paranoia and Homosexuality," Freud offers an eye-opening discussion of jealousy that includes the very homosexual twist suggested in *The Winter's Tale*.

There is not much to be said from the analytic point of view about normal jealousy. It is easy to see that essentially it is compounded of grief, the pain caused by the thought of losing the loved object, and of the narcissistic wound, in so far as this is distinguishable from the other wound; further, of feelings of enmity against the successful rival, and of a greater or lesser amount of self-criticism which tries to hold the subject's own ego accountable for his loss. Although we may call it normal, this jealousy is by no means completely rational, that is, derived from the actual situation proportionate to the real circumstances and under the real control of the conscious ego; for it is rooted deep in the unconscious, it is a continuation of the earliest stirrings of the child's affective life, and it originates in the oedipus or the brother-and-sister complex of the first sexual period. *Moreover, it is noteworthy that in some people it is experienced bisexually. That is to say, a man will not only feel pain about the woman he loves and hatred of the man who is his rival, but also grief about the man, whom he loves unconsciously, and hatred of the woman as his rival; and this latter set of feelings will add to the intensity of his jealousy. .*

(Freud 1922/1998: 216, italics added)

In a 1965 essay, "Reflections on the Notion of Kinship," anthropologist George Devereux provides a fascinating psychoanalytic reading of the exchange model of kinship derived from his teacher Marcel Mauss. He sees marriage as "chiefly a means of resolving conflicts between the 'takers' and the 'givers' of women" (Devereux 1978: 208). For Devereux, the exchange relations established with a marriage involve primarily deeply ambivalent relations between the men who are doing the exchange—fathers or brothers, as the case may be. Underlying the overt heterosexual relations between the bride and the groom lies a quite different set of relations, more ambivalent and therefore less explicitly manifested.

> [T]he principal regulations do not concern the relationship between men and women but the relation between the men themselves, since such transactions occur between men; women are simply their objects. The institution of marriage which stands with kinship, both consanguine and affinal, in a relationship of co-emergence has as its goal not the socially advantageous resolution of the heterosexual problem but the repelling of the threatened specter of latent homosexuality, product of the Oedipus complex.
>
> (*ibid.*: 211)

There is little in Devereux's or Freud's comments that would have surprised Shakespeare's contemporaries. In "Ganymedes and Kings: Staging Male Homosexual Desire in *The Winter's Tale*," Nora Johnson suggests how thoroughly Foucault's influential *History of Sexuality* has revised our understanding of Elizabethan views of male homosexual behavior. The homoeroticism implied in the two princes' intimate bond and "rooted affections" in *The Winter's Tale* is in line with current scholarship on Elizabethan male sexuality. Alluding to the work of Alan Bray (1990) on homosexuality and male friendship in Elizabethan England, Johnson writes:

> What emerges from Bray's study is more than simply the absence of what twentieth-century historians would call "homosexuality." These accounts suggest that homosexual practice was part of an aristocratic sexual esthetic, a "fashion," in which the courtier sampled at will from an array of erotic practices, none of which could impose itself upon him as a rigid identity. Even Ashley's apparent preference for boys seems to have been compatible with his role as a husband and father. To reiterate the point that has become associated with Foucault's work, sodomy in early modern England is an act, not an identity.
>
> (Johnson 1998: 188) [9]

Johnson focuses on the place of the boy "sodomite" and more generally on the slipperiness of gender and of sexual relations in Elizabethan theater, where boys and young men played the female roles. *The Winter's Tale* allows the tensions and potential competition between homosexual and heterosexual intimacy to motivate what looks like a conventional jealousy story. The suggestion that it is Polixenes rather than Hermione who is the primary object of Leontes' jealous attention was made early on by W.H. Auden, who proposed that Leontes' jealousy against Hermione was a defense against acknowledging the unspeakable truth that his real desire was for his lost childhood friend. This defense drives Leontes to insist, "I do not love him, she does" (Auden 1962: 246).[10] In her essay "'Boy Eternal': Aging, Games, and Masculinity in The Winter's Tale," Gina Bloom sees *The Winter's Tale* as challenging conventional assumptions about male development. Her analysis focuses on how *The Winter's Tale* deals with male development. She sees the play as implicitly questioning the linear model of male psychosexual development that we associate with Freud. This is the vision of the inevitable development of early homoerotic attachments for boys into mature heterosexual relations. *The Winter's Tale* presents such a model of development, Bloom suggests, but only to throw it into question. She argues that, while Leontes' appears by the end of the play to have reconciled his ambivalence about aging and assuming adult relationships and responsibilities, Polixenes betrays psychological regression in his attempts to remain "a boy eternal."

Reading *The Winter's Tale* through the sonnets

In *Impersonations*, Stephen Orgel notes the significance of themes from the Dark Lady sonnets in *The Winter's Tale* (Orgel 1996b: 17). In fact, *The Winter's Tale* reveals a striking resonance with Shakespeare's early sonnets. Shakespeare's 154 sonnets were likely composed between 1592 and 1598 but were only published in 1609, just a year or two before Shakespeare wrote *The Winter's Tale*. *The Winter's Tale* was likely Shakespeare's attempt to work critical themes from his Sonnets into a single story, a story that seeks to resolve major contradictions in Shakespeare's poetic reflections on time, love, art, and reproduction. While the Petrarchan sonnet tradition generally had a male poet addressing an elusive mistress, Shakespeare's primary love object in the early sonnets is male. The first 17 sonnets are addressed to a "faire youth," the object of the poet's love. This unnamed youth is possibly the "Mr. W.H." whom Shakespeare's dedication provocatively calls "the only begetter of these ensuing sonnets." [11]In this first group of sonnets, Shakespeare laments the toll that time will have on the boy's beauty. Several of the early poems stress the "immortality through reproduction" theme, urging the youth to have children to evade the ravages of time.

> If thou couldst answer "This fair child of mine
> Shall sum my count, and make my old excuse,"
> Proving his beauty by succession thine!
> This were to be new made when thou art old,
> And see thy blood warm when thou feel'st it cold.
>
> (Sonnet II)

Other sonnets turn from the restorative powers of nature to those of culture, praising the power of the poet's art to preserve the youth's beauty. A well-known example comes from Sonnet XVIII.

> Nor shall death brag thou wander'st in his shade,
> When in eternal lines to time thou grow'st,
> So long as men can breathe, or eyes can see,
> So long lives this, and this gives life to thee.

Sonnet XVII acknowledges the potential synergy of culture (poetry) and nature (biological reproduction) in countering time ravages.

If I could write the beauty of your eyes,
And in fresh numbers number all your graces,
The age to come would say "This poet lies;
Such heavenly touches ne'er touch'd earthly faces."
But were some child of yours alive that time,
You should live twice, in it, and in my rhyme.

The clearest reference to the hidden problem of *The Winter's Tale* is found in Sonnet XX, which addresses the androgynous attractions of the fair youth whom Shakespeare calls "the master-mistress of my passion." He laments the impossibility of his consummating physically his love for the boy who, "prick'd . . . out for women's pleasure," will inevitably seek a woman's love.

A woman's face with nature's own hand painted,
Hast thou, the master mistress of my passion;
A woman's gentle heart, but not acquainted
With shifting change, as is false women's fashion:
An eye more bright than theirs, less false in rolling,
Gilding the object whereupon it gazeth;
A man in hue all hues in his controlling,
Which steals men's eyes and women's souls amazeth.
And for a woman wert thou first created;
Till Nature, as she wrought thee, fell a-doting,
And by addition me of thee defeated,
By adding one thing to my purpose nothing.
But since she prick'd thee out for women's pleasure,
Mine be thy love and thy love's use their treasure.

Equipped by nature for the pleasure of women, the fair youth can only be loved platonically by the poet. Sonnet XLII brings us to the heart of *The Winter's Tale*. It is a double jealousy poem that has remarkable resonance with Freud's reflections on the bisexuality inherent in certain forms of jealousy. The poet and the fair youth both love the same woman. The poet fears losing his mistress to his friend. The poet's jealousy over losing the woman to the friend is doubled by his jealousy over losing the youth to the woman. The poet struggles to make sense of the double loss. The resolution comes in the final couplet by way of a logical twist: since the poet and the youth are one, he cannot truly lose the mistress' love since she cannot love the youth without also loving him. And so, he keeps them both (while possessing neither).

That thou hast her it is not all my grief,
And yet it may be said I loved her dearly;
That she hath thee is of my wailing chief,
A loss in love that touches me more nearly.

Loving offenders thus I will excuse ye:
Thou dost love her, because thou know'st I love her;
And for my sake even so doth she abuse me,
Suffering my friend for my sake to approve her.
If I lose thee, my loss is my love's gain,
And losing her, my friend hath found that loss;
Both find each other, and I lose both twain,
And both for my sake lay on me this cross:
But here's the joy; my friend and I are one;
Sweet flattery! then she loves but me alone.

The sonnets promising to immortalize the youth in verse and those urging pro-creation set up a contrast that echoes the debate between Perdita and the disguised Polixenes in Act IV of *The Winter's Tale* about the relative power of art versus nature in horticulture. This debate was familiar in Shakespeare's day, perhaps the most famous example coming from Montaigne's essay "Of the Caniballs," first trans-lated into English in 1603. [12] While hybridization through cross-pollination was unknown in Shakespeare's day, the grafting of one plant onto another was practiced. With specific reference to artificially modified carnations and "streak'd gillyvors," Perdita objects to such practices as unnatural, preferring flowers that have not ben-efitted from the intervention of human grafting arts. She argues that being artifi-cial, hybrid plants produced through the horticultural arts are "nature's bastards." In defense of the benefits of human arts supplementing nature's creations, Polixenes proposes a dialectical resolution to the problem. The dichotomy between art and nature on which Perdita's argument is based is false, he says, since "over that art/ Which you say adds to nature, is an art/That nature makes" (IV, iv, 107–109). Art, Polixenes proposes, should be understood as an expression of the natural order rather than its negation. [13] Throughout *The Winter's Tale,* Shakespeare works his way to a subtle reconciliation of art and nature, a problem to which structuralists like Lévi-Strauss returned in the mid-20th century in their focus on the nature–culture dichotomy. [14] This resolution is most dramatically on display in the play's famous final scene, where Hermione is brought back from the dead as a synthesis of nature (alive after an absence of 16 years) and art (a statue).

Another way the play proposes a reconciliation of opposition between nature and art comes close to the Sonnets' solution. In Act I, Leontes had conceived of his son Mamillius as a work of art, a vision in which the son perfectly reproduces the father. Mamillius represents for Leontes a kind of compensation for the loss of his childhood connection to Polixenes. Recall how in Shakespeare's procreation sonnets, conceiving a child is proposed as the fair youth's compensation for the loss of his poet/lover. However, the child can serve as compensation only if he can reproduce the father both in appearance and through biological regeneration. Just as Polixenes replicated Leontes in their youth as his twin, Mamillius will function as his father's twin in his adult life. It is in this light that Leontes responds to Florizel when, in Act V, he first lays eyes on Polixenes' son:

> Your mother was most true to wedlock, prince;
> For she did print your royal father off,
> Conceiving you: were I but twenty-one,
> Your father's image is so hit in you,
> His very air, that I should call you brother,
> As I did him, and speak of something wildly
> By us perform'd before.

(V, i, 157–163)

Leontes views Florizel as Polixenes' double, both his air (appearance/double) and his heir, reproducing his father by both art and nature. So Florizel compensates Polixenes for the loss of Leontes, just as Mamillius compensates Leontes for his loss of Polixenes. Nature's reproduction not only "prints" the son off the father, but links Polixenes' son by a double replication to Leontes himself, who recalls his childhood self as Polixenes' twin. Through these tortured twists of replication, Leontes can fashion himself as Florizel's "brother" (revealing the hidden specter of doubly displaced incest in Florizel's marriage to Perdita). When he looks at Florizel, he sees not just Polixenes, but also himself in his early relationship with his friend. Choplogic this may be, but it is an argument powerfully prefigured in the early Sonnets. If this logic sounds familiar, we need to only recall the final couplet of Sonnet XLII:

> But here's the joy; my friend and I are one;
> Sweet flattery! then she loves but me alone.

This concern with immortalization through faithful reproduction is behind Leontes' obsession with Mamillius' resemblance to him. The notion of a child as a perfect reproduction of a parent is a parent's narcissistic fantasy. Cloning is not nature's path to reproduction. With biological reproduction, every child is a new roll of the dice, a novel remix of two parents. In human histories, linear time and its contingencies inevitably trump the replication of cyclical time. But Perdita argues that the recombination of natural reproduction amount to the bastardized grafting of which she disapproves in the cultivation of flowers. It is, in Perdita's terms, "unnatural" in its mixing. But it is also "natural" in its bio-logic. If biological reproduction can never fully replicate a parent, picture-perfect replication can be approached in the domain of art ("*Art* thou my boy?"). This is where art triumphs over nature. Except, of course, that it lacks life. This desire for perfect replication lies behind Leontes' frequent use of the metaphors of art to characterize a father's relations to his sons. And it is just this power of art to create a perfect copy that astounds Leontes when he confronts the statue of Hermione in the play's closing scene.

By the end of *The Winter's Tale*, the action returns to Sicilia and delivers a satisfying restoration. The exchange cycle is complete. Tragic losses triggered by Leontes' jealousy in Act I are restored in Act V by the unexpected return of his wife and lost child and his reconciliations with Polixenes and Camillo. The story, a tale of the seasons, has, like the year, traced a circle. But it is not quite a full circle. As noted earlier, cyclical time with its perpetual restorations can never completely evade history's linear contingencies in human lives. And so, this exchange "cycle" is inherently imperfect because it includes life as well as art. Mamillius is gone, incompletely replaced by a surrogate "son," Florizel. Camillo is betrothed to the widowed Paulina, yet Camillo is not Antigonus. Hermione is restored as Leontes' Queen, but her 16 missing years are inscribed on her brow and in her memory. As for that buried problem that powers the play, Leontes finally recovers his lost relationship with Polixenes. But they are now linked as in-laws rather than as the "twinn'd lambs" of their youth. Once "rooted together" in youthful affection, the two kings have finally found a way to transplant the common tree that was dislodged in the breach of their friendship. But this family tree is made possible by their children's marriage rather than by a more direct relationship between the two kings. The union of Florizel and Perdita is, after all, a compromise and a replacement. It represents both a restoration and a transformation of an earlier desire. If, through the power of art, the fair youth and Shakespeare can jointly "beget" The Sonnets, then in *The Winter's Tale*, through the natural power of biological reproduction wedded to the cultural trick dynastic marriage, the union of Florizel and Perdita can allow their fathers to beget jointly the heirs of their kingdoms.

Here we find the missing echo of cross-cousin marriage. Recall that cross-cousin marriage represents a cultural compromise, requiring a brother and a sister to marry "out" rather than directly reproduce their own families. But what is forbidden in one generation returns as preferred in the next. Brother and sister go their own ways in marriage so that their children can unite in the following generation. Social reproduction pulses with an out-again-in-again rhythm. Through the artifice of cross-cousin marriage, a sibling set can reproduce their own descent group through their children's marriage. Compare this with the marriage of Florizel and Perdita. The "twinn'd lambs," Polixenes and Leontes, once rooted together, cannot continue their "tree" directly with each other. The homoerotic/incestuous union of the brother-princes, blocked both socially and biologically from producing offspring, recalls the prohibited reproductive destinies of brother and sister. Both are a turning in when nature calls for a turning out. The one is sexual incest, the other a sort of gender incest. Each prince must go his own way in marriage. But what is impossible in nature can be accomplished through social and theatrical artifice. In a kind of atavistic fantasy, *The Winter's Tale* has the wives disappear (we never get to see Polixenes' wife), and even Perdita, true to her name, is lost for 16 years. [15]And when Leontes' women reappear in Act V, it is in anticipation of the impending union of the children of Leontes and Polixenes, who, through the long gap of time, are reunited through the dynastic marriage of their children.

Mediation

The unusually long delay between loss and restoration in *The Winter's Tale* involves more than just an unfolding plotline. As with many cycles of ritual exchange, a delay in reciprocity allows for the resolution of the buried problem to work itself out through a slow reworking of the troubled relationships. The long way home is the cost of coming to terms with the realities of the adult world. By the end of the journey through *The Winter's Tale*, we know what has been resolved in the play's five acts. Less clear is how that resolution takes place. Whether as wealth objects like economic exchange or as people as in marriage arrangements, the gift is more than just a single act or a thing. The "change" in "exchange" generally calls for a carefully orchestrated ritual process. In the *kula*, the gap between a gift and its eventual return is filled with mediating acts: magic spells to increase the partner's generosity, intermediate gifts as holding places for the return, and short-term circulations of the *kula* valuable among family members. Marriage exchange often involve mediating processes like bride-service, the bride's ceremonial transfer to her new home, extended bridewealth negotiations, or transfers of animals, cash, or wealth objects. Reciprocal exchange is often an attenuated and highly mediated process.

Mediation of the troubled relationships is essential to restoration in *The Winter's Tale*, and it is not surprising that the play features numerous go-betweens. Camillo initially acts on behalf of Leontes, later for Polixenes, and finally serves as a mediator between the two kings. Paulina negotiates with Leontes on behalf of Hermione. Cleomenes and Dion serve as intermediaries between the Delphic Oracle and Leontes' court. The old Shepherd, who adopts Perdita and serves as her surrogate father for 16 years, is also effectively an intermediary, a temporary father for Perdita before she is restored to her birth parents. Time's gift of 16 years bridges the two halves of the play, allowing events to slowly circle back from Bohemia to Sicilia.

Of all the mediations that bridge the losses of Act I and the restorations of Act V, two are important enough to consider in detail. The first is an event, the sheep-shearing festival. Sheep, shepherds, and the rich web of associations linked to hair-cutting dominate the long fourth act of *The Winter's Tale* and oversee the play's transition from tragic to comic mood. The second important mediator in *The Winter's Tale* is Autolycus, the peddler/tinker/singer/thief who "haunts wakes, fairs and bear-baitings." Despite his roguish nature and his thoroughgoing dishonesty, there is something life-giving about Autolycus, something exhilarating and mysterious that helps propel the play to its resolution. Both the sheep-shearing festival and Autolycus are Shakespeare's innovations on Greene's story.[16] While the sheep-shearing motif only enters the play in full force in Act IV, pastoral imagery is ubiquitous in *The Winter's Tale*. We find pastoral references even in Leontes' court, far from the world of sheep-shearing. Polixenes and Leontes are characterized as twinn'd lambs in Act I. Leontes admonishes Mamillius, "We must be neat; not neat, but cleanly, captain:/And yet the steer, the heifer and the calf/Are all call'd neat" (I, ii, 159–161), where "neat" means both "tidy" and "cattle." The pastoral mood intensifies as soon as the action shifts from Sicilia to Bohemia. Act III opens with the entrance of the Shepherd and his son. As his son relates the ghastly scene of Antigonus being devoured by a bear, the Shepherd comes upon the basket containing the infant Perdita. From this moment, the play's downward movement reverses, as the emphasis on death is replaced by the arrival of new life:

"Heavy matters! heavy matters! but look thee here boy. Now bless thyself: thou met'st with things dying, I with things newborn" (III, iii, 118–120). In one brilliant moment, the play enters the green world of Shakespearean comedy. Pastoral themes triggered familiar associations for Shakespeare's contemporaries. England was an agrarian society, and the world of sheep and shepherds provided much of the imagery in art and prayer. Moreover, Shakespeare's father was a part-time wool-stapler, a middleman in the wool trade. His family would have been familiar with the shepherd's world.

The image of The Good Shepherd was familiar in Christian liturgy and shaped conventional understandings of pastoral care.[17] "The Lord is my Shepherd" made perfect sense in a society with a thriving pastoral economy. The frequent references in the play to shepherds and sheep link the court and the countryside. They also resonate with the Biblical theme of The Good Shepherd, the idiom that modeled for Elizabethans all forms of pastoral care. The contrast between Leontes in Act I, who imprisons his wife, indirectly kills his son and abandons his daughter to the elements and the wolves, and the lowly Shepherd who rescues and cares for Perdita in Act III, vividly evokes the stock Christian distinction between the bad and good shepherd familiar to Elizabethan audiences.

The theme of sheep-shearing, which emerges explicitly only in Act IV of *The Winter's Tale*, is anticipated from the start of the play, but only indirectly. Through his genius for wordplay, Shakespeare weaves a subtle web of associations among the words "heir," "hair," and "air" in such a way as to link Leontes' loss of his heir with shearing—the sheep's loss of hair. The Oracle announces in II, ii, "and the king shall live without an heir, if that which is lost be not found" (144–135). The imagery is repeated in V, i, when Leontes acknowledges that the injuries he inflicted on Hermione were such "that heirless it has made my kingdom" (10). As the play approaches its conclusion, Paulina urges Leontes not to despair about the loss of his children, promising "The crown will find an heir" in which the intended double sense of the phrase becomes apparent. In Act IV, this web of associations grows more complex with the addition of "air" to the mix, where it signifies appearance produced by clothing. Garments creates a person's "air," covering and reshaping the human form like hair covers animals. In scene iv, Autolycus comes across the Shepherd and his son, who are on their way to find Polixenes to confess to having found Perdita abandoned when she was an infant.

CLOWN
We are but plain fellows, sir.

AUTOLYCUS
A lie; you are rough and hairy. Let me have no
lying: it becomes none but tradesmen, and they
often give us soldiers the lie: but we pay them for
it with stamped coin, not stabbing steel; therefore
they do not give us the lie.

CLOWN

Your worship had like to have given us one, if you
had not taken yourself with the manner.

SHEPHERD

Are you a courtier, an't like you, sir?

AUTOLYCUS

Whether it like me or no, I am a courtier. Seest
thou not the air of the court in these enfoldings?
hath not my gait in it the measure of the court?
receives not thy nose court-odor from me? reflect I
not on thy baseness court-contempt? Thinkest thou,
for that I insinuate, or toaze from thee thy
business, I am therefore no courtier? I am courtier
cap-a-pe; and one that will either push on or pluck
back thy business there: whereupon I command thee to
open thy affair.

(IV, iv, 847–866)

Here "air" refers to an impression created by one's clothing. And finally, there is Leontes' greeting to Florizel upon arriving in Sicilia: "Your father's image is so hit in you, /His very air, that I should call you brother" (V, i, 160–161). Leontes recognizes in Florizel his father's heir/air, where replication of appearance certifies the son's legitimacy. The multiple associations among "heir," "hair," and "air" might be dismissed as cheap wordplay if their intersections did not point to interconnected themes central to the play.

There are also strong conventional links between the shaving or cutting of the hair and ascetic practices of penance, self-abasement, and loss of power. While found worldwide, these associations have seminal Biblical foundations in the Samson story (Leach 1957; Obeyesekere 1984). Losing his heir is ultimate recognized as Leontes' punishment for his sins. Autolycus recreates and extends this association when he describes his technique of "fleecing" unsuspecting victims:

'twas nothing to geld a codpiece of a
purse; I could have filed keys off that hung in
chains: no hearing, no feeling, but my sir's song,
and admiring the nothing of it. So that in this
time of lethargy I picked and cut most of their
festival purses; and had not the old man come in
with a whoo-bub against his daughter and the king's

son and scared my choughs from the chaff, I had not
left a purse alive in the whole army.

(IV, iv, 725–734)

Autolycus is a professional pickpocket, a figure also known in as a "cutpurse" who
fleeces his victims, taking their (money) "bags." In the slang of Shakespeare's time, to
cut a purse or a bag suggested not only theft but castration. This loss of a generative
power is, of course, the very punishment endured by Leontes in losing his children.
An extraordinary semantic network in the play links fleecing, shearing, (dis)robing,
robbing, and gelding. Consider that Autolycus boasts that, by "fleecing" (shearing/
robbing) his victims, he can turn the shearers into sheep.

Prosper you, sweet sir. Your purse is not hot enough
to purchase your spice. I'll be with you at your
sheep-shearing too: if I make not this cheat bring
out another, and the shearers prove sheep, let me
be unrolled and my name put in the book of virtue!

(IV, iii, 124–129)

This virtuoso wordplay generates undercurrents of symbolic association, producing
an implicit commentary on the "good shepherd" theme threading its way through
the metaphorical fabric of Shakespeare's text.

Hair and the staging of gender

Shakespeare's play with ideas often works indirectly, through the network of tropes
that infuses the text.[18] But not all tropes work the same way. Witty and amusing as
puns on "heir," "here," "hear," "air," and "hair" may be, they are a relatively tepid sort
of word-craft in the context of Shakespeare's impressive linguistic arsenal.[19] Puns may
amuse (or irritate) an audience, but they rarely move the audience to unexpected
insight. However, in *The Winter's Tale,* Shakespeare's "hair play," entangled as it is with
the theme of sheep-shearing, is different, reaching deep into the heart of the play.
Inexplicably, the wordplay involving hair and shearing in *The Winter's Tale* has been
largely overlooked by critics. Yet it works as a master trope, bringing together many
of *The Winter's Tale*'s central themes, linking sheep-shearing, penitential hair-cutting,
stripping a victim of clothes, stealing, castrating, and the tragic loss of one's heirs.

Facial hair has a special significance in *The Winter's Tale*. For Elizabethans, facial
hair was strongly implicated in the performance of gender. In his essay "The
Renaissance Beard: Masculinity in Early Modern England," Will Fisher surveys the
role of facial hair as a marker of masculinity in Elizabethan England (Fisher 2001).
Beards are mentioned in all but four of Shakespeare's plays. They are visible in almost
all portraits of adult males of Shakespeare's day. Facial hair was more than an abstract

symbol of adult masculinity. Fisher quotes the Elizabethan physiognomer Thomas Hill who described facial hair as a form of excrement linked directly to seminal fluid:

> The bearde in man . . .beginnith to appear in the nether jaw. . . through the heat and moisture, carried into the same, drawn from the genitours: which draw to them especially, the sperm from those places.
>
> (*ibid.:* 174)

When Autolycus refers to his false beard as his "pedlar's excrement," (IV, iv, 840) which he removes to trick the Shepherd and his son, the term highlights the idea of facial hair as a kind of seminal excretion representing the adult male's generative capacity. Additionally, facial hair has the ambiguous character of both belonging and not belonging to the face that produces it. Unlike the more permanent features of the human anatomy, the beard can be grown, shaved, and shaped at will. Like all body hair, the beard has a liminal status in relation to the self. It is at once an accessory *to* the self, like a garment, and an emanation *from* the self.

For Elizabethans, the beard was important as a double boundary marker, distinguishing men from women and also men from boys. Stephen Orgel notes that boys in Shakespeare's day were considered a kind of intermediate gender between the male and female, suggesting the ambiguous "master-mistress" that excites Shakespeare's passion in Sonnet XX.

> This hardly needs to be demonstrated: Rosalind reminds Orlando that in matters of love the two are all but identical- "boys and women are for the most part cattle of this colour" (1.2.388–389). Handsome boys were praised in Renaissance England by saying that they looked like women – "A woman's face, by Nature's own hand painted / Hast thou the master-mistress of my passion." Even Gaveston, [Jonathan] Goldberg's prime example of the masculine love object in the period, entertains his beloved Edward with lascivious dances performed by "a lovely boy in Dian's shape:" the cross-dressing is clearly not irrelevant to the lasciviousness. So it cannot be the case that the love of boys has *nothing* to do with the love of women in this culture.
>
> (Orgel 1996b: 51–52)

These associations explain the use of boy actors to play the parts of women on the Elizabethan stage. The appearance of facial hair on a young actor was enough to render him a problematical choice for playing women. When the hair in question was a beard, the act of growing or shaving a beard often represented a form of gender-play in Shakespeare's day, a negotiation among the mutable statuses of male and female. Since boy actors on the Elizabethan stage would frequently use prosthetic beards to assume a masculine role, Autolycus' putting-on and taking-off of his beard suggest not just the power of disguise but the kind of gender negotiation afforded by the Elizabethan stage.

This gender juggling can be seen in *The Winter's Tale*'s memorable final scenes, which, like the dramatic resurrection of Hermione, depend on the illusions of stage-craft. *The Winter's Tale* ends with the anticipated marriage of Florizel and Perdita. Within the fictional world of the play, Leontes' daughter marries Polixenes' son. But within the world of the stage, the union is something else, something masked. From the perspective of the Elizabethan stage, the audience actually witnesses the union of two boys, one of whom, unbearded, is disguised as a girl. *The Winter's Tale* concludes by producing a compromise only possible on the stage: an ambiguous boy-girl/boy-boy couple. While Perdita's role-identity is feminine, the gender ambiguity of the transvestite boy playing Perdita was no secret to Elizabethan audiences. Perdita's would be clearly seen as a boy playing a girl. Stephen Orgel notes the complex erotic psychology of transvestism in Elizabethan Puritan tracts. Gender identification and sexual attraction were both understood in Shakespeare's day to depend on both the actor's body and his costume. Orgel suggests that the fundamental erotic ambiguity of the inside-outside gender reversal of the transvestite actor was also understood to have significant implications for sexual attraction:

> But the argument against transvestite actors warns of an even more frightening metamorphosis than the transformation of the boys into a monster of both kinds. Male spectators, it is argued, will be seduced by the impersonation, and losing their reason will become effeminate, which in this case means that not only will they lust after the women in the drama, which is bad enough, but also after the youth beneath the woman's costume, thereby playing the woman's role themselves.
>
> (Orgel 1996b: 27)

By the play's end, the lost love of the royal princes is recovered twice-over, once as a union of boy and girl (their children) within the story, and once as the union of two young men, within the performance. In this way, Shakespeare gives us a theatrical compromise formation, an indirect restoration of the lost "twinn'd lambs" of the kings' youth. We are treated at long last to a resolution of the play's central problem through the magic of masks and the long delay in completing the cycle of reciprocity.

Autolycus on the margins and in the heart

Finally, there is the extraordinary mediating role of Autolycus. One of Shakespeare's brilliant but underappreciated comic creations, Autolycus bursts upon *The Winter's Tale* in III, iii, singing what appears to be a conventional pastoral ditty praising the end of winter and the first signs of spring:

AUTOLYCUS
When daffodils begin to peer,
With heigh! the doxy over the dale,

> Why, then comes in the sweet o' the year;
> For the red blood reigns in the winter's pale.

(III, iii, 1–4)

In his song's next lines, we learn his true identity as a rogue:

> The white sheet bleaching on the hedge,
> With heigh! the sweet birds, O, how they sing!
> Doth set my pugging tooth on edge;
> For a quart of ale is a dish for a king.
> The lark, that tirra-lyra chants,
> With heigh! with heigh! the thrush and the jay,
> Are summer songs for me and my aunts,
> While we lie tumbling in the hay.

(III, iii, 5–12)

Autolycus is a petty thief, a pickpocket, and an unrepentant womanizer. Turning to address the audience directly, Autolycus states that at one time, he "wore three pile" (rich velvet) as a servant of Prince Florizel. But, having been sacked for some unspecified offense, he is now "out of service." Shedding his old garments, he assumes a new identity. His father, he tells us, named him Autolycus "who, being as I am littered under Mercury, was likewise a snapper-up of unconsidered trifles" (III, iii, 24–26).

Shakespeare's most likely source for Autolycus was William Golding's translation of Ovid's *Metamorphosis*. Autolycus is introduced in Book XI as the child of Chione (Chyone) and Hermes (Mercury). Hermes triumphs over Apollo in a competition for the love of the beautiful Chione. Autolycus was conceived through Hermes' rape of Chione. Taking after his father, Ovid's Autolycus was a virtuoso thief and sweet-talker who could convince his victims that white was black and black, white. Shakespeare appears to have merged Autolycus' identity with that of his half-twin brother Philammon, whose talents lay in singing and poetry. Autolycus' abilities as a thief and seducer are closely linked with his words and music. Shakespeare's Autolycus claims to have been "littered under Mercury," the father of his mythical namesake. In classical mythology, Mercury (or Hermes) was a messenger god associated with a patchwork of traits that resonate strongly with Shakespeare's Autolycus: theft, shape-shifting, trickery, poetry, breaching boundaries, and commerce. Autolycus presides over *The Winter's Tale* as its spirit of improvisation and exchange, overseeing transfers of money, clothes, goods, and even identities, all exchanged in a spirit of roguish eloquence.

Autolycus literally means "self-wolf." In the context of the Good Shepherd theme and Autolycus' penchant for disguising himself in false hair, the wolf reference suggests that Autolycus, who haunts festivals to prey on the unwary, is a kind of wolf in sheep's clothing (Matthew 7:15). Moreover, the name "self-wolf" evokes the venerable Latin saying *Homo Homini Lupus* (Man is a Wolf to Man).[20] Once he appears in Act III of *The Winter's Tale*, Autolycus is set loose on the play, haunting the stage just as he haunts festivals and bear-baitings. He pops up repeatedly within the context of the sheep-shearing festival, sometimes singing, sometimes stealing, always scheming. Continually assuming and shedding disguises, Autolycus is either selling ribbons and other decorative accessories for the women, hawking printed copies of songs, or thinking up new ways of relieving people of their money or their garments. Though an inveterate schemer, Autolycus works on-the-fly, impulsive and free-form.

> I understand the business, I hear it: to have an
> open ear, a quick eye, and a nimble hand, is
> necessary for a cut-purse; a good nose is requisite
> also, to smell out work for the other senses. I see
> this is the time that the unjust man doth thrive.
> What an exchange had this been without boot! What
> a boot is here with this exchange! Sure the gods do
> this year connive at us, and we may do any thing
> extempore.

(IV, iv, 793–800)

In his exuberant embrace of a life of masquerade and trickery, Autolycus effectively deconstructs "honesty" for the audience and puts to question the ultimate trustworthiness of everyone around him. Autolycus may be "utterly" dishonest, but, in his many asides, where he takes us into his confidence, Autolycus is always honest. Even as he hides his identity, he uses his disguises to reveal the truth about himself. In a play where so much remains undisclosed, there is no problem understanding Autolycus. Where many characters are deceitful in their professed honesty, Autolycus manages to be honest in his deceitfulness. His candor and the pleasure he takes his trickery afford the audience relief from a world dominated by self-delusion. When in IV, iii he meets the old Shepherd's son, Autolycus, true to his name, masquerades as his own victim (a self-wolf), pretending to have been robbed by Autolycus, concealing himself to the Clown while revealing himself to the audience.

CLOWN
What manner of fellow was he that robbed you?

AUTOLYCUS
A fellow, sir, that I have known to go about with
troll-my-dames; I knew him once a servant of the
prince: I cannot tell, good sir, for which of his
virtues it was, but he was certainly whipped out of the court.

CLOWN
His vices, you would say; there's no virtue whipped

out of the court: they cherish it to make it stay
there; and yet it will no more but abide.

AUTOLYCUS
Vices, I would say, sir. I know this man well: he
hath been since an ape-bearer; then a
process-server, a bailiff; then he compassed a
motion of the Prodigal Son, and married a tinker's
wife within a mile where my land and living lies;
and, having flown over many knavish professions, he
settled only in rogue: some call him Autolycus.

CLOWN
Out upon him! prig, for my life, prig: he haunts
wakes, fairs and bear-baitings.

AUTOLYCUS
Very true, sir; he, sir, he; that's the rogue that
put me into this apparel.

(IV, iii, 89–109)

Every word Autolycus utters is simultaneously a lie and the truth. Autolycus'
unique gift is his ability to use the truth as a means of deception, but he also
serves the larger vision of the play by using deception as a means to the truth.
This confounding of the conventional opposition of lying and honesty is clearest
when, in Act IV, Autolycus, disguised by a false beard as a beggar, comes across
the Shepherd and his son on their way to Polixenes' palace. Hoping to escape
Polixenes' wrath, they plan to confess to the king how they had found Perdita
sixteen years earlier.

AUTOLYCUS
[Aside] Though I am not naturally honest, I am so
sometimes by chance: let me pocket up my pedlar's excrement.
Takes off his false beard
How now, rustics! whither are you bound?

SHEPHERD
To the palace, an it like your worship.

AUTOLYCUS
Your affairs there, what, with whom, the condition
of that fardel, the place of your dwelling, your
names, your ages, of what having, breeding, and any
thing that is fitting to be known, discover.

CLOWN

We are but plain fellows, sir.

AUTOLYCUS

A lie; you are rough and hairy. Let me have no
lying: it becomes none but tradesmen, and they
often give us soldiers the lie: but we pay them for
it with stamped coin, not stabbing steel; therefore
they do not give us the lie.

(V, iv, 838–852)

The exchange bristles with ironic commentary on lying and honesty. The only truly honest man turns out to be Autolycus, who, in a delightful twist on the idea of deceit, disguises himself by *removing* his false beard. And in the bluntness of his deception, Autolycus suggests why *The Winter's Tale* needs no Iago to underwrite Leontes' jealousy. The real source of jealousy in the play is not the false clues laid by others, but the human proclivity for self-deception: *Homo Homini Lupus*. As an ironic exemplar of Polonius' famous advice to Laertes in *Hamlet*, it is Autolycus who proposes a twisted sense in which a person, both falsely honest and truly deceitful, may know himself. Autolycus embodies, in an exhilarating way, one of philosophy's classic paradoxes: the truthful liar.[21] Shakespeare recruits Autolycus to dislocate the status quo. The trickster-poet-thief presides over the deconstruction and reformation of relationships in the play. Trusting in the power of surfaces, playfully locating character in appearance and costume rather than in the essence of things, Autolycus offers a theatrical path to a revision of life's possibilities. To an anthropologist, Autolycus is the classic anti-hero of anti-structure. He is to *The Winter's Tale* what the Lord of Misrule was in medieval England during the Christmastide, when a professional disrupter was appointed to preside over the Feast of Fools.

Shakespeare frequently uses such comic disrupters as The Gravedigger in *Hamlet*, Lear's Fool, Touchstone in *As You Like It*, or Feste in *Twelfth Night*. Such licensed "fools" figure not just in literary contexts, but in rituals throughout the world, lending to the status quo the life-giving power of change.[22] The theatrical embodiment of improvisation, Autolycus haunts the margins, inhabiting the borders separating and connecting conventional categories. Straddling the distinctions between self/other, shepherd/sheep, victim/victimizer, the trivial/the profound, virtue/vice, honesty/deceit, and tragedy/comedy, Autolycus energizes *The Winter's Tale* by scrambling its categories, temporarily replacing the rule of law and convention with the power of improvisation and reversal. The quintessential mediator, Autolycus enters the play after the plot's descent into utter dissolution in the first two "Sicilian" Acts. He dominates the "Bohemian" second half of the play, reigniting a dying world and cheating the troubled social order back into shape. As the play's master spirit of change through exchange and order through disorder, Autolycus both sets and upsets the stage for the miraculous transformations that bring the tangled web of *The Winter's Tale*, spun out over wide gaps of time and space, to a powerful and art-felt resolution.

Notes

1 For an anthropologically oriented treatment of these themes in Shakespeare's early sonnets, see Paul 2000.

2 For an extended discussion on the exchange of hospitality in *The Winter's Tale*, see Ruiter 2007.

3 The inherent ambiguity of exchange relationships and the ambivalence of the obligations they entail are suggested by the double meaning of "Gift" in German and Swedish, which translates as both "present" and "poison."

4 Lévi-Strauss' approach to studying marriage systems became known in Anthropology as "Alliance Theory."

5 There are exceptions, such as in many Arab societies where children of brothers (patrilateral parallel cousins) are encouraged to marry. This strongly endogamous form of marriage privileges keeping a girl within the safety and comfort of her own descent group when she marries and also prevents the dispersion of valuable descent group assets.

6 Patrilateral cross-cousin marriage (where a man marries his father's sister's daughter) should also provide a good compromise. But it occurs very rarely. Lévi-Strauss goes to great lengths to demonstrate why patrilateral cross-cousin marriage does not produce the same kind of alliance chains as its matrilateral version. His argument is quite involved and would take us well beyond the scope of this essay.

7 The term sublimation means literally "a lifting up" of an impulse or desire to a higher level in seeking an outlet for its expression. Sublimation is a mature defense in the Freudian arsenal of ego defenses by which the ego mediates between the id and the constraints of the real world.

8 In his Introduction to *The Oxford Shakespeare* edition of *The Winter's Tale*, Stephen Orgel criticizes commentaries on the obscurity of this passage, concluding that the passage is simply a muddled articulation by a crazed speaker of something that has an underlying lucid meaning.

9 Elucidation assumes that behind the obscurity and confusion of the text is a clear and precise meaning, and that the obscurity, moreover, is not part of the meaning. And since the editorial process is committed to elucidation, it is largely helpless before a genuinely obscure text. But what does it mean that a play speaks incomprehensibly? What are the implications for a drama of a text that works this way? — as *The Winter's Tale* undeniably does, if we think of it as a transaction between actors and audiences rather than between editors and readers . . . . (Orgel 1996a:9), see also Bray 1990.

10 Auden's insight appears to come directly from Freud's "Notes on a Case of Paranoia" (Standard Edition, 12:9–82), his extended analysis of a judge, Dr. Schreber, suffering from paranoia. In this case study, Freud identified four distinct kinds of delusional psychosis as alternative psychotic responses to repressed homosexual attraction. One of the four he calls "Pathological Jealousy," a delusional denial based on a double twist: the defensive reversing of the sex of the subject and projection onto another. It is not unfrequently disappointment over a woman that drives a man to drink, but this means, as a rule, that he resorts to the public-house and to the company of men, who afford him the emotional satisfaction which he has failed to get from his wife at home. If now these men become the objects of a strong libidinal cathexis in his unconscious, he will ward it off with the third kind of contradiction: 'It is not I who loves the man, she loves him' and he suspects the women in relation to all the men whom he himself is tempted to love. (p. 64) I am indebted to Robert Paul for drawing my attention to this case study and its relevance to my understanding of *The Winter's Tale*.

11 The identity of "the fair youth," who is the primary object of Shakespeare's love sonnets, has been the subject of considerable scholarly debate. One of the most frequently named candidates is Henry Wriothesley, the 3rd Earl of Southampton, one of Shakespeare's patrons. The case for Wriothesley is supported by the fact that Shakespeare dedicated his two longer poems, "The Rape of Lucrece" and "Venus and Adonis," to the young Earl. If the sonnets were also dedicated to him, then the initials W.H. must have been reversed in the dedication at some point in the publication of The Sonnets, perhaps to protect the youth's anonymity.

12   They [the American Indians] are even savage, as we call those fruites wilde, which nature of hir selfe, and of hir ordinarie progress hath produced: whereof indeede, they are those which our selves have altered by our artificiall devices, and diverted from their common order, which we should rather terme savage. In those are the true and the most profitable vertues, and natural proprieties most alive and vigorous, which in these we have bastardized, applying them to the pleasure of our corrupted taste.

(Montaigne 1966:169)

13 Critics have widely heralded Shakespeare's resolution (via Polixenes) of the debate between the virtues of nature and culture as a stroke of Shakespearean genius. It is interesting to note that, without indicating any debt to Shakespeare's insight, Claude Lévi-Strauss hit upon the same solution to resolving the structuralist's antinomy between nature and culture in the closing chapter of his well-known book *The Savage Mind*:

The pre-eminent value of anthropology is that it represents the first step in a procedure which involves others. Ethnographic analysis tries to arrive at invariants beyond the empirical diversity of human societies, and, as the present work shows, these are sometimes to be found at the most unforeseen points. Rousseau. . . foresaw this with his usual acumen: 'One need look near at hand if one wants to study men; but to study man one must look from afar; one must first observe differences in order to discover attributes'. However it would not be enough to absorb particular humanities into a general one. This first enterprise opens the way for others which Rousseau would not have been so ready to accept and which are incumbent on the exact natural sciences: the reintegration of culture in nature and finally of life within the whole of its psycho-chemical conditions.

(Lévi-Strauss 1966:247)

Here Lévi-Strauss adds the following footnote: "The opposition between nature and culture to which I attached much importance at one time . . . now seems to be of primarily methodological importance."

14 Lévi-Strauss 1966; Boyd and Richerson 1988; Paul 2016.

15 I am grateful to Stephen Orgel who suggested to me the significance of the women's disappearance in the play.

16 Where Shakespeare stages an elaborate sheep-shearing festival, *Pandosto* mentions only a meeting of all the farmers' daughters in Sicilia, whither Fawnia was also bidden as the mistress of the feast, who, having attired herself in her best garments, went among the rest of her companions to the merry meeting, there spending the day in such homely pastimes as shepherds use.

17 Alpers 1996; McFarland 1972; Laniac 2006.

18 See Chapters 8 and 9 for discussions of Shakespeare's treatment of metaphor.

19 On Shakespeare's use of homonyms of "hair" see Berry 2002:20 and Kökertiz 1966.

20 This well-known Latin phrase can be traced to a proverb quoted in Plautus' play *Asinaria* (495).

21 "The liar's paradox," *pseudómenos lógos* (ψευδόμενος λόγος) in Ancient Greek, is treated as a significant problem in modern philosophy, but was first raised by the ancient Greeks. The earliest statement of the paradox is often attributed to Eubulides of Miletus, who lived in the 4th century BC. Eubulides is reported to have asked, "A man says that he is lying. Is what he says true or false?"

22 On the role of clowns and other disrupters in the context of "rituals of reversal," see Babcock 1978; Turner, Victor, *The Ritual Process: Structure and Anti-Structure*, Livingston, N.J.; Transaction Publishers 1969; Hillerman 1993.

5

AND THE FLESH WAS MADE WORD

Romeo and Juliet in the kingdom of Cratylus

Nor shall death brag thou wander'st in his shade,
When in eternal lines to time thou grow'st:
So long as men can breathe or eyes can see,
So long lives *this*, and *this* gives life to thee.

(Shakespeare, Sonnet XVIII)

Romeo and Juliet begins in a fierce volley of words and ends in silence. Between the words and the silence lies Shakespeare's tragic meditation on the relationship between language and love. Act I opens on a street in Verona. We are treated to an exchange of insults and gestures between servants of the Capulets and Montagues, which escalates into a brawl, quelled only by the arrival of Prince Escalus. Outraged by the repeated history of clashes between the two families, the Prince decries the ancient feud that, he claims, was "bred of an airy word" (I, i, 87). Swords follow words as the repartee triggers a deadly duel. The exchange of insults rekindles an old feud between the families, along with a confusion of discourse in Verona's streets. The puns hurled back and forth, using *choler*, *collar*, and *collier*, are primitive, exploiting the humor in overlapping sounds but are ultimately meaningless. With language in low play, words are reduced to mere sound. A single word is set free to carry several unrelated meanings, and even a single sound can stand for several distinct words. The confusion of signs spills over from words to gestures, as Samson, aiming at insult, "bites his thumb" at Abram:

ABRAM
Do you bite your thumb at us, sir?

SAMPSON
I do bite my thumb, sir.

DOI: 10.4324/9781003179771-8

ABRAM
Do you bite your thumb at us, sir?

SAMPSON, *aside to Gregory*
Is the law of our side if I
say "Ay"?

GREGORY, *aside to Sampson*
No.

SAMPSON
No, sir, I do not bite my thumb at you, sir,
but I bite my thumb, sir.

(I, i, 45–52)

The servants are uncertain about even their crude gestures. What is the difference between a bodily movement and a sign? Is the gesture conventional enough to be properly read? Does a gesture have to be intentional to be considered an insult? From the outset, *Romeo and Juliet* presents a world of unsteady and potentially lethal communication. Uncertain signs are loose on the streets, to be read and misread.

By the second scene, calm has returned to Verona, but words are still in question. Capulet has drawn up a guest list for "an old accustomed feast" (I, ii, 20) that evening at his house. Handing the list to two servants, he orders them to seek out the listed guests and deliver the invitation. But again, words fail. Neither of the servants can read. One expresses his exasperation with Capulet's order.

SERVINGMAN
Find them out whose names are written here! It is written that the shoemaker should meddle with his yard, and the tailor with his last, the fisher with his pencil and the painter with his nets, but I am sent to find these persons whose names are here writ, and can never find what names the writing person has here writ. I must to the learned. In good time.

(I, ii, 37–43)

Lamenting his inability to read, the servant complains that reading is above his paygrade. The scene looks to be one of Shakespeare's comic moments, like the pun-filled banter at the play's start. But the perils of reading and misreading turn out to be at the heart of the story. Quoting an unnamed authority, the servant attempts to produce a proverb on the tradesman's proper use of tools to support his claim that Capulet's request is beyond his skill. The passage highlights a double failure of reading: the servant's inability to read Montague's list, and his humorous misreading of a quoted text.

No one paid attention to this passage until 1926, when Morris Tilley published a short article in *Modern Language Notes* titled "A Parody of *Euphues* in *Romeo and*

Juliet" (Tilley 1926). Tilley revealed the passage to be a parody of words found in the dedicatory epistle of John Lyly's 1578 prose romance *Euphues: The Anatomy of Wit*. Tilley provides a convincing comparison of the passages from *Romeo and Juliet* and *Euphues*, carefully showing how Shakespeare's quote can be brought into line with its source from Lyly's text. But what is Lyly's proverb, mangled or otherwise, doing in Shakespeare's play? Tilley proposes that it not only illuminates the confused mind of the servant, but it is also Shakespeare's chance to aim a critical dart at Lyly himself by suggesting that his pretentiously ornate romance might not demonstrate the verbal skill expected of a celebrated literary wit.

Shakespeare was probably poking fun at the fashion of his day for "euphuistic" writing and speaking, a language style named for Lyly's hero. Euphuism is characterized by a pretentious elaboration of traditional rhetorical devices like balance, antithesis, rhetorical questions, alliteration, metaphor, and simile and the overuse of classical and mythological references. Celebrating form over substance, euphuism was in vogue in London throughout the 1580s and had become the speech style of choice at Elizabeth's court. Euphuism exhibited what rhetoricians of the day called *copia*—"abundance" considered essential to good writing and oratory. Desiderius Erasmus, the renowned Dutch scholar, published *De Copia* in 1522, an influential treatise widely read in Elizabethan England. Though a champion of elaborated style in prose and poetry, Erasmus also recognized that resort to florid language was easily subject to abuse. The relationship between style and substance, rhetoric and truth, was clearly on Shakespeare's mind as he composed *Romeo and Juliet* sometime between 1591 and 1595.

Euphues' proverbs and their echo in *Romeo and Juliet* may have their roots in an older and more venerable text, Plato's *Cratylus*. *Cratylus* is Plato's Socratic dialogue on the nature of language, more specifically on names. A conversation among Socrates, Hermogenes, and Cratylus, *Cratylus* takes up the question that Juliet poses from her balcony: *What's in a name?* Plato treats the issue in terms of what modern linguistics call arbitrariness. The dialogue debates whether names stand for things by resemblance (*physis*) or arbitrary conventions (*nomos*). Are the words for things based on divine contrivance or human whim?[1] Socrates asks whether the names of things are to be understood as "correct" names or whether any arbitrary label will do just as well. Hermogenes answers first, supporting the "nominalist" view that words are merely conventional and arbitrary representations.[2] Cratylus, on the other hand, appears to support Socrates' claim that only a thing's *correct name* will suffice, a name that resembles or directly evokes the thing named. In his initial defense of the natural realism of names, Socrates leads his interlocutors to acknowledge that names must have a creator. The law-maker, he goes on, is best suited to the making of words since words are the tools appropriate to legislating. It is in the context of this argument that Socrates introduces the section from which Lyly's proverbs may have been derived.

SOCRATES

And how does the legislator make names? and to what does he look? Consider this in the light of the previous instances: to what does the carpenter look in making the shuttle? Does he not look to that which is naturally fitted to act as a shuttle?

SOCRATES
And whatever shuttles are wanted, for the manufacture of garments, thin or thick, of flaxen, woollen, or other material, ought all of them to have the true form of the shuttle; and whatever is the shuttle best adapted to each kind of work, that ought to be the form which the maker produces in each case.

Socrates argues that the craftsman must use the tools that are best adapted for the job they are doing.

SOCRATES
And the same holds of other instruments: when a man has discovered the instrument which is naturally adapted to each work, he must express this natural form, and not others which he fancies, in the material, whatever it may be, which he employs; for example, he ought to know how to put into iron the forms of awls adapted by nature to their several uses?

Socrates concludes that names, the mind's tools, should be naturally suited for their work. Many readers of Cratylus assume that Plato supports Cratylus' view that words do indeed have natural names, names linked to their referents by deep resemblance (i.e., essential nature) rather than by arbitrary convention (i.e., culture or personal whim).[3] Elizabethan scholars and theologians recognized Plato as a strong supporter of the realist rather than the conventionalist view of language. For Elizabethans, Plato was merely affirming the God-given nature of names as revealed in Genesis.

In her study of Elizabethan understandings of language, Anne Ferry quotes Richard Mulcaster, a 16th-century schoolmaster and generally credited as the founder of English lexicography. Mulcaster explains how the Bible supports Cratylus' vision of the origin of names.

> We need not approved by *Platoe's Cratylus*, or Aristotle's proposition as by best autorities, (tho men may be sufficient to proue their own inuentions) that words be voluntary, and appointed vpon cause, seeing we have better warrant. For euen God himself, who brovght the creatures, which he had made, vnto that first man, whom he had also made, that he might name them, according to their properties, that planelie declare by so doing, what a cunning thing it is to giue right names, and how necessary it is, to know their forces, which be allredie given, bycause the word being known, which implyeth the property the thing itself is half known, whose propertie is employed.
>
> (Ferry 1988: 30)

Ferry suggests that this linking of words directly to their referents was based on an understanding of "reading" not based on the decoding of language but on the direct physical experience of seeing something (*ibid.*: 23). The Elizabethan world was filled with signs of all kinds. Understanding the world meant learning to read them.

A superficial reading of *Cratylus* seems to support the Elizabethan belief in the divine origin of words and their direct tie to things, as proposed in *Genesis*. But a closer reading suggests that Plato does not come down unequivocally on the side of linguistic naturalism. *Cratylus* proposes a more qualified and complex view. The dialectical spin in Plato's argument is precipitated by an unexpected twist of Socrates' argument when, with self-conscious irony, his etymological wizardry to demonstrate the natural character of names hits a wall. He fails to come up with a convincing origin for *techné* (τέχνη), the Greek term for "art" or "craft" (Plato *op. cit.*: 74). Socrates' attempt to show the natural roots of names founders on a Greek word for "cultural artifact." Plato's argument takes a dialectical detour, acknowledging the truth in Hermogenes' nominalist argument without simply rejecting Cratylus' intuitions about the analogical resonance between sound and sense. Backing off the claim that words are all naturally motivated, Socrates acknowledges that words float and change on the corrupting currents of history and usage. Names wander from their "natural" roots. Socrates is forced to confess that the "correct" resemblance-based grounding of words is often hidden or transformed in the unstable currents of time. In his careful explication of *Cratylus*, John Joseph concludes that Cratylus' naturalistic understanding of word origins represents an ideal for Plato rather than an account of how people actually use words: "He has accepted a view of what language *should be*, not what it is" (Joseph 2000: 72).

Cratylus' theory of names could never have been right. If words pictured reality directly, philosophers' arguments could be verified simply by reference to their words, which would be assumed to mirror the nature of what they described. By implication, philosophical discourse would be right by definition since words could never lie. No argument could be wrong. Plato clearly knew this was an untenable argument, no matter how appealing the imitative view of words was. Though philosophy rests on language as its primary tool, language is not equipped to reflect truth by naming it. Truth must be discovered *through* language, but not *in* it. If words are tools for *reflecting on reality*, they cannot do so by *reflecting reality*. The proper job of words is to *talk about* things. Words work best when they are different from what they represent. In *Philosophy in a New Key,* Susanne Langer vividly makes the point that language signs must be different from what they represent rather than picturing their meaning.

> A symbol which interests us also as an object is distracting. It does not convey its meaning without obstruction. For instance, if the word "plenty" were replaced by a succulent, ripe, real peach, few people could attend entirely to the mere concept of quite enough when confronted with such a symbol. The more barren and indifferent the symbol, the greater is its semantic power. Peaches are too good to act as words; we are too much interested in peaches themselves.
>
> (Langer 1957: 61)

Moreover, language forms are too unsteady to mirror the truth of things. Words are designed to lie as well as tell the truth. Their relation to truth must be indirect, which implies that language can mislead us from the path of truth as readily as lead us there. Sweet words can mask a bitter truth. A single word can mean several different things. How are we to know the difference between the correct use of words and the ever-present possibility of deception or misunderstanding? Given the human penchant for misreading, we can never be sure we have it right. Apparent opposites like virtue and vice or medicine and poison can be hard to tell apart. Appearances can be deceptive, as Friar Lawrence suggests in his long speech in Act II of *Romeo and Juliet*, where he argues that only "fair use" can distinguish medicine from poison, a confusion that will ultimately have fatal consequences for *Romeo and Juliet*.

> O, mickle is the powerful grace that lies
> In plants, herbs, stones, and their true qualities.
> For naught so vile that on the Earth doth live
> But to the Earth some special good doth give;
> Nor aught so good but, strained from that fair use,
> Revolts from true birth, stumbling on abuse.
>
> (II, iii, 1–6)

Recognizing both the power and the limitation of words, Plato seems to move, in dialectical fashion, from Cratylus' naturalist view of language to Hermogenes' conventionalism. In insisting upon the inherent superiority of representation by resemblance but acknowledging the contingent effects of history, Plato both affirms and moves beyond Cratylus' position.

The Petrarchan tradition

In our excursion through Plato's *Cratylus,* we seem to have strayed far from Shakespeare's Verona. But we never really left the neighborhood of the Capulets and Montagues. From the opening scene of the play, language is the star of the show. Sounds, words, names, rhetorical, and poetic devices command the stage, as if poetry were at once the literary means and the ultimate theme of the tragedy. This attention to form is most evident in the language of Romeo. Not your typical teenage lover, Romeo is a lover-poet, modeled on the Italian poet-scholar Francesco Petrarch, who devoted his artistic life to celebrating his unrequited love for his mistress Laura in his collection of 366 sonnets, *Il Canzonieri*. The Petrarchan tradition of courtly love features a rejected suitor composing sonnets to an elusive or unattainable "mistress." Shakespeare makes Romeo's connection with Petrarch's forlorn lover clear in Mercutio's mocking welcome to Romeo in Act II.

BENVOLIO
Here comes Romeo, here comes Romeo.

MERCUTIO
Without his roe, like a dried herring. O
flesh, flesh, how art thou fishified! Now is he for the
numbers that Petrarch flowed in.

(II, iv, 38–41)

The Petrarchan sonnet tradition was a literary fashion in Shakespeare's day. Over 30 collections of sonnets were published during or near the reign of Elizabeth. Shakespeare's sonnets were published after Elizabeth's death in 1609. Sir Phillip Sidney's collection of 108 poems collectively called *Astrophil and Stella* was first published in 1591. Edmund Spenser's sonnet sequence, *Amoretti*, was written in 1594 and published a year later in London. Though influenced by Petrarch, Spenser's sonnets were unusual in that they were about Spenser's reciprocated passion for a woman he would marry. The 89 sonnets of *Amoretti* were dedicated to Elizabeth Boyle, whom Spenser courted and married in the year that the poems were written, a rare case of a sonnet series celebrating requited love. *Romeo and Juliet* was composed in part as a celebration of the Petrarchan tradition. It is the only Shakespeare play to open with sonnet.[4] The opening sonnet encapsulates the story that is about to unfold, disclosing its tragic end and effectively reducing the rest of the play to a staged recapitulation of its opening poem. A sonnet spoken by the Chorus also introduces the second act, but from Act III on, the sonnet disappears.

Romeo and Juliet treats the Petrarchan tradition with deadly seriousness. To understand how Shakespeare is playing with the tradition, it is worth noting an often overlooked feature of the Petrarchan tradition. These love sonnets are not intended merely to evoke or celebrate lovers. *Petrarchan sonnets are commonly written to replace an unattainable lover.* The elusive beloved is remade through the poet's words and "sonnetized" into verse. Elizabethan sonnets conventionally work as a "textified" surrogate for a mistress unattainable in the flesh. As we saw in the last chapter, many of Shakespeare's early sonnets celebrate the poet's power to bestow on flesh a second life. Consider Sonnet 15, where Shakespeare's immortal words are said to replace ephemeral flesh.

> Then the conceit of this inconstant stay
> Sets you most rich in youth before my sight,
> Where wasteful Time debateth with Decay,
> To change your day of youth to sullied night;
> And all in war with Time for love of you,
> As he takes from you, I engraft you new.

Using the image of artificially reproducing plants through grafting, Shakespeare proposes a way that words can be seen as a way of creating new life. Other sonnets celebrate the power of words to replace a lover unable or unwilling to reciprocate the poet's passion.

Romeo and Juliet is probably the world's most famous love story. But the play is not just Shakespeare's tribute to young love. It also sets up a contest between words and the world, a literary experiment to craft a surrogate world of love constituted entirely by rhetoric, words that, in the spirit of Cratylus, mimic the world's forms and aspire to take their place. But the play is a tragedy, and the world ultimately overwhelms the word. The experiment fails in the end. But in its brilliant attempt at linguistic realism, turning flesh to words, *Romeo and Juliet* is a tale of love set loose in the kingdom of Cratylus. Questions about the value of rhetoric are central to the play. Shakespeare's immediate source for the story, Arthur Brooke's *Tragicall History of Romeus and Juliet*, was based on well-known Italian versions of the story popularized in prose novellas in the middle of the 16th century and translated into English between 1559 and 1567 (Levenson 2004). Brooke's version of the tragedy self-consciously questions the value of rhetoric and associates it with the capacity for self-deception.

> Oh how can we perswade ourself to what we like,
> And how we can diswade our mynd, if aught our mynd mislyke.
> Weak arguments are stronge, our fancies streyght to frame
> To pleasing things, and eke to shone, if we mislyke the same.
>
> (Brook 1957: 429–432)

Brooke was trained in rhetoric, and his story is rich in the use of rhetorical devices, particularly anaphora (the repetition of a word or phrase at the beginning of successive clauses) and polyptoton (repetition of different forms of the same root word) (Levenson 2004: 125). The complexity of his language is in part a result of his self-conscious imitation of Petrarchan models. Shakespeare took Brooke's already florid text and pumped up the rhetorical play with unparalleled virtuosity. Particularly in the play's first act, Shakespeare floods the text with arcane rhetorical figures, including less well-known devices such as arteismus, zeugma, anaphora, and synoechiosis (*ibid.*). Punning wordplay is equally abundant in *Romeo and Juliet*. M.M. Mahood has provided a conservative estimate of 175 distinct "quibbles" (word plays) scattered throughout the text (Mahood 2004: 56).

One rhetorical device has been recognized as having special prominence in the play: the oxymoron, the union of opposites. Romeo's first long speech on love uses the oxymoron lavishly to illustrate love as a tempest of conflicting passions:

ROMEO
Alas, that love, whose view is muffled still,
Should, without eyes, see pathways to his will!
Where shall we dine? O me! What fray was here?
Yet tell me not, for I have heard it all.
Here's much to do with hate, but more with love.
Why, then, O brawling love! O loving hate!
O any thing, of nothing first create!

O heavy lightness! serious vanity!
Mis-shapen chaos of well-seeming forms!
Feather of lead, bright smoke, cold fire,
sick health!
Still-waking sleep, that is not what it is!
This love feel I, that feel no love in this.

(I, i, 169–180)

Critics have noted how the oxymoron structurally mimics the play's plot structure, the tragic conjoining of opposites. In its early scenes, *Romeo and Juliet* is pure rhetoric in action.

> The function of the contraries and reversals in R&J is to sustain what Simon O. Lesser terms *"a sense of the opposite"* The play possesses what Lesser calls "the sublime ambivalence of narrative art." We are constantly aware of the double face of the action.
>
> (Shapiro 1964: 501)

In the opening act, we encounter Romeo as a poet-lover, the frustrated and downcast suitor of the elusive Rosaline. Romeo's solace is his poetry, presumably sonnets dedicated to Rosaline. The "textified" world of *Romeo and Juliet* is on display even before we meet Romeo. Before he appears in the flesh, we encounter Romeo as just words, reported speech, in the form of a long exchange between his friend Benvolio and Romeo's parents, who ask Benvolio about Romeo's whereabouts.

LADY MONTAGUE
O, where is Romeo? Saw you him today?
Right glad I am he was not at this fray.

BENVOLIO
Madam, an hour before the worshiped sun
Peered forth the golden window of the east,
A troubled mind drove me to walk abroad,
Where underneath the grove of sycamore
That westward rooteth from this city side,
So early walking did I see your son.
Towards him I made, but he was 'ware of me
And stole into the covert of the wood.
I, measuring his affections by my own
(Which then most sought where most might not be found,
Being one too many by my weary self),
Pursued my humor, not pursuing his,
And gladly shunned who gladly fled from me.

MONTAGUE
Many a morning hath he there been seen,
With tears augmenting the fresh morning's dew,
Adding to clouds more clouds with his deep sighs.
But all so soon as the all-cheering sun
Should in the farthest east begin to draw
The shady curtains from Aurora's bed,
Away from light steals home my heavy son
And private in his chamber pens himself,
Shuts up his windows, locks fair daylight out,
And makes himself an artificial night.
Black and portentous must this humor prove,
Unless good counsel may the cause remove.

(I, i, 118–145)

In performance, this exchange is a straightforward account of a lovesick youth heading home in the early morning hours to the comforting refuge of his bedroom. But carefully read, these lines paint a far more interesting picture. A second world appears, a world of poetic forms systematically replacing the physical world. The rhetoric mimics natural space and motion, suggesting the capacity of poetry to replace nature.

As the Montagues' *son* makes his way from west to east, the heavenly *sun* moves east to west. Each natural feature of the environment is paired with a metaphoric counter. Romeo stops under a sycamore that is at once a tree and a trope, poetically evoking the young man's sad condition (sick *amour*). Romeo's tears mimic the morning dew, and his sighs replicate heaven's clouds. Rather than confront the sad realities of the world, Romeo retreats to the physical protection of the wood, which doubles as the imaginary protection of the "would." Arriving home, Romeo "pens" himself in his room, locking out the world physically and writing away his pain by creating a text lover. He has made himself "an artificial night" twice over. First, unable to endure the daylight, Romeo counters the morning sun by closing the shutters, creating an artificial night. And, second, through his verse, Romeo transforms himself into a Petrarchan "knight of artifice," the courtly lover of the sonnet.[5]

When Romeo first sets his eyes on Juliet at the Capulet's reception, it is Rosaline, his reluctant lover and muse, whom he hopes to see. But at the sight of Juliet, all thoughts of Rosaline vanish:

ROMEO, *to a Servingman*
What lady's that which doth enrich the hand
Of yonder knight?

SERVINGMAN
I know not, sir.

ROMEO
O, she doth teach the torches to burn bright!
It seems she hangs upon the cheek of night
As a rich jewel in an Ethiop's ear,
Beauty too rich for use, for Earth too dear.
So shows a snowy dove trooping with crows
As yonder lady o'er her fellows shows.
The measure done, I'll watch her place of stand
And, touching hers, make blessèd my rude hand.
Did my heart love till now? Forswear it, sight,
For I ne'er saw true beauty till this night.

(I, v, 41–52)

The sympathetic reading of this passage recognizes love at first sight, elegantly set out in rhymed couplets. But in the previous scene, we have just heard Mercutio's more cynical view of love. Inclined to view Romeo's passions as barely concealed lust whose flames can be quickly doused through crude sexual release, Mercutio advises: "Romeo, "If love be rough with you, be rough with love./Prick love for pricking and you beat love down" (I, iv, 27–28). Romeo justifies his plan to crash the Capulets' party that evening by his dream of the previous night. But Mercutio reminds him that "Dreamers often lie" (I, iv, 51).

True, I talk of dreams
the children of an idle brain
Begot of nothing but vain fantasy,
Which is as thin of substance as the air,
And more inconstant than the wind who woos
Even now the frozen bosom of the north,
And, being angered, puffs away from thence,
Turning his side to the dew-dropping south.

Benvolio adds "This wind you talk of blows us from ourselves…" (I, iv, 96–104). This exchange provokes Mercutio's Queen Mab speech in which he interprets Romeo's youthful passion as a fanciful delusion under the spell of the fairies' midwife, Queen Mab. Romeo, Mercutio suggests, has talked himself into love.

Having substituted Juliet for Rosaline, Romeo approaches his new love interest at the feast. The famous initial exchange between them takes on the form of a jointly composed lovers' sonnet, capped by a kiss:

ROMEO, *taking Juliet's hand*
If I profane with my unworthiest hand
This holy shrine, the gentle sin is this:

My lips, two blushing pilgrims, ready stand
To smooth that rough touch with a tender kiss.

JULIET
Good pilgrim, you do wrong your hand too much,
Which mannerly devotion shows in this;
For saints have hands that pilgrims' hands do touch,
And palm to palm is holy palmers' kiss.

ROMEO
Have not saints lips, and holy palmers too?

JULIET
Ay, pilgrim, lips that they must use in prayer.

ROMEO
O then, dear saint, let lips do what hands do.
They pray: grant thou, lest faith turn to despair.

JULIET
Saints do not move, though grant for prayers' sake.

ROMEO
Then move not while my prayer's effect I take.
He kisses her.

(I, v, 92–105)

Juliet shares Mercutio's suspicion of Romeo's motives, urging Romeo to reframe his signs of passion as sacred acts so that his kisses become "holy palmers kiss" and his lover's pleas can be read as prayers. She complains that he kisses "by the book," following the courtly lover's conventional script, which, she fears, has replaced genuine feeling. Aspiring to make the flesh into poetry, Romeo attempts, in Gayle Whittier's memorable phrase, to "sonnetize" the body of his lover (*ibid.*: 30). When faced with a crisis, Romeo is predisposed to edit rather than act. When Friar Lawrence informs him of his banishment for having killed Tybalt, he takes the idea of the Prince's "sentence" literally, responding not to his fate but to the Friar's word choice:

FRIAR LAWRENCE
I bring thee tidings of the Prince's doom.

ROMEO
What less than doomsday is the Prince's doom?

FRIAR LAWRENCE
A gentler judgment vanished from his lips:
Not body's death, but body's banishment.

ROMEO
Ha, banishment? Be merciful, say "death,"
For exile hath more terror in his look,
Much more than death. Do not say "banishment."

(III, iii, 9–15)

Initially skeptical of Romeo's word-magic, Juliet is quickly drawn in to his conception of the world as a text. As the first light of dawn approaches the bedroom where Romeo and Juliet have spent their wedding night, the couple panics and tries to talk away the light that means Romeo's banishment by calling day night, repeating Romeo's earlier attempt to poetically "lock fair daylight out."

JULIET
Yond light is not daylight, I know it, I.
It is some meteor that the sun exhaled
To be to thee this night a torchbearer
And light thee on thy way to Mantua.
Therefore stay yet. Thou need'st not to be gone.

ROMEO
Let me be ta'en; let me be put to death.
I am content, so thou wilt have it so.
I'll say yon gray is not the morning's eye;
'Tis but the pale reflex of Cynthia's brow.
Nor that is not the lark whose notes do beat
The vaulty heaven so high above our heads.
I have more care to stay than will to go.
Come death and welcome. Juliet wills it so.
How is 't, my soul? Let's talk. It is not day.

(III, v, 12–25)

Juliet has entered Cratylus' domain where reality is subject to the power of words. When she discovers that her new lover is both a boy and a name—a Montague—she begins to learn just how much there is in a name. Following her first encounter with Romeo at her father's party, Juliet asks her Nurse to find out the boy's name.

JULIET
Go ask his name. *The Nurse goes.* If he be married,
My grave is like to be my wedding bed.

NURSE, *returning*
His name is Romeo, and a Montague,
The only son of your great enemy.

JULIET
My only love sprung from my only hate!
Too early seen unknown, and known too late!
Prodigious birth of love it is to me
That I must love a loathèd enemy.

(I, v, 148–155)

From this point on, names will play a central role in Romeo and Juliet. Juliet's question "What's in a name?" sets in motion one of the best-known speeches in any Shakespeare play. Hoping to talk her way out of her dilemma, she proposes that she and Romeo deny their names.

JULIET
O Romeo, Romeo, wherefore art thou Romeo?
Deny thy father and refuse thy name,
Or, if thou wilt not, be but sworn my love,
And I'll no longer be a Capulet.

ROMEO, *aside*
Shall I hear more, or shall I speak at this?

JULIET
'Tis but thy name that is my enemy.
Thou art thyself, though not a Montague.
What's Montague? It is nor hand, nor foot,
Nor arm, nor face. O, be some other name
Belonging to a man.
What's in a name? That which we call a rose
By any other word would smell as sweet.
So Romeo would, were he not Romeo called,
Retain that dear perfection which he owes
Without that title. Romeo, doff thy name,
And, for thy name, which is no part of thee,
Take all myself.

(II, 11, 38–49)

Like Hermogenes, Juliet now treats names as arbitrary labels subject to human desire.[6] But her argument raises more questions about names than it answers. "What's in a name?" eventually produces some unwelcome answers, answers that seriously challenge the idea of arbitrariness. In "The Name of the Rose in *Romeo and Juliet,*" Catherine Belsey points out the contradictions in Juliet's attempt to transcend the constraints of the sign:

> Identity, the speech acknowledges, exists in the symbolic as the Name of the Father. Juliet imagines a succession of (im) possibilities should he repudiate his father's name, or she hers; that he should be named differently; and finally that he should simply remove his name, as if it were extrinsic, separable from identity. In place of Romeo's name Juliet offers her "selfs," implying that beyond their names, as beyond the name of the rose, the lovers could exist as unnamed selves. This move to transcend the signifier, however, the play at once makes clear, is precisely a contradiction. In offering to take what she urges *literally*, Romeo can only propose punningly to assume another *name*, to adopt a different location in the symbolic.
>
> Oh, tell me, friar, tell me,
> in what vile part of this anatomy
> does my name lodge? Tell me, that I may sack
> The hateful mansion.
>
> (Belsey 1993: 132)

Oddly, when she begs Romeo, "deny thy father and refuse thy name," Juliet skips over the name that matters—Montague—focusing instead on her lover's given name, Romeo. To deny Romeo's father, the line would need to read, "Montague, Montague, wherefore art thou Montague?" Juliet's error suggests her dilemma. Her friend may be *called* Romeo, but he *is* a Montague. It is possible to deny a given name (what is given can also be taken back). But Montague, the family name, is not "given" in the same way since it implies both a family history and an unalterable biological endowment. One is *born into* a family name. As for Juliet, when she suggests to Romeo: "be but sworn my love, /And I'll no longer be a Capulet" (ll. 38–40), she unintentionally suggests the one path she has for changing her family name: marrying Romeo. That sort of swearing is the marital vow, the word of law, not the couple's sworn love for each other.

More subtle semantic issues are at stake in Juliet's insistence on the arbitrariness of names. Consider her claim: "That which we call a rose/ By any other word would smell as sweet" (ll. 46–47). In a modern context, where linguistics largely supports the arbitrariness claim, it sounds reasonable to propose that any sound will do for a rose. But Shakespeare's view of language was different and subtler; he had a poet's understanding of words. To English speakers, "rose" is not experienced as an arbitrary sound that can be replaced with any other. It lives within a network of established associations.[7] In the context of this play, the word cannot help but trigger an association with Juliet's cousin Rosaline, Romeo's original love interest, and the possibility that Juliet is merely "A Rosaline by another name." If we take Juliet at her word and assume that a rose called anything else would smell the same, we encounter other problems. It is tough for English speakers to get past the name "rose" in imagining or identifying a rose. Whatever new label one might arbitrarily assign would not evoke the rose the way its "real" name does. Would a flower renamed "cockroach" still smell as sweet as "a rose?" In the short run, it is hard to imagine. Because names have both social and psychological histories of use, we are, for the time being, stuck with "rose."

Recall that Plato suggested that the social use of words gradually increases their arbitrariness (the nominalist view). However, for individuals, language use increases the perceived "naturalness" of our words through a dense web of associations that forms over time between a name and its referent. Shakespeare evokes these associations by playing on the diffusion of the "ro" sound in many directions: Romeo, Rosaline, Rosemary, among others. These association networks are not just acoustic but multi-sensory. We can recall the smell of a rose by hearing its name, viewing its picture, or merely seeing the color pink or red. Through use, the name "rose" and its acoustic qualities become part of the experience of the flower. Names have a dual history: a social life in which words come to be part of a collective language, and a personal life by which individuals make words their own and imbue them with sensory meaning. Through use, words gradually lose their arbitrary character. It becomes virtually impossible for a native speaker to hear a word as pure sound as a foreigner might. Over time, words become more than stand-ins for things. For the speaker, the word *becomes* the thing, assuming the "naturalness" that Plato sought to demonstrate.[8] This is why we do not speak *in* our language, but *through* it.

While linguists may understand the social history of words, it is poets who grasp their sensory history. And no poet better exploited the semantic power of the word as a sensory object than Shakespeare. In *Romeo and Juliet*, he plays with the undercurrent of associations linking sound and sense in names and even in seemingly random sounds. Shakespeare's evocation of the sound-power of the word is his Cratylus muse at work. It is not just in their primitive acoustic associations that names convey meaning. Many of the characters in *Romeo and Juliet* have names whose meanings are deeply connected to their characters. Tybalt, whom Mercutio repeatedly calls "The Prince of Cats" is derived from Tibalt or Tybert, the Prince of Cats in *Renart the Fox*. Benvolio is Latin for "wishing well," a fitting name for Romeo's faithful friend. Also appropriate is the name Mercutio which means "unpredictable" or mercurial, after the god Mercury. Juliet's connection to her name is also not arbitrary. We learn from the Nurse that Juliet was born on Lammas eve, which would be the last day in July, linking her name directly to her birth. Moreover, the Nurse's nickname for her, Jule, evokes the bright gem to which Romeo compares her in his gush of couplets upon first laying eyes on her:

> O, she doth teach the torches to burn bright!
> It seems she hangs upon the cheek of night
> *As a rich jewel* in an Ethiop's ear—
> Beauty too rich for use, for Earth too dear.

(I, v, 51–34)

"Brief sounds determine my weal or woe"

In other cases, the significance of names rests more on sound connections than dictionary derivations. Pure sounds haunt *Romeo and* Juliet, creating dense connections between names and emotions central to the play. Shakespeare establishes shadowy but powerful links among various uses of the sounds "ro," "woe," and "O" that connect Romeo, Rosaline, rosemary, roses, and other words in such a way as to draw attention to the poetic power of sound connections and undercut any sense of arbitrariness of names. In Act II, Scene iii Friar Lawrence asks Romeo if he has spent the night with Rosaline, Romeo answers "With Rosaline, my ghostly father/ I have forgotten that name and that name's woe" (II, iii, 41–42). Friar Lawrence, dismayed at the speed with which Romeo has exchanged lovers, comments: "If ere thou wast thyself and these woes thine/ Thou and those woes were all for Rosaline" (ll. 73–74). In the following scene, Benvolio and Mercutio make fun of Romeo, using his name as their weapon:

BENVOLIO
Here comes Romeo, here comes Romeo.

MERCUTIO
Without his roe, like a dried herring.
Flesh, flesh, how art thou fishified! Now he is for the
Numbers that Petrarch flowed in.

(II, iv, 36–39)

The play of sound here creates complex associations. Romeo without his roe suggests a "meo" a mere pussy cat who, like a dried fish emptied of its sperm (roe), is a poor match (and easy prey) for Tybalt, the Prince of Cats. Even the initial letter of a name is given an odd weight in the play. As she tells Romeo that Juliet's parents have arranged her marriage to Paris, the Nurse assures Romeo that Juliet has no interest in that match and thinks only of Romeo:

NURSE
I anger her sometimes and tell
her that Paris is the properer man, but I'll warrant you,
when I say so she looks pale as any clout in the
versal world. Doth not rosemary and Romeo begin with a letter?

ROMEO
Aye, nurse, what of that both with an 'R'.

NURSE
Aye, mocker, that's the Dog's name. R is for
the— no, I know it begins with some other letter, and

she hath the prettiest sententious of it, of you and
rosemary, that it would do you good to hear it.

(II, iv, 195–204)

Rosemary was traditionally thought to symbolize both remembrance and marriage, and R was sometimes called the "dog letter" to celebrates its connection to the "arr" of the dog's growl. These "R" associations suggest a hidden onomatopoetic resonance with the first letter of Romeo's name.

One acoustic theme which preoccupied Shakespeare in writing *Romeo and Juliet* has gone largely unnoted by critics.[9] It involves the cluster of homonyms aye/eye/I, which acoustically are midway between a word and the vocalized emotion "ay." The initial use of the sound comes in the third scene of Act I in the Nurse's long speech in which she reminisces about Juliet's childhood:

NURSE
And then my husband--God be with his soul!
A' was a merry man--took up the child:
'Yea,' quoth he, 'dost thou fall upon thy face?
Thou wilt fall backward when thou hast more wit;
Wilt thou not, Jule?' and, by my holidame,
The pretty wretch left crying and said 'Ay.'
To see, now, how a jest shall come about!
I warrant, an I should live a thousand years,
I never should forget it: 'Wilt thou not, Jule?' quoth he;
And, pretty fool, it stinted and said 'Ay.'

LADY CAPULET
Enough of this; I pray thee, hold thy peace.

NURSE
Yes, madam: yet I cannot choose but laugh,
To think it should leave crying and say 'Ay.'
And yet, I warrant, it had upon its brow
A bump as big as a young cockerel's stone;
A parlous knock; and it cried bitterly:
'Yea,' quoth my husband,' fall'st upon thy face?
Thou wilt fall backward when thou comest to age;
Wilt thou not, Jule?' it stinted and said 'Ay.'

JULIET
And stint thou too, I pray thee, nurse, say I.

(I, iii, 40–59)

It is difficult to know what all these deliberate repetitions of ay/I are doing here. The nurse effectively creates a thread of sound associated with Juliet in the way that Richard Wagner and Giacomo Puccini create short musical leitmotifs as musical tags for their focal opera characters. The word "ay" and its homonyms keep reappearing throughout the play and, after many apparently arbitrary appearances in the text, the sound takes on weight. The Nurse vaguely predicts, "Thou wilt fall backward when thou comest to age;/ Wilt thou not, Jule?" Juliet's response is equally mysterious: "it stinted and said 'Ay.'" But when Juliet encounters Romeo at the Capulets' party, we see an echo of the Nurse's prediction in the couple's first exchange of words:

ROMEO
Have not saints lips, and holy palmers too?

JULIET
Ay, pilgrim, lips that they must use in prayer.

(I, v, 99–100)

The sound reappears doubled over early in Act II when Mercutio parodies Romeo's poetic love-making attempts to conjure Rosaline through the power of rhymes.

MERCUTIO
Nay, I'll conjure too.
Romeo! humours! madman! passion! lover!
Appear thou in the likeness of a sigh:
Speak but one rhyme, and I am satisfied;
Cry but 'Ay me!' pronounce but 'love' and 'dove;'
Speak to my gossip Venus one fair word,
One nickname for her purblind son and heir,
Young Adam Cupid, he that shot so trim,
When King Cophetua loved the beggar-maid!
He heareth not, he stirreth not, he moveth not;
The ape is dead, and I must conjure him.
I conjure thee by Rosaline's bright eyes,
By her high forehead and her scarlet lip,
By her fine foot, straight leg and quivering thigh
And the demesnes that there adjacent lie,
That in thy likeness thou appear to us!

(II, I, 6–21, italics added)

The syllable again shows up in the balcony scene:

ROMEO
It is my lady, O, it is my love!

O, that she knew she were!
She speaks yet she says nothing: what of that?
Her eye discourses; I will answer it.
I am too bold, 'tis not to me she speaks:
Two of the fairest stars in all the heaven,
Having some business, do entreat her eyes
To twinkle in their spheres till they return.
What if her eyes were there, they in her head?
The brightness of her cheek would shame those stars,
As daylight doth a lamp; her eyes in heaven
Would through the airy region stream so bright
That birds would sing and think it were not night.
See, how she leans her cheek upon her hand!
O, that I were a glove upon that hand,
That I might touch that cheek!

JULIET
Ay me!

(II, ii, 10–25, italics added)

Finally, in the farewell bedroom scene between the lovers, Juliet uses the repeated "I" sound as a sort of incantation aimed at turning day into night.

JULIET
Yond light is not daylight, I know it, I.
It is some meteor that the sun exhaled.
To be to thee this night a torchbearer.
And light thee on thy way to Mantua.
Therefore stay yet. Thou need'st not to be gone.

(III, v, 12–16, italics added)

The common sound linking the words *I, ay,* and *eye* runs just beneath the text, creating the sort of diffuse associations that Edward Sapir characterized as "condensation symbolism."[10] As with puns, attention is drawn not only to names but also to the basal pulse of pure sound.

The proliferation of eddies of sound suggests a world in which language is charged with nondiscursive meaning carried through primitive sound correspondences. Modern linguists have generally marginalized such effects of sound-symbolic associations in language. However, in 1930, John Firth, in his book *Speech*, proposed the significance of family resemblances of sounds in language (e.g., the association of *gl* words with light). Firth coined the term *phonaestheme* for phonemes that carry networks of semantic associations.[11] Such meaningful sound streams were not just recognized but were of great interest to Shakespeare three-and-a-half centuries earlier. In *Romeo and Juliet*'s exploitation of the hidden connections of sound and sense, we are back on Cratylus' home ground, the linguistic landscape in which names shimmer with hidden resonances. These strange resonances of sounds do not have "meaning" for the play in the way that ordinary language does. They serve as an intimation of a kind of non-arbitrary and mystical connection between sound and sense beyond the ordinary use of words, pointing to what Friar Lawrence, at the end of the play, calls "A greater power than we can contradict" (V, iii, 158).

An Elizabethan view of language

Though modern audiences might view the primitive play of sound in *Romeo and Juliet* as trivial and of marginal interest, Shakespeare's audience was prepared to respond quite differently.[12] Early modern English views of the original perfection and current corruption of language were somewhat like Plato's, though filtered through scripture. Elizabethans believed that God initially endowed humans with a perfect form of language, what the Spanish humanist Juan de Vives called "the true appellations of things:"

> For that language, whose words should make clear the nature of things, should be the most perfect of all; such as it is probable was the original language in which Adam attached the names to things. For these are the true appellations of things, as to which it is written in the sacred psalm: "Great is the Lord who counteth the multitude of the stars and calleth them all by their names. Great is His power, and of His wisdom there is no end."
> The *Cratylus* of Plato points to this opinion, though Aristotle gives another sig-nification to it in his book *Die Interpretatione*. This discovery of the right appel-lation of things, beyond everything else, caused the admiration of Pythagoras.[13]
> (Vives 1913: 92)

Shakespeare's contemporaries believed that this original language had become cor-rupted with the Fall of Adam. This postlapsarian imperfection of language only increased with the overreaching pride of Nimrod, grandson of Ham and builder of the Tower of Babel.[14]

   This understanding of words and even sounds as sacred objects is an important aspect of the life of language in *Romeo and Juliet*. Having attempted to deny the power of names, Juliet is forced to recognize in her interview with her nurse in III, ii that her fate can rest on the most primitive units of speech.

JULIET
What devil art thou that dost torment me thus?
This torture should be roared in dismal hell
Hath Romeo slain himself? Say thou but "Ay,"
And that bare vowel "I" shall poison more
Than the death-darting eye of cockatrice
I am not I if there be such an "I,"

> Or those eyes shut that makes thee answer "Ay."
> If he be slain, say "Ay," or if not, "No."
> Brief sounds determine my weal or woe.

(III, ii, 43–51)

I have suggested that Shakespeare makes much of "brief sounds" in *Romeo and Juliet* as he explores the nexus of language forms that control human lives. The potential significance of the primitives of speech and writing, along with names and more elaborate language forms like prayer, proclamations, curses, and letters, is an important aspect of the Elizabethan view of language. The modern view of language, influenced by the Swiss linguist Ferdinand de Saussure (Saussure 1983), conceives of words as abstract and more-or-less arbitrary labels for concepts. But Shakespeare's contemporaries tended to see words more as things, sound objects, or written signs endowed with substantial properties. Words took their place in a broader universe of signs, including a wide variety of nonverbal signifiers (Ferry 1988: 38). Making sense of these signs was understood as an act of reading. The reification of word-as-objects was also true for smaller language units like sounds, syllables, and alphabetic letters.

> Often the components of language are referred to as if they were things, objects are compared to verbal signs, and sentences about language slip without distinction into discussion of nonverbal matters. Demonstration of this blurring of words and things can begin with concepts of letters, and by some theorists to be "first to be aduised, onelie to resemble, and expresse the sound by their aspectable figur." The literalness of this notion that the actual shape of letters have significant signifying power is shown by the visual terms habitually used to describe letters. Letters are said by John Hart to be "the Images of manne's voice," so that "what writer doth nearest and most iustly dicerne the diuers voices of the speach, he is best able to describe and paint the same with his pen."

(Ferry 1988: 32)

The powers attributed to names were grounded in the belief that Hebrew was the Bible's original language. The names that God bestowed in creation were understood to contained essential elements of identity. Protestant writers of the period shared with their Catholic peers the assumption that, in the right circumstances and the right hands, some words and sounds had the power to perform miracles. Sacred names and words were assumed to have an inherent potency. Like the power of prayer, word-magic and curses were taken to be potential attributes of sacred language. *Romeo and Juliet* is haunted by such magical undercurrents of sound as well as by names. The flow of pure sound in the text contributes to the sense that more than just names are implicated in the tragedy of the two families and their "star-crossed" children. In her essay on the fate of the Petrarchan sonnet in *Romeo and Juliet*, Gayle Whittier reflects on how the language of the sonnet is let loose from its conventional form within the play and in Shakespeare's deft hand comes to assert an agency of pure sound over the fates of the Montagues and Capulets.

If sonnet form has lost its furor, however, the living volatility freed from it, erupts in the play's first dialogue, Sampson inelegant chain of "coals," "colliers," "choler," and "collar." Were these four terms contracted, they might comprise a quadruple pun. Unlike a true pun, the sequence evolves in and through felt time. Like a true pun, however, it generates meaning out of sound... above the intentionality of the speakers. They do not choose their words; the words, in a sense, choose them.

(Whittier 1989: 28)

To the Elizabethan ear, sounds and even individual letters could carry special meanings. For example, letters were often treated as sacred symbols with their own mystical powers. So that in schoolbooks, the recitation of the ABCs was generally followed by the Lord's Prayer. The mystical power of letters, numbers, and hieroglyphs was emphasized in the various forms of Neoplatonism, Cabalism, and Hermeticism fashionable in Shakespeare's day, fashions that attracted Shakespeare, Spencer, Nashe, Marlowe, and other writers.[15] Underscoring the alphabet's sacred associations for Elizabethans was the fact that printed alphabets were organized as rows of letters with crosses at the end of each row. Alphabet books were known as "crossrows" or "Christcross-rows." Set out in this way, they conveyed the aspect of a sacred text.

A world colonized by words

In Shakespeare's Verona, there is no escaping the dominion of language. The world of *Romeo and Juliet* is constituted and governed by sound-shapes, word-forms, and a host of literary devices. The literal has been colonized by the figurative. We have seen how Romeo "pens" himself in his room, attempting to create a literary substitute for a lover. We recall that the old feud between the Capulets and Montagues that powers the plot of *Romeo and* Juliet stems from an ancient "airy word," a word that is both unremembered and unforgettable. Verona's citizens are subject to Verona's laws, while the Prince's "sentence" seals Romeo's fate. Misreading can be amusing, but it can also prove fatal. The Capulet servants lament their inability to carry out Old Montague's orders if they cannot read the names on his invitation and ask Romeo for his help deciphering the invitation, while Romeo has reading problems of his own. When he first confesses his love of Juliet to the Friar, the Friar chides Romeo for having so quickly forgotten Roseline. But Romeo insists that his love for Juliet is genuine and that Roseline never reciprocated his love.

ROMEO
I pray thee, chide me not. Her I love now
Doth grace for grace and love for love allow.
The other did not so.

(II, iv, 91–93)

Friar Lawrence responds, "O, she knew well/ Thy love did read by rote, that could not spell" (ll, iv, 93–94). Juliet's mother offers her daughter reading lessons. Trying to convince Juliet to consider Paris' offer of marriage, Lady Montague urges her to read her suitor's face carefully:

LADY CAPULET
What say you? Can you love the gentleman?
This night you shall behold him at our feast.
Read o'er the volume of young Paris' face,
And find delight writ there with beauty's pen.
Examine every married lineament.
And see how one another lends content,
And what obscured in this fair volume lies.
Find written in the margent of his eyes.
This precious book of love, this unbound lover,
To beautify him only lacks a cover.

(I, iv, 75–89)

Like stars and words, faces must also be read. The lovers' fate is tied as much to the unread as to the misread. Friar Lawrence sends a letter to the banished Romeo in Mantua informing him of his plan to fake Juliet's death through a potent sleeping drug that simulates death so that the two lovers can be secretly reunited in the Capulet tomb when Juliet wakes. But the letter never arrives, since Mantua's houses have been closed by plague to outsiders. Having never received the Friar's letter, Romeo arrives at the tomb before Juliet awakes, misreads the situation, and assumes she is dead. Horrified at the sight of his "dead" bride, Romeo kills himself with the poison he had purchased in Mantua, rechristening the toxic liquid as a "cordial and not poison" (V, ii, 90) in a tribute to the Friar's warning about the interchangeability of medicine and poison. When Juliet wakes and finds Romeo dead beside her, she stabs herself, continuing the cascade of deaths that brings the play to its conclusion. At this point, we witness the play's most unexpected and consequential wordcraft in the delayed realization of Mercutio's dying curse: "A plague 'o both houses" (III, i, 94).

As a literary creation, *Romeo and Juliet* seems to celebrate the triumph of language, realizing through Shakespeare's deft hand Romeo's dream of creating a world controlled by pure rhetoric. Deploying almost every rhetorical device in the writer's toolkit, Shakespeare demonstrates a formidable mastery of poetic language. The play begins in low comedy, and the audience dares to hope that the lovers' tale will also end as comedy. The play is an invitation to fantasy, provoking the audience to conjure its own false "nightingale."

Yet the question remains: has *Romeo and Juliet* managed to confirm Cratylus' conviction that, perfectly mimicking the world, poetic forms are a credible replacement for reality? I think not. The couple's tour through the Kingdom of Cratylus takes a more complicated path. Plato was seeking the relation of words to truth. But *Romeo and Juliet* is about the relation of language to desire. And this complicates matters enormously. So long as the Petrarchan lover can romance the sonnet rather than the lover, poetry can rule. But once the couple moves beyond the couplet into the world of flesh and blood and power, things become more difficult. After they consummate their marriage, daylight intrudes. Romeo and Juliet struggle to reconcile their love with the realities of their world, a world where language serves much more than just desire. As the sun forces its way into their bedchamber, poetry can no longer work its magic of making day into night, or transforming the nightingale into a lark. At this point, the rhetorical engine sputters, as the play's language shifts from rhyme, the enchanted idiom of night, to the blank verse of day.

"What's in a name?" has no simple answer. Names have many kinds of meaning. Like the Kingdom of Cratylus, Verona is a heterogeneous landscape of contending language forms with which its inhabitants must contend. The language world is not limited to Plato's ideal names, nor to Shakespeare's rhetorical wizardry. Human communication is irreducibly polyphonic, an idea most famously associated in modern language theory with the Russian linguist and literary critic Mikhail Bakhtin. Bakhtin reshaped the appreciation of the language of the novel by seeing it as a field for displaying the great variety of speech styles and dialects at play in any society. These different forms of speech meet up in the interchange of everyday conversation, which he called "dialogized heteroglossia," noting that linguists and critics have generally overlooked it. "One might even say outright," he argued, "that the dialogic aspect of discourse and all the phenomena connected with it have remained to the present moment beyond the ken of linguistics" (Bakhtin 1981: 273). While early literary critics may not have emphasized the heteroglossia of Shakespeare's world, Shakespeare surely did. His plays offer up a kaleidoscopic view of Elizabethan speech forms in conversational play, highlighting the intersection of class, gender, social status, and regional dialect.

Language also betrays significant variations in its capacity to free our speech and to constrain it. *Romeo and Juliet* highlights this diversity of constraint in different speech genres. The characters in Shakespeare's Verona use diverse language forms bearing different kinds of authority, different degrees of arbitrariness, and different relations to "the truth" of things. Navigating this patchwork of language genres presents the most significant challenge for the play's characters in correctly "reading" their world. Three distinct kinds of language can be seen at work in the play.

(1) *Playful Language.* Some of the play's language is relatively unconstrained, such as the playful punning banter between the servants at the play's start. Such open talk, including the language of everyday conversation, is always subject to being misread. The language of poetry is more formally constrained but also semantically free. As we see with Romeo, virtuosity with tropes and other poetic devices permits the imagination considerable scope and ambiguity in refiguring reality and demonstrates language at the service of desire and only conditionally at the service of truth.

(2) *Institutional Language.* More constraining is the language of legal and political authority, represented in *Romeo and Juliet* by the laws governing Verona, and the weighty proclamations and "sentences" of the Prince. Even more authoritative,

perhaps, is the language of the Church, represented in the play by prayer, marriage vows (the "holy words" that Romeo urges the Friar to use to "close our hands") and of the thread of wise counsel from Friar Lawrence that runs through the play. Both law and prayer are grounded in powerful institutions like government and Church that claim transcendent authority but are still subject to human manipulation.

(3) *Sacred Language.* While *Romeo and Juliet* proposes the tragic unreliability of language, the play evokes another more mysterious possibility, the shadowy operation of a transcendent form of language, idealized by Plato as beyond human control and desire. The clearest suggestion of the hidden work of sacred language comes near the play's end as Friar Lawrence tries to convince Juliet to abandon her dead husband and flee the tomb.

JULIET
O comfortable friar, where is my lord?
I do remember well where I should be,
And there I am. Where is my Romeo?

FRIAR LAWRENCE
I hear some noise. — Lady, come from that nest.
Of death, contagion, and unnatural sleep.
A greater power than we can contradict.
Hath thwarted our intents.

(V, iii, 153–161, italics added)

Transcendent authority is also suggested by the delayed power of Mercutio's curse, which hovers just offstage and exerts a decisive and unexpected effect on the lovers' fate. Such sacred signs are the ideal coin of the realm in the Kingdom of Cratylus, language linked directly to ultimate authority and beyond the power of humans to talk away. The working of sacred symbols in the play undercuts the impression of the fallibility of language that the play initially presents. It represents the Cratylus neighborhood of Hermogenes' world. While the Friar makes the operation of sacred signs explicit, they have been hinted at throughout the play by insistent patterns of sound symbolism that run through the text, just below the level of conscious awareness, the origin of the "brief sounds" that Juliet says determine "her weal or woe."

Returning to the original question, "What's in a name?" that ties *Romeo and Juliet* to Plato's *Cratylus,* we see why it is such a difficult question to answer. Names figure prominently in *Romeo and Juliet,* but not in any single determinate way. Names are taken apart and subject to teasing wordplay, as when Benvolio and Mercutio play sarcastically with the syllables of Romeo's name, deconstructing the name into sounds, only to have those sounds come back in the underbelly of the text to haunt the play. Personal names are relatively open to parental choice, but over time tend to reshape identity so that the name can come to seem like an intrinsic evocation of the person, as Benvolio or Mercutio or Juliet are closely tied to their names.

Apparently arbitrary, names become increasingly "naturalized" through use, even suggesting a transcendent connection between the name and the named. The family name is even less arbitrary. In the play, the lovers discover the impossibility of wishing away their names, linked as they are to social and biological identity. Unable to control or even comprehend the language forms that intrude on their self-created world and unable to evade the prison-house of language, Romeo and Juliet ultimately fail to read their world correctly. And in the end, it swallows them alive.

Starting with an unrealistic sense that the world might be subordinated to desire through the human ability to control language, Romeo and Juliet come to realize that reading and writing the world into submission is an impossible dream. While we encounter sacred forms of language tied directly to transcendent powers in the play, such sacred signs turn out not to operate in ordinary human time and are not under human control. Sacred language exerts its force in the world of *Romeo and Juliet* in a way that human words cannot "contradict." And so, while the play opens with a display of rhetorical bravura, by the play's tragic ending, speech has begun to close down. Having been informed of Juliet's "death" by Balthazar, and having never received the Friar's letter clarifying the ruse to fake Juliet's death, Romeo returns to Verona, determined to join Juliet in her grave. He opens the door to the Capulet tomb with the following words:

ROMEO
Thou detestable maw, thou womb of death,
Gorged with the dearest morsel of the earth,
Thus I enforce thy rotten jaws to open,
And, in despite, I'll cram thee with more food!

(V, iii, 45–48)

Initially an agent of language creation, Romeo ends up as an agent of silence as he seeks to close up the mouth of the tomb with his own body. This image of the closing down of speech and the stopping up of breath is taken up by the rest of the characters. When Friar Lawrence arrives at the tomb, too late to save Romeo, he confronts the silence of the blood-stained entrance to the tomb, exclaiming, "Alack, alack. What blood is this which stains/ The stony entrance to this sepulcher?" (V, iii, 140–141). The Prince enters, followed by Old Montague who announces, "Alas, my liege my wife is dead tonight; Grief of my son's exile has stopped her breath." (210–211).

Prince Escalus continues the closing down of speech: "Seal up the mouth of outrage for a while/ Till we can clear these ambiguities" (216–217). And, finally, Friar Lawrence, asked to explain the tragic scene confronting them, begins: "I will be brief, for my short date of breath/Is not so long as is a tedious tale" (229–230). In straightforward prose, stripped of all rhetorical and poetic flourish, Friar Lawrence summarizes the events that led up to the present deaths. It is a fitting testament to their love that Romeo and Juliet are resurrected as statues by the two families at the play's end as a sign of their reconciliation. And, in its limited way, the promise of Petrarchanism has also been realized. Flesh has been replaced and immortalized by art. But it must also be noted that this art is mute, the memorial evoking, in its golden glow, only the proverbial color of silence.

Notes

1 For an insightful discussion of *The Cratylus* in relation to the history of the more general debate between supporters of *physis* and *nomos* in answering this question, see Joseph 2000.

2 All Plato quotes are from Plato 1982.

3 Under the influence of the writings of Swiss linguist Ferdinand de Saussure—who famously proposed that the hallmark of the linguistic signifier was that it is arbitrarily linked to its referent (what he termed "the signified")—linguists today seem to mostly subscribe to the nominalist view of language as systems of largely conventional signs. While acknowledging a minor role for analogy in linguistic forms like onomatopoeia, the modern tendency is to treat the lexicon of a language (Plato's focus) as mostly arbitrary human invention (*nomos*), while assuming that the general human language capacity is grounded in psycho-biological nature (*physis*). See Saussure 1983. But the search for significant signs of naturalistic imitation in language is very much alive in certain corners of literary theory, poetics, linguistics, and cognitive anthropology. These scholars often cite Plato's *Cratylus* as their inspiration. Roman Jacobson, taking off from Plato, identifies analogical processes and forms in language not only in word sounds but also in grammatical features and word order (Jacobson 1965). The most elaborate modern version of Cratylus' naturalist argument for the analogical nature of language is the magisterial volume *Mimologics* by the French literary critic Gérard Genette. Starting with a detailed analysis of *The Cratylus*, *Mimologics* seeks to demonstrate the central role of analogy and imitation in almost every aspect of language and literature (Genette 1995). See also Shore 1996, especially Chapters 12–13.

4 Gayle Whittier (Whittier 1989) contrasts Shakespeare's narrative use of the sonnet form in the Preface to *Romeo and Juliet* with the more personally expressive character of the Petrarchan model.

> In fact Romeo and Juliet opens with a Petrarchan inheritance in the reliquary of the Prologue's English sonnet, an inheritance that endures structurally but endures emptied of its traditional lyric lovesick persona, dense metaphor, emotional extremity, song have been supplanted by public narrative. "Two households," lovers," opens the poem; "story" rather than lyric is the dramatized. Even the liquidity of Petrarchan time-liturgical, sonal, and aesthetic-cramps to an explicit reckoning of reducing the brief lifespans of the lovers and their even briefer countable theatrical "traffic." The surviving sonnet itself sustains burden more fitting for an entire sequence. No longer poetic the sonnet serves as a means to a dramatic issue. Some Petrarchan lingers in the loose and ironic paradox of "civil blood making unclean" and in the tighter oxymoron "fatal loins," but the emphasizes a triumph of the prosaic over the lyrical, bequeathing theatrical appeal in wooden prosody:
> The which if you with patient ears attend,
> What here shall miss, our toil shall strive to mend.
> (Prologue, 11. 13–14)
>
> (Whittier 1988: 27–29)

5   Romeo himself springs forth from the mouth of his father as a recitation inherited from the pages of a courtly miscellany, described but not seen as the topos of the languishing lover. In this persona he suffers less from love than from his desire to live out artistic imitation, to make himself "an artificial [k]night," in worried Montague's pun (1.1.140). Petrarch's is the book he kisses by, but La Rochefoucauld perhaps makes the better case for him: "There are people who would never have fallen in love but for hearing love discussed" (maxim 136). (Whittier 1989: 29)

6   In *Henry IV, part I,* Fallstaff makes a similar argument about the word honour:

FALSTAFF
'Tis not due yet; I would be loath to pay him before
his day. What need I be so forward with him that
calls not on me? Well, 'tis no matter; honour pricks
me on. Yea, but how if honour prick me off when I
come on? how then? Can honour set to a leg? no: or
an arm? no: or take away the grief of a wound? no.
Honour hath no skill in surgery, then? no. What is
honour? a word. What is in that word honour? what
is that honour? air. A trim reckoning! Who hath it?
he that died o' Wednesday. Doth he feel it? no.
Doth he hear it? no. 'Tis insensible, then. Yea,
to the dead. But will it not live with the living?
no. Why? detraction will not suffer it. Therefore
I'll none of it. Honour is a mere scutcheon: and so
ends my catechism.

(V, ii, 128–142)

In this case, Falstaff appeals to the nominalist argument that *honor* is merely an arbitrary word to evade the undesirable obligations that honor would impose on him.

7   As apprentice lover-poet, Romeo yearns for a suitably unattainable lady. Rosaline, always a word rather than a presence, bears a name that might entitle a sonnet cycle and that resonates with the love tradition (the Romance of the Rose, the rose-form vision of the Paradiso, and the ubiquitous symbol of feminine beauty). Like the rose in her name, she will be nominal and brief. (Whittier 1989: 29)

8   In their seminal psychological study of symbol formation, Werner and Kaplan call this synthetic process whereby a symbol becomes increasingly attached to its referent by a web of associations, "the physiognomic apprehension of symbols." According to the authors, this web of internal associations, undercutting the perception of arbitrariness of the sign, is central to language development. It appears to be intuitively understood by poets and was likely on Shakespeare's mind in some way as he wrote *Romeo and Juliet*. See Werner and Kaplan 1984.

9   For an exception, see Mahoot 2004: 70.

10 In condensation symbolism . . . richness of meaning grows with increased dissociation. The chief developmental difference, however, between this type of symbolism and referential symbolism is that while the latter grows with formal elaboration in the conscious, the former strikes deeper and deeper roots in the unconscious and diffuses its emotional quality to types of behavior or situations apparently far removed from the original meaning of the symbol. (Sapir 1934: 493–494)

11 On phonaesthemes, see Firth 1930; Shore 1996; Padraic et al. 2014; Bergen 2004.

12 For an interesting discussion of the way Elizabethans understood language, see De Grazia 1978.
13 See also Donawerth 1984: 4.
14 De Grazia, Magreta, "Shakespeare's View of Language: An Historical Perspective," *Shakespeare Quarterly,* Vol. 29, No. 3 (Summer 1978), pp. 376–377.
15 Ferry, Anne, *The Art of Naming*, Chicago: The University of Chicago Press 1988, p. 132.

6

JUST FOR PLAY

Unmasquing *A Midsummer Night's Dream*[1]

A Midsummer Night's Dream is generally acknowledged as Shakespeare's most popular play by far. Over the last decade, it has accounted for over 7% of all Shakespeare productions both in the United States and abroad (Kopf 2016). In addition to its many professional stage productions, the play has spawned untold high school and college productions and at least six TV and film adaptations, starting in 1909 with a ten-minute silent film version. Shakespeare's fairytale has also inspired music: a famous overture and incidental music composed over 15 years by Felix Mendelsohn, a ballet choreographed by George Balanchine, and an opera by Benjamin Britten. Despite its popularity (or, perhaps because of it), critics have sometimes complained that *A Midsummer Night's Dream* is theatrical fluff, Shakespeare's "lightest play," lacking the substance of his more serious work. Consider the following condescending comment from an anonymous online review of Michael Hoffman's 1999 Hollywood film production of *A Midsummer Night's Dream*:

> That's not to say that this film is bad. For whatever time it takes most movie-goers to fit into its "groove," once they do they'll be treated to a cute and charming, but lightweight diversion that looks great – courtesy of Oliver Stapleton ("One Fine Day," "The Grifters") and despite the "enchanted" forest obviously being a set – and which features a well-known and talented cast of performers. It's that the story itself -- despite the testing of time over several centuries – just isn't that exciting or, for that matter, very interesting to mainstream viewers. While there's enough there to keep one from being bored, the plot isn't exactly one of Shakespeare's strongest and seems to meander a bit too often. At times one can't help but get the feeling that the well-known cast is partially present simply to hold the viewer's interest.[2]

DOI: 10.4324/9781003179771-9

The reviewer has clearly not considered the possibility that the failure here is his rather than Shakespeare's. Insubstantial as the play may appear on the face of it, the public has always been enchanted by this lovers' romp through fairyland. Conceived as a feast for the eyes and ears, the play is a stage director's and costume designer's dream. I suspect that, in addition to the play's primal theatrical charms, there is also something elusively profound about *A Midsummer Night's Dream* that pulls audiences in. In this chapter, we view *A Midsummer Night's Dream* through the lenses of the anthropology of marriage, the psychology of love, and performance theory, in an effort to unearth the play's perennial popularity. In addition to the seductive power of the fairy forest on the imagination, Shakespeare accomplishes something else in *A Midsummer Night's Dream*, something remarkable. He orchestrates our excursion through fairyland to shed a fascinating light on one of the major challenges people everywhere confront: how to reconcile love, erotic attraction, and marriage. This, I think, is where the real magic of the play lies.

A Midsummer Night's Dream has no single source, being spun out of many threads. Shakespeare created his fairy forest and its inhabitants from so many different sources that scholars have had a field-day mapping them: Chaucer's "The Knight's Tale and "The Merchant's Tale," John Lyly, Spenser's *The Shepherd's Calendar*, Marlowe, Montemayor's *Diana,* Apuleius' *The Golden Ass*, Plutarch by way of North, Ovid by way of Golding, *Corinthians* from *The King James Bible,* and Erasmus are just some of the play's supposed sources. Assembling these sources in a loose and shifting patchwork, the play has been put together remarkably like a dream. First performed between 1595 and 1596, *A Midsummer Night's Dream* was written around the same time as *Romeo and Juliet*, whose plot the play anticipates in the play-within-a-play, *Pyramus and Thisbe*. While *Romeo and Juliet* is a tragedy that begins in a comic mode, *A Midsummer Night's Dream* turns these genres inside-out, starting out in a tragic key, but eventually ending up as comedy. The play was probably staged initially as a wedding masque, a theatrical performance accompanying a marriage ceremony. Harold Brooks claims that the likely occasion was Lady Elizabeth Carey's wedding to Thomas, son of Lord Berkeley in February of 1596. But we know that other notable weddings also took place around that time that might have been the setting for the play's first performance. Whatever the facts, the play was clearly composed as a wedding masque, giving it a double life as a play about weddings and as a performance serving as an actual part of a wedding celebration.

The play begins with the impending wedding of Duke Theseus and Hippolyta, moves through a chaotic chain of mismatched amorous relationships, and ends with three couples retiring to their bedrooms to consummate their marriages. The original performance of the play-as-masque, along with its embedded play-within-a-play, can be considered theatrical "foreplay," a fanciful, erotically charged appetizer, preceding the consummation of the marriages. *Midsummer Night's Dream* was written as *"comedus interruptus,"* the same role that *Pyramus and Thisbe* serves for the three weddings within the play. The play moves in a circle from the Athenian court's troubled relationships to the (psychedelic) "green world" of the forest, and then back to the court for the weddings. In the process, the play enacts a mysterious rite of passage that allows the marriages both within the play and outside the play to be consummated. To understand what Shakespeare is doing in *A Midsummer Night's Dream*, we need to turn our attention to the puzzle that Shakespeare presents at the start of the play. It opens in the Athenian court of Duke Theseus, who is struggling to sort out troubled relations of love, marriage, and desire, not just for his subjects, but for himself and his intended bride, Hippolyta. From the outset, *A Midsummer Night's Dream* prepares us for some kind of significant transformation. Anticipating his imminent marriage, Theseus instructs his servant Philostrate to transform the mood of Athens:

> Go Philostrate,
> Stir up the Athenian Youth to merriments:
> Awake the pert and nimble spirit of merriment;
> Turn melancholy forth to funerals;
> The pale companion is not for our pomp.
>
> (I, i, 11–15)

This movement, from a tragic to a triumphant key, is already implicit in Theseus's courtship of Hippolyta. The couple anticipates marrying "in four happy days," but Theseus makes it clear that this happy union was born of violence, not romance. Before he captured Hippolyta's heart, Theseus had captured her body:

> Hippolyta, I woo'd thee with my sword,
> And won thy love, doing thee injuries;
> But I will wed thee in another key,
> With pomp, with triumph and with revelling.
>
> (I, i, 16–19)

Such fierce "courtship" is known to anthropologists as "marriage by capture." The bride is "won" by the groom as a conquest of war. So Hippolyta is both a happy bride-to-be and a wounded captive of her future husband. The challenge of transforming this "romance" from its dark beginnings as a military triumph to a joyous celebration of romance is no small feat. It will require, as Theseus suggests, a change of key.

For all its devotion to reason and law, Athens is an emotionally unsteady place. Enter Egeus and his daughter Hermia, followed by a pair of competing suitors. Egeus is determined to reserve for himself the power to choose his daughter's husband by right of local law and custom. His choice is Demetrius, but Hermia will have none of it. She has set her sights on Lysander, who, Egeus insists, has "bewitch'd the bosom of my child." Egeus solicits Theseus to support his paternal right to have his daughter put to death or banished to a nunnery for disobedience to his wishes. Once again, marriage is to be accomplished by a potentially lethal force. Theseus and Hippolyta are to be united by past violence and future love. If Egeus is to have his way, Demetrius and Hermes are to be joined by the force of law and the threat of death. From Egeus's perspective, marriage has nothing to do with love but with the father's will. This leaves Hermia and Lysander, who are linked by a passionate love lacking social legitimation. This web of romantic dysfunction grows even more tangled when we learn that Hermia's best friend, Helena dotes on Demetrius and stalks him in the hope of winning him back from Hermia. Demetrius, who once had eyes only for Helena, now worships Hermia. We struggle to keep the couples straight, much as they do themselves. In this world, the heart is fickle and love is fleeting, producing only shifting alliances and unsteady feelings.

Love and marriage

In 1955, Sammy Kahn and Jimmy Van Heusen wrote a song made famous by Frank Sinatra whose lyrics proclaimed the inseparable union of "Love and Marriage:"

> Love and marriage, love and marriage
> They go together like a horse and carriage
> This I tell you brother
> You can't have one without the other…

Despite the appeal of these lyrics, the psychology of love and the sociology of marriage tell a much more complicated story, suggesting that the relation between love and marriage is far from straightforward. Consider the problematical status of love and marriage (and sex!) in anthropological theory. Anyone interested in the world's diverse marriage traditions can always consult an introductory anthropology textbook that is also likely to offer examples of cultural variations in sex practices and taboos. What you will not find, however, is much about love. Romance does not figure as an important topic in classic ethnography. Generations of anthropology students have learned that in so-called "traditional societies," marriage occupies (and often preoccupies) center stage, but love, if it is found at all, is sequestered away in the wings of ethnography. In these traditional societies, the bread-and-butter of classic ethnology, marriage is mostly seen as a way to legitimize a couple's offspring and to create political alliances between families. Romantic feelings rarely make an entrance, and when they do, it often means trouble.

Born of the prohibition of incestuous mating *within* families, the institution of marriage alliances *between* families has proliferated into numerous local forms. From African polygyny (one man marries multiple wives) to Tibetan polyandry (one woman marries a group of brothers), marriages are primarily social and not personal relationships serving economic and political functions. Tina Turner popped the question back in the '90s, "What's love got to do with it?" To which the anthropologist replied: "Not much." In addition to marriage, anthropologists have always been interested in sex. Social theory proposes that social systems channel sex in different directions by prohibiting relations between some people, permitting it between others, and even prescribing sex for special relationships. While prohibitions and taboos worked to keep certain people apart, sex was also the glue that tied families together. The loss of the estrus period for Homo sapiens meant that couples could have year-round sex, potentially bonding man and woman permanently and creating the conditions for the family to develop. Sex was also harnessed to prevent societies from fragmenting into warring factions. By prohibiting sex within the family beyond husband and wife, the sexual drive forced people to search for mates in other groups that were potential enemies. We call this imperative to marry out "*exogamy*." "Marry out or die out" is how we put it (Lévi-Strauss 1969; Kang 1982). But, as sexually active teenagers and cheating spouses can attest, sex and marriage are not the same things. Not only did sex underlie human pair-bonding, but it was also a potential disrupter of marriage relations. Legalizing sex might encourage social cohesion among potential enemies, but illicit sex could also prove to be the great fly in the ointment that greased the wheels of all those socially arranged marriages. In the orderly world of arranged marriage, lust can mean trouble, often violent trouble.

In contrast to the well-documented anthropological interests in sex and marriage, I know of no introductory anthropology text that devotes so much as a single chapter to love. When love is mentioned, it is often in its role as a marriage-disrupter. We learn that marriage is hardly ever about love and almost always about political alliances, economic exchange, and social hierarchy. Anthropologists seem to derive pleasure from assuring students that love doesn't count for much in the long history of marriage. Yet, there are a few anthropologists who have demurred, insisting that romantic love is far more universal and far more important around the world than we have claimed. A notable example is William Jankowiak, who has spent his career insisting that we pay more attention to the importance of love and romantic intimacy in societies where we had assumed it was absent. Jankowiak has documented the importance of romantic love in Asian "arranged marriage societies" like China and Mongolia, warning us that the avoidance of public expressions of love does not necessarily demonstrate an absence of romantic feelings and relationships.

Jankowiak's most influential paper is a 1992 article in the journal *Ethnology* he co-authored with Edward F. Fischer titled "A Cross-Cultural Perspective on Romantic Love" (Jankowiak and Fischer 1992). The authors aim to remedy the discipline's lack of attention to romantic love. "The anthropological study of romantic (or passionate) love," the authors argue, "is virtually nonexistent due to the widespread belief that romantic love is unique to Euro-American culture" (p. 149). Reviewing the theoretical literature on love and marriage in anthropology and sociology, the authors note the widely shared assumption that the sentiments we commonly recognize as love are inherently malleable and subject to social and cultural construction. In most traditional societies where families arrange marriage, society's demands are assumed to determine individual emotional experience, preventing the emergence of romantic love.

> The premise of much of this research is apparent: cultural traditions bind the individual emotionally into a web of dependency with others, thereby rechanneling or defusing the intensity of an individual's emotional experience.

> This web of dependency, in turn, undermines the individual's proclivity to
> fantasize about a lover or the erotic. . . .
>
> *(ibid.*: 149)

The assumption here is that cultural norms are enough to block the emergence
of feelings of romantic love, which the authors define as "any intense attraction
that involves the idealization of the other, within an erotic context, with the
expectation of enduring for some time into the future . . . ." (p. 150). Jankowiak
and Fischer assume that romantic love is distinct from the sort of calm and de-
eroticized attachment that characterizes "companionate" relationships. Moreover,
they seek to show, by scouring the ethnographic record, that romantic love is a
universal experience, a biologically grounded emotion, even where social norms
do not encourage it. Combing through Murdock and White's 1969 Standard
Cross-Cultural Sample (SCCS) of 186 societies for ethnographic examples of
romantic love, they were able to find at least one instance of passionate love
recorded in 147 out of the 186 societies, or 88.5%. No recorded evidence of
romance was found for 11% of the societies surveyed.[3] Note that the authors were
not arguing that romantic love is valued or emphasized in all societies, only that
it appears to be present (though often suppressed) in the societies where we had
assumed it was absent.

In the introduction to his 2008 edited collection of articles on romantic love
around the world, titled *Intimacies: Love and Sex Across Cultures,* Jankowiak revisits
the question of the universality of romantic love. However this time, he moves
beyond the emphasis on romantic love as a universal experience to focus on a universal dilemma of conflicting desire, which he calls "a tripartite conundrum."

> [W]hat human communities have in common is a universal compulsion
> to make a working peace with the three-way conflict between romantic/
> passionate love, comfort/attachment love, and physical sex. Every culture
> must decide whether to synthesize, separate, blend, discount, stress, ignore one
> or the other.
>
> (Jankowiak 2008: 2)

In this view, the differences between cultures do not lie in whether or not they create the possibility of romantic love, but how each culture orchestrates the expression
of the tensions between different kinds of love:

> The emotional tug between the competing and often contradictory desires
> insures every generation will revisit, renegotiate, and modify their "traditions"
> that account for the relationship between love and sex. Less known, and
> even less recognized, are the social constraints placed on the expression of
> different types of love and sex. Because the demands of comfort love and pas-
> sionate love often differ from the push of sexual desire, their interrelationship
> or separation presents different structural and psychological dilemmas for the

individual and his or her community who must deal with the often competing tugs produced by these dueling forces.

(*ibid.*: 5–6)

It is striking that Jankowiak's love conundrum does not reserve a seat for marriage
at the negotiating table, especially considering that the author is an anthropologist.
But when, in the fashion of mainstream anthropological theory, we add marriage to
the volatile mix of conflicting priorities governing the intimate relations between
(or, indeed, within) the sexes, we can see the real complexity of the entanglements
we casually gloss as "love."

Why are anthropologists so enthusiastic about marriage and so hard on romantic
love as human universals? Anthropology has long specialized in the study of "traditional societies." The message "marriage trumps love" underwrites the very idea of
traditional society. Marriage represents the triumph of what Emile Durkheim called
"social facts" over individual ones. The marriage-trumps-love position might even
be said to justify the whole enterprise of cultural anthropology and the credibility
of the idea of "the cultural construction of reality."

Claude Lévi-Strauss provides an interesting twist on Durkheim when he distinguishes between elementary and complex marriage systems, or in other words,
between them and us. Explicit marriage rules or preferences govern elementary or
arranged marriage. Personal inclinations are subordinated to political necessity. By
contrast, Lévi-Strauss' "complex marriage" (love marriages) emphasizes individual
choice in establishing marriages and is explicitly governed by personal preferences
and not by sociological rules. We have come to assume that love marriages and
romantic love itself are cultural inventions with their own sociology and history. The
roots of romantic love are held to lie in the development of a courtly love tradition
that has been traced to Arabic literature of the ninth and tenth centuries, and from
there to the ballads of 10th-century French troubadours. For modern readers, the
medieval history of romantic love was summarized for us in C.S. Lewis' influential
1936 book *The Allegory of Love* (Lewis 1936). An aestheticized and idealized love
was linked to the courtier, the dashing lover-knight whose character was vividly
traced in Castiglione's influential 1528 treatise *Il Cortigiano* ("The Courtier"). Not
coincidently, its author was also an accomplished sonneteer. The anthropologist's
suspicions that romantic love has a particular history as a joint European/Arabic
invention has long appealed to our predisposition to see even the most intimate
dimensions of human experience as artifacts of history and culture.

One way of rescuing romantic love from a total determination by culture and
history is by acknowledging the universal developmental foundation of love in what
psychologists call "attachment," that is a child's first-love experience of dependence
on its mother for protection and security.[4] "Secure attachment" of an infant to its
mother is seen as a precondition for later successful "love" relationships, while pervasive insecure attachment prevents the infant from forming love bonds throughout
his or her life. While attachment theory focused on mother-infant relationships,
some later researchers sought to extend the idea of a distinct infant attachment style

to other adult forms of attachment, including romantic love. Jankowiak clearly distinguishes adult attachment relations (which he calls "comfort love") from romantic love's eroticized passions. But others have seen primitive attachment needs as the common source of all love relationships. In a 1987 study titled "Romantic Love Conceptualized as an Attachment Process," Cindy Hazen and Phillip Shaver hypothesized that differences in adult styles of romantic love would be linked to developmentally earlier maternal attachment styles. In their study, they proposed that:

> romantic love is an attachment process—a biosocial process by which affectional bonds are formed between adult lovers, just as affectional bonds are formed earlier in life between human infants and their parents. Key components of attachment theory, developed by Bowlby, Ainsworth, and others to explain the development of affectional bonds in infancy, were translated into terms appropriate to adult romantic love.
>
> (Hazen and Shaver 1987: 511)

While understanding romantic love as a developmental extension of maternal attachment is not universally accepted by psychologists, attachment theory does have the advantage of grounding the capacity for romantic love as a developmental trait which is universal for humans, suggesting that different forms of psycho-social attachment, including romantic love, may have a common foundation in universal processes of human development.

Whatever the boundary lines of love's different neighborhoods, it is clear that the relations among these neighborhoods depend on local cultures' emotional maps. The cultural influences on love include the rules and norms for its expression or repression, its overall value and salience within a cultural context, and the key relationships that define the most culturally emphasized form of love in a community. Distinct cultural models produce different readings of love, foregrounding certain attachment relationships, and backgrounding others. Variations in incest prohibitions would shape how the emotions linking different attachment ties among kin would be socially regulated. In a society with a rule requiring marriage between a man and his mother's brother's daughter, norms governing relations between these cousins would be eroticized, distinguishing them dramatically from those relations between the children of two brothers or two sisters, where the cousins would be considered more like brothers and sisters than potential lovers. While the default reading of love might be culturally malleable, this is far from claiming that romantic love does not exist where it is not culturally emphasized. What is foregrounded in one setting may well be a significant part of background experience in another.

The issue is not so much whether "romantic love" is or is not universal. The answer to that question is as slippery as the question is ambiguous since the term "romantic love" comes with lots of historical and cultural baggage. What is universal is that love and marriage do not naturally go together, like a horse and carriage or anything else. *Romeo and Juliet*'s universal appeal is precisely that the tragedy of forbidden love is so widely recognized. The story evokes the wall that humans have so often erected between love and marriage. But why erect a wall and not a bridge? We have noted how natural selection hit on an ingenious way to cement relations between the sexes as a foundation for child-rearing units: get rid of the estrus cycle and use year-round mutual erotic attraction as a kind of social glue. However, this solution had one problem. Sexual attraction might bring male and female together, but it could not keep them together. As Finnish sociologist Edvard Westermarck reminded us, familiarity generally does not breed. Dubbed the Westermarck Effect, this principle proposed that, once domesticated, erotic attraction tends to decrease with time and familiarity. So culture intervenes to stabilize unions, adding to sexual access purely social and legal norms. Mating becomes marriage. While they some-times coexist, love and marriage always belong to different orders of experience. Love is largely a private matter, while marriage belongs to the family and society more broadly. Erotic love may lead to marriage, but it is also a serious threat to a marriage's stability. The human struggle has been how to reconcile love, sex, and marriage to promote stable relationships.

Finding ourselves back in the opening scenes of *A Midsummer Night's Dream*, we witness a parade of dysfunctional unions that anatomize before our eyes the incom-patibility of love and marriage. In Shakespeare's Athens, romantic love is squarely opposed to custom and law, where it remains the right of fathers to determine their children's spouses. Sexual desire is left to run its own course. Though we might sup-pose that love has a prior claim on our sympathy, neither love nor law seems to work very well on its own. Socially sanctioned marriage is underwritten by force, even violence. And passion looks more like witchcraft than genuine feeling, providing no solid foundation for a long-term relationship.

The idea of *discordia concors*, harmony won out of discord, is the play's implied promise.[5] From the troubled court of Athens, the script quickly delivers us into the Fairies' world, where we are led to expect romance to have its day (or, more precisely, its night). The expectation, born of conventional romance tales, is that the forest, powered by *mythos* rather than Athens's rigid *logos,* will ultimately redeem the court and point the way for the lovers to rescue marital concord from lovers' discord. But as soon as we enter the forest, we discover that this fairyland is no Arden, but a turbulent realm of erotic dreams and nightmares presided over by the fairy King and Queen Oberon and Titania, the nocturnal doubles of Theseus and Hippolyta. Here, with the help of a drop of love juice, sex and love can be coupled or de-coupled in the twinkle of an eye. Love in the fairy forest is no tidier than it had been back in Athens. Right away, we learn that Titania and Oberon's relationship is currently on the rocks:

OBERON
Ill met by moonlight, proud Titania.

TITANIA
What, jealous Oberon! Fairies, skip hence:
I have forsworn his bed and company.

(II, i, 60–62)

In a parody of the love triangles confounding the Hermia/Lysander, Helena/ Demetrius pairings, Oberon and Titania each resent the other's past amorous attachments to Hippolyta and Theseus. An old history of desire links the court and the forest. The current source of discord however turns out to be the royal pair's competing desire for a young boy, a child, born to an "Indian votress" of Titania who had died in childbirth. Oberon wants the boy as his page and Titania covets him as her foster child. Oberon and Titania rule over the forest's sprites and fairies, while Oberon's servant Puck is its Lord of Misrule. Puck, also known as Robin Goodfellow, is pure pastiche: part-Cupid, part-devil, part-child, part-animal. Like Ariel in *The Tempest*, he appears to do his master's bidding but quickly proves to be a skilled master of forest dreamwork, setting in motion much of the mischief that rules in the fairy kingdom.

If Athens is dominated by rigid law and social convention, the forest is its contrary. Erotic impulse rules the night world of the play, just as sober law and custom hold sway over the day. In Fairyland, relationships mutate as emotions run wild. Until the brilliant and eccentric readings of the play by Polish director and critic Jan Kott in the mid-1960s, *A Midsummer Night's Dream* was generally staged in a major key as light romance. The darker aspects of the Forest were either underplayed or ignored completely. Kott's influential essays "Titania and the Ass's Head" (Kott 1969) and his 1987 article "The Bottom Translation" (Kott 1987) draw our attention to the disturbing underbelly of the play, to its darker, erotic elements. Kott does not deny that the play is open to a light staging. "There will always remain," he wrote,

> two interpretations of *A Midsummer Night's Dream*: the light and the somber. And even as we choose the light one, let us not forget the dark one... In both interpretations of *A Midsummer Night's Dream,* the bottom translation is full of different meanings. All of them, even their contradictions, are important.
>
> (Kott 1987: 64)

Ultimately, the lovers' experiences in the forest make no more sense than they did back in Athens. The realm of pure desire does not redeem love and marriage from the grip of pure law. Both realms equally dislocate desire from the self, the one allocating it to legal and paternal authority, the other to the power of love juice. Like us, Puck struggles to distinguish Lysander from Demetrius and he misapplies his potion, scrambling the lovers' desires even worse than they had been back in Athens. Oberon, still angry with Titania for refusing to hand over the boy, orders Puck to bewitch Titania in her sleep with a drug that will impel her to fall in love with the first creature she sees upon awakening. Latent pedophilia will be pharmacologically recast as bestiality. To seal Titania's humiliation, Puck transforms Bottom into a kind of inverted satyr, a man with an ass's head. It is this Bottom with this "top" that Titania first sees on waking. Thus follows the disarming tryst between Titania and Bottom. Half-man, half-ass, Bottom has been "translated" into himself.

Eventually, the action of the play takes its predictable course and returns us to Athens. While we have assumed that the forest will redeem the court's excesses, the journey through the forest does not work out that way. As Kott put it:

> The Forest in Arden always represents Nature. The escape to the Forest of Arden is an escape from the cruel world in which the way to the crown leads through murder, brother robs brother of his inheritance, and a father asks for his daughter's death if she chooses a husband against his will. But it is not only the Forest that happens to be Nature. Our instincts are also Nature. And they are as mad as the world.
>
> (Kott 1969: 235)

Though obviously very different, Athens and the fairy forest are ultimately hard to tell apart. Regarding love and marriage, the forest is more a replication of Athens than its antithesis. An anti-rational world dedicated to the power of desire is every bit as crazy as the world dedicated to patriarchal power and law.

Theatrical bricolage

Despite all these roadblocks, at the end of the play, the newly united couples exit the stage to consummate their marriages. We must have missed something. It seems that Fairyland has somehow rescued the court from its excesses, allowing the weddings to proceed. Yet, even as we applaud the triumph of love over law, it is hard to see what has made all this concord possible. This is the real puzzle of *A Midsummer Night's Dream*, which directors of the play often fail to solve. Most productions of the play I have seen do not help us figure out what has made the marriages possible. The answer is surely not found in Puck's love juice. Nor is it found in the law books of Athens or the insistent demands of Hermia's father.

Shakespeare's answer is right before our eyes, but somehow, we miss it. For the source of the play's resolution of the problem of reconciling sex, marriage, and love, we need to turn our backs on both the court of Athens and the forest and look to the play's margins, to the third world of the play, the troop of actors who are struggling to mount *Pyramus and Thisbe*. The mechanicals (village tradesmen) occupy a liminal world of rehearsal as they attempt to enter the script, neither fully in the play nor beyond it. Until the final act, the mechanicals live on the outskirts of *A Midsummer Night's Dream*. Their rehearsals repeatedly intrude on the play's main action, but only, it seems, as comic relief. From *Hamlet,* we recall Shakespeare's predilection for dislocating the center of his play to its margins and so we might wonder whether these rehearsal scenes might constitute the displaced heart of the play.

In the tradition of Elizabethan wedding masques, the mechanicals are ordinary folks who come together as an *ad hoc* troupe of actors. Their everyday roles are as tradesmen. Unlike a professional acting troupe, the mechanicals are left to their own devices in assembling a play's elements, using whatever is at hand. They approach putting together the play as an act remarkably close to what Lévi-Strauss, in *The Savage Mind*, called *bricolage*.

> There still exists among ourselves an activity which on a technical plane gives us quite a good understanding of what a science we prefer to call 'prior' rather than 'primitive', could have been on the plane of speculation. This is what we commonly call 'bricolage' in French. In its old sense the verb *'bricoler'* applied to ball games and billiards, to hunting, shooting, and riding. It was however always used with reference to some extraneous movement: a ball rebounding, a dog straying or a horse swerving from its direct course to avoid an obstacle. And in our own time a 'bricoleur' is still someone who works with his hands and uses devious means compared to those of a craftsman. The characteristic feature of mythical thought is that it expresses itself by means of a heterogeneous repertoire which, even if extensive, is nevertheless limited. It has to use this repertoire, however, whatever the task at hand because it has nothing else at its disposal. Mythical thought is therefore a kind of 'intellectual bricolage' . . . .
> (Lévi-Strauss 1966: 16–17)

As amateur actors, the tradesmen are theatrical bricoleurs. Their performance is cobbled together rather than ready-made. *The Savage Mind* is a long and ethnographically packed rumination about the logic of myth. It treats myth-making as an early species of science, a quest for ordered understanding that Lévi-Strauss calls the "science of the concrete." The materials of the myth world are a heterogeneous assortment of found objects in the world: events, plants, animals, marginal beings. What holds these foundational elements together as elements of philosophical speculation is that they assume a natural order expressed by elements of classification. It is not the individual elements that propose an order to the world, but their fit with other elements.

> When he began his study of the classification of colours among the Hanunoo of the Philippines, Conklin was at first baffled by the apparent confusions and inconsistencies. These, however, disappeared when informants were asked to relate and contrast specimens instead of being asked to define isolated ones. There was a coherent system, but this could not be understood in terms of our own system which is founded on two axes : that of brightness (value) and that of intensity (chroma). All the obscurities disappeared when it became clear that the Hanunoo system also has two axes but different ones. They distinguish colours into relatively light and relatively dark and into those usual in fresh or succulent plants and those usual in dry or desiccated plants.
> (*ibid.*: 55)

Whether guided by scientific observation or a mythic imagination, classification is, for Lévi-Strauss, the key to understanding the fundamental rationality of human thought. His many works on myth suggest how classificatory schemes can serve as elementary philosophical schemata dealing with fundamental contradictions of existence and their mediations. Before the dawn of modern science, mythos is how humans cobbled together coherent understandings of their world using the materials they had at hand. Like theatrical rehearsal, myth-making for Lévi-Strauss is a kind of sense-making that imaginatively exploits the confluence of more-or-less random means and more-or-less rational ends.

In its reflections on this human quest for mediation in a world dominated by opposing forces of personal passion and social necessity, *A Midsummer Night's Dream* anticipates *The Savage Mind* by almost 350 years. Theseus' Athens, with its rigid adherence to a patriarchal legal code controlling human passions, would seem to represent the extreme vision of an ordered society. But it is a social order ruled by death. Athenian law has no place for human sentiment, empathy, or desire. Its equation of marriage, patriarchal power, violence, and death suggests the madness of total law-driven rationality. The usual antidote to over-reaching *logos* would seem to be a neutralizing dose of *myth*. And Shakespeare gives us plenty of *mythos* in the night world of the fairies, a fluid landscape of shape-shifting beings and unfettered feeling under the unstable dominion of love juice. But unconstrained fantasy is as dangerous as a world governed by pure rationality. Like Athens's court, the forest ultimately fails to provide the desired *discordia concors*, offering no viable resolution for the lovers.

That leaves just the theatrical world of the mechanicals. Here there would seem to be some hope of finding a proper order that might reconcile the conflicting demands of law and passion. The fact that all the actors are called "mechanicals," representing not only themselves but also their professions, suggests a basic template for social order, what sociologists call "the division of labor." In addition, their striking names suggest other dimensions of classification. The names Francis Flute, Tom Snout, Nick Bottom, Peter Quince, Snug the joiner, and Robin Starveling are grounded in a variety of classificatory domains: musical instruments (flute), fruit (quince), body parts (snout, bottom), directions (bottom), birds (robin), and isolated parts of speech (snug). The problem is that they are classificatory isolates, drawn from disparate domains. Together, they constitute a world of discrete singles with no common framework to bring them together as a whole. Through rehearsal, the mechanicals will struggle to make their parts into a collective whole in the form of a coherent drama.

The mechanicals have a long way to go in figuring out how theater works. Peter Quince's first job is to assign the actors their roles in the play. This task does not prove to be easy. Bottom wants to play all the roles, from top to bottom, anticipating Puck's shape-shifting and preparing the way for his own eventual grotesque translation. Reluctantly, Bottom settles for the part of Pyramus. Francis Flute balks at playing Thisbe, Pyramus' lover, in drag, claiming that he is too old to play the female parts. But he also comes to accept his part and will eventually grow into it. The players keep showing up in rehearsal, trying to embody their roles and learn their lines. Until the very last moment, all the mechanicals can manage is a parody of failed theater. The players mangle the play, forget their lines, mispronounce words, and fail to distinguish stage directions from their spoken parts. Unable to produce theatrical concord out of the script's unintegrated parts, the actors seem to be stuck outside the heart of the play. The play remains a pure externality, a dead script. Though the play is inherently tragic, the muddled production becomes unintentionally comic. The wedding guests can only laugh, not at the script as intended, but at the actors' ludicrous failure to credibly embody the play.

    This failure of the actors starts from the very opening lines of the play when Peter Quince opens the performance with a prologue whose phrasing is so unsteady as to humorously transform its meaning:

> If we offend, it is with our good will.
> That you should think we come not to offend
> But with good will.[6] To show our simple skill,
> That is the true beginning of our end.

(V, i, 8–11)

The noble audience finds only unintentional satire in the butchered reading. They are amused by Quince's failure to pay attention to the script's punctuation, a reading which leaves the script sounding like disordered words rather than meaningful speech.

THESEUS
This fellow does not stand upon points.

LYSANDER
He hath rid his prologue like a rough colt; he knows
not the stop. A good moral, my lord: it is not enough
to speak, but to speak true.

HIPPOLYTA
Indeed he hath played upon this prologue like a child
on a recorder: a sound but not in government.

THESEUS
His speech was like a tangled chain; nothing impaired,
but all disordered.

(V, i, 118–125)

Because the actors cannot enter into the script, the wall that blocks the audience from true engagement with the performance can never be breached, a failure which is repeatedly highlighted by the central role of Snout as the actor/wall separating the lovers in Pyramus *and Thisbe*. Rather than being internalized as a moving performance, the play has been fully externalized as script, props, and actors. This deconstruction of theater into its component externalities is a kind of anti-theater, the reverse of the normal flow of actors into characters and audience into participants. This externalization is best exemplified by the performance of Starveling as Moonshine. A terse paraphrase of the role replaces his performance of the man-in-the-moon:

MOONSHINE
This lanthorn doth the horned moon present;
Myself the man i' the moon do seem to be.

THESEUS
This is the greatest error of all the rest: the man
should be put into the lanthorn. How is it else the
man i' the moon?

DEMETRIUS
He dares not come there for the candle; for, you
see, it is already in snuff.

HIPPOLYTA
I am aweary of this moon: would he would change!

THESEUS
It appears, by his small light of discretion, that
he is in the wane; but yet, in courtesy, in all
reason, we must stay the time.

LYSANDER
Proceed, Moon.

MOONSHINE
All that I have to say, is, to tell you that the
lanthorn is the moon; I, the man in the moon; this
thorn-bush, my thorn-bush; and this dog, my dog.

DEMETRIUS
Why, all these should be in the lanthorn; for all
these are in the moon.

(V, i, 235–251)

As Demetrius notes, this man-in-the-moon is not a man who seems to be *in* the moon. The actor has failed to embody his role. This failure to bring either the actors or the audience into the play's imaginative space means that the audience, unable to suspend disbelief, is not experiencing the tragedy of the play but rather the comedy of its mis-performance. Their attention is not on the characters but on the actors as actors, not on the meaning of the dialogue but on the script's words, including stage directions. Were *A Midsummer Night's Dream* to conclude with this artistic travesty, our only choice would be to accept it as light comedy and throw up our hands in laughter. But even though the mechanicals do offer to conclude their performance with a satirical, rustic bergomask dance, the performance does not end in burlesque but in an unexpected moment of theatrical magic. At the very edge of disaster, the play suddenly catches fire as principals find their voices and fuse the script's pure externality with the pure internality of the actor's emotion.

Pyramus makes his final entry on the stage to discover Thisbe's blood-stained shawl. Assuming the lion has killed her, Pyramus bemoans the loss of his love.

> **PYRAMUS**
> But stay, O spite!
> But mark, poor knight,
> What dreadful dole is here!
> Eyes, do you see?
> How can it be?
> O dainty duck! O dear!
> Thy mantle good,
> What, stain'd with blood!
> Approach, ye Furies fell!
> O Fates, come, come,
> Cut thread and thrum;
> Quail, crush, conclude, and quell!
>
> (V, I, 265–276)

Skillfully delivered, this speech has a transformative effect on both audiences watching the performance. The change in Theseus and Hippolyta's engagement with the play is especially notable:

> **THESEUS**
> This passion, and the death of a dear friend, would
> go near to make a man look sad.
>
> **HIPPOLYTA**
> Beshrew my heart, but I pity the man.
>
> (V, i, 277–279)

True to the Aristotelian understanding of successful tragedy, the play begins to produce pity in the audience, sharing a profound sense of empathy with the character and action before them. The culminating moment comes when Thisbe enters the stage and, like Juliet, discovers her dead lover who, convinced that she was dead, has killed himself. Suddenly the script takes on new emotional and rhetorical power, shedding all signs of its comic estrangement. Thisbe slays herself while uttering the first truly heartfelt speech of the play.

Thisbe
Asleep, my love?
What, dead, my dove?
O Pyramus, arise!
Speak, speak. Quite dumb?
Dead, dead? A tomb
Must cover thy sweet eyes.
These My lips,
This cherry nose,
These yellow cowslip cheeks,
Are gone, are gone:
Lovers, make moan:
His eyes were green as leeks.
O Sisters Three,
Come, come to me,
With hands as pale as milk;
Lay them in gore,
Since you have shore
With shears his thread of silk.
Tongue, not a word:
Come, trusty sword;
Come, blade, my breast imbrue:
Stabs herself
And, farewell, friends;
Thus Thisby ends:
Adieu, adieu, adieu.
Dies

(V, i, 311–334)

Not all productions of *A Midsummer Night's Dream* take Shakespeare's cues from Theseus and Hippolyta's empathetic reactions or the sudden heat of the language. Some directors do not seem to note the theatrical magic that Shakespeare has hidden in the script. Whenever directors fail to notice what has happened, the play tends to end emotionally flat, reinforcing the impression of theatrical fluff. But the best productions make the magic clear, such as the scene's superb staging in Adrian Noble's eccentric 1995 Royal Shakespeare Company production, made into a captivating 1996 film. Perhaps most impressive is the brilliant performance by Sam Rockwell as Thisbe in Michael Hoffman's 1999 film version of *A Midsummer Night's Dream* where the Flute/Thisbe/Rockwell character throws off his wig at the height of his grief, revealing himself to be a man in drag, but a man convincingly and powerfully moved by the loss of his love. Such insightful performances of the play capture *A Midsummer Night's Dream*'s real magic, where theater momentarily takes hold of the audience and transforming slapstick into unexpected empathy as the actors move *into* the text, carrying the audience along with them.

In such insightful productions of *A Midsummer Night's Dream*, great acting rescues the tragedy and unexpectedly grips the audience, producing both aesthetic pleasure and credible emotion. The externality of script and stagecraft is wedded to emotional realism. The actors and the audience are momentarily carried away on a wave of theater magic. Upon entering the theater for the performance, Theseus ruminates on the unpredictable course of artistic imagination:

> And as imagination bodies forth
> The forms of things unknown, the poet's pen
> Turns them to shapes and gives to airy nothing
> A local habitation and a name.
> Such tricks hath strong imagination,
> That if it would but apprehend some joy,
> It comprehends some bringer of that joy;
> Or in the night, imagining some fear,
> How easy is a bush supposed a bear!

But it is Hippolyta's reply that recognizes the radical possibilities of social transfiguration inherent in the act of publicly recounting imaginative stories:

> But all the story of the night told over,
> And all their minds transfigured so together,
> More witnesseth than fancy's images
> And grows to something of great constancy

At the play's end, Bottom assures his audience that "the wall is down." Many walls have fallen: the one keeping Pyramus from Thisbe, the wall separating the actors from embodying their lines, the wall preventing the audience from emotional engagement with the play, and, at last, the wall separating love, sex, and marriage.

A theatrical resolution

The promised resolution to the conundrum of love and marriage was not to be found in devotion to law alone. Convincing theater cannot be reduced to its governing script without its convincing embodiment by the actors. But neither could the demands of love and marriage be reconciled in a world shaped by personal desire alone. Discarding the script in favor of pure improvisation will rarely produce convincing theater. Instead, Shakespeare points the way to an unexpected resolution of love and marriage in the idea of theatrical rehearsal. Learn your lines and stage directions well and keep rehearsing until the magic takes hold and you enter the text with full heart, transforming inert lines into living theater. Play *by* the rules, the play proposes until you can play *with* the rules. *A Midsummer Night's Dream* ends with the three couples' successful marriage. But the fourth successful marriage enacted in *A Midsummer Night's Dream* is the marriage of script and feeling, the marriage that makes possible all the others. The curtain falls before we can ever know whether the successful performance of a wedding can really turn into the successful performance of a marriage. We are left with the suggestion that rehearsal might be the key to marriage, just as it was to a wedding.

How seriously are we to take Shakespeare's fairy tale? Can rehearsal serve as a path to a resolution of love and marriage? Perhaps not, if love has to come first. In a love-match society that privileges internal authenticity over conventional forms, it may be hard for us to understand such an outside-in vision of love in marriage. William James understood it when he argued that much of our inner emotional life is shaped by our outward displays of feeling.

> Our natural way of thinking... is that the mental perception of some fact excites the mental affection called the emotion, and that this latter state of mind gives rise to the bodily expression. My thesis, on the contrary, is that *the bodily changes follow directly the perception of the exciting fact, and that our feeling of the same changes as they occur IS the emotion.* ...We feel sorry because we cry, angry because we strike, afraid because we tremble.
>
> (James 1890: 449, italics in the original)

Physical behavior—emotional gestures—he suggests, may actually precede feeling, rather than follow it. In this view, motion precedes emotion.[7] This notion of marriage as a continuous rehearsal of love is at the heart of the argument that matchmakers give for the superiority of arranged marriage. Love does not need to precede marriage, they insist. Let the carriage drive the horse, allowing love to develop gradually out of the daily performance of being married. Practice, not passion, makes perfect. A version of this argument recently appeared in *The Daily Mail* in London:

> They are seen by many as business deals that have little to do with love. But arranged marriages are far more likely to lead to lasting affection than marriages of passion, experts claim. According to research, those in arranged marriages – or who have had their partner chosen for them by a parent or matchmaker – tend to feel more in love as time grows, whereas those in regular marriages feel less in love over time. And within ten years, the connection felt by those in arranged marriages is said to be around twice as strong. Relationship experts claim this is because arranged matches are carefully considered, with thought going into whether potential partners' families, interests and life goals are compatible. This means they are more likely to commit for life – and to stick together through rocky patches.
>
> (Bentley 2020)

We know from other times and other places that the relation between performance and feeling may be credibly conceived in a different key than our own. After all, arranged marriages were common in Shakespeare's day. From a different cultural tradition, consider that the Japanese have a term *makoto* that means both "sincerity" and "faithfulness," by which they mean a role performed with such heart that the gap between the role and the player disappears. The outside, flawlessly performed, can bring the inside into alignment. A theatrical *concors* rescues an existential *discordia*.

The idea that acting is merely a simulation of life, such that living must precede acting, is a conventional understanding of theater. But Shakespeare often explored the possibility that the relationship might be reversed, that life itself was acting, a performance in continuous rehearsal. Jaques most famously articulates this performative vision of life, the idea that "all the world's a stage" in *As You Like It*. Shakespeare explores the relations between theater and life in many other plays. In *Richard II*, for instance, Richard contemplates his many roles as performances:

> Thus play I in one person many people,
> And none contented: sometimes am I king;
> Then treasons make me wish myself a beggar,
> And so I am: then crushing penury
> Persuades me I was better when a king;
> Then am I king'd again: and by and by
> Think that I am unking'd by Bolingbroke,
> And straight am nothing:
>
> (V, v, 31–38)

In *Henry IV, 1*, Falstaff helps prepare the young Prince for his future as King by putting on a "play extempore" where Falstaff plays Hal's father, and young Hal plays himself being examined by the King. Here the theatrical idiom is explicitly a kind of rehearsal for kingship. In Chapter 1, we have seen how *Hamlet* deals with the theme of acting versus being, throwing into question the idea that acting merely mirrors life rather than constituting it.

A theatrical conception of human action as ongoing rehearsal has been developed in modern times in performance theory. Perhaps the most influential thinker who pursued the idea of social interaction as a kind of acting is the sociologist Erving Goffman who, influenced by George Herbert Mead's notion of the "social self," developed a conception of the self that was an ongoing creation of social interaction where self and other cooperate in the creation of an individual's public face, what Goffman calls "a line" (Goffman 1959, 1982). Social life is in continuous dress rehearsal for one's staging of a self. In Goffman's theater of the self, it is rehearsal all the way down. Influenced by Goffman, theater director and scholar Richard Schechner sees in the idea of rehearsal a kind of "restored behavior," repeatable behavioral scripts central to all human performance from stage drama, dance, ritual, and the interactions in the theater of everyday social life. For Schechner, performance and rehearsal are not discrete attempts to imitate life, but the process of continual creation and restoration of life by trying on new roles and masks, revising the idea of who one is. In personal terms, restored behavior is "me behaving as if I am someone else" or "as if I am 'beside myself,' or 'not myself,'" as when in a trance. But this "someone else" may also be "me in another state of feeling/being," as if there were multiple "me's" in each person.

> The difference between performing myself—acting out a dream, reexperiencing a childhood trauma, showing you what I did yesterday—and more formal "presentations of self" (see Goffman 1959)—is a difference of degree, not kind. There is also a continuum linking the ways of presenting the self to the ways of presenting others: acting in dramas, dances, and rituals. The same can be said for "social actions" and "cultural performances": events whose origins can't be located in individuals, if they can be located at all. These events when acted out are linked in a feedback loop with the actions of individuals.
>
> (Schechner 1985: 37–38)

Schechner surveys the variety of performance types in human societies and suggests that the close relation between theater and religious ritual throws into question the modern assumption that performance is always understood as imitation rather than as becoming. He provides a vivid account of a Native American deer dance he watched performed by a Yaqui dancer in Arizona. The description comes remarkably close to the kinds of blurred lines between acting and being that Shakespeare proposes in his vision of Bottom's "translation" into an ass:

> While watching the deer dance of the Arizona Yaqui in November 1981, I wondered whether the figure I saw was a man and a deer simultaneously . . . ; or, to say it in a way a performer might understand , whether putting on the deer mask made the man "not a man" and "not a deer" but somewhere in between. The top of his head (man's/deer's), with its horns and deer mask is a deer; the bottom of his head below the white cloth, with its man's eyes, nose, and mouth, is a man. The white cloth the dancer keeps adjusting is the physicalization of the impossibility of a complete transformation into the deer. At the moments when the dancer is "not himself" and yet "not not himself," his own identity, and that of the deer, is locatable only in the liminal areas of "characterization," "representation," "imitation," "transportation" and "transformation" . . . . All these words say that performers really can't say who they are. Unique among animals, humans carry and express multiple and ambivalent identities simultaneously.
>
> (*ibid.*: 4)

"How," wonders Theseus, reading the advertisement of the plot for the performance of *Pyramus and Thisbe*, "shall we find the concord of this discord" (V, i, 48)? The question of *discordia concors*, finding harmony in opposition, weaves its way through *A Midsummer Night's Dream*.[8] It is as relevant to the problem of staging believable theater as it is to the resolution of love and marriage. In theater, a script with all of its rhetorical and staging constraints (an externality) must be brought into a workable relationship with a set of actors who are charged with infusing it with credible life and passion (an internality). Similarly, a successful marriage must reconcile the external legal and political demands of family and society with the bride and groom's emotional and sensual impulses. Little wonder that perfect theatrical productions and perfect marriages are so elusive.

In *A Midsummer Night's Dream*, Shakespeare proposes rehearsal as a common resolution to both dilemmas, using the mechanicals' struggles to mount *Pyramus and Thisbe* as its model. But as a seasoned director and playwright, Shakespeare knew that rehearsal does not guarantee a successful performance. No amount of rehearsal could assure the players that the hobbled production of *Pyramus and Thisbe* would eventually blossom into living theater. *Discordia concors*, when it works at all, is, by its paradoxical nature, a struggle, not a formula. In itself this is to say, something of a miracle. This is why Shakespeare's theatrical tour of Fairyland, written to marry a performance *at* a wedding with a performance *of* a wedding, has been so often staged but so rarely realized.

Notes

1 This chapter was originally presented as a lecture in honor of Prof. Benson Saler delivered in the Anthropology Department at Brandeis University on Valentine's Day, 2008.
2 http://www.screenit.com/movies/1999/william_shakespeares_a_midsummer_nights_dream.html
3 Murdock, G. P., and D. White, "Standard Cross-Cultural Sample," *Ethnology* 8:329–369, 1969.
4 For classic works on attachment theory, see Bowlby 1969, 1988, Ainsworth 1967, 1968 Harlow 1961.
5 The notion of *discordia concors* can be traced back to the pre-Socratic Greek philosophers Pythagoras, Heraclitus, and Empedocles. It refers to a harmony won out of discord, but this harmony is not produced despite the discord but because of the initial discord. In its original Greek formulation, *concordia discord* referred to a harmony in the world born of the discord between the four primary elements of air, earth, fire, water. The idea that the eventual concord requires an initial discord is central to Shakespeare's understanding of the role of rehearsal in *The Midsummer Night's Dream*.
6 "Good will" here is a likely ironic reference to the ironic hand of the playwright. The pun is conventional in Shakespeare's work.
7 I am grateful to Rudolph Makkreel for suggesting this wonderful phrase to me.
8 On the relation of the Neoplatonist question of *discordia concors* to *A Midsummer Night's Dream* see Brown, Jane, "*Discordia Concors:* On the Order of *A Midsummer Night's Dream, Modern Language Quarterly,* v. 48, no. 1, pp. 20–41, 1987.

7

THE BODY POLITIC, THE BODY POETIC

Julius Caesar and legacy of "The King's Two Bodies"

Shakespeare's interest in ideas grew from his insights into the intractable dilemmas into which people, great and ordinary, might be led. Ideas were not abstractions to him. They were part of life, implicit in conflicting desires, circumstances, and interpretations. Shakespeare did not occupy himself with the formulaic resolution of those dilemmas since his imagination was stirred by great questions rather than tidy answers. In every sense, Shakespeare's plays are works of wonder. This celebration of life's paradoxes and contradictions has led some critics to charge him with moral weakness and indecision (Platt 2009). However, it is not a moral or intellectual defect that fired up Shakespeare's imagination but the interest in human dilemmas in real-time (or, more accurately, stage-time). Anthropologists would say that Shakespeare favored "experience-near" evocations of human problems.

In his own time, Shakespeare was not alone in this close-up perspective on ideas. Chapter 2 discussed the two distinct rhetorical traditions that emerged in Elizabethan theater, one didactic and moralistic, the other, evident in more radical playwrights like Kyd and Marlowe, more open and explorative. Temperamentally, Shakespeare was drawn to explorative drama, not despite, but because of its ambiguities (Altman 1978). Explorative theater grows out of a tradition of discourse featuring the casual-wear of story-telling rather than the formal attire of didactic philosophy. The narrative tradition of philosophy, associated with Plato and Socrates, made its arguments through stories exploring moral dilemmas and other intellectual puzzles, stories that juxtaposed conflicting characters and viewpoints. Often these stories offer no simple resolution to the discord, leaving the untidy and unresolved debate for audiences to contemplate. Rather than alienating the audience, this unfinished business tends to lure people back to the plays for another look. Shakespeare's theoretical untidiness underlies his enduring popularity.

This chapter explores some of this unfinished business in Shakespeare's tragedy *Julius Caesar*. While the play's ambiguities are most evident in Shakespeare's

DOI: 10.4324/9781003179771-10

handling of character and motive, we will move beyond the focus on the play's dramatis personae to examine how uncertainties about character and motive in Caesar's murder can be seen as an entryway to a more expansive landscape of ideas. More than a tragedy of flawed character, *Julius Caesar* is an example of social theory staged amid civil unrest, the story of a society at war with itself, at war over loyalty to Caesar, over loyalty to the Roman Republic, and finally, over the very nature of society itself. As a work about a city caught between incompatible conceptions of itself, *Julius Caesar* deserves a place among the world's most engaging works of social thought. Only *Hamlet*, written just after *Julius Caesar*, challenges the Roman drama in its exposition of life's ambiguities.

Viewers and critics have puzzled over *Julius Caesar's* equivocations, debating the identity of its hero and whether this tragedy can be said to have a hero at all.[1] In her 1966 article "The Complexity of *Julius Caesar*," Mildred Hartsock nicely sums up the interpretive challenges of *Julius Caesar*:

> From the eighteenth century to the present, editors, critics, and directors have recognized special problems in the interpretation of Shakespeare's *Julius Caesar*. Every major play has been extensively debated, to be sure, but discussions of this play have been marked by an unusual perplexity. There is little agreement about the most elementary elements of interpretation. Is Caesar a dangerous dictator–a genuine threat to Rome; or is he the "noblest man / That ever lived in the tide of times," as Antony says he is?' Is Brutus the mistaken idealist, strong in abstract principle but weak in human perceptive-ness; or is he, as Swinburne thought, the "very noblest figure of a typical and ideal republican in all the literature of the world"? Is he the Aristotelian hero, noble but flawed, recognizing at last that he has erred? Or is he the willful egoist, embodying the very traits of Caesarism which he professes to hate?
>
> (Hartsock 1966: 56)

The play's title suggests that its leading man is Caesar, whom Elizabethans were taught to view as a Roman superhero, a mythic figure approaching the status of a god. Yet in Shakespeare's account, Caesar is given remarkably little stage time, speaking a mere 43 lines compared with Brutus' 194 (or Hamlet's 1569!). Killed off less than halfway through the play, Caesar returns briefly to the stage only as a ghostly apparition. Still, the play's title would seem to nominate Caesar as its star. And Shakespeare is far from kind in his depiction of his assassins. But ultimately, Shakespeare remains uncommitted, making a case both for and against Caesar, just as he does for Brutus. Each is viewed through a prism, diffracting them into contending images of virtue and weakness. In the long history of critical commentary on *Julius Caesar*, the Brutus and Caesar readings have each had their champions. The play's first two acts keep shifting perspective, attracting both sympathy and antipathy for the play's main characters. Underlying this question of the play's hero lies an even more fundamental problem: evaluating the conspirators' motives. Do we celebrate Caesar's assassination as a defense of republicanism or denounce it as treachery? Whom does Shakespeare intend us to see as the "good guys" and the "bad guys?" He clearly finds the conspirators' motives suspect, saving some of his most caustic irony in depicting them. However, Caesar fares no better than his conspirators and is equally viewed with suspicion.

To appreciate the enigma, we only need to examine Shakespeare's portrayals of Brutus and Caesar. Initially, Brutus' motives seem honorable enough as he agonizes about whether to join in the conspiracy against Caesar. He had been Caesar's close friend, the beneficiary of Caesar's generosity. Brutus was even rumored to be Caesar's illegitimate son. But Brutus is troubled by Caesar's arrogance and fears that Caesar is about to allow himself to be crowned Emperor by the Senate, effectively turning the Roman republic into an autocratic monarchy. Characteristically, he ends up siding with principle rather than friendship. Brutus' speech is solemn and carefully measured, verging at times on bombast. It betrays both nobility of mind and a generous measure of self-righteous pride, a pride that Cassius exploits to his advantage. Though a well-respected urban praetor before the assassination (thanks to Caesar's appointment), Brutus shows himself to be not only principled but also naïve, indecisive, and a poor judge of character. Shakespeare's Brutus is initially of two minds about Caesar. As he himself puts it, he is "with himself at war" (I, ii, 52). Despite his apparent flaws, Brutus' noble intentions, concern for the republic and love of Caesar all seem heartfelt, attracting audience sympathy over the centuries. But even at his best, Brutus makes for a compromised hero. Acceding to Cassius' arguments to join an assassination plot against a close friend and an indisputably great general, Brutus falls in with the conspirators because of what he fears Caesar might do, rather than anything that Caesar has actually done.

> And for my part
> I know no personal cause to spurn at him,
> But for the general. He would be crowned:
> How that might change his nature, there's the question.
> It is the bright day that brings forth the adder,
> And that craves wary walking. Crown him that,
> And then I grant we put a sting in him
> That at his will he may do danger with.
>
> (II, ii, 10–17)

Characteristically, Brutus frames his intentions in abstract terms inflated by flowery language. Attracted more to principle than to people, his understanding of others is often surprisingly shallow. "If it be aught toward the general good," he assures Cassius, in a voice reminiscent of textbook oratory:

> Set honor in one eye and death i' th' other
> And I will look on both indifferently;

> For let the gods so speed me as I love
> The name of honor more than I fear death.
>
> (I, ii, 92–96)

The obsession with honor upstages Brutus' more humane virtues. It will be rhetorically turned back against him later in the play in Antony's famous speech. In his self-consciously stoic self-presentation, he comes off as too cerebral, self-consumed, and emotionally remote. Brutus' coolness extends to his treatment of his wife. At the start of Act II, Portia appeals to her husband's sense of compassion and marital faith in attempting to get Brutus to confess to her what has been troubling him.

> Within the bond of marriage, tell me, Brutus,
> Is it excepted I should know no secrets
> That appertain to you? Am I your self
> But, as it were, in sort or limitation,
> To keep with you at meals, comfort your bed,
> And talk to you sometimes?

"Dwell I" she asks her husband, "but in the suburbs/Of your good pleasure?" (I, ii, 303–309). Upon hearing Messala's report of Portia's gruesome suicide (she swallows burning coals!), Brutus' reaction is muted, and he ends up using the announcement of Portia's death more to magnify himself rather than to mourn his dead wife:[2]

MESSALA
Then like a Roman bear the truth I tell,
For certain she is dead, and by strange manner.

BRUTUS
Why, farewell, Portia. We must die, Messala.
With meditating that she must die once,
I have the patience to endure it now.
Even so great men great losses should endure.

> (IV, iii, 216–221)

Does Brutus' *sang froid* suggest a stoic response to too much suffering or self-centered detachment? It is hard to tell.[3]

Shakespeare's unsteady portrait of Brutus would seem to leave Caesar as the presumptive star of the show. But Caesar's heroic credentials as the play's leading man are no more convincing than Brutus'. Not only is Caesar eliminated from the play early on, but Shakespeare's portrait of Caesar is drawn too close for comfort. Like Brutus, Caesar is fond of referring to himself in the third person. Caesar attempts to present himself as a title rather than a man, a transcendent figure distinct from the human Julius: "I rather tell thee what is to be feared /Than what I fear" Caesar tells Antony, "for always I am Caesar" (I, ii, 221–222). This is language deployed to turn a man into a god. If Shakespeare's Brutus is too pompous to cast as a god, Caesar is too frail. His next words undercut any illusion of impending divinity: "Come on my right hand, for this ear is deaf," he bids Antony, "And tell me truly what thou think'st of him" (223–224). However great the title and the reputation that accompanies it, the man himself is fragile, grown weak with the infirmities of age and subject to epilepsy, what Elizabethans called "the falling sickness." Even as Casca recounts to Brutus and Cassius the scene he witnessed of Caesar refusing the crown offered to him by Antony, the image of Caesar's power is immediately undercut by the description of physical frailty:

CASCA
And then he offered it the third time. He put it the
third time by, and still as he refused it the rabblement
hooted and clapped their chopped hands and
threw up their sweaty nightcaps and uttered such a
deal of stinking breath because Caesar refused the
crown that it had almost choked Caesar, for he
swooned and fell down at it. And for mine own part,
I durst not laugh for fear of opening my lips and
receiving the bad air.

CASSIUS
But soft, I pray you. What, did Caesar swoon?

CASCA
He fell down in the marketplace and foamed at
mouth and was speechless.

BRUTUS
'Tis very like; he hath the falling sickness.

(I, ii, 253–265)

In the second scene of Act I, Cassius seeks to convince Brutus to join the conspirators in assassinating Caesar. But his argument does not focus so much on Caesar's misdeeds or his abuse of power, as on Julius' physical weaknesses as an ordinary mortal puffed up by divine pretensions:

CASSIUS
I was born free as Caesar; so were you;
We both have fed as well, and we can both
Endure the winter's cold as well as he.
For once, upon a raw and gusty day,
The troubled Tiber chafing with her shores,
Caesar said to me "Dar'st thou, Cassius, now

Leap in with me into this angry flood
And swim to yonder point?" Upon the word,
Accoutered as I was, I plungèd in
And bade him follow; so indeed he did.
The torrent roared, and we did buffet it
With lusty sinews, throwing it aside
And stemming it with hearts of controversy.
But ere we could arrive the point proposed,
Caesar cried "Help me, Cassius, or I sink!"
I, as Aeneas, our great ancestor,
Did from the flames of Troy upon his shoulder
The old Anchises bear, so from the waves of Tiber
Did I the tired Caesar. And this man
Is now become a god, and Cassius is
A wretched creature and must bend his body

(I, ii, 104–124)

Shadowed by his frailties, Caesar never appears as the hero we had expected. In Act II, scene ii, his wife Calphurnia tries to convince Caesar to cancel his trip to the Senate House, fearful that the comets and other strange apparitions that have been reported are omens of Caesar's impending death. Caesar's initial response is fierce defiance of the omens:

Caesar shall forth. The things that threatened me
Ne'er looked but on my back. When they shall see
The face of Caesar, they are vanishèd.

(II, ii, 10–12)

As Calphurnia continues to press him with her fears, Caesar's arrogance turns into fatalism:

CAESAR
What can be avoided
Whose end is purposed by the mighty gods?
Yet Caesar shall go forth, for these predictions
Are to the world in general as to Caesar.

CALPHURNIA
When beggars die there are no comets seen;
The heavens themselves blaze forth the death of princes.

CAESAR
Cowards die many times before their deaths;
The valiant never taste of death but once.

Of all the wonders that I yet have heard,
It seems to me most strange that men should fear,
Seeing that death, a necessary end,
Will come when it will come.

(II, ii, 27–39)

At last, Calphurnia seems to prevail, and Caesar decides not to proceed to the Senate House. He makes a feeble attempt to mask his fear by insisting that the decision comes from his iron will.

CAESAR

And you are come in very happy time
To bear my greeting to the Senators
And tell them that I will not come today.
Cannot is false, and that I dare not, falser.
I will not come today. Tell them so, Decius.

CALPHURNIA

Say he is sick.

CAESAR

Shall Caesar send a lie?
Have I in conquest stretched mine arm so far,
To be afeard to tell graybeards the truth?
Decius, go tell them Caesar will not come.

DECIUS

Most mighty Caesar, let me know some cause,
Lest I be laughed at when I tell them so.

CAESAR

The cause is in my will. I will not come.
That is enough to satisfy the Senate.
But for your private satisfaction,
Because I love you, I will let you know.
Calphurnia here, my wife, stays me at home

(II, ii, 65–80)

But Caesar changes his mind once again, making his fatal decision to proceed to the Senate House. In his characterization of Caesar, Shakespeare has painted a portrait combining vacillation, frailty, and pomposity, matching the ambivalent portrayal of Brutus.

While early critics often defended either the Brutus or the Caesar reading of the play, modern criticism has been more willing to accept the play's equivocations on their own terms. One of the earliest modern scholars to have proposed that *Julius Caesar*'s ambiguities are at the heart of the play is Ernest Schanzer, a mid-century critic who focused on Shakespeare's "problem plays." Reviewing the history of the play's interpretation, Schanzer notes the tendency of critics to support either the Brutus or the Caesar reading of the play. To these interpretive orientations, he proposes a third reading, arguing that:

> Fortunately for the less resolute spirits there is a third tradition in relation to which the play may be viewed, made up of writers whose reaction to Caesar and the conspiracy is not simple and undivided . . . but of a complex and sometimes bafflingly contradictory nature.
>
> (Schanzer 1955: 298)

Schanzer sees Shakespeare as intentionally taking the audience down one interpretive path only to reverse course and wander into another, disrupting the viewers' certainty of the meaning of what they are seeing and creating a moral quandary. This is the same kind of dislocation of interpretation that Shakespeare would further refine in *Hamlet*, as we shall see in Chapter 9.

Tyrannicide

While Shakespeare's fascination with moral dilemmas would probably have been enough to discourage him from taking sides in the plot to assassinate Caesar, there were also political considerations predisposing him to keep to the middle of the road. In staging Caesar's assassination, Shakespeare was stepping into the heart of what was known as the "tyrannicide debate" over the right of a private citizen to kill a tyrannical leader. Renaissance thinkers had inherited this idea from classical and medieval philosophers and theologians. It shaped political discourse about kingship among European scholars and theologians for almost two thousand years.[4] "Tyrant" derives from the Greek word *tyrannos* (τύραννος), originally meaning "monarch" or "leader of a polis." A tyrant came to refer to an absolute ruler believed to have seized power illegitimately or who exercised power cruelly or unjustly. Tyrannicide is the assassination of this darker sort of tyrant. The earliest use of the term "tyrannicide" can be traced back to Harmodius and Aristogeiton concerning the killing of Hipparchus of Athens in 514 BC. Hipparchus was one of the last Greek leaders to call himself a "tyrant," before the term took on its current negative association. Killing a tyrant would seem to be uncontroversial. But killing a king, even a bad one, created some profound dilemmas and generated political and philosophical disagreement for two millennia.[5]

Early Greek writers approved of tyrannicide by private citizens in the case of a ruler who had usurped power and whose rule thus lacked legitimacy (*tvirannus ex endefectu tituli*). This tradition of supporting the assassination of usurping tyrants continued through the medieval period (Jászi and Lewis 1957:7). For Plato, a tyrant was the worst kind of ruler. But neither Plato nor Aristotle stressed the illegitimate path to power as the defining aspect of tyranny, focusing instead on the abuse of that power in cruel and selfish governance. So in Greek philosophy, the term came to imply less about the legal status of the tyrant's rule than his abuse of power. While Aristotle strongly disapproved of tyrants, he was also skeptical of those committing tyrannicide, noting that the practice generally attracted people whose motives were more selfish than civic. From its early use in Greek political discourse, the issue of tyrannicide was clouded over by ambiguity, questions of definition, and interpretation. The meaning of tyranny was up for debate, including the criteria for determining the legitimacy of rule and what constitutes misrule. One man's tyrant was another man's hero.[6] So from the outset, the issue of tyrannicide provoked disagreement. Those defending the right of subjects to resist tyrannical power commonly invoked Cicero's defense of Caesar's assassination, which had an enduring influence on the debates. With obvious allusion to the assassination of Caesar, Cicero wrote:

> What can be a greater crime than to kill a man, especially one who is an intimate friend? Is he a criminal who has killed the tyrant, even if the tyrant was his friend? It does not seem so to the Roman people, who regarded this as the finest of all glorious deeds.
>
> (Jászi and Lewis 1957: 10)

His comments, widely quoted in later centuries, became texts for those who sought to enlist the authority of classical tradition in their struggle against arbitrary rule.

By the Renaissance, the tyrannicide debate had become even more complicated. Caesar's assassination still had a special place in the debate, but by this time, Caesar's status as a tyrant was seen as much more problematical than Roman leaders like Caligula or Nero, whose outrageous abuses of power were universally acknowledged. In other words, Julius Caesar's assassination had become the decisive case in arguments both for and against tyrannicide. Seizing absolute power, while contrary to republican ideals, was not by itself convincing evidence of tyranny. After all, what constituted "seizing power" was far from clear even in the Roman Republic. A Roman leader could lawfully be appointed temporary "dictator" in troubled times, so even Caesar's anticipated crowning could be justified by his supporters as a natural extension of his dictator status. Caesar had already been appointed to a dictatorship in 49 BC, a position which he had held for only 11 days. He had been reappointed to another temporary dictatorship for the year 48/47 BC. In 46 BC, he was made dictator for the next ten years, and in February of 44 BC, this appointment was changed to *dictator perpetuo*, dictator for life, a position Caesar held at the time of his assassination in March of the same year. Was this legitimate authority or not? Furthermore, it had become evident that these Senatorial appointments were a prologue to Caesar's elevation to divine status as *Divus Iulius*, a Roman conception of divine kingship that anticipated the "the divine right of Kings" in Shakespeare's England (Weinstock 1971).

Caesar's status as a military hero was beyond dispute. His victories in the Gallic Wars, which ended in 51 BC, extended the Roman Empire beyond the Rhine and across the English Channel to Britain. So impressive were his conquests that they cast a shadow on the military reputation of Caesar's rival and son-in-law Pompey. Pompey and Caesar (along with Marcus Licinius Crassus) had formed the three-way military alliance in 60 BC that became known as The First Triumvirate, triggering a civil war whose conclusion at the Battle of Pharsalus in 48 BC marked the end of Pompey's power (and eventually, as an exile in Egypt, the end of his life). These are the historical events that set the stage for the opening scene of Shakespeare's play. So the question of whether Caesar's death was tyrannicide or regicide was inevitably going to be a matter of opinion, open to being construed as political expediency dictated.

By the 16th century, the tyrannicide debate had become inextricably tied up with Reformation politics. As much a political as a theological revolution, the Reformation sought to undo the Roman Catholic claims of universal authority embodied in the Pope. As John Neville Figges put it in his 1907 Birbeck Lectures at Cambridge: "The imaginative vision of the Middle Ages could see but one state worthy of the name upon earth, the Civitas Dei. Everything else, including the rights of kings is mere detail and has but a utilitarian basis." (Figges 2012: 19). The political revolution accompanying the theological reformation required rethinking power relations in Europe and a new emphasis on Europe as a collection of autonomously governed states. According to Figges, this European political reformation, no longer conceived under Rome's dominion, was at once a revolutionary and a conservative vision. It looked back to the Middle Ages for its model of religious authority, but also forward to the modern nation-state.

> So far as the Reformation helped to produce the compact, omni-competent, territorial, bureaucratic state, so far as it directly or indirectly attended to individual liberty, it must be regarded as modern in its results. But so far as it tended to revive theocratic ideals, theological politics, and appeals to Scripture in regard to the form of Government, it was a reversion to the ideals of the earlier Middle Ages, which were largely disappearing under the combined influence of Aristotle and the Renaissance.
>
> (*ibid.*: 24)

During the Reformation, the divergent political and theological views inevitably confronted the thorny issues inherent in the tyrannicide debate. Luther disapproved of tyrannicide, even as he preached resistance to the religious authority of Rome. Despite his status as a church reformer, Luther's views of political resistance to a prince were notably conservative.

> Luther rejected the doctrine of tyrannicide not only by inference but very explicitly. He acknowledged that the Greeks, the Romans, and even the Jews had held tyrannicide praiseworthy. But, he said, one should not ask what the heathens or Jews had done, but rather what was right and permissible. Resistance to authority was not permissible. If a prince did not allow the true

gospel to be preached and practiced, Christian subjects should move to a land where it was allowed.

(Jászi and Lewis 1957: 20–21)

Calvin also supported submission to the prince's authority, asserting the wickedness of rebellion against constituted authority, even in cases where authority was abused. In this rejection of rebellion, Calvin supported what Figges called "the merest commonplace of the time." (Figges op. cit.:55). But not every Reformation voice saw tyrannicide as an act of insubordination. Support for tyrannicide came from the radical Monarchomach branch of Calvinism among the French Huguenots and other contrarians who became known as "resistance theorists." These included the Scottish historian and humanist George Buchanan and his fiery compatriot John Knox, who was the founder of the Presbyterian Church. These dissenting voices did not merely condone resistance to tyrannical rule but saw such resistance as obedience to God rather than any kind of insubordination.

In Shakespeare's England, the tyrannicide debate inevitably wrestled with the question of the subject's right to resist oppressive royal authority. In this context, arguing for the right of tyrannicide could not avoid clashing with the Tudor doctrine of the king's divine right to rule. Public acceptance of absolute royal power was central to the Tudor project of state creation throughout the 16th century. The first obstacle to this concept was the Roman Church's universalist claim of hegemony, and the King's entailed subordination to Papal authority. Underlying the conflict between the Roman papacy and the English throne that came to a head in Henry VIII's reign lay the more general claims of the primacy of secular (state) power over ecclesiastical (church) authority, claims extending beyond England.

> By the end of the fifteenth century, consolidated national monarchies of varying degrees of stability had been established in England, Spain, and France. The kingship of this period had obviously become something very different from the medieval kingship. The suppression of feudal restraints and the active role which the king began to assume in the promotion and protection of industry and trade are obvious signs of developing absolutism. Further important characteristic of the new monarchy was the increasing efficiency of a permanent royal bureaucracy. And finally, as evidence of royal power, we find the subjugation of the church itself to the demands of national policy.
>
> (Jászi and Lewis: 43)

Having asserted the preeminence of state power over ecclesiastical authority by the 1536 parliamentary law titled "An Act Extinguishing the authority of the bishop of Rome," Henry VIII was faced with a dilemma. His rebellion against the Pope's authority could be construed more generally as subjects' right to resist their sovereign when they felt oppressed by his rule. The solution was to maintain the claim of absolute authority but shift it from the Church to the State. The sovereign's power could be seen as coming directly from God, bypassing ecclesiastical authority. Under the establishment of Henry's new Church "The divine right of Popes" became "the divine right of Kings," who were now understood as head of both State and Church. In England, John Neville Figges argues, kings' divine right was not a matter of explicit political doctrine but asserted as self-evident truth underlying the subject's duty of submission and obedience.

> The doctrine of the religious duty of political obedience as expounded and believed under Henry VIII and Elizabeth, involved no theory of monarchy in especial and no theory of the origin and nature of political authority. It was only out of discussion of the nature of political authority and obligation that any theory of the divine right of kings could possibly arrive. But in England ... under Henry VIII the question was barely touched upon.
>
> (Figges 2012: 121)

By Shakespeare's time, most English subjects took for granted their monarchs' divine right to rule. But the divine right of the King to *absolute* rule had become controversial. The defense of tyrannicide had become so influential that it could not be ignored.

Not only did the right of resistance implied by tyrannicide have the vocal support of the Monarchomach wing of the reformation, but in Scotland, John Knox and John Buchanan were publishing influential treatises proposing a divine right of resistance to unjust rule as a counterweight to the divine right of kings. "Resistance Theory" carried the weight of classic writers like Plato, Aristotle, and Cicero and also had the more qualified support of influential medieval scholars like John of Salisbury in *Polycraticus* and Thomas Aquinas in his commentary on *The Sentences of Peter Lombard* and his 1267 treatise *De Regno* (On Kingship) (Wyllie 2018:154–160). With the idea of significant limitations on royal power up for public debate, the principle of absolute submission to the Crown needed more explicit justification.

Was the King, after all, to be thought of as a man or a god? In 1598, just a year before Shakespeare wrote *Julius Caesar*, King James VI of Scotland (who would become James I of England upon Elizabeth's death) published a treatise titled *The True Law of Free Monarchies*, setting forth the principles underwriting the absolute rule of the Monarch and his effective ownership of his realm and his subjects. The treatise begins with a sonnet, comparing the subject's obligation to obey his King to the King's obligation to follow God's precepts in ruling:

> GOD giues not Kings the stile of Gods in vaine,
> For on his Throne his Scepter doe they swey:
> And as their subiects
> ought them to obey,
> So Kings should
> feare and serue their God againe

If then ye would enioy a
happie raigne,
Obserue the Statutes of your heauenly King,
And from his Law, make all your Lawes to spring:

"Kings are called Gods by the propheticall King Dauid," James asserts, "because they sit vpon GOD his Throne in the earth, and haue the count of their administration to giue vnto him." (4.2) In the same section, James asserts that a subject's role is not to pass judgment on whether any sovereign acts might be considered acts of tyranny. With the tyrannicide debate clearly on his mind, he writes:

[W]hat liberty can broiling spirits, and rebellious minds claime iustly to against any Christian Monarchie since they can claime to no greater libertie on their part, nor the people of God might haue done, and no greater tyranny was euer executed by any Prince or tyrant, whom they can obiect, nor was here fore-warned to the people of God, (and yet all rebellion countermanded vnto them) if tyrannizing ouer mens persons, sonnes, daughters and seruants; redacting noble houses, and men, and women of noble blood, to slauish and seruile offices; and extortion, and spoile of their lands and goods to the princes owne priuate vse and commoditie, and of his courteours, and seruants, may be called a tyrannie ?

James argues that, while obliged to govern in God's place according to God's precepts, the King effectively owns his subjects and wields absolute power over them and their property. James continued to assert these claims after assuming the English throne in 1603. Ironically, despite these extreme claims of divine right by its King, Scotland had never accepted the idea of absolute monarchy, viewing the monarch as a *primes inter pares*, "the equal" of his subjects. These beliefs notwithstanding, James still insisted that, as King, he was effectively God on earth and not subject to questioning or any form of resistance by his subjects, no matter how he ruled.

In choosing to write about Caesar's death, Shakespeare could not avoid the politically sensitive tangle of the tyrannicide debate. Not only did he have to deal with the historical complexity of interpreting both the conspiracy and the actors' motives, but he had to consider the current political implications of any position he took on the assassination. In 1599, staging the assassination of Caesar was no casual matter. The Court was sure to take a keen interest in the representation of royal power on the stage. Any stage production or even the printing of a play required a government license from the Master of the Revels (and de facto government censor), Edmund Tylney, who carefully studied theatrical scripts for evidence of heresy or sedition. The only choices left to a playwright were a clear denunciation of the Roman conspiracy or leaving the matter ambiguous. Presumably, out of both intellectual predisposition and political pragmatism, Shakespeare chose ambiguity over advocacy.

Suicide

One of the great ironies surrounding *Julius Caesar* is its reputation as a play about murder. Other than the assassination of Caesar, who is quickly dispatched in Act III, murder does not figure prominently in the play. True enough, most of the main characters die in *Julius Caesar*, but their deaths are all suicides. Could it be that *Julius Caesar* was conceived as a tragedy, not about murder, but suicide? Might the play's real theme be a great society on the brink of self-destruction? Once we view the play from this perspective, we know the identity of the play's tragic hero and Shakespeare's perspective on Caesar's killing. While Brutus, Cassius, and Portia all die by their own hand, the play's ultimate tragic hero is Rome itself. Self-destruction is everywhere in *Julius Caesar*. We can see this pattern in both the opening and the conclusion of the play. The play opens amid a holiday celebration, but it turns out that the celebration is for Caesar's defeat of Pompey at the battle of Pharsalus. The tribune Marullus chides the workingmen who have gathered to celebrate Caesar's triumphant return:

MARULLUS
Wherefore rejoice? What conquest brings he home?
What tributaries follow him to Rome
To grace in captive bonds his chariot wheels?
You blocks, you stones, you worse than senseless things!
O you hard hearts, you cruel men of Rome,
Knew you not Pompey? Many a time and oft
Have you climbed up to walls and battlements,
To towers and windows, yea, to chimney tops,
Your infants in your arms, and there have sat
The livelong day, with patient expectation,
To see great Pompey pass the streets of Rome.
And when you saw his chariot but appear,
Have you not made an universal shout,
That Tiber trembled underneath her banks
To hear the replication of your sounds
Made in her concave shores?
And do you now put on your best attire?
And do you now cull out a holiday?
And do you now strew flowers in his way
That comes in triumph over Pompey's blood?
Be gone! Run to your houses, fall upon your knees,
Pray to the gods to intermit the plague
That needs must light on this ingratitude.

(I, i, 36–60)

The play opens on a Rome in disarray. The populace is dressed for celebration while their tribunes tell them they should be mourning. Here is a mighty Rome, mightily disordered. It is a world unable to distinguish a hero from a villain, a win from a loss, a friend from a foe. Moreover, the signs of the workers' professions that signal the economic basis of the local social order are missing. For example, in Act I, scene i Marcella asks the Carpenter "Where is thy leather apron and thy rule?" (line 7), suggesting through double-entendre the link between a clear division of labor in society and proper governance.[7]

Confusion is everywhere, including in their over-burdened words. Puns spill in all directions, confusing communication between the commoners and tribunes. The chaos begins to take shape when it becomes apparent that the war, whose conclusion the commoners are supposed to celebrate/mourn, is a civil war, pitting Roman against Roman and father-in-law (Caesar) against son-in-law (Pompey). Celebrating victory in a civil war is a paradox masquerading as a triumph. Winners are indistinguishable from losers. Caesar's defeat of his daughter's husband may celebrate a victory against his military rival, but it is equally the story of a family turned against itself. Caesar's triumph over his daughter's husband is also the potential end of Caesar's legitimate bloodline. So we can understand why the play shifts in scene ii from a victory celebration to the Lupercal festival, a Roman fertility ritual marshaled to help Caesar's barren wife Calphurnia produce offspring.

This inability to distinguish friend and foe is ubiquitous in *Julius Caesar* and is central to both its opening scene and its tragic conclusion. In Act V, scene iii, Cassius and Titinius attempt to gauge the outcome of the battle between the armies of Brutus and Antony, but from their vantage point cannot tell the good guys from the bad ones.

CASSIUS
Go, Pindarus, get higher on that hill.
My sight was ever thick. Regard Titinius
And tell me what thou not'st about the field.
This day I breathèd first. Time is come round,
And where I did begin, there shall I end;
My life is run his compass.—Sirrah, what news?

PINDARUS
O my lord!

CASSIUS
What news?

PINDARUS
Titinius is enclosèd round about
With horsemen that make to him on the spur,
Yet he spurs on. Now they are almost on him.
Now Titinius! Now some light. O, he lights too.
He's ta'en. And hark, they shout for joy.

(V, iii, 21–37)

By the time the audience learns that Cassius and Titinius had misinterpreted the battle's outcome and that Brutus had defeated Antony's army, it is too late. Believing their cause had failed, Cassius dies at the hand of Pindarus, just as Brutus will die in scene v at the hand of Strato. But their deaths are a form of suicide where an individual kills himself using another's hand. It is a civil war in miniature.

The king's two bodies

Julius Caesar comes to us from Roman history by way of Plutarch. However, Shakespeare's treatment of Caesar's murder was also shaped by current political and theological issues in late 16th-century England. One issue was the legal status of royal power in relation to the doctrine of divine right. Rather than simply relying on a taken-for-granted acceptance of the idea of divine right, jurists were attempting to formulate an explicit doctrine of sovereign power consistent with the need to solidify the identity and sovereignty of the English state. One of the most significant doctrines supporting this project emerged from a legal dispute involving Queen Elizabeth early in her reign. The theory, now known as "The King's Two Bodies," is the subject of a well-known 1957 study of medieval political theology by Ernst Kantorowicz. He traces the medieval roots of a legalistic conception of royal power articulated by Elizabethan lawyer and political theorist Sir. Edmund Plowden (see Chapter 2 for a further discussion of this).

In 1577, Plowden published in French a collection of legal cases gathered in a volume titled *Les Commentaries ou Reports de Edmund Plowden*.[8] One of these cases involved a dispute involving Queen Elizabeth over control of the Duchy of Lancaster, which arose in the third year of her reign. The Lancastrian kings had owned the Duchy as their private property, not as a Crown holding. Elizabeth sought to invalidate the 21-year lease established by her half-brother Edward VI of the Duchy of Lancaster to an individual because the young King had granted the lease before he had come of age. The Court decided to uphold the legality of the lease, despite the age of the King. The legal opinion emphasized the principle that a King inherently possesses dual personhood conceived as "the body natural" and "the body politic." This doctrine, stressing the Monarch's double personhood, attempted to work out specific issues stemming from the doctrine of a king's divine right. As a matter of political theory, the doctrine acknowledged the mortal and humanly fallible "body natural" of royalty but only insofar as it is understood as a necessary vessel for executing the transcendent, eternal, and infallible powers of the royal office. The doctrine proclaimed that royal power was lodged in the blood and soul—the "body mystical"—of the legitimate titleholder. The doctrine recognized that the sovereign might hold some possessions as a private person (i.e., in his "less ample" body natural) while others were owned by the royal office (i.e., in his "more ample" body politic). The two-bodies doctrine, symbolized in royal discourse by the monarch's use of "the royal we," was also useful for clarifying the transfer of sovereignty upon the incumbent's death or abdication. According to the doctrine, the transfer of sovereignty involved the "migration of the soul" of the monarch to a legitimate successor, guaranteeing continuity of royal power. The transcendent aspect of royalty—the royal soul—never dies and is the conceptual basis of succession. The notion of two-bodies underwrites the traditional proclamation "The King is dead, long live the King."[9]

The double character of kingship has great relevance for *Julius Caesar* as it illuminates contending conceptions of Roman society conceived as a "body politic." Shakespeare's recounting of Caesar's assassination might well have been titled "Rome's Two Bodies." If the play's real tragic hero is indeed Rome, it is, in Shakespeare's vision, a city that is (to borrow Brutus' phrase) "at war with itself," portraying clashing models of how to conceive of a society in Shakespeare's shape-shifting portrait of Rome. This double representation of Rome as a body politic was Shakespeare's literary idiom for social theory, his vision of alternative ways of conceiving society. His interest in modeling society places Shakespeare in the company of some of the influential social theorists of modern times.

Models of society: Maine, Durkheim, Tönnies, and Dumont

The most basic job of social theory is to propose general models that clarify the institutions and processes on which human society is based. Social theories are theories of human connection, and the history of social thought is a procession of such influential models. These models never picture actual societies. Max Weber called such abstract models "ideal types," simplifications of actual societies that shed light on actual societies' salient characteristics or the direction of change within a single society. Many of the most significant social models were developed in the 19th century under the influence of evolutionary thought and are framed as historical phases or stages of social evolution. In this section I will outline a few of these classic theories to illuminate how Shakespeare anticipates modern social theory as he portrays Roman society in *Julius Caesar*.

For Sir Henry Maine (1822–1888), the key distinction was between traditional societies based on "status" and more modern societies based on "contract" (Maine 1861). In Maine's theory, ancient societies bound individuals tightly to traditional groups based on inherent statuses such as family, residence, age, or gender. According to Maine, such societies were organized by "ascribed status," offering relatively little mobility for individuals and little choice over their associations. By contrast, in modern societies, ascribed status is replaced mainly by voluntarily contractual relations between individuals and groups. Here individuals are seen as autonomous agents, acting out of self-interest. A social evolutionist, Maine, assumes that the direction of development of progressive societies in his time involves the shift in emphasis from status to contract (Graveson 1941).

Writing a generation after Maine, French sociologist Emile Durkheim (1858–1917) focuses on the nature of "social solidarity," meaning the "glue" that holds a society together. Durkheim distinguishes between the solidarity of small-scale societies held together by what he termed "mechanical solidarity" and that of large-scale, complex societies, where the division of labor produces a necessary interdependence, which he termed "organic solidarity" (Durkheim 1893/1997). Mechanical solidarity is "cultural" solidarity based on shared concepts, experiences, values, and social representations. Sharing these representations, members are assumed to be like each other. Organic solidarity, produced by the division of labor, defines an economically based "external" solidarity. Based on people's economic interdependence, organic solidarity unites people not by their similarities but through their differences. Solidarity shifts from a subjective to an objective fact, from a shared world of representations to a shared-in world of interdependent roles. In complex societies characterized by organic solidarity, people are linked through practical needs and contractual relations.

A similar distinction was made by German sociologist Ferdinand Tönnies (1855–1936) between societies based on a Gemeinschaft (community) model and a Gesellschaft (society) model (Tönnies 1887/1955). Much like Durkheim's societies based on "mechanical solidarity," a Gemeinschaft is a community emerging from common family ties, collective values, and shared sentiments. It is marked by a "unity of will," comparable to Durkheim's collective social representations. In contrast, a Gesellschaft is based on depersonalized, instrumental ties based on self-interest, where family ties are secondary to impersonal relationships mediated by economic interests. Gesellschaft is essentially a market-model of society in which the common interest is understood only as an emergent property of the interaction of individual interests.

A more recent contribution to social theory comes from French anthropologist Louis Dumont, who emphasizes contrasting models of social organization in contemporary civilizations (Dumont 1970, 1986). Nonetheless, Dumont's tendency to describe Western individualism as a "modern" ideology and his historical treatment of the gradual emergence of individualism in Western thought suggests that Dumont's typology also has evolutionary roots. Dumont distinguishes between two different meanings of the term "individual." The empirical individual, the single person, is found in every human society. But the ideological individual, the conceptual basis of modern individualist ideology, has a particular history and only emerges in European thought starting in the Renaissance.

Dumont seeks to make sense of Indian hierarchy by focusing on the cultural assumptions about inequality that underlie the caste system. In contrast to Western (often unrealized) ideals of social equality and personal liberty, Indian society is more "holistic," recognizing hierarchy as an ideal model of ordered social relations. For Dumont, these ideological differences produce two distinct kinds of society, calling for different sociologies with contrasting assumptions.

> [W]e have to recall that there are two kinds of sociology distinguished by their starting point and their global approach. In the first kind, one begins, as is natural for modern scholars, by positing individual human beings, who are then seen as living in society; sometimes one even attempts to show society as arising from the interaction of individuals. In the other kind of sociology, one starts from the fact that men are social beings, that is, one takes society

as a global fact irreducible to its parts–and here it is not a matter of "Society" in the abstract but always of a particular, concrete society with all its specific institutions and representations. Since one speaks of methodological individualism in the first case, one might speak of methodological holism in the second. In fact, every time we confront a foreign society the holistic approach is called for, and the ethnologist or anthropologist cannot do without it: he will only be able to communicate with the people he wants to study when he has mastered the language they have in common, for that is the vehicle of their ideas and values, of the ideology through which they think of everything, including themselves.

(Dumont 1986: 1–2)

Dumont sometimes contrasts Indian and Western models of society using an old scholastic distinction between *universitas* and *societas*. *Universitas* represents a form of social holism in which the society is understood to precede and encompass the individual, who, in an important sense, does not exist except through social relationships. By contrast, *societas*, the individualist model, sees the individual with private interests and desires as preceding and engaging with rather than embedded in the society. The modern individual participates in society contingently, through a social contract entered into voluntarily. Dumont's models are distinctive in focusing on the importance of cultural values and ideology in their origin. Nonetheless, they bear close kinship with the classic theoretical distinctions described above.

Shakespeare's depiction of social relation in Rome

Long before the 19th century and its theories of social evolution, Elizabethans had inherited a metaphorical vocabulary for conceptualizing society from classical philosophy that captivated the political imagination in Europe for 1500 years. Most influential was Plato's use of the body metaphor in his *Politics*. His conception of the *polis* as a "body politic" was repeated by Aristotle in his *Politics*, where he uses the metaphor to provide the classic articulation of what Louis Dumont meant by a "holistic" society:

We may now proceed to add that [though the individual and the family are prior in the order of time] the polis is prior in the order of nature to the family and the individual. The reason for this is that the whole is necessarily prior in nature to the part. If the whole body be destroyed, there will not be a foot or hand except in that ambiguous sense in which one uses the same word to indicate a different thing, as when one speaks of a 'hand' made of stone. ; for a hand, when destroyed [by the destruction of the whole body] will be no better than a stone' hand'. All things derive their essential character from their function and their capacity; and it follows if they are no longer fit to discharge their function, we ought not to say that they are the same things, but only that, by an ambiguity, they still have the same names.

We thus see that the Polis exists by nature, and that it is prior to the individual . . . . Not being self-sufficient when they are isolated, all individuals are
so many parts equally depending on the whole [which alone can bring about
self-sufficiency]. The man who is isolated – who is unable to share in the
benefits of political association, or has no need to share because he is already
self-sufficient – is no part of the polis and must be either a beast or a god.

(Aristotle 1952 I, ii: 12–14)

In Aristotle's *polis*, there are no (ideological) "individuals" in Dumont's sense of
the modern term. People are, by nature, social beings. Their primary identities are
defined through their relationships and their institutional affiliations. This organic
vision of society as a political body became a key metaphor for political and religious hierarchy throughout the middle ages (Nederman, Green, and Mews 2005).
Borrowing from Plutarch's letter to Trajan, John of Salisbury developed the corporate metaphor in his political treatise *Polycraticus*:

[A] republic is, just as Plutarch declares, a sort of body which is animated by
the grant of divine reward and which is driven by the command of the highest equity and rule by a sort of rational management . . . . The position of the
head in the republic is occupied, however, by a prince subject only to God
and to those who act in His place on earth, inasmuch as in the human body
the head is stimulated and ruled by the soul. The place of the heart is occupied
by the senate, from which proceeds the beginning of good and bad works.
The duties of the ears, eyes, and mouth are claimed by the judges and gover-
nors of provinces. The hands coincide with officials and soldiers. Those who
always assist the prince are comparable to the flanks. Treasurers and record
keepers (I speak not of those who supervise prisoners, but of the counts of
the Exchequer) resemble the shape of the stomach and intestines; these, if they
accumulate with great avidity and tenaciously preserve their accumulation,
engender innumerable and incurable diseases so that their infection threatens to ruin the whole body. Furthermore, the feet coincide with peasants
perpetually bound to the soil, for whom it is all the more necessary that the
head take precautions, in that they more often meet with accidents while they
walk on the earth in bodily subservience; and those who erect, sustain and
move forward the mass of the whole body are justly owed shelter and support.
Remove from the fittest body the aid of the feet; it does not proceed under its
own power, but either crawls shamefully, uselessly and offensively on its hands
or else is moved with assistance of brute animals.

(John of Salisbury 1990: 65)

This organic image of the polity as a "body politic" is not merely a metaphor. As
Dumont has shown, it represents an implicit theory of society, a *universitas* model
of holistic association in which the whole body of society precedes and defines
the individual who is understood as a part of the whole. This model of political

association has no legitimate place for notions of individual liberty or self-interest. While the metaphor is not a description of an actual society, the body politic is a conceptual model of an ideal society.

Shakespeare exploits the body politic metaphor throughout *Julius Caesar* but distorts its traditional symbolism and throws its conventional meaning into question. The first reference to the city as a body comes in the second scene of Act 1, but it is buried in a metaphoric double entendre. As the scene opens, the city is celebrating the Feast of Lupercal, an ancient pre-Roman fertility rite where several young men act as priests (known as Luperci, "brothers of the wolf"), responsible for sacrificing a goat and a dog. The Luperci run a circuit around the old boundary of the Palatine hill, the highest of Rome's seven hills. As they run, the Luperci whip barren women with leather thongs called *februa*, conveying fertility on the women. In this running of the Lupercal circuit, Mark Antony is one of the runners. Caesar, desperate for an heir, urges his wife Calphurnia to take advantage of the opportunity to get whipped. Shakespeare's word for the race circuit is "course," a word whose evocation of "corpse" figures throughout the play. In this case, Shakespeare exploits a triple reference in which the meanings of "course," "corpse," and "curse" overlap in a disharmonic chord that grotesquely plays with the body politic image. In their sacred race, Shakespeare represents the Luperci circling the heart of the city.

In Act II, scene i, the wordplay resurfaces as the conspirators plan the assassination. Cassius and Brutus are debating whether to kill Caesar's supporter Mark Antony along with Cesar. Cassius wants Antony eliminated:

DECIUS
Shall no man else be touched, but only Caesar?

CASSIUS
Decius, well urged. I think it is not meet
Mark Antony, so well beloved of Caesar,
Should outlive Caesar. We shall find of him
A shrewd contriver; and, you know, his means,
If he improve them, may well stretch so far
As to annoy us all; which to prevent,
Let Antony and Caesar fall together.

BRUTUS
Our course will seem too bloody, Caius Cassius,
To cut the head off and then hack the limbs,
Like wrath in death and envy afterwards;
For Antony is but a limb of Caesar.
Let's be sacrificers, but not butchers, Caius.
We all stand up against the spirit of Caesar,
And in the spirit of men there is no blood.

(II, I, 167–181)

The body politic is evoked by Brutus, not to suggest a sacred political whole, but as an object of dismemberment. The association of "corpse" with a dead body becomes apparent. In an important passage to which we shall return, Brutus asks that the hacking of Caesar's body be construed as a sacrifice rather than as butchery.

In Act III, following the assassination, the ritual act of "circling the course" that opened the play is metaphorically repeated, but with a gruesome twist. Following Caesar's assassination, Antony invokes the same double entendre when he asks the commoners to circle the body of Caesar before as a prelude to his reading of Caesar's will:

> **ANTONY**
> You will compel me, then, to read the will?
> Then make a ring about the corpse of Caesar,
> And let me show you him that made the will.
> I descend? And will you give me leave?
>
> (III, i, 169–172)

Relying on the body-politic notion, medieval political theory stressed the "corporate" nature of social-political units such as the family, the Church, or the State. Shakespeare marshals imagery of "incorporation" in several places in *Julius Caesar*. In Act I, scene ii, Cassius uses the image of a body grown too big in his response to Caesar's being offered the crown by the Senate.

> **BRUTUS**
> Another general shout!
> I do believe that these applauses are
> For some new honors that are heaped on Caesar.
>
> **CASSIUS**
> Why, man, he doth bestride the narrow world
> Like a Colossus, and we petty men
> Walk under his huge legs and peep about
> To find ourselves dishonorable graves.
>
> (I, i, 139–145)

Later in the same speech, Cassius looks into the history of Rome for a legitimate precedent and finds none:

> When went there by age, since the great flood,
> When it was famed with more than with one man?
> When could they say, til now, that talked of Rome,
> That her wide walks encompassed but one man?
>
> (I, ii, 151–4)

For Cassius, the apotheosis of Caesar means the end of the Roman republic. The old body-politic imagery is discredited, evoking only the usurpation of power. There can be no legitimate monarch for Rome. At issue is not the legitimate succession to the throne as in most of Shakespeare's political dramas, but rather the throne's very existence as a threat to a republic of free citizens. Gradually, the imagery of incorporation is being infused with the rhetoric of self-interest. Rome no longer knows itself as a single social body. This tragic confusion of models is the most basic sense in which Shakespeare's Rome is at war with itself. In Act II, scene i, the corporal metaphor is inverted. Brutus, agonizing over his decision to participate in the killing of Caesar, represents his inner conflicts as "Like to a little kingdom" broken by civil war:

BRUTUS
Since Cassius first did whet me against Caesar,
I have not slept.
Between the acting of a dreadful thing
And the first motion, all the interim is
Like a phantasma or a hideous dream.
The genius and the mortal instruments
Are then in council, and the state of man,
Like to a little kingdom, suffers then
The nature of an insurrection.

(II, i, 65–72)

Later in the same scene, the incorporation metaphor appears again in a speech by Brutus' wife Portia, as she invokes the nature of their marital bond in trying to convince Brutus to reveal what is troubling him.

PORTIA
You have some sick offense within your mind,
Which by the right and virtue of my place
I ought to know of. And upon my knees
I charm you, by my once commended beauty,
By all your vows of love, and that great vow
Which did incorporate and make us one,
That you unfold to me, your self, your half,
Why you are heavy, and what men tonight
Have had resort to you; for here have been
Some six or seven who did hide their faces
Even from darkness.

BRUTUS
Kneel not, gentle Portia.

PORTIA

I should not need, if you were gentle Brutus.
Within the bond of marriage, tell me, Brutus,
Is it excepted I should know no secrets
That appertain to you? Am I your self
But, as it were, in sort or limitation,
To keep with you at meals, comfort your bed,
And talk to you sometimes? Dwell I but in the suburbs
Of your good pleasure? If it be no more,
Portia is Brutus' harlot, not his wife.

(II, i, 288–310)

Portia uses an urban variation of the *polis* metaphor to characterize her marriage to Brutus, underscoring the resonance of the body-politic image with Rome's city. And, as a microcosm of the burning city, Portia kills herself by swallowing fire.

Many of the relationships in *Julius Caesar* which are described in the metaphoric idiom of a universitas world are compromised by images of war, internal conflict, and even dismemberment. Lacking the clearly articulated dichotomies of the Victorian theorists, Shakespeare opts to manipulate the traditional rhetoric of social holism to picture its unraveling. In Portia's plea in the speech above, she distinguishes between being Brutus' wife and his harlot. In the conventional Elizabethan view of marriage, a wife and a husband form a relationship based on the mystical incorporation of two into one. But a harlot's relationship is with a customer, based on a mutual negotiation of self-interest rather than on any common interest, and is a purely commercial transaction. Metaphors suggesting holism gradually give way to images of fragmentation. A discourse of commerce and self-interest overlays the language of incorporation, suggesting an emerging societas model of social relations. Through the power of Shakespeare's word-magic is born a poetics of social theory. "[H]onour," says Cassius, as he works to persuade Brutus to join the conspiracy,

is the subject of my story.
I cannot tell what you and other men
Think of this life, but for my single self
I had as lief not be as live to be
In awe of such a thing as myself.
I was born free as Caesar, so were you;

(I, ii, 92–97)

"A single self" has a distinctly modern ring. It is not a part of anything, but apart from everything. In the discourse of political holism, the term "part" suggests the sort of interdependence of social relations emphasized in Aristotle's organic view of the polis, where parts cannot legitimately exist outside the whole. But in Shakespeare's hands, the word "part" turns on itself and comes to suggest the self-interest by which individuals are separated from one another. So it is no coincidence that "part" appears in the text of the play 18 times, with numerous additional variants on the word. In six of those 18 cases, the conspirators use the word in variations of the phrase "For mine own part," where it specifies action motivated by self-interest. The play ends on the downbeat, punctuated by a final ironic use of "part." Having defeated Brutus and Cassius' armies and avenged Caesar's murder, Octavius, Caesar's nephew and heir, and Antony, Caesar's loyal friend, are informed of Brutus' suicide. Antony eloquently praises Brutus in a famous speech:

ANTONY
This was the noblest Roman of them all.
All the conspirators save only he
Did that they did in envy of great Caesar.
He only in a general honest thought
And common good to all made one of them.
His life was gentle and the elements
So mixed in him that nature might stand up
And say to all the world "This was a man."

(V, v, 74–81)

Antony's eloquent eulogy sounds to my ears like an apt concluding speech for a conventional tragedy. But Shakespeare gives the play's final words to Octavius, whose words have the feeling of an afterthought, a clear downbeat to Antony's uplifting eulogy.

OCTAVIUS
According to his virtue, let us use him
With all respect and rites of burial.
Within my tent his bones tonight shall lie,
Most like a soldier, ordered honorably.
So call the field to rest, and let's away
To part the glories of this happy day.

(V, v, 82–87)

The effect is jarring, particularly Octavius' ambiguous and ominous use of "part," which should provoke a double-take from any careful reader.

In Roman history, the victors, Octavius (who became Augustus Caesar), Mark Antony, and Marcus Lepidus, formed a new government known as The Second Triumvirate, which turned out to be no more stable than the First Triumvirate. Under the Second Triumvirate, the Empire was divided into what was supposed to be three parts: the eastern provinces were controlled by Antony and the Western provinces by Octavius. Lepidus was by far the weakest of the three and was promised control of Africa, but he came into conflict with Octavius, who accused him of fomenting discord and rebellion. Lepidus was eventually removed from power.

The Triumvirate was beset by competing ambitions and jealousies of the Triumvirs, eventually leading to a war between Octavius and Mark Antony, who had fled to Egypt. Antony's double suicide with Cleopatra left Octavius (soon to rename himself Augustus) as the first Emperor of Rome. [10]

Ritual inversion[11]

The doctrine of the King's Two Bodies splits the monarch down the middle, dividing a sacred, spiritual persona from a secular self. As a divinely appointed monarch, the ruler represents the whole of the kingdom and defines the nation's collective interest. As a secular being, the titleholder is understood as an individual with human frailties and private interests like everyone else. The two bodies doctrine proposed a division in the monarch, much like the distinction between the universitas and societas models of the *polis*. While the holistic and individualistic models of society were intended to characterize two different societies or two stages in the historical evolution of a society, the two-bodies model locates the sacred and secular dimensions within the same person and proposes a paradoxical conception of the King, a person at war with himself.

Sixteenth-century England was a society in the throes of social and cultural change, looking at once backward to a powerful medieval legacy of social, political, and religious ideas, and forward to an emerging early modern commercial society with increasingly secular interests and values. Both the universitas and societas models were in contention for people's understanding of themselves and their relationships.[12] When Shakespeare characterizes Rome as a society beset by civil war, he is thinking as much about the internal contradictions of his own society as he is about Roman history. It is not just a conflict between individuals or armies that engages Shakespeare's attention in *Julius Caesar*. In this context, it is not unreasonable to consider the body politic of Rome as the true tragic hero in the play.

Shakespeare uses ritual in *Julius Caesar* as a powerful idiom for exposing the contradictions between these models of society and personhood.[13] Rather than directly invoking alternative models, he shows how contradictory models can coexist by ritually inverting and ritually undoing the holistic vision of Rome. Brutus is intent on convincing himself and his fellow conspirators that their actions are honorable, based not on personal jealousy or self-interest, but on noble, disinterested ideals of preserving the Republic. He therefore proposes a ritual handshake by which the conspirators seal their pact and render it sacred.

> **BRUTUS** (coming forward)
> Give me your hands all over, one by one.
>
> **CASSIUS**
> And let us swear our resolution.

(II, I, 23–24)

But in Elizabethan English, the word "resolution" meant both "solidarity" and "dissolution," in which case this ritual moment enacts simultaneously the coming together and coming apart of the conspirators as a group. The ritual undoes itself in the acting. After the murder, this ritual of solidarity is repeated, but this time the conspirators collectively wash their hands in Caesar's blood.

CASSIUS

Stoop then, and wash. How many ages hence
Shall this our lofty scene be acted over
In states unborn and accents yet unknown!

BRUTUS

How many times shall Caesar bleed in sport,
That now on Pompey's basis lies along
No worthier than the dust!

CASSIUS

So oft as that shall be,
So often shall the knot of us be called
The men that gave their country liberty.

(III, i, 123–132)

The noble intentions of the rite are inscribed in the "lofty" eloquence of the language. But the meaning of the ritual is again undercut by Cassius' ambiguous reference to the conspirators as "the knot (not) of us," a double reference that simultaneously asserts and unravels the bond uniting them. Shakespeare skillfully deploys "self-consuming metaphors" (see Chapters 8 and 9).

The most obvious reference to ritual in *Julius Caesar* comes in the debate between Cassius and Brutus about whether to kill Antony along with Caesar. Brutus couches his argument against killing Antony in the metaphorical idiom of political holism, invoking the body politic. Consistent with that model, he urges his fellow conspirators to view the assassination as a sacrifice rather than as butchery. The conflict between sacred and secular readings of the act could not be more clearly delineated.

BRUTUS

Our course will seem too bloody, Caius Cassius,
To cut the head off and then hack the limbs,
Like wrath in death and envy afterwards;
For Antony is but a limb of Caesar.
Let's be sacrificers, but not butchers, Caius.
We all stand up against the spirit of Caesar,
And in the spirit of men there is no blood.
O, that we then could come by Caesar's spirit
And not dismember Caesar! But, alas,

> Caesar must bleed for it. And, gentle friends,
> Let's kill him boldly, but not wrathfully.
> Let's carve him as a dish fit for the gods,
> Not hew him as a carcass fit for hounds.
>
> (II, i, 175–187)

Whether to view the assassination as sacrifice or butchery is a memorable meta-phoric evocation of the underlying conflict troubling both the assassins' motives and the vision of their society. The line between sacrifice and butchery is fearfully thin.

The issue reemerges following the murder, as Brutus and Antony address Rome's citizens, each attempting to sway the mob to its side. The speeches are delivered in the marketplace, an ambiguous space that is both a sacred site of political oratory and a secular center of commerce. The irony intensifies when Antony gets his turn to speak and effectively purchases the crowd's support by reading Caesar's will, where he bequeaths 75 drachmas to each Roman citizen. The discrediting of the ritual is clear in the double meaning of "utter" in Elizabethan English, which means both "to speak" and "to offer up for sale." Exploiting this double meaning, Cassius had warned Brutus of the dangers of letting Antony speak.

CASSIUS
> Brutus, a word with you.
> You know not what you do. Do not consent
> That Antony speak in his funeral.
> Know you how much the people may be moved
> By that which he will utter?
>
> (III, I, 255–259)

While Antony purchases the crowd's support, Brutus appeals to the mob's ability to reason subtly about a complex act, asking them to "split hairs," so to speak. As usual, his language is high-minded, an attempt to model honor in the contours of his speech, but his words suggest something entirely different. Brutus is not content to split just hairs. The crowd cannot follow this kind of subtle reasoning, but what they do hear is Brutus verbally dismembering Caesar. Brutus recounts his motives for Caesar's murder in a parody of subtle legal reasoning, syntactically hacking Caesar to pieces. Once again, the ritual inverts itself, revealing what it is supposed to deny, as seen in the extract below. The relevant lines here have been italicized.

BRUTUS
> Romans, countrymen, and lovers, hear me for my
> cause, and be silent that you may hear. Believe me
> for mine honor, and have respect to mine honor
> that you may believe. Censure me in your wisdom,
> and awake your senses that you may the better

judge. If there be any in this assembly, any dear
friend of Caesar's, to him I say that Brutus' love
to Caesar was no less than his. If then that friend
demand why Brutus rose against Caesar, this is my
answer: *not that I loved Caesar less, but that I loved*
Rome more. Had you rather Caesar were living, and
die all slaves, than that Caesar were dead, to live all
freemen? *As Caesar loved me, I weep for him. As he*
was fortunate, I rejoice at it. As he was valiant, I
honor him. But, as he was ambitious, I slew him.
There is tears for his love, joy for his fortune, honor
for his valor, and death for his ambition.

(III, ii, 14–31)

While Antony divides up Caesar's cash estate, Brutus concentrates on carving up Caesar himself. In the process, Brutus unwittingly answers the question as to whether the murder was better conceived as sacrifice or butchery.

Conclusion

Elizabethan jurists formulated the doctrine of the King's Two Bodies to deal with a specific issue linking English property law and political theory. As it involved the rights of ownership by English monarchs Edward VI and Elizabeth I over royal lands, it inevitably involved an explicit reformulation of the English monarch's legal identity. While it may have resolved a specific legal issue related to the Duchy of Lancaster, the notion of the monarch's dual personhood also brought forward a paradoxical vision of the state as both a sacred whole, encompassing a sacred body politic (a universitas model), and a secular federation of self-interested individuals. The secular state anticipates the "market model" of the modern societas state, an atomistic revision of the *polis*, constituted through individuals' voluntary contracts.

It is conventional to see the Tudor era as a turning point in English political history, signaling the transition from an essentially medieval society to an early modern state. In this view, an older hierarchical conception of the polis, which we have characterized as a universitas, began to give way to a secularized model of society in which the importance of self-interest was openly acknowledged. From this perspective on English history, Shakespeare's reading of Caesar's murder is at once his reading of Plutarch's Rome and his meditation on his own society in which a profound historical shift emerged in how Elizabethans understood their society.[14] Our analysis of the play in light of the concept of the King's two bodies paints a broader picture than usual of the play's thematic terrain. But it also suggests that the time is ripe for a widening of our vision, not only of *Julius Caesar*'s significance as a play but of Shakespeare as a social theorist.

Notes

1 For a good discussion of the long-standing debates about the hero of *Julius Caesar*, see Daniel 1998.

2 Commentators often note that Brutus acknowledges Portia's death some 60 lines earlier in the scene. The double revelation of Portia's death is either an author's error, an editorial mistake, or else a strong suggestion of Brutus' distracted state of mind and his state of denial of Portia's suicide.

3 A.D. Nuttal, in his study of the philosophical dimensions of Shakespeare's plays, *Shakespeare the Thinker*, views Brutus' response to the news of Portia's death as a forgivable consequence of his stoicism, revealing at least as much to admire in Brutus as to condemn:

> [A] messenger arrives and tells Brutus – what? – that his wife has just died. Brutus behaves as if he were hearing the news for the first time and puts up a tremendous show of serene acceptance. The messenger is duly impressed: "Even so great men great losses should endure" (IV.3.193). We who know that Brutus was informed in advance of the bad news may be tempted to say, "You fraud!." But Cassius, who knows all, says, "I have as much of this in art as you,/But yet my nature could not bear it so" (IV.3.194–195). I think this means, "I am as good as you are at artificial performance, but I haven't got your sheer guts." He notes the artifice and, vividly aware as he is of the courage Brutus is showing in the midst of terrible grief, has no difficulty in forgiving it. Cassius loves Brutus even more than Brutus loves Brutus. But Brutus evidently loved Portia. His love for his wife and his grief at her death, "affections" Brutus is proud to be able to repress, actually redeem him as a human being."
>
> (Nuttall 2007: 184–185)

This is clearly a more generous account of both Brutus and Cassius than I am proposing here. I think a close reading of Shakespeare's portrayal of Brutus suggests a less heroic and more qualified evaluation of Brutus' character. In any case, these contrasting readings surely speak to the subtlety and the equivocation in Shakespeare's portrayal of his Roman "heroes."

4 Not all Elizabethan playwrights were as equivocal as Shakespeare about Caesar's murder. In 1607 William Alexander published his play *Julius Caesar* in London, portraying Caesar as a tyrant *ex parte exercita* ("in execution"), as opposed to merely *ex defectu tituli* ("through usurpation"). This version of Caesar's assassination poses no interpretive dilemma, clearly supporting the murder as a righteous act of tyrannicide. See Lovascio 2016.

5 For good discussions of the history of these debates, see Jászi and Lewis 1957, Daniel 1998: 29–38. and Clarke 198.

6 It is telling that John Wilkes Booth, Abraham Lincoln's assassin, considered Lincoln to be a tyrant and saw his act as an instance of tyrannicide.

7 We noted in the last chapter that Shakespeare uses a similar metaphor for disorder in *A Midsummer Night's Dream*, where the rag-tag troupe of amateur actors is made up of "mechanicals" whose crafts and names produce incoherent sets, an incoherence resonating perfectly with their inability to put together a coherent theatrical performance.

8 The full title of Plowden's book is *Les Commentaries, ou, Les Reportes de Divers Cases en les Temps des Raignes le Roy Ed. le size, le Roigne Mary, le Roy & Roigne Philip & Mary, & le Roigne Elizabeth*.

9 When I first taught *Julius Caesar* to Samoan high school students during my Peace Corps stint in Western Samoa in the late 1960s, the students had no problem grasping

Shakespeare's understanding of the distinction between Julius and Caesar. Traditional Samoan political culture has its own version of the "two bodies" distinction in relation to chiefs, who can each be formally referred to with the dual pronouns 'oulua (you two), distinguishing the transcendent dignity (afio) of the title from the persona of the titleholder.

10 For the history of the Triumvirate, see Eck 2002 and Eder 2005.

11 For an influential essay on the use of ritual in *Julius Caesar*, see Stirling 1956.

12 On emerging forms of self-awareness in Shakespeare's time, see Trilling 1973, Greenblatt 2005.

13 On the significance of contradictory cultural models within a society see Shore 1996, Chapters 11–12.

14 While I am arguing that *Julius Caesar* represents Shakespeare's response to a historical change in the English understanding of society, there is another possible way of framing my argument. The publication in 1978 of *The Origins of English Individualism* by Cambridge anthropologist Alan MacFarlane throws the medieval/early modern binary into question for English history and proposes a different picture. MacFarlane is a social anthropologist interested in comparative family structure and property rights, especially in the origins of individualism. His early work focused on the English family in the context of European society. MacFarlane's thesis is that England represents an exception to the widely held idea that the modern individual emerged around the late 16th century with incipient industrialization and the growth of capitalism. In this view, individualism was absent in the middle ages, where people were tied to family-based communal land, property, and labor systems. But MacFarlane finds evidence of English individualism well before the English Renaissance.

> The majority of societies conceive of the transmission of wealth to the next generation as an automatic process. All children (or at least all males) are born as 'heirs' who co-share their parents' property. There is no concept of singling out one heir as opposed to others or of 'disinheriting' children. The parents and children can be seen as co-partners; there is no 'private property' which the parents hold, no choice they can exercise over who will get their property or the family's headship when they die. The English system has been different, at least in the ranks below the higher aristocracy since the thirteenth century. As Bracton in the thirteenth century put it, *'Nemo est heres viventis'*, no-one is the heir of a living man. Children do not have a right by birth alone, in any 'family property'. There is no such thing as a 'family estate'. Although they may hope to inherit, and although there is a preference for the oldest male child, a person may sell or dispose of his or her property as he or she wishes. There is no 'family property', no restraint of the line (*'restrait lignager'*). Inheritance is based on an optional and flexible system. This is again both unusual and old, dating back in England to the thirteenth century, at least.
>
> (MacFarlane 1978: 260–261)

MacFarlane does not deny the importance of the Renaissance for the historical emergence of individualism for Europe in general. But he sees the English family system as a case of exceptionalism, where a distinctive thread of individualism runs through English family histories from long before the Age of the Tudors. MacFarlane's work is clearly outside the mainstream of historical thought. It has inspired both critical praise from scholars who suggest his data requires a reformulation of English family history and considerable skepticism from some family historians and demographers, who question the accuracy of his data and the validity of the inferences he draws from his data (see White and Vann 1983 and Snell 1989). I am not competent to judge between the claims of MacFarlane's supporters and critics. Whether the individualist conception of society was the product of the English Renaissance or a much older part of English culture does not change the importance of the contradiction in models of society at the heart of *Julius Caesar*. What it does affect is the historical status of that contradiction. If MacFarlane's reading of English history turns out to be right, then it implies that the contradiction between universitas and societas models of social relations is an English example of conflicting cultural models that Shakespeare transposed from England to Rome. If MacFarlane's analysis turns out to be wrong, it suggests that we can usefully read *Julius Caesar* as a commentary on a genuine historical revolution in Tudor England in the way in which society was imagined.

PART III
Shakespeare's craft

8

JUST NOTHING

How *King Lear* means

King Lear is a royal retirement tragedy, a harrowing tale of abdication, not without parallel in the modern British monarchy. An aging king, wishing to cast aside the burdens of his office, divides his kingdom among his two eldest daughters, calculating the division proportional to their disingenuous expressions of love for him. In the process, he disinherits his youngest daughter, the only honest one, for what he sees as her insufficient expression of filial love. In his attempt to stage the final act of his long life as King, Lear's abdication backfires, to the utter ruin of himself, his family, and the kingdom. Because of Lear's royal status, his advanced age, and the consequences of his misjudgment, King Lear's bungled retirement must rank as one of literature's great "senior moments." Though *King Lear* is one of Shakespeare's numerous plays about royal succession gone sour, it is far from a typical succession story. So harrowing is the story that it pulls the audience down along with Lear and his daughters. By itself, the plot does not account for the uncanny power of this play, arguably Shakespeare's bleakest and most unsettling work. The play offers commentators many possible avenues to explore. This chapter approaches *King Lear* by focusing on Shakespeare's craftsmanship, specifically the relationship between the play's language and form, and its effect on its audience. What is it about this play that produces the disturbing experience of watching or reading it?

King Lear brings together several themes: the tragedy of growing old, the question of social legitimacy, Lear's appalling judgment, an aged father's vanity and folly, a king's confounding of affairs of state and those of the heart, filial ingratitude and greed from two daughters, and, arguably, a too-rigid devotion to abstract principle from the virtuous third daughter. The Gloucester-Edmund-Edgar subplot, borrowed from the book *The Countess of Pembroke's Arcadia*, echoes the main storyline but throws into relief dilemmas of family succession springing from conflicting claims of succession by nature, civil law, and loyal devotion. Those themes suggest

DOI: 10.4324/9781003179771-12

what King Lear means. But *how King Lear* means is something different, referring to how its plot structure and its language contribute to what Maynard Mack calls:

> the effect the play has produced on readers and audience throughout the years: as a strange, powerful, yet sometimes uneasy union of high-flown parable and vision with a homely verisimilitude such as Shakespeare was never to surpass.
>
> (Mack 1965: 47)

We will examine Shakespeare's brilliant use of buried and intersecting metaphors that rhetorically perform Lear's "undoing" on its characters as well as its audience, as *King Lear* enacts *for* us and *within* us the unraveling of the world.

Metaphor and meaning

The problem of meaning construction bookends the opening and closing acts of this volume. Like *Hamlet, King Lear* deals with its main character's struggle to make sense of a world that does not readily disclose itself. But if the problem in *Hamlet* is too much meaning, too many interpretations to make sense of things, *King Lear* proposes the possibility of a world that offers up too little meaning. Chapter 1 explored how *Hamlet* disrupts three fundamental cognitive strategies for meaning-making: similarity, contrast, and observation, and makes the audience share in Hamlet's disorientation.[1] Similarly, *King Lear* plays with the audience's cognition of the story, but it works mainly through metaphorical manipulation, the subtle interaction of the dominant metaphors crisscrossing its text. Making this claim is asking a lot from metaphor and raises the question of how metaphor works on the reader of a literary text.

Of the many tropes available to the writer, metaphor has long held a privileged place as a device harnessing the power of language for making meaning. No trope has been better studied or more exploited for its evocative power. Indeed, the term metaphor has sometimes been used in the literature on rhetoric as a stand-in for literary tropes in general (Nöth 1990: 128). In Shakespeare's day, metaphor was understood through Aristotle's *Poetics* and his *Rhetoric* and Quintilian's treatises on oratory. Quintilian saw metaphor as a form of comparison, known in classical grammatical theory as *similitude*, the qualitative similarity between two different things. The Aristotelian conception of metaphor was subtler. In his *Poetics*, Aristotle defines metaphor as an analogical transfer connecting two different ideas or things. Metaphor is thus a kind of word-based analogy. But Aristotle did not require that the things compared be linked through a high degree of objective iconicity. He recognized the capacity of the imagination to discover or create links between two entities that were only moderately similar. A metaphor for Aristotle was a kind of riddle to be resolved by the imagination (*ibid.*: 132). Until recently, our understanding of metaphor was dominated by the work of the philosopher Max Black. "Metaphor," Black argued, "plugs the gaps in the literal vocabulary,"

So viewed, metaphor is a species of *catachresis*, which I shall define as the use
of a word in some new sense in order to remedy a gap in the vocabulary, the
putting of new senses into old words. But if a catachresis serves a genuine
need, the new sense introduced will quickly become part of the literal sense.

(Black 1962: 33)

For Black, metaphor was an inherently *linguistic* device, using a verbal analogy to
create new words and expressions in a language when the available resources were
inadequate. But in 1980, this understanding of metaphor was fundamentally challenged with the publication of a slim volume by linguist George Lakoff and philosopher Mark Johnson (metaphorically) titled *Metaphors We Live By* (Lakoff and
Johnson 1980). In that volume and the many that have followed it, Lakoff and
Johnson made a radical proposal. Metaphor, they argued, is not merely a linguistic
device, a matter of rhetorical style at the surface of a text as the classical rhetoricians
had suggested. It cannot be accounted for by its status as a stand-in for an absent
synonym, extending an impoverished lexicon through analogy. Lakoff and Johnson
claim that metaphor is really a mode of thinking. In fact, they argued that metaphor
is *the* human mode of thinking. Concepts, they propose, are metaphorical all the
way down.

The most important claim we have made so far is that metaphor is not just a
matter of language, that is, of mere words. We shall argue, on the contrary, that
human *thought processes* are largely metaphorical. That is what we mean when
we say that the human conceptual system is metaphorically and defined.
Metaphors as linguistic expressions are possible precisely because there are
metaphors in a person's conceptual system. Therefore whenever in this book
we speak of metaphors, such as ARGUMENT IS WAR, it should be understood that *metaphor* means *metaphorical concept*.

(*ibid.*: 6)

Rather than locating metaphor in language, Lakoff and Johnson move metaphor
indoors as a component of mind. Metaphorical statements are merely (to use a
common metaphor) "the tip of the iceberg," the outward manifestation of a mental
model that the mind was manipulates as its way of understanding things. We understand abstract concepts by performing mental manipulations on imagined concrete
entities: objects, containers, and bodily movement. They argue that a metaphorical
representation is more concrete than the concept it stands for, allowing a transfer of
structure from a more concrete to a more abstract concept.

Metaphorical manipulation is accomplished on mental models that mediated
human cognition. For example, "structural metaphors" organize a more abstract
concept using a more concrete and readily graspable concrete structure. Lakoff and
Johnson's example of "AN ARGUMENT IS WAR" is an example of such a structural metaphor. One way we can make sense of "an argument" is to picture it using
the mental model of warfare. Of course, there might be other understandings of an

argument that use a different mental model, such as ARGUMENT IS PLAY. We might well switch models when invoking the idea of argument in different contexts to highlight different features of an argument. In addition to "structural metaphors," Lakoff and Johnson propose another kind of metaphor, "orientational metaphor," which uses spatial modeling.

> [T]here is another kind of metaphorical concept, one that does not structure one concept in terms of another but instead organizes a whole system of concepts with respect to one another. We will call these *orientational metaphors*, since most of them have to do with spatial orientation: up–down, in–out, front–back, on–off, deep–shallow, central–peripheral. These spatial orientations arise from the fact that we have bodies of the sort that we have and that they function as they do in our physical environment. Orientational metaphors give a concept a spatial orientation; for example, HAPPY IS UP. The fact that the concept of HAPPY is oriented UP leads to English expressions like "I'm feeling up today."
>
> (*ibid.*: 14)

Lakoff and Johnson insist that while these metaphorical manipulations are an aspect of the imagination, they are far from arbitrary since they are derived from our physical interactions in the world and our experience with the bodies housing our minds. Different cultures and languages will produce variations in how these manipulations are structured and what aspects of an experience are salient, but they all have a common source in our shared bodily experience of reality. In this new understanding, what had been called "metaphors" become "metaphorical expressions," surface representations of underlying mental models shaping our understanding of things.

This new version of metaphor theory is an essential component of what came to be known as cognitive linguistics. Cognitive linguists treat all of language—not only metaphoric expressions but rules of syntax and word order—as ways of manipulating underlying cognitive models. Cognitive Linguistics resulted in the 1980s from the intersection of Lakoff's understanding of metaphor and Ronald Langacker's studies of cognitive grammar (Langacker 1987, 1991, 1999, 2008). In 1987, the same year that Langacker published the first volume of his foundational handbook on cognitive linguistics, Lakoff published his major work on human classification *Women, Fire and Dangerous Things*. In that volume, Lakoff took up questions about human categorization that had inspired Lévi-Strauss' structuralist account in *The Savage Mind*. But he approached the problem from the perspective of Cognitive Linguistics and Cognitive Psychology (Lakoff 1987). In Cognitive Linguistics, meaning-making is understood to be a central function of language. Semantics, the study of meaning, formerly sidelined by Chomskian linguistics, is resurrected as a primary focus of linguistics. Linguistic structures are understood as ways of producing meanings by mappings physical and sensory experience onto linguistic forms. Linguistic forms are closely linked to the semantic structures they are designed to express, manifesting the same analogical mappings as metaphor, but at an even more abstract level. This cognitive understanding of language is consistent with the basic assumptions of metaphor theory and brings language forms into a close relationship with the contours of human perception and experience.

These trends in metaphor theory have had a significant impact on our understanding of how metaphor works in literary texts (Lakoff and Turner 1989; Semino and Steen 2008; Cook 2010; Fauconnier and Turner 2008). Particularly significant is Giles Fauconnier's theory of how metaphors use complex blends of what are termed "mental spaces." Mental spaces are coherent cognitive domains in which the mind simulates certain meaningful experiential situations. A mental space is an idealized cognitive model of "a possible world." George Lakoff provides a more technical definition, grounded in neuroscience:

> A "mental space" . . . is a mental simulation characterizing an understanding of a situation, real or imagined. The entire space is governed by a gestalt node, which makes the mental space an "entity" which, when activated, activates all the elements of the mental space.
>
> (Lakoff 2008: 30)

Mental spaces can include an almost unlimited stock of meaningful experiential domains like "food preparation," "flying in a plane," "making love," or "Saturday morning." Mental spaces (e.g., "cooking") can have other mental spaces embedded within them (e.g., "making scrambled eggs"), giving them a potentially complex structure. In early versions of modern metaphor theory, a metaphor was conceived as a simple mapping from one conceptual structure onto another so that, in the case of the LOVE IS A JOURNEY metaphor, the more concrete journey schema is mapped onto the more abstract love schema. But with the development of the idea that mappings create a network of blends of various mental spaces (idealized cognitive simulations of possible worlds), the work of metaphor became richer and more complex. Turner and Fauconnier describe an example of how the idea of mental spaces produces meaning as a dense network of associated mental spaces:

> Conceptual products are never the result of a single mapping. What we have come to call "conceptual metaphors," like TIME IS MONEY or TIME IS SPACE, turn out to be mental constructions involving many spaces and many mappings in elaborate integration networks constructed by means of overarching general principles. These integration networks are far richer than the bundles of pairwise bindings considered in recent theories of metaphor.
>
> (Fauconnier and Turner 2008: 55)

In this view, metaphoric language works by activating a set of experiential schemas. Understanding a text is accomplished by mentally simulating a blend of models, reproducing the experiential basis of the blend for the knower.

When we look at how Shakespeare develops key metaphors in *King Lear*, this cognitive approach can help clarify the play's unusual power over its audience. If metaphor lived just at a text's surfaces, playing a merely ornamental role would simply serve as literary eye-candy. But if the new metaphor theorists are right, the metaphorical expressions in a text serve a much more profound function, controlling the deepest reaches of an audience's imagination as they experience the text. Metaphor controls some of the fundamental processes of meaning-making, triggering imaginary situations that bring the story to life. Skillfully deployed, the metaphoric landscape of a text shapes the translation of words to multisensory mental imagery, and from there to a viewer's experience. The writer in control of metaphor has a powerful tool for playing with the reader's inner life. While Shakespeare obviously did not benefit from these modern theories of metaphor cognition, his sophisticated intuitions about the potential powers of language are unmistakable. Shakespeare clearly knew how metaphor could dig into the human heart and mind and how a writer might pull the audience into a story by playing with the most basic imaginative processes. Through its extraordinary use of metaphoric language, *King Lear* anticipates contemporary metaphor theory by three and a half centuries.

An emptying out of meaning

In *King Lear*, Shakespeare wanted to stage the step-wise unraveling of a life and the world that gave that life its meaning. The play was composed as a great undoing, where the undoing is cleverly embedded in the very textures of the play's language so that the audience would, consciously and unconsciously, experience this unraveling viscerally. *King Lear* enacts a terrifying evacuation of meaning for a king who, approaching the end of a long life, attempts to bring his life to significant closure. We never learn why Lear's life ends this way, other than perhaps his lack of wisdom in giving away his kingdom prematurely and picking the wrong heirs.[2] But *these* consequences seem far out of proportion to *those* errors of poor judgment. Railing against the injustice of his fate, Lear protests, "I am a man/More sinned against than sinning" (III, ii, 62–63). That lack of balance is just the point. Lear counted on justice in the way we all do when we expect things to make sense, to add up in the end, while the world responded with—just nothing.

Rhetorically, *King Lear* is a dazzlingly complex fabric, loomed from intertwining metaphoric strands. The variation in the degree of surface development of these metaphoric strands, their more-or-less "buried" character, contributes substantially to the uncanny effect *Lear* can evince in audiences. Not all metaphors are equally visible. Metaphor lives at various levels of removal from awareness. Some are fully developed and out in the open in a text. Others can exist as partial images or as mere traces. In *King Lear*, this layering of metaphor creates complex images, multiple eddies, and currents of incomplete and incompatible meanings, running throughout the text and intersecting in significant and often disturbing ways. *King Lear* assaults its audience by grandly dis-quantifying itself. Stephen Greenblatt has suggested that "*King Lear* is haunted by a sense of rituals and beliefs that are no longer efficacious, that have been *emptied out*" (Greenblatt 1988: 177). The play both reports and enacts that emptying-out. A king, unwitting and foolish, manages to rip a hole in the fabric of his world at the very moment he seeks closure and completeness to his life. And step-wise, scene by scene, piece by piece, this world is drained of its sense.

The first hint that something is wrong comes straightaway in the play's opening exchange between Kent, Gloucester, and Edmund. It is not so much in *what* they say—that is innocent enough and mainly informational. We are introduced to the King's impending division of the kingdom and then to Gloucester's two sons. The unease does not reside in the action but the language, an unsettling fusion of imagery drawn from the incompatible worlds of intimate feeling, legal reasoning, and mercantile calculation. "I thought the King had more *affected* the Duke of Albany than Cornwall," says Kent, a reference to Lear's feelings for his two sons-in-law. The comment draws from Gloucester the following odd clarification.

> It did always seem so to us; but now in the
> division of the kingdom, it appears not which of
> the Dukes he values most, for equalities are so
> weigh'd that curiosity in neither can make
> choice of either's moiety.

> (I, i, 3–7)

No longer in the realm of human feeling, our minds are confronted by an idiom legalistic or mercantile in feel. This conjunction of incompatible imagery is then echoed in Gloucester's comments about his two sons. Of Edmund, the bastard, Gloucester acknowledges: "His breeding, Sir, hath been at my charge," where "breeding" and "charge" are the meeting points of three incompatible mental spaces. Gloucester's "breeding" lives at the intersection of education and animal copulation, while "charge" similarly draws on intersecting spaces of legal authority, sexual assault, and mercantile exchange. Instead of blending and reinforcing each other, these layers of metaphor pull us in mutually exclusive directions. The result is semantic chaos. When Gloucester describes his elder son, Edgar, as his son "by order of law," he immediately tries to assure Kent that this legal status does not diminish his natural feelings for Edgar, who remains, he says, "yet no dearer in my account." But "dearer" and "account" trigger the mental space of buying and selling in addition to their intended space of paternal affection. Trapped in metaphoric gridlock, the double-dealing imagery speaks a language beyond the speakers' conscious intentions, setting up a chain of disturbingly incompatible associations. Unable to disengage the language of mercantile reckoning and legal wrangling from the idiom of intimate feeling, Kent assures Edmund, "I must love you, and sue to know you better." Taking his cue, Edmund replies: "Sir, I shall, study deserving" (I, i, 27–28).

With our sensibilities thus confounded by the metaphoric anomalies of the opening scene, we enter Lear's court and find a world in which a madness speaks the language of businesslike rationality and legal nicety, where desire is framed as cool calculation, material greed as love, obligation as affection, and political power as paternal care. Confounding his roles of king and father, Lear both commands and purchases his daughters' affections, auctioning off chunks of his kingdom in exchange for verbal assurances of love: so much kingdom for such-and-such a quantity of adoration. These conceptual blends produce a sense, not just of disorientation, but of growing repulsion. "Beyond all manner of so much I love you," insists Goneril, her tongue quite unable to articulate both affection and accounting. Sister Regan echoes the rhetorical dilemma: "I am made," she insists, "of that self metal as my sister/And prize me at her worth" (I, i, 69–70), where metal/mettle becomes a metaphoric alloy uniting the domains of personal character (mettle), strength of will, hardness, and, of course, money. Regan professes herself "an enemy to all other joys/Which the most precious square of sense possesses." What sort of affectionate feeling can be imagined as "a precious square of sense?" In a world of such promiscuous metaphor, Cordelia can only keep silent. When she does speak, it is an oddly detached profession that she loves her father "according to her bond." The language of love has been corrupted almost unto silence. In a foolish parody of King Solomon's legal reasoning, Lear lops his kingdom in half. Banishing and cursing to sterility his one true daughter, while serving up the kingdom piecemeal for her scheming sisters, Lear's actions set in motion a disruption of the natural order that is born by metaphor before it literally consumes the old King.

If disease comes dressed as calculating reason, then the cure should take the form of reason clothed as madness. Gradually Lear is reduced by his scheming daughters to nothing. In Goneril's bizarre formulation, his train (entourage) is gradually "disquantitied" from 100 to 50 to 25, and, finally, to nothing, as if a person, or a kingdom, could be dismembered by the numbers. Stripped of all the trappings of his conventional humanity, of his fatherhood, his manhood, his kingship, Lear upstages his daughters. In a desperate attempt to assert what remains of his humanity, he takes upon himself the final stages of his undoing, casting himself out of his office, out of his house, and, eventually, out of his mind. As Cordelia is silenced, Lear's Fool emerges with an increasingly lunatic tongue, a crazed tongue that unfailingly speaks the truth. Lear follows suit as his language grows ever more fantastic, and his sense of himself—his *qualities* of humaneness—grows clearer. The unjustly outlawed Edgar, disguised as the poor madman Tom-o-Bedlam, can only mimic their madness. It is an attempt at a homeopathic curing-rite. The *performance of madness* acknowledges the deranged world and attempts to undo it. By Act IV, with Lear in high rage, Edgar marvels aloud at the mad King's lucidity, calling his ravings "matter and impertinency mix'd; Reason in Madness" (IV, vi, 176–177), a fitting antidote to the Madness-in-Reason that gets the play going.

The world is turned on its head. With madness passing for reason, man becomes woman, the king becomes beggar, the father becomes the child, and the fool becomes the wise man. Lear does not just go mad. He suffers from *Hysterica passio*— the rising of the womb, which Shakespeare's contemporaries knew as "the climbing mother," a condition which was believed to choke women and bring on "hysteria." Images of menstruation begin to leak through the text's surface, running together with images of a world-destroying flood. Lear's doomed arrangement to alternate monthly visits with Goneril and Regan become his "monthly courses." When the fool sings the ditty, "Come over the bourn, Bessy to me," he adds a new twist, "Her boat hath a leak and she must not speak," blending metaphor models of drowning and menstruation. "Pour on, I will endure," bellows the mad king. The unstoppable rain carries the menstruation-as-flood imagery beyond Lear to nature itself as if in sympathy with Lear's cursing of his daughters' fecundity, transforming flow into flood. Fullness and emptiness converge. Anticipating what is to come, the metaphor proposes a self-consuming oxymoron. A life-giving image (like maternal blood) is converted into a death-dealing trope. Lear, ever the king, attempts to command the life-giving forces of nature to turn back in destruction upon the world:

> Blow, winds, and crack your cheeks! Rage! Blow!
> Your cataracts and hurricanoes spout
> Till you have drenched our steeples, drown'd the cocks!
> You sulfurous and thought-executing fires,
> Vaunt couriers of oak-cleaving thunderbolts,
> Singe my white head! And thou all shaking thunder,
> Strike flat the thick rotundity o' th' world!
> Crack nature's moulds, all germens spill at once
> That makes ingrateful man.

> (III, ii, 1–9)

Shakespeare's use of self-negating metaphor enacts at the level of discourse structure the evacuation of meaning that Lear has unwittingly triggered in the plot. *King Lear* swarms with self-consuming metaphors: not just metaphors of consumption, but metaphors that ingest themselves. These are paradoxical conceptual blends that both exploit and undo the very basis of metaphoric cognition.

The image of self-consumption breaks through the text's surface in a metaphoric *pas-de-deux* of its very own. The frequent references to "serving" Lear alternate as "feeding him" and "eating him." Dining, serving, and cannibalizing metaphors are scattered helter-skelter throughout the text at various levels of remove. None is developed as surface metaphor, but they are unmistakably there. Cursing Cordelia in the play's opening court scene, Lear invokes the cannibalistic image of the "Barbarous Scythian,/ That makes his generation messes/To gorge his appetite" (I, i, 120). Lear gives Cordelia's third of the kingdom to her sisters' husbands with the admonition "Cornwall and Albany,/With my two daughters' dowers digest the third" (I, i, 144). The eating metaphor disappears, re-emerging with a new twist in I, iv, when a banished and disguised Kent (who, like the metaphor in question, has gone underground) offers to "serve" Lear truly, and "to eat no fish" (I, iv, 18). Here "service" as the duty owed to one's master becomes blended with the imagery of eating, anticipating its transformation into the metaphor in which Lear becomes "served" for dinner as both the guest and the meat course. By line 41, the metaphoric implications of the horrific blend have begun to emerge when Lear tells Kent: "Follow me; thou shalt serve me; if I like thee no worse after dinner, I will not part from thee yet. Dinner, ho! dinner." (I, iv, 41–43). It is left to the Fool to give voice to the darker implications of the serving imagery. Alluding to Lear's lethal division of his kingdom, he tells his master:

FOOL
Give me an egg,
nuncle, and I'll give thee two crowns.

KING LEAR
What two crowns shall they be?

FOOL
Why, after I have cut the egg i' the middle, and eat
up the meat, the two crowns of the egg. When thou
clovest thy crown i' the middle, and gavest away
both parts, thou borest thy ass on thy back o'er
the dirt: thou hadst little wit in thy bald crown,
when thou gavest thy golden one away.

(I, iv, 159–167)

At least seven mental spaces run together in the Fool's prattle: crown as head, crown as money, crown as a sign of royal power, crown as half of broken egg, and parents feeding upon their young. Later in the same passage, the fool explicitly refers to Goneril as one of the egg pairings, an image that interacts with the earlier eating reference, blending it into an implicitly cannibalistic vision. The Fool picks up the metaphoric thread of cannibalism once again—this time inverted so that the offspring devour the parent: "The hedge-sparrow fed the cuckoo so long" he says, "That it had its head bit off by its young" (I, iv, 221–222). The images of head, crown, service, feeding, and ingestion refract and recombine so that their senses become thoroughly entangled. The meanings of the resulting blend are emergent in the disconcerting confluence of these various metaphoric threads. These metaphoric threads snake through the play beneath its surfaces, emerging now and again in uncanny places and unsettling combinations. By Act III, scene iv, Edgar turns to his father and Lear and, taking the literary voice of the Fool, breaks into verse:

Child Rowland to the dark tower came,
His word was still: Fie, foh, and fum,
I smell the blood of a British man.

(III, v, 195–197)

At first, this seems to be a nonsensical intrusion of childhood fantasy into the play. But note again the disturbing confluence of metaphoric imagery that has emerged from the play's underbelly: images of cannibalism, of dangerous blood set loose, and of unspeakable dread. Echoing these images is Albany's pronouncement, "Humanity must perforce pray on itself,/Like monsters of the deep" (IV, ii, 60–61).

The play's master trope

The play's master trope is built into its plot structure. *King Lear* promises us a conventional plot familiar to both anthropologists and Elizabethan audiences: the ceremonial humiliation of the king, who leaves the comforts of the Court, undergoes a set of trials in the wilderness, and returns wiser and ready to be elevated into his office. This is the venerable theme of the "ritual killing of the king," which Sir James Frazer popularizes in *The Golden Bough*, and anthropologist Tom Beidelman describes in its African incarnation in his essay "Swazi Royal Ritual."[3] This archetypal theme of a king's suffering, and eventual redemption underlies the medieval archetypal morality tale that Maynard Mack calls "The Abasement of the Proud King." "In one common form of this archetype," Mack tell us:

> the king comes from swimming or his bath to find his clothes and retainers gone. His role has been usurped by an angel sent from heaven to teach him, in the words of the Magnificat, that God humbles the proud and exalts the humble. In his nakedness, he finds that the evidence of his kingliness, indeed his whole identity, is gone. Assertions that he is in fact the king and efforts to regain his throne lead those around him to mock him as a madman. Standing at last among the beggars outside his own palace, wind-torn, tormented by hunger and thirst, he acknowledges his true position, repents his former arrogance, and is then enlightened by the angel and restored to power.
>
> (Mack 1965: 49–50)

Mack reminds us that the Renaissance version of this redemption scenario was a pastoral romance where

> the protagonist moves in a sweeping arc from the world of everyday. . . to some sort of Arcadian countryside forest which is more in sympathy with human feelings and states. . . [H]aving undergone in the process something like a ritual death and rebirth, he is able to return to the everyday world restored to serenity and often to temporary felicity
>
> (*ibid.*: 63–64).

Both medieval and Renaissance versions of the sin-and-redemption scenario echo the Christian cyclical journey from blessing to fall to redemption. In Chapter 4, we explored the pastoral version of this scenario in *The Winter's Tale*. In that play, the pastoral theme is developed by metaphors of seasonal change and return hinted at in the play's title. In *The Winter's Tale*, King Leontes, self-deluded and jealous, has convinced himself that his wife is an adulteress and that his daughter is not his child. Over a period of 16 years, he is ultimately humbled, made to "prove a sheep" by being shorn of his *heir*.

The parable's promised structure is cyclical, a journey from blessing to humiliation to humility and back to blessing. In *King Lear*, however, the audience's expectation of this sort of moral walkabout is complicated by the fact that, at the play's outset, this King seems to have already come full-circle. The play starts at the end of his life's journey, and we meet Lear in the winter of his reign, not at its outset. So the play's opening already establishes a false expectation, proposing an already-completed journey. This false beginning turns into the first of several false endings to the story. It is at the *end* of his life that Lear begins his journey of self-knowledge. So while Shakespeare furnishes us with a comfortingly familiar scenario, he subverts its form and fails to deliver on the promise of the genre. For the audience, as for Lear, this is a story of failed expectations. Lear never makes it home, dying wiser perhaps but still unfulfilled, having seen his one honest daughter die before him. Though set in pagan England, the play is Christian in form, a form that promises its audience a proper Christian conclusion. However, *King Lear* is no conventional Christian morality play.[4] It has the wrong shape. For Lear, there is too much punishment for too little sin. What is missing in Lear's journey is the circling back, the coming home.

"Is this the promis'd end," Kent laments, as the just-dead Cordelia is carried on stage by her crazed father. But the promised end finally eludes both Lear and the audience. There is no balance in all of this, no wheel of justice come full circle. "I am," Lear laments, "more sinned against than sinning." The balance at the heart of the Christian morality tale is missing. Even Christ in his suffering and death, which superficially parallel Lear's, is understood as the second Adam, redeeming an original sin and fall through compensatory suffering and ascension. For Lear, there is no such balance. We are not just told about this failure of conventional moral closure. Shakespeare builds it into the play's language, so the audience *experiences* the undoing of its expectations in much the same way that Stanley Fish demonstrates how Milton makes the reader experience the Fall of Man in *Paradise Lost* (Fish 1971). As Stephen Booth puts it: "An audience's experience of *King Lear* persistently reflects its characters' experience of the events depicted in it. The play makes its audience suffer *as audience*. . . ." (Booth 1983: 11).

Shakespeare produces this experience of moral undoing for his audience by developing a set of structural metaphors in the play that takes the form of a self-consuming trope. This metaphor-blend engages the multiple mental spaces shared by the single image of the circle. In Shakespeare's hands, the circle, that rich conventional image of completeness and justice, is looped back upon itself as its negation, giving birth to its hollow twin as it gradually reveals itself as the picture of "nothing." Promising *in its forms* and *its metaphors* a fullness of life and a completion of a journey, the play finally gives us zero. Cordelia's answer to Lear's demanded accounting of her love in exchange for a piece of the kingdom is "Nothing, my Lord." To which Lear responds, portentously: "Nothing will come of nothing: Speak again." Proposing in its balanced rhetorical form a circle of justice, the content of Lear's pronouncement undoes the form. As contrasted with an exchange signaling justice or fulfillment, this circle is just nothing: nothing doubled back upon itself. "Thou hast pared thy wit o' both sides, and left nothing i' th' middle," the Fool chides his master. "I am better than thou art. I am a fool, thou art nothing" (I, iv, 185–186). Towards the end of the play, Edmund uses the wheel image to acknowledge the possibility of transcendent justice. "The wheel," he says, "has come full circle" (V, iii, 205). But the audience is about to learn how little justice this world has to offer up and just what this particular circle will amount to. Nothing shows up everywhere in *King Lear*, becoming palpable as images of circles appear suggesting a dizzying array of metaphoric models: monthly courses (circuits); the "operation of the orbs"; "bleeding rings"—sockets emptied of their eyes; cracked eggs, "the thick rotundity of the world" laid flat. "I am bound," says Lear "upon a wheel of fire." The metaphoric power of these diverse images is linked to their paradoxical blend of fullness and emptiness. Lear's world is glutted with vivid images of empty fullness, of all the circles becoming zeros.

The *circle as metaphor*, a fundamental orientational schema that typically suggests completion, is ultimately realized and undercut as the *circularity of metaphor*. The metaphoric joke, the grotesque double-entendre of turning an image of complete-ness into an image of zero, is enacted not only in the trope's content but in the very constitution of the intersecting metaphoric blend. As images of fullness are subverted into images of emptiness, audiences are forced to simulate one gestalt gobbling up its sibling gestalt, as self-consuming tropes circle back upon themselves in an act of linguistic cannibalism. Shakespeare deploys his mastery of metaphor to terrifying effect on both Lear and his audiences.

"Nothing" is set loose in the play to do and to undo. "Nothing," Lear assures his Fool, in an echo of his warning to Cordelia, "can be made out of nothing." The Fool responds literally, with his story of the egg being emptied out of itself, leaving nothing in the middle. Lear's emptying out assumes a literal form as his daughters "disquantity" him, reducing step-by-step to nothing his allotted retinue, initiating a baring of the self. "Oh ruined piece of nature," exclaims the blinded Gloucester, when he comes upon Lear in the full bloom of his suffering. With an ironic ref-erence to his own empty orbs, his eyes having been violently "plucked" out by Cornwall, Gloucester moans, "This great world/ Shall so wear out to naught."

Just as completion can turn to nothing, so "nothing" can consume itself back into something: a homeopathic circling back of the disease upon itself as cure. The self-consumption of disease by imitation of itself—think of Donne's famous "death thou shalt die"—might be called "tropic" medicine, curing through metaphor. To regain his honor and his self, Edgar, like Kent, must undo himself. To cure madness, one imitates it, performs it, putting out the fire by playing with fire. The paradox exists not only in action but in the ironic play of metaphor. In Act II, as Edgar undoes himself, transforming himself into Poor Tom, he says: "That's something yet: Edgar I nothing am." But the word "nothing" consumes itself since Edgar is saying both "I nothing am" and "I no thing am."

But ultimately, the homeopathic remedy fails. *King Lear* is not to be rescued by the restorative promise of its form. As Act V comes to its bloody close, the play seeks a form to complete itself, but stumbles. "Is this the promis'd end?" a horrified Kent asks aloud, as the dead Cordelia is borne on stage. To which Edgar quickly adds, "Or image of that horror?" taking momentary refuge in the possibility that Cordelia has merely performed her death and thus overcome it. "I know when one is dead and when one lives," Lear insists. "She's dead as earth" (V, iv, 305–306). But then Lear falls back into imagining that Cordelia again breathes and speaks. Some 20 lines later, we get another false finish. Albany parodies the expected end of a Shakespearean tragedy by hauling out a set speech, conventional for this genre of tragedy, reconstituting the powers that are left in the wreckage of the play and proclaiming that justice has been served:

> You lords and noble friends, know our intent;
> What comfort to this great decay may come
> Shall be applied. For us we will resign,
> During the life of this old Majesty,
> To him our absolute power: *[to Edgar and Kent]*
> you, to your rights,
> With boot and such addition as your honours
> Have more than merited. All friends shall taste
> The wages of their virtue, the cup of their deservings.
>
> (V, 111, 296–304)

Were it to end here, we would have closure, and balance, a full circle of justice, and a restoration of order. In other words, we would have the promised end. But Albany's performance falters as the play crawls on. Lear interrupts Albany's proclamation, jolted from his delusions that Cordelia lives:

> O see, see
> And my poor fool is hang'd. No, no, no life!
> Why should a dog, a horse, a rat have life,
> And thou no breath at all? Thou'lt come no more,
> Never, never, never, never, never!
>
> (ll. 304–308)

But then, she's back to life in what Stephen Booth calls the "now-dead, now-alive pattern."

> Pray you, undo this button: thank you, Sir.
> Do you see this, look on her, her lips.
> Look there, look there!
>
> (ll. 306–308)

At which point, Lear dies. In the end, there is for Lear no heroic performance of his end, just death, just nothing. The play does not close; it sputters out. As Booth says, "*King Lear* ends but does not stop." (*ibid.*: 15)

So the power of *King Lear* is tied in part to its way with words. From the play's opening scene, truth has no direct voice that does not unspeak itself. Unable to speak directly, the play goes underground and speaks to us from its metaphoric underbelly. The dismal message of *King Lear* is embedded in its language. Its buried metaphors do not blend: they consume themselves, breaking through the text's surface, connecting in bizarre, paradoxical combinations with other images, playing with our imagination in alarming ways. The play's dark movement is carried by its metaphors and performed by the meta-metaphorical emptying-out and through the audience's repeated experience of the self-consuming trope. In this way, the unimaginable idea of something becoming nothing and a circle becoming zero is rendered an imaginable *experience* for both those in the play and those watching it. *King Lear*'s often-noted emotional power can be traced not only to its harrowing story but to the chaotic rhetoric that boils in its belly.

Notes

1 For an interesting analysis of how *Hamlet* plays with metaphors of mirroring, see Cook 2010.
2 In his Japanese adaptation of the Lear story in his great film *Ran*, Akira Kurosawa proposed that the old king in that story is being punished in retribution for past unspecified transgressions. Kurosawa attempts to salvage the story as a morality tale in which suffering is understood as ultimate justice. But in framing the story in this way, Kurosawa fundamentally changes Shakespeare's story by providing a rationale for the king's suffering, Part of the stinging power of *Lear* lies in its structural appeal to the audience's expectations of justice while showing us a fundamentally unjust world.
3 Frazer 1922; Beidelman 1966.
4 For a defense of *King Lear* as a fundamentally Christian story, see Miller 1993.

9

SHAKESPEARE AND THEORY IN PERSPECTIVE

Watching Shakespeare plays on stage is one thing. Reading Shakespeare is something else. In this book, I have made a case for why close reading of Shakespeare's plays can yield insights not readily available to the theater audience. While watching the plays is more likely to convey the dramatic power of story and character, careful attention to the texts can reveal a landscape of ideas cultivated by Shakespeare but not always apparent to the viewer. Shakespeare had found ways to create texts that seamlessly accommodate both narrative engagement and theoretical reflection. In the previous chapter, we saw how Shakespeare's manipulation of metaphor in *King Lear* could induce cognitive chaos in the audience, simulating Lear's deteriorating state of mind. This chapter concludes the book by going deeper into Shakespeare's literary craft. While developing character and storyline is essential to drama, adding an elaborate theoretical layer to theatrical productions is less common. Bringing the two perspectives together without compromising either poses a significant technical challenge for a playwright. Theory and narrative naturally speak in very different voices. The chapter will examine how Shakespeare layered his plays to reconcile the conflicting demands of drama and social theory. Shakespeare possessed an acute sense of irony often expressed by manipulating conventional literary forms to accommodate multiple and sometimes veiled meanings. By playing with conventional structures, he was able to develop unexpected commentary on philosophical issues transcending a scene's immediate meanings. This book has uncovered some of these more theoretically oriented layers of meaning in the plays. This final chapter will summarize some of the significant literary devices Shakespeare used to create a play of ideas.

Word-play

The sounds of words can motivate multiple readings, giving apparently simple speech ambiguity and semantic complexity. This potential of language to convey

DOI: 10.4324/9781003179771-13

more than one reading was not lost on Shakespeare. The vitality of his word-play suggests not only his inventiveness but also the multivocality of a world in the throes of radical transformation. As one translator of Shakespeare put it, the challenge of translating Shakespeare's plays requires an acknowledgment of the creative energy underlying the utter density and the untidy vigor of his language:

> In my experience, translating Shakespeare implies not only an investigation into the extraordinary thickness of his theatrical inventions but also a voyage inside the dramatic turbulence of a language confronting a world, a culture, an episteme, which were undergoing a vertiginous transformation. There lies the secret of his terrible energy, of his hybridization of registers, styles, grammatical patterns, and of course, pictures of the world. One must always be ready to acknowledge a blurring in the recesses of Shakespeare's texts, a subterraneous meaning peeping through the accepted sense, and apparently semantic confusion which may soon reveal the creation of a new perspective on things and on human beings.
>
> (Serpieri 1998: 65)

Serpieri's sense of the "terrible energy" of Shakespeare's language is echoed by Russ McDonald in his study of Shakespeare's language, *Shakespeare and the Arts of Language*. McDonald celebrates Shakespeare's sensitivity to the rhetorical possibilities inherent in word-play. For example, he offers a close reading of Shakespeare's Sonnet 138 ("When my love swears that she is made of truth/I do believe her though I know she lies. . . ."), demonstrating the poet's mastery of word-play and his exploitation of the ambiguities of language (McDonald 2001: 138). The sonnet uses subtle word-play both to reveal and mask its truth. The incompatibility of poetic truth and human passion become the sonnet's central theme.

The power and ambiguity of language were important themes in classical treatises on rhetoric, which were familiar elements of the humanist curriculum for schoolboys in Shakespeare's day. The most influential of these works for Elizabethans was Quintilian's *Institutio Oratoria*, where the Roman rhetorician wrote: "I turn to the discussion of ambiguity, which will have countless species: indeed, in the opinion of philosophers there is not a single word which has not a diversity of meanings" (Quintilian 1921: 138). The influence of Quintilian's treatise is evident in George Puttenham's 1589 treatise *The Art of Poesy*, where the author lays out for readers an extensive landscape of poetic tropes for the use of a poet in pursuit of florid word-play. Book III of Puttenham's work deals specifically with the functions of ornament in poetry where, it treats the subject of poetic ornamentation by conceiving of poetic language metaphorically as accouterment.

> [T]he good proportion of anything doth greatly adorne and commend it, and right so our late remembred proportions doe to our vulgar Poesie, so is there yet requisite to the perfection of this arte another manner of exornation, which resteth in the fashioning of our makers language

and style, to such purpose as it may delight and allure as well the mynde as the eare of the hearers with a certain noueltie and strange manner of conveyance, disguising it no little from the ordinary and accustomed. . . .

(Puttenham 1904, Book III: 1)

The formidable arsenal of classical tropes included amphibology (double entendre), agnominatio (the echoing of a sound of one word in another in close relationship with it), syllepsis (applying a word to two others in different senses), polypoton (use of multiple words derived from the same root), antanaclasus ("the rebound," repetition of a word but with different meanings), as well as more familiar figures such as metaphor and alliteration. Shakespeare had an acute sensitivity to the links between sound and sense. The titles of several of Shakespeare's comedies employ plays on words. *Much Ado About Nothing* is much about "noting," while *The Comedy of Errors* deals with "eros" as much as with "errors." Even the simple title *Hamlet* is a kind of double entendre since it refers ambiguously both to the Hamlet the father and the son—and ultimately to the chain of Hamlets that constitutes the very idea of succession to the Danish throne. Shakespeare's words are alive with ambiguity and hermeneutic possibility.

Critics have sometimes seen Shakespeare's attraction to puns as a stain on his genius. In his 1765 *Preface to Shakespeare*, Samuel Johnson saw Shakespeare's fascination with "quibbles" as a weakness in his writing, claiming that Shakespeare's obsession with word-play wielded a "malignant power over his mind," leading him to stray from "reason, propriety and truth."

A quibble is to Shakespeare what luminous vapours are to the traveller; he follows it at all adventures, it is sure to lead him out of his way, and sure to engulf him in the mire. It has some malignant power over his mind, and its fascinations are irresistible.

(Johnson 1968: 74)

Indeed, puns are often treated as low humor, trivial detours from intelligent discourse. The most common kind of pun, the simple homonym, draws attention away from meaning to the surface of speech so that language is no longer experienced as a transparent vehicle for conveying concepts or experiences. This kind of attention to an overlap of sounds with different meaning draws attention to the sonic dimension of language over its capacity to convey meaning. At worst, a focus on surface sound interferes with rather than enhances speech's communicative power. This unwelcome disruption of meaning-making by shifting attention to pure sound is reflected in the rolled eyes and other conventional signs of annoyance that often greet puns.

Shakespeare was not above using these sorts of primitive puns, but he also used double entendre in a much more powerful way. Sometimes the profundity is not in the pun itself but in the context in which it is used. At the start of Chapter 5, we noted the barrage of punning banter by the Capulets' servants Gregory and

Sampson that opens *Romeo and Juliet*. Were this banter merely a verbal slapstick device for opening the play, we would be justified in feeling that the cheap word-play was not worthy of Shakespeare. But in this case, we are not dealing with just a *play on* words, but also a *play about* words. *Romeo and Juliet* is a story about the complex relations between love and poetry. Questions about the power and fallibility of language are central to the play, whose action turns on what the Prince calls "Three civil brawls bred of an airy word" (I, i, 80). In the context of this play, it is far from trivial that we enter the play in a scene at once tragic and comic marked by the confusion wrought by words whose overlapping sounds keep shifting and confounding the meaning of discourse. This banter introduces the reader to a world where confusion of tongues underwrites violent conflict, a place where the most ordinary language has become a problem. The puns themselves may be trivial, but they actually serve as an introduction to the play's profound theoretical question.

The play of sound and sense in puns does not always subvert meaning. In the hands of a writer gifted with sensitivity to the relation between sound and meaning, word-play can become a window onto unexpected and intriguing concordances of sound expanding rather than disrupting meaning. Where correspondences of sound point to hidden connections between things that had appeared unrelated, we enter an enchanted realm of heightened significance, a world where the normal arbitrariness of the linguistic sign is momentarily suspended. Kenneth Muir calls these "uncomic" or "serious" puns (Muir 1977).[1] Frequently Shakespeare uses a word whose sound evokes another word, each of the words suggesting a different metaphor. Muir suggests that the ambiguities produced by the simultaneous evocation of different metaphors create in Shakespeare's texts parallel currents of meaning which add to the complexity and the richness of the text. Muir cites, for example, Lady Macbeth's announcement in Macbeth of her intention to implicate the grooms in Duncan's death by smearing them with Duncan's blood:

> If he do bleed
> I'll gild the faces of the grooms withal.
> For it must seem their guilt.
>
> (II, ii, 71–73)

The similarity in sound between "gild" and "guilt" creates a hybrid image (what modern metaphor theorists would call "a conceptual blend") that Shakespeare later exploits when Macbeth, describing Duncan's corpse in the following scene, refers to "His silver skin, laced with his golden blood" (II, iii, 131). These subtle word-plays are found throughout Shakespeare's work. Clearly, they are not the kind of "eye-roller puns" intended to provoke comic relief. These sonic twins resonate with each other to produce evocative streams of metaphoric mixing, are a common source of Shakespeare's rhetorical complexity and semantic richness.

Shakespeare goes beyond even these serious puns to an exalted realm of word-play that produces a kind of "magical pun." No writer has equaled Shakespeare in exploiting the semantic possibilities of a word's multiple meanings, where apparently superficial correspondences in sound turn out to be matched by surprising correspondences in meaning. We noted one of these brilliant uses of word-play in the first Act of *Romeo and Juliet* where Benvolio recounts to Romeo's parents his recent encounter with his love-sick cousin, making his way home with a heavy heart at sunrise. The word-play in that exchange is both dense and subtle and is easily overlooked. It exploits the multiple links between son/sun, wood/would, sycamore/sick amor, pen (as in write)/pen (as in imprisonment), and night/knight. A supplementary perspective, initially overlooked in the direct experience of the scene, is skillfully embedded in the text in such a way that missing it still leaves the emotionally charged conventional reading of the lines intact. However, once the supplementary perspective is recognized, it radically changes the significance of the exchange. The scene becomes less a simple recounting of Romeo's love-sickness than a powerful revelation about a less obvious source of his problem, Romeo's affinity—the poet's affinity—for attempting to control the world by manipulating language.

Shakespeare's linguistic virtuosity is put at the service of his predisposition for recognizing multiple sides of any issue or situation. As Russ McDonald puts it: "The key to Shakespeare's use of word-play is that he finds the instability of language analogous to the ambiguities of human experience generally, and his gift for manipulating the verbal sign permits him to register the intricacies and implications of characters; motives and actions with extraordinary subtlety" (McDonald 2001: 145). Other critics have also highlighted Shakespeare's gift for manipulating language with word-play both aesthetic and conceptual. Stephen Booth describes the delight of Shakespeare's double-talk, his ability to juice complex meaning from concordances of sound and sense in apparently simple words:

> There is great joy to be had from puns, but all of it ordinarily belongs to the person who senses the opportunity in the linguistic situation. The joy, I suggest, is in sensing the availability of a simultaneously likely and unlikely connection, and unexpected opportunities for articulating to contexts that are and remain essentially unconnected.
>
> (Booth 2004: 33)

A special form of the magical pun Shakespeare used to great effect is the self-consuming pun, a word-play that turns a word or a phrase back upon itself to reverse its meaning, proposing that something both is and is not. The pair of words of the self-canceling pun is like an oxymoron. But rather than using two different words with opposite meanings, the self-canceling pun uses a single word or phrase with a common meaning plus a second less familiar meaning or a homonymic double that reverses the original sense of the word. Since the audience typically grasps only the more common meaning of the word, the self-canceling pun is an effective covert device. The unexpected reversal of meaning embeds a radical reading of the scene, which can effectively reverse or qualify its conventional meaning.

Shakespeare uses the self-consuming pun several times in *Julius Caesar*, where a buried second meaning acts as a choric echo, alerting a careful reader that all is not what it first appears to be. For example, in Act III, as the conspirators plot Caesar's assassination, Cassius proclaims:

> So oft as that shall be,
> So often shall *the knot of us* be call'd
> The men that gave their country liberty.

(III, i, 130–133)

"The knot of us" intends to convey a tight bond among the conspirators. But the knot unravels when its shadow twin springs into view and the phrase becomes "The *not* of us," suggesting that, in killing Caesar, the conspirators are effectively undoing themselves. This conversion of unity into dissolution has already been anticipated in the text in Act II when Brutus, seeking a ritual to seal the pact of the conspirators, says: "Give me your hands all over, one by one," to which Cassius adds "And let us *swear our resolution*" (II, i, 123–124). "Resolution's" primary meaning is a collective affirmation, but it also means "dissolution." The self-consuming pun introduces a hidden resonance between the state of language and Roman politics, an implicit commentary that literally *predicts* the ultimate irony of their pact and the tragic end it will produce.

This sort of self-canceling pun is also at work in the first act of Hamlet. Scene ii opens with Claudius making clear the strange circumstances that brought him the crown:

KING
> Though yet of Hamlet our dear brother's death
> The memory be green, and that it us befitted
> To bear our hearts in grief, and our whole kingdom
> *To be contracted* in one brow of woe,
> Yet so far hath discretion fought with nature
> That we with wisest sorrow think on him
> Together with remembrance of ourselves.

(I, ii, 1–5)

In the context of a royal wedding, "contracted" would normally suggest a marriage alliance that expanded the kingdom's political reach. But it also suggests the opposite, a turning inward. Specifically, the phrase Claudius uses, "contracted in one brow of woe," plays a perspective trick, converting the reference to a contracted marriage into an image of a contracted brow.

A particularly interesting example of the self-canceling pun is found in Act II of *King Lear* when Edgar, betrayed by his brother, forced to flee his home and now hunted like an animal, assumes the persona of a madman Poor Tom to save himself, and claims, "Poor Turlygod! Poor Tom!/That's something yet. 'Edgar' I nothing am" (II, iii, 20–21). Like Lear, Edgar must undo himself in order to try and save himself. The connections between going mad, being thrown out of one's house, having one's retinue reduced, being stripped naked, and reducing oneself to nothing are powerfully developed in *King Lear*. Being forced to become nothing in order to be reborn as something is a ritual form central to *King Lear*. And in this speech the paradox of nothing and something is linguistically embodied in the double meaning of Edgar's final words, "'Edgar' I nothing am," where "nothing" may be read as both "I nothing am" and its negation "I no thing am." The second, submerged reading, proposing redemption, is supported by the sentence that precedes it: "That's something yet." Here "no thing," "nothing" and something" are semantically twisted together in a linguistic knot/not.

As seen in the detailed analysis in Chapter 8, in *King Lear* Shakespeare took the idea of the self-consuming pun even further in deploying self-consuming metaphors. Chapter 8 traced the development of a complex of self-consuming metaphors in *King Lear* that joined images of fullness and completion with images of emptying. The metaphorical expressions come fast-and-furious, especially from the mouth of Lear's Fool, creating a dizzying and chaotic cloud of paradoxical images that are virtually impossible for an audience to process cognitively. This literary technique was shone to be consistent with modern cognitive linguistic theories of metaphoric cognition that emphasize complex metaphors as blends of "mental spaces" that usually create rich textures of meaning. However, in this case, Shakespeare has created self-canceling blends that are nearly impossible to process cognitively, simulating for the audience the experience of the emptying out of meaning that is the thematic heart of *King Lear*. *King Lear* beautifully illustrates Shakespeare's linguistic virtuosity and how he put it to powerful use in his plays. Finally, we saw how Shakespeare works the paradox of "completion as emptying" into the play's structure by designing the play around the expectations of a conventional dramatic circuit from sin to suffering to redemption, only to subvert the form and have it end as nothing. The architecture of the play is itself a self-consuming structural metaphor, the circle-becoming-zero.

Buried metaphor

Closely related to Shakespeare's use of puns and other forms of word-play is his handling of metaphor. Shakespeare's writing is replete with unusually vivid metaphoric expressions. Not only did Shakespeare use metaphor liberally. He even wrote poems *about* metaphor. Several of Shakespeare's sonnets were about the difficulty of finding an apt metaphor to compare his lover. Consider, for example, the opening lines of Sonnet 130.

> My mistress' eyes are nothing like the sun;
> Coral is far more red than her lips' red;
> If snow be white, why then her breasts are dun;
> If hairs be wires, black wires grow on her head.

His most famous sonnet, Sonnet 18, begins with a similar quest for an appropriate metaphor to capture the beauty of his love. The poem begins with a poet's question:

> Shall I compare thee to a summer's day?

But in this instance, he finds the conventional poetic tropes for beauty to be inadequate.

> Thou art more lovely and more temperate:
> Rough winds do shake the darling buds of May,
> And summer's lease hath all too short a date:
> Sometime too hot the eye of heaven shines,
> And often is his gold complexion dimm'd;
> And every fair from fair sometime declines,
> By chance, or nature's changing course, untrimm'd;

The metaphor of the seasons is inadequate for the job. The world's beauty in spring and summer is ephemeral compared with his love's eternal charms.

> But thy eternal summer shall not fade
> Nor lose possession of that fair thou ow'st;
> Nor shall Death brag thou wander'st in his shade,

Yet, this claim seems to contradict the conventional view of the fragility and ephemeral nature of human beauty. But in an unexpected twist on the convention, Shakespeare clarifies that his lover will live forever, but only

> When in eternal lines to time thou grow'st;

Initially, it is not completely clear what kinds of "eternal lines" Shakespeare is alluding to. But by the final couplet, the sonnet reveals the real object of his love, the "thee" referenced in "thy eternal summer."

> So long as men can breathe or eyes can see,
> So long lives *this*, and *this* gives life to *thee*.

So long as the voice can recite the poem and eyes can read it, both the poem and the beloved will live forever. "This" and "thee" converge. If nature cannot preserve his lover's beauty, a literary analog of nature—the sonnet—can do the trick. Art mimics nature and also preserve and replaces it. While the beauty of nature is transient, the beauty of poetry endures. Working in subtle tension with the message of the conventional love sonnet, this sonnet concludes as a tribute to itself, celebrating the life-preserving power of the poetic trope.

Shakespeare also devised a more extensive and subtle use of metaphor for embedding theoretical commentary in his plays. We normally think of poetic metaphors as single images proposing a comparison for some specific object (e.g., "My love is a rose."). But Shakespeare mastered the creation of a diffuse metaphoric stream subtly infiltrating the entire text of a play. The "soft" use of such buried metaphors distinguishes Shakespeare's use of metaphor from the more literal associations of allegory. Lightly distributed throughout a play's text, buried metaphors are not always immediately apparent, gradually building up a presence in a text. Often they are mere hints at metaphor rather than fully fleshed out tropes. Buried metaphors might be thought of as a semantically provocative shadow that haunts the subtext of the play, rarely intruding on the play's surfaces but an emergent current of unexpected meaning. Once noticed by the reader, buried metaphor can significantly impact the interpretation of the play.

Consider the way such buried metaphor works in the opening scene of *Julius Caesar*. The play opens with the tribunes Flavius and Marullus confronting a group of commoners in the streets who are not dressed in such a way as to reveal their professions. Flavius orders the commoners to head home since it is a working day.

> **FLAVIUS**
> Hence! home, you idle creatures get you home:
> Is this a holiday? what! know you not,
> Being mechanical, you ought not walk
> Upon a labouring day without the sign
> Of your profession? Speak, what trade art thou?
>
> (I, i, 1–5)

When they learn that the working men have declared a holiday for themselves to celebrate the triumph of Caesar against Pompey, Marullus explodes in anger:

> You blocks, you stones, you worse than senseless things!
> O you hard hearts, you cruel men of Rome.
>
> (I, i, 35–36)

Note the imagery Marullus employs to describe what he sees as the unthinking mob of commoners in Rome. He calls them, "You blocks, you stones," employing one possible metaphor for parts of a city. To conceive the citizens of a state as blocks and stones is to see them as senseless things with "hard hearts," inert components of the polis. What starts as an innocent reference will eventually become important in the play as one of the competing metaphor models for imagining the polis. Later in the play, competing metaphors for the city will be introduced. Most important is conceiving Rome as a "body politic" comprising a head, a trunk, and limbs. In Act II, scene i, the conspirators meet in Brutus' orchard to formulate their plans for killing Caesar. When Cassius proposes that they kill Mark Antony as well, Brutus objects:

> **BRUTUS**
> Our course will seem too bloody, Caius Cassius,
> To cut the head off and then hack the limbs,
> Like wrath in death and envy afterwards;
> For Antony is but a limb of Caesar:
>
> (II, I, 175–178)

Using conventional medieval political imagery, Brutus imagines the city as a body, with Caesar as its head. Mark Antony is viewed as a limb (Caesar's right hand). But in the current context of planning a regicide, the imagery of the body politic creates a problem of conceptualizing the killers. When Brutus says, "Our course will seem too bloody," the word "course" also suggests a bloody "corpse," which leads Brutus to conceptualize the murder as a sacrifice. "Let's carve him as a dish fit for the gods," Brutus insists, "Not hew him as a carcass fit for the hounds" (II, i, 186–187). Trying his best to evade the butchery metaphor entailed by conceptualizing Rome as a body, Brutus struggles to reshape the metaphor to conceptualize the killing as a sacred rite. Throughout the play, conflicting metaphors for Roman political association highlight the Elizabethan world's contested political landscape.

Another example of buried metaphor we have examined comes from *The Winter's Tale*. *The Winter's Tale* is a play about both fatherhood and kingship, and their connection. Two "buried metaphors" shape the meaning of the story, the conventional biblical metaphor of the good shepherd as an image of pastoral care, and the cutting of hair, conventionally used as a symbol of punishment and penance. The two mental spaces are linked through the theme of sheep-shearing, which dominates the second half of the play. Autolycus, whose name means "Self-Wolf," is one of Shakespeare's great choric characters both fascinating and baffling, whose significance in the play is often overlooked. A theatrical rendering of the proverbial "wolf in sheep's clothing," Autolycus intends "to make the shepherds prove sheep" by "cutting their purses," blending the mental spaces of the good shepherd and the shearing of hair. The currents of embedded metaphor gradually converge, lending an unexpected unity to what initially seems like a disjointed play with two poorly connected plots. A powerful and coherent set of themes dealing with sin, redemption, humility, fatherhood, and kingship are linked through the metaphoric power of the good shepherd theme.

The Winter's Tale nicely illustrates how Shakespeare can weave together seemingly unrelated strands of buried metaphor to produce in the play unexpected thematic unity. In the play's first half, Leontes' destruction of his family, born of irrational jealousy, results in his own punishment. Leontes is left heirless in part through his own doing. But this was also the punishment meted out to him by the Oracle at Delphi, which proclaims, in direct, unambiguous language:

> Hermione is chaste, Polixenes blameless,
> Camillo a true subject, Leontes a jealous tyrant,
> his innocent babe truly begotten; and the King shall
> live without an heir if that which is lost be not
> found.

(III, ii, 141–146)

The King's punishment is to lose his heir, a pun which also suggest losing his hair, a classic act of humility and penance. It is a punishment that anticipates redemption. The word-play is made even clearer by the play's conclusion when lost relationships are restored, and Leontes is reunited with his lost daughter as well as his wife (in a famous miracle of theatrical resurrection). With his daughter comes her husband, Florizel. Their marriage reconciles Leontes and Polixenes. The return of his daughter restores Leontes' lost heir. Paulina's proclamation signals the climax to the long-delayed resolution of the play: "The crown will find an heir" (V, i, 55), bringing the buried metaphor to the surface of the text in a moment of linguistic and theatrical magic. Throughout the play, the metaphorical blends of "crown," "heir," and "hair" are left largely hidden from view. But, once the metaphor surfaces in Paulina's simple statement, Shakespeare's word-craft brings together several undercurrents of buried metaphors in The Winter's Tale, contributing to this play's dramatic resolution and its haunting emotional and philosophical power.

What's in a name?

In addition to his play with metaphor, Shakespeare often uses names to introduce subtle commentary into the text. In perhaps the most quoted lines of *Romeo and Juliet*, Juliet famously tries to dismiss the importance of names, in particular the name of her new lover:

> O Romeo, Romeo! wherefore art thou Romeo?
> Deny thy father and refuse thy name;
> Or, if thou wilt not, be but sworn my love,
> And I'll no longer be a Capulet. . . .

$$(\text{II, ii, } 35\text{--}38)^2$$

While audiences watching the play tend to take Juliet at her word, in sympathy with her claim that names are just labels that may be attached or detached at will, a close reading of her lines suggests something quite different. Shakespeare's answer to Juliet's question "What's in a name?" would seem to be a mystery. At every step, names dog her tracks. Her question "Wherefore art thou Romeo" includes a play on the word "art" where the name Romeo is identified as a work of "art"—the poet's art. Not initially grasping the extent to which the power of names constrains her world, Juliet she asks Romeo why his name is "Romeo." To save their own relationship, Juliet urges Romeo to deny his father and refuse his name. If he denies his father, then it is not "Romeo" at issue but "Montague," his family name, a name to which Romeo is bound by blood and history. Juliet cannot escape the legacy of names. Even as Juliet claims that "that which we call a rose/By any other name would smell as sweet" (II, ii, 46–47), she unknowingly evokes Rosaline, Romeo's love interest at the start of the play, ironically suggesting that lovers themselves might prove interchangeable. Even her own name Juliet (July) is oddly linked to her birth, since, as her nurse reveals, she was born on Lammas Eve (the last day of July).

While it is a focal theoretical concern of *Romeo and Juliet*, Shakespeare's interest in the interplay of sound and sense in his characters' names is found throughout his work. In *Twelfth Night*, Viola and Olivia are parallel female characters whose links are reflected in the fact that their names are near anagrams of each other.

Underscoring their bond is the fact that Olivia falls in love at first sight with Viola, who has disguised herself as a young man, Cesario. We may not know right away what this all means, but once we see it, we know that something important is at stake. The near-anagram reappears in the name of Olivia's servant Malvolio, a name which literally means "ill will." Olivia's household is also populated by Feste, a clown, and Olivia's uncle Sir Toby Belch. These names link Olivia's household to images of feasting and digestion, an odd association for a household until we realize that this household's mistress is paralyzed by mourning for Olivia's brother. Shakespeare's link predates Freud's classic *Feasting and Melancholia* by over three centuries. Again, the web of associations in the names directs readers to pay attention, suggesting that these connections are not coincidental and that the play may be understood from a new perspective.

The same can be said for the odd names of the would-be actors in *A Midsummer Night's Dream* who reappear at key points in the play, struggling to stage the play *Pyramus and Thisbe*. Consider the striking collection of names: Snug (a joiner), Frances Flute (a bellows mender), Peter Quince (a carpenter), Robin Starveling (a tailor), Nick Bottom (a weaver), and Tom Snout (a tinker). At face value, the names convey a comic note, but they are also evocative in potentially significant ways. Each name is drawn from a different semantic domain (carpentry, birds, fruit, musical instruments, anatomy), and each player hails from a different profession. They propose a world ordered by multiple dimensions of classification. But the classifications are all disjunctive, coming from incompatible domains. Shakespeare uses an elaborate form of word-play to elevate and deepen the significance of what appears on the surface to be little more than entertaining farce.

Shakespeare's naming practices are not always memorable. Sometimes he develops a pair of characters so that their names do not stick in memory, and the audience has trouble recalling who's who. In some cases, characters' names are so close as to be easily confused. In other cases, the characters are sufficiently indistinct that their names do not function well in keeping them apart. Aside from Olivia and Viola (as well as Malvolio) in *Twelfth Night*, there are the sisters Goneril and Regan[3] and the brothers Edmund and Edgar in *King Lear*, Rosencrantz and Guildenstern in *Hamlet*,[4] Helena and Hermia, as well as Demetrius and Lysander in *Midsummer Night's Dream*. In *A Midsummer Night's Dream*, the pairing of Theseus and Hippolyta in Athens is paralleled by their night-time doubles, Oberon and Titania. In some productions of the play, the two pairs are played by the same characters. In every case where Shakespeare deliberately blurs the distinction between a pair of characters, there is a significant point to the conflation of identity. Once again, names, including name confusions, turn out to be far from arbitrary. To the discerning reader, these patterns of blurred identity are not just dramatically important but are philosophically significant as well.

Disrupting genre

A final technique that Shakespeare perfected to produce a reflexive, theoretical mood in his plays is to disrupt the reader's expectations of form. Shakespeare's plays often appeal to the audience's anticipation of familiar theatrical and literary conventions but then disrupt those expectations. Tension between the audience's anticipation of a literary form or genre and what actually happens produces an unexpected space in the play for theoretical commentary and reflection.

One of the most common ways Shakespeare manipulates genre in his plays is with the closely allied performance genres of ritual and theatre. While the correct performance of a ritual or a drama is a powerful signal that all is at it should be, a failure of expected performance is a powerful signal that something is wrong. As discussed in Chapter 1, *Hamlet* is a play full of rituals that are inevitably incomplete, interrupted, or otherwise "maimed." The play opens with a changing of the guard. Bernardo's "Who's there?" are the first words we hear. Old Hamlet's funeral is interrupted by his brother's wedding to his wife. Prince Hamlet is trapped in a mourning rite that will not end. Ophelia's funeral rites are twice-maimed, first because, having committed suicide, she is denied burial in the Church graveyard, and secondly because Hamlet and Laertes both jump into her grave and convert the burial rites into an oratorical competition. And finally, the plot itself is interrupted by Fortinbras' arrival to complete his revenge story and replace Hamlet's succession tale with his own.

Hamlet is the not the only example of ritual and performance at play within Shakespeare's works. *King Lear* begins with the old king dividing up his kingdom among his daughters and apportioning territory based on a grotesque calculus of how much each daughter claims to love him. This auctioning off of his kingdom using the currency of love is not a conventional ritual, but it suggests a reading of a last will and testament. Lear is performing a kind of funeral rite for himself. Moreover, the rite that should mark the end of life and the play's conclusion is the start of the play. By distorting ritual and implicating that distortion in the disruption of a story-line's expected shape, Shakespeare propels the audience into a grotesquely distorted world. Before we come to know the content of this world, we know that its forms do not make sense. In *King Lear*, disrupted ritual is paralleled by the disruption of the expected theatrical genre. On the face of it, the play promises a familiar story: the ceremonial humbling of a foolish king, who is forced from his court and must undertake a journey into the forest or other wild place, suffering physical as well as spiritual torment, only to return at the end of the story to his court, having gained from the ordeal some kind of wisdom and humility. This journey suggests a familiar rite of passage for kings with many variations that have been well studied by anthropologists.

At first, the play seems to follow its anticipated path, and the audience has a right to expect that Lear will be returned at the play's end to his rightful place in his court, in the embrace of his one faithful daughter Cordelia. But the play fails to complete itself in the anticipated manner. Instead, Cordelia is captured and put to death, and Lear dies holding her in his arms, protesting that he can see her breathe. Watching the pitiful spectacle of Lear attempting to revive his dead daughter, Kent articulates the audience's own sense that the play has betrayed them when he asks, "Is this the promised end?" (V, iii, 278), a question which implicates both the promised end of the world (doomsday) and the expected conclusion for this kind of story. This rupture of form is a violation of both a ritual process and a theatrical genre. As with any violation of expectation, the absence of "the promised end" of *King Lear* both draws attention to the conventional norms that have been breached and opens a space—a theoretical moment—for reflecting on the larger implications of what this violation might mean. The ultimate meaning of this disturbing play, and even the question of whether Shakespeare gives us any reason to expect meaning from this play are issues deeply contested by scholars and audiences alike. However, these deliberate disruptions of conventional form serve to open the play to theoretical interrogation in a way that a play that was true to genre would not.

Genre issues involving ritual also pervade *Julius Caesar*, raising questions about the conspirators' motives in killing Caesar. In Act II, when Cassius insists that Mark Antony be killed along with Caesar, Brutus relents but says, "Let's be sacrificers, but not butchers, Caius" (II, i, 183). The issue is how to frame the act. Brutus wants the killing of Caesar to be viewed as a ritual sacrifice, not as butchery. These questions of how to frame Caesar's death continue after the assassination as the conspirators and Mark Antony negotiate plans for Caesar's funeral. The conspirators' challenge is whether to allow Caesar's friend Mark Antony to speak:

ANTONY
Friends am I with you all and love you all,
Upon this hope, that you shall give me reasons
Why and wherein Caesar was dangerous.

BRUTUS
Or else were this a savage spectacle.

(III, i, 241–244)

Antony insists that Caesar's body be "produced" in the marketplace, where he can offer a eulogy for his friend. While the marketplace may be an appropriate gathering place for civic events, it is also a center of commerce. The ambiguity is crucial, though audiences do not always notice it. In the context of the marketplace, the eulogies begin to lose their status as parts of a sacred funeral rite and are transformed into a kind of auction or theatrical production, purchasing the populace's hearts and minds. The currency in play is initially words. But Antony understands as Brutus does not, that words alone might not suffice to purchase the people's support. And so he produces not only Caesar's body but his will and offers in Caesar's name 75 drachmas to every Roman citizen. It was not lost on Shakespeare that in Elizabethan English, "to utter" meant not only "to speak" but "to purchase." The "utter ambiguity" created by the uncomfortable proximity of sacred and commercial discourse produces a shadow of doubt in Julius Caesar, an unexpected opening for theoretical reflection in the play.

Anamorphosis

All of the literary devices we have discussed involve subtle manipulations of the reader's point of view. Shakespeare's skill in orchestrating plays that are equally effective from two points of view reflects his genius for controlling perspective. This concern with perspective is evident throughout *Hamlet*, where Shakespeare repeatedly manages to lure the attention of "the distracted globe"—the audience—away from the consequential action "offstage" to pay attention to the wrong thing. Shakespeare's fascination with point-of-view is not merely an abstract literary concern, but emerges from technical developments in optics and mirrors in Shakespeare's day, as well as the changing cosmology that accompanied the Copernican revolution discussed in Chapter 3. The Copernican revision of the cosmos was a radical "perspectival revolution," producing for the Elizabethans a new "world view." When seen from the sun's perspective, the universe looked very different from what it had been when Earth was its focal point.

Developments in optics reinforced the notion that perspective mattered. The first compound optical microscope was developed in 1595 in the Netherlands, followed 13 years later by the refracting telescope (Watson 2007). Both scale and angle of view were dramatically relativized. In Shakespeare's day, scholars and artists were fascinated by catoptrics and dioptrics and the various kinds of perspective glasses produced by early Renaissance optical science.

> In 1533, Agrippa von Nettesheim, master of occult science, had written that experiments with mirrors and lenses were "daily seen," and listed an impressive variety: "Hollow, Convex, Plane, Pillar-fashion'd, Pyramidal, Globular, Gibbose, Orbicular, full of angles, Inverted, Everted, Regular, Irregular, Solid and Perspicuous. . . . There is a sort of Glass wherein a man may see the Image of another man, but not his own . . . [etc.]."
>
> (Shickman 1978: 219)

Seen from a proliferating array of new perspectives, the world as people understood it took on new meanings, forcing a revision of old understandings of how the cosmos was ordered. Like any significant paradigm shift, the combination of the Copernican revolution and the science of optics was unsettling, not only in its specific effects on cosmology but more generally in relativizing people's understanding of their world. Any account of how we see would now have to account for the role of perspective (Edgerton 2009).

This relativity of perspective had profound theological and psychological implications for Shakespeare's contemporaries. The perspectival revolution affected not only philosophers and theologians but also artists. Renaissance artists became increasingly engaged by perspectival issues. Increasingly, a painting was understood to encompass a particular point of view. The Sienese artist Ambrogio Lorinzetti's 1344 painting *Annunciation* is generally recognized as the first image employing linear perspective. The discovery of linear perspective in painting was based on a paradox with far-reaching implications for the Renaissance. Superficially, linear perspective suggests painting's mimetic function, the reproduction in two dimensions of how the eyes perceive three dimensions. This superficial attention to perceptual realism was achieved by a visual trick and actually represented a growing interest in illusion and the fallibility of human vision:

> Among the multitude of claims for linear perspective, the relevant ones here are not just that it became "the naturalized visual culture of [a] new artistic order," or that it led to a wholly different way of seeing the world, but that it was essentially illusionary.
>
> (Clark 2007: 83)

The human eye was understood to be subject to perceptual manipulation, underscoring the relativity of perception. Perspective was recognized more as a dimension of local culture and history than a human universal (Panofsky 1991).

Artists devised techniques for drawing attention to the angle at which a painting is viewed as a central component of its meaning. These techniques for controlling point of view attracted the attention of writers. To create an explicitly theoretical space in his plays, Shakespeare appears to have been influenced by a perspective trick adopted from Renaissance painting and adapted for literature. This technique, called *anamorphosis*, developed from the interest in perspective that emerged in Renaissance art and architecture. Deriving from a Greek word meaning "transformation," the word "anamorphosis" is composed of terms meaning "again" or "back" (*ana*) and "shape" or "appearance" (*morph*). Anamorphic projections are distorted images that are difficult to discern when viewed straight on but become more evident when viewed from an angle or through a reflection from a cylindrical object or mirror. Anamorphosis invites the viewer to "look again" at a painting from a new angle, gaining a novel perspective on the image, both literally and figuratively. For anyone assuming that the new attention to perspective in painting implied a decisive turn to perceptual realism, anamorphosis comes as a surprising revelation:

> More than anything else, anamorphosis can now be seen to threaten any assumption that perspectival art somehow brought appearance and reality successfully together. According to Baltrušaitis, anamorphosis was nothing less than "an effective medium for producing optical illusion and a philosophy of false reality." Under its impact perspective ceased "to be a science of reality and [became] an instrument for producing illusions." .
>
> (Baltrušaitis 1977)

The first generally acknowledged anamorphic representation was Leonardo Da Vinci's 1485 drawing *The Eye*, a distorted and elongated representation of an eye which, when rotated at a sharp angle, looks like a normal eye. The image is drawn as an accurate image but only from an oblique angle of observation. The most famous example of anamorphic representation is *the double portrait of Jean de Dinteville and Georges de Selve, "The Ambassadors"* painted by Hans Holbein the Younger in 1533 and now owned by the National Gallery in London. The painting is reproduced below in Figure 9.1.

FIGURE 9.1 "The Ambassadors." Jean de Dinteville and Georges de Selve ("The Ambassadors") Hans Holbein the Younger. The Ambassadors. 1533. © The National Gallery, London

Viewed straight on, the painting is a formal portrait of two men. *Jean de Dinteville* (1504–1555), Seigneur of Polisy and French ambassador to the court of Henry VIII, is dressed in sumptuous secular garments while *Georges de Selve, Bishop of Lavaur,* wears clerical attire.[5] The men stand on either side of a table displaying an assembly of scientific instruments of the day, two globes (one terrestrial, one celestial), an oriental rug, several open books (including a Lutheran Psalm Book), and a lute. The painting conveys an upbeat initial impression, a testament to the harmonious partnership of the Church, science, and global trade. But the exact meaning of this assemblage of objects has been the subject of much scholarly debate. Closer examination of the intricately detailed painting throws into question the simple and optimistic interpretation. For example, the lute is painted with a broken string, a common symbol of discord in Renaissance iconography that suggests that the assemblage we are staring at may not be as harmonious as we had thought. See Figure 9.2 below.

FIGURE 9.2 Broken lute string in "The Ambassadors". Detail from Jean de Dinteville and Georges de Selve ("The Ambassadors"), Hans Holbein the Younger. The Ambassadors. 1533. © The National Gallery, London

Most startling is the distorted image joining the two men at their feet *(Figure 9.3)*.

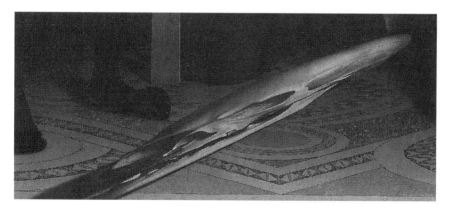

FIGURE 9.3 Distorted shape at the base of "The Ambassadors," Detail from Jean de Dinteville and Georges de Selve ("The Ambassadors"), Hans Holbein the Younger. The Ambassadors. 1533. © The National Gallery, London

Easily overlooked as a shadow upon an initial viewing of the picture, the form becomes clear only when it is viewed with the painting rotated sharply clockwise. Viewed up close from this angle, the shadow reveals itself as a human skull, a common symbol of human frailty, transience, and mortality. The "corrected" image, the ultimate *memento mori,* is seen below in *Figure* 9.4.

FIGURE 9.4 The "corrected" image. Photo courtesy of Thomas Shahan

The image of death is represented anamorphically. It is always right before our eyes, but we do not readily notice it. Once recognized, the knowledge of human mortality and vanity implied by the skull revises our vision, lending new and unanticipated meaning to the display of the achievements of human art, science, and culture. The "meaning" of the painting becomes much more complicated than first imagined and has to be understood as encompassing *both* the conventional first impression the painting conveys, and the startling re-vision of the image derived from the second glance and the new perspective. Ilya Kliger nicely summarizes the implications of the "look-again" experience of viewing Holbein's *The Ambassadors:*

> The viewer of *The Ambassadors* is encoded into the logic of the painting as a protagonist to whom something happens in time. In the sequential acts of perceiving and then deciphering the blot, the viewer replaces the depicted figures as the painting's true hero. Looking at a partially anamorphic image, the viewer is, as it were, split into two: called upon to seek an answer to a riddle on the one hand, and, on the other, to remember the riddle when the answer is received. In this sense, the viewer must fulfill the double task required of readers – namely to join the protagonist's movement through narrative and to make sense of that movement in its entirely.

(Kliger 2007: 295)

Kriger's double task necessitated by the split representation of anamorphosis is the one we have been considering in these pages: simultaneous attention to the action at hand and the ultimate theoretical interpretation of that action. Note that this painting employs partial rather than total anamorphosis. Most of the image seems to be comprehensible from direct viewing. The immediately available image displays a coherent and solid world grounded in cultural, theological, and scientific achievement. In this world, the skull's anamorphic image appears as a shadow or stain on the floor that is all but invisible. However, the skull is decoded once the angle of vision is shifted and the viewer's perspective on what this image means becomes inverted. What had been initially perceived as a direct apprehension of a conventional truth reveals itself as a distorted image. As Stuart Clark puts it, "[T]he dominant visual order is painstakingly naturalistic, and yet it is rendered utterly formless once the naturalism of the anamorphic skull is restored by its being seen from the required viewpoint" (Clark 2007: 92). Conversely, what had appeared as the distorted image turns out to propose a more accurate perspective. The painting can never be viewed—or understood—the same way again.

A similar use of the human skull with a different anamorphic technique appears in a 1587 anamorphic portrait of Mary Queen of Scotts, which is composed of painted slats that continually rotate together so that a conventional portrait of Mary constantly morphs into a death's head image and then back to the Queen in an effect similar to modern holographic images.[6] The "skull view" of this painting appears below in Figure 9.5.

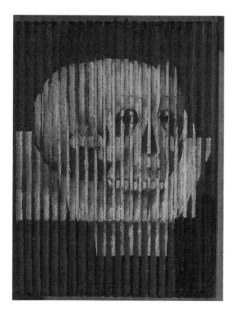

FIGURE 9.5 Anamorphosis, called Mary, Queen of Scots, 1542–1587. Reigned 1542–1567. Anonymous. © The National Galleries of Scotland. Given by A.H. Mayor 1962. Skull perspective.

The "Mary view" of the painting appears below in Figure 9.6

FIGURE 9.6 Anamorphosis, called Mary, Queen of Scots, 1542–1587. Reigned 1542–1567. Anonymous. © National Galleries of Scotland. Given by A.H. Mayor 1962. Mary perspective.

Artists employed various kinds of anamorphic representation throughout the Renaissance.[7] Anamorphic projection was an important part of the attempt to represent perspective on a two-dimensional surface accurately. But it could also serve other, less obvious functions. Anamorphic representations could be used to hide a politically dangerous or controversial image in an otherwise conventional painting. A notorious example of such use of anamorphic projection is the secret portrait of "Bonnie Prince Charles" now at the Westgate Museum. Painted on a tray in such a distorted manner that the image was unrecognizable when viewed normally, the corrected image would appear when viewed in reflection on a cylindrical object. Following the Battle of Culloden in 1746, where the Hanoverian loyalists defeated the Jacobite supporters of Charles Edward Stuart (known as Bonnie Prince Charlie), it became treasonable to show any support for the Stuart Prince. Using the anamorphic projection of his portrait on the tray, his supporters could raise a glass and secretly toast his portrait as it appeared on the cylindrical glass.

As a cultural phenomenon, anamorphic representation in Shakespeare's day could be understood in two very different ways. Most obviously, it reflects the relativizing effect of new attention to perspective and suggests the dislocation of a privileged point of view. Though it showed up in painting, anamorphism was spawned by revolutions in optics, astronomy, and cosmology, all of which drew attention to multiple ways of seeing and ordering the world. Throwing into question the distinction between appearance and reality, anamorphic painting contributed to a decentered universe, one that was increasingly moving away from understanding itself from a monolithic point of view.

Like all play with perspective, anamorphism thrived in a culture fascinated by magic, illusion, and *trompe l'oeil* painting. It is important to remember that magic and illusion were not yet clearly distinguished from emerging developments in science and technology. This fascination with magic, illusion, and the play of perspective were prominently on display on the Elizabethan stage:

> The optical playing on perspectives thus becomes a metaphor for Shakespeare's theatrical use of illusions, deceptions, errors, equivocations, and metatheatrical side-effects added onto the stage fiction, within the frame of the dialectic – central to his work and within the whole epoch of Baroque sensibility— between seeming and being, surface and depth, shadow and substance, *something and nothing*
> … On the relativism of the eye is founded the web of the theatrical illusion itself, which represents reality and at the same time questions it by providing both the characters and the audience with unusual perspectives through which new insights into reality can be obtained beyond the layers of experience. New insights which, once caught, are nevertheless soon distrusted, since reality is ultimately only appearance to human eyes, according to Neoplatonic philosophy.
>
> (Serpieri 1998: 61–62)

But the double-imaging of anamorphosis also had a more conservative face. While the most obvious implication of anamorphosis for Renaissance culture was how it supports a relativizing of perspective, its message was more complex. Despite the initial disruption of interpretation caused by the discovery of the anamorphic image, many of the "hidden" images turn out not to contradict the conventional view so much as to deepen it.

Even ironic forms of anamorphism could reorient perception away from conventional truths to a less easily accessible higher truth. Literary versions of anamorphism were often used in religious poetry to emphasize the distinction between a deceptive appearance and a more reliable apprehension of divinely ordained reality. Here relativism was clearly not the message of the anamorphosis used to conceal secret images. The same was true for political uses of hidden anamorphic images. For example, the use of cylindrical anamorphosis in concealing from all but his secret supporters the hidden portrait of Bonnie Prince Charlie in a distorted swath of paint on a serving tray does not de-center the world so much as it re-centers it on the man presumed by his supporters to be the legitimate King.

Even the classic example of deceptive anamorphosis, the hidden image of the death's skull in Holbein's portrait *The Ambassadors*, is not intended simply to multiply possible perspective on the scene. Holbein clearly added it to provide a perspective that, while less conventional, was understood to be a revelation. In this use of anamorphism, the asymmetry is double: what is less obvious is also more real. This constructive (rather than deconstructive) use of anamorphism is paradoxical in that the hidden portrait and the shadow skull both use a relativistic perspective trick to underwrite a committed point of view. Once it is recognized, the oblique view is understood to convey a truer representation than the misleading direct perspective.

This constructive use of anamorphosis is what we noted in the language of the scenes we from *Romeo and Juliet* discussed at the beginning of the chapter. Here the play of language may seem initially to be refracting the world into incoherence, but a coherent theoretical point of view is rescued by the brilliant hidden double meanings that emerge from the conversation between Montague and Benvolio. This is anamorphosis used to impart a coherent, if submerged, theoretical point of view at the intellectual heart of a powerful love story. For Shakespeare, it served as a perfect technique for adding a theoretical perspective to a more conventional story. Just as painters produced visual representations of anamorphic projections, early modern writers were inspired to mimic this in their own art form. Stuart Clark notes that the anamorphic techniques of early modern painters were "[e]xtended by analogy to the often 'oblique' strategies adopted by early modern writers" (Clark 2007: 92). The development of a literary anamorphosis required writers to find a way to produce word analogs to the distorted images of anamorphic art.

There are many ways that anamorphosis can be adapted to a literary text. In this chapter, I have discussed a variety of techniques Shakespeare uses analogous to visual anamorphosis and that serve to embed a complex philosophical point of view in a conventional story without interfering with or interrupting the straight-on narrative. This claim implies that Shakespeare had a sophisticated grasp of anamorphosis in painting. Anamorphosis already had a long history in painting when Shakespeare started writing. Numerous anamorphic paintings existed in Shakespeare's day, but it is unlikely that he had direct contact with many of them. An anamorphic portrait of Edward VI now hanging in the National Portrait Gallery in London was probably on display in Whitehall Palace when Shakespeare performed there in 1591–1592 (Shickman 1978: 218).

From his plays and poetry, we know that Shakespeare was aware of the kind of perspective tricks in painting and drawing that included anamorphic projection. His plays make several allusions to perspective painting. For example, in *Antony and Cleopatra*, Cleopatra uses the image of an anamorphic painting to account for her complex apprehension of Antony:

> Let him forever go, Let him not—
> Though he be painted one way like a Gorgon,
> The other way's a Mars.

(II, v, 115–117)

However, this is not the only example of Shakespeare referencing anamorphic imagery. The most subtle reference in Shakespeare to anamorphic imagery is found in Act II, scene ii of Richard II. Richard has fled to Ireland, leaving his Queen behind in deep melancholy not only for someone real (her lost husband) but for the absent presence of someone only imagined, the heir that she will never bear.

THE QUEEN
Some unborn sorrow, ripe in fortune's womb
Is coming toward me and my inward soul
With nothing trembles; at something it grieves,
More than with parting from my lord the king.

(II, ii, 10–13)

Bushy prevails on the Queen to "lay aside life-harming heaviness/And entertain a cheerful disposition." He compares the false images of "sorrow's eye" to an anamorphic image, hoping to convince her that her melancholy is an illusion:

BUSHY
Each substance of a grief hath twenty shadows,
Which shows like grief itself, but is not so.
For sorrow's eye, glazed with blinding tears,
Divides one thing entire to many objects;
Like perspectives, which rightly gazed upon
Show nothing but confusion, eyed awry
Distinguish from: so your sweet majesty,
Looking awry upon your lord's departure,
Find shapes of grief, more than himself, to wail;
Which, look'd on as it is, is nought but shadows
Of what it is not. Then, thrice-gracious queen,
More than your lord's departure weep not. More's not seen;
Or if it be, 'tis with false sorrow's eye,
Which for things true weeps things imaginary.

(II, ii, 14–27)

According to Allan Shickman, Shakespeare's reference here is to the anamorphism of the pleated or corrugated panel whose slats turn continuously to reveal multiple images. This is the kind of "turning anamorphism" used in the 1587 portrait of Mary Queen of Scotts discussed above.

In a fascinating essay on Andrew Marvell's use of anamorphic imagery in his poem "Eyes and Tears," Gary Kuchar discusses this passage, emphasizing Shakespeare's use of anamorphism in describing the effects of the Queen's blinding tears which create in her field of vision "nothing but confusion" by dividing "one thing entire to many objects." [8] This evocation of anamorphic tears is also found in Shakespeare's "Venus and Adonis" where Venus' eye and the tears it sheds mutually reflect each other's images, each seeing, each seen:

> O! how her eyes and tears did lend and borrow;
> Her eyes seen in the tears, tears in her eye;
> Both crystals, where they view'd each other's sorrow,
> Sorrow that friendly sighs sought still to dry;
> But like a stormy day, now wind, now rain,
> Sighs dry her cheeks, tears make them wet again.
>
> (961–966)

Shakespeare's interest in perspective tricks went far beyond these few direct references to anamorphic painting in his plays. Shakespeare's frequent use of disguise and deception attests to his interest in the fallibility and manipulability of human perception. Hamlet was conceived as a virtuoso showcase of anamorphic deception. In Chapter 1, I suggested that *Hamlet* was not staged so much by Shakespeare as it was "off-staged," by which I mean that the play is constantly drawing the attention of both characters and audience to an apparent center of action, while, in fact, the real action is taking place somewhere else. From his first words in the play, Hamlet's language suggests that we have entered a world where language has lost its conventional mooring.

> Shakespeare's Perspectivism and polyphony are displayed through a vast range of devices. The play on perspectives is thematized in the hints of the contemporary figurative practice of anamorphosis. It may also, and much more frequently, find an objective correlative in the metalogical use of language as a means of displacing and distorting accepted meanings and codes. Hamlet is the master of this procedure: given a codified acceptation of words, idioms, phrases, formulas, in the language that all the other characters use, he is always displacing the conventional meaning, either literal or metaphorical, starting from his very first words in reply to the King and a bit everywhere in the play. As in the trick of anamorphosis, which deconstructs the central perspective with its assumption of the objective reality of any given thing, Hamlet's metalogical procedures are a way of *looking awry* at the alleged significance of conventional language.
>
> (Serpieri 1998: 64)

In *Hamlet*, Shakespeare exploits the radical potential of perspective tricks to convey a disconcerting sense of a world coming unhinged. By the play's conclusion, we know that there is no hidden center in this kingdom. The play opens with the question "Who goes there?" uttered on Elsinore Castle's parapet by the night watch guard Bernardo. We enter the play in a place from which we cannot see. "There" turns out to be both invisible and indeterminate. In Scene iv, Hamlet will experience yet another interruption on the parapet, this time in the form of his father's ghost, emerging from somewhere unspeakable. The play stages a succession of characters spying on other characters. In II, i, Polonius charges Reynaldo to spy on his son Laertes in Paris. Polonius plants himself behind the arras in the Queen's bedroom to spy on Hamlet's interview with his mother. Meanwhile, the entire bedroom scene is being watched by the Ghost of Old Hamlet. Claudius dispatches Rosencrantz and Guildenstern to spy on Hamlet in Wittenberg. Claudius prays in his closet, unaware that Hamlet is watching him. Hamlet stages *The Mousetrap*, conceived by him as a mirror to catch and reflect the guilty conscience of his uncle and mother. On the face of it, we might assume that Hamlet's notion of his play "mirroring" Claudius's crime and reflecting his guilty conscience implies that a mirror reflects an accurate image.

In his essay on the place of mirrors in Shakespeare's work, Arthur Kinney suggests that this conventional reading of Hamlet's claim misses the complexity of what mirror images implied in Shakespeare's day:

> Leonardo da Vinci remarked that images in mirrors exist only for those look-ing at them, whether they see their own reflections there or not. . . . A mir-ror, Anthony Miller tells us, then as now "may be designed so as to *distort*, a series of mirrors may be arranged so as to multiply images, and even a mirror otherwise faithful must reverse an object as it reflects it." In Shakespeare's day, too, mirrors were most frequently used as metaphorical means of displaying exemplary or infernal images rather than direct reflections.
>
> (Kinney 2004: 3)

What the audience actually sees in the performances of *The Mousetrap* is not a direct reflection of the King and Queen's guilt. There is also an emergent supplementary perspective. The royal audience to the theatrical performance watches the dumb show followed by the play, while Hamlet secretly watches the King and Queen's reactions. Meanwhile, we, the audience, watching both *Hamlet* and *The Mousetrap*, are afforded a spectacle diffracted into numerous angles, an irresolvable profusion of viewpoints. In the end, Hamlet's play offers no reliable mirror on the rot of Denmark. What it has afforded us is more like a prism.

This sense of dislocation is underscored in the final scene of *Hamlet*. With Hamlet, Laertes, Claudius, and Gertrude all lying dead, killed one by one in a bloody circuit of revenge, the young Norwegian Prince Fortinbras leads his army into Elsinore Castle, having marched from Norway, via Poland, and from beyond what we had assumed were the Danish boundaries of the play, to claim the throne of Denmark. The play ends with its focus suddenly shifted to a kind of side-show. The Norway revenge story, which had been summarized in the opening scene of the play in a tedious and long-winded speech by Horatio, begging to be ignored by the audience, reappears in the final minutes of the play to reveal itself as the overlooked heart of the play. We had all been attending to the wrong country and the wrong revenge. In *Hamlet*, Shakespeare has constructed an elaborate theatrical analog to the painter's perspective trick. In attending straight on to the business at hand, the audience and the central characters have all missed the point of the play because, as it turns out, they have been viewing the action from the wrong perspective. The anamorphism of Hamlet is no simple literary analogy of *The Ambassadors*. Holbein's double/triple portrait is only partially anamorphic since it has an easily comprehensible straight-on perspective and a single oblique shadow image that finally discloses a deeper meaning. But the world of Hamlet's Denmark has no shadow focal point on which to rest its revelation. Its world is a continuous unfolding of an unending anamorphosis. There is no privileged angle from which we can resolve the ambiguity and derive a final understanding of the play. Consequently, *Hamlet* is radically anamorphic, a kind of "muse-trap" where the fundamental human need to locate oneself in a point of view is frustrated at every turn.

Shakespeare applied what he had likely learned from anamorphic imagery, focusing his audience's attention on a compelling conventional story while embedding a theoretically disruptive shadow at the margins of the plays. We have seen how this anamorphic technique works in *Hamlet* and, in part, accounts for its distinctive power and its apparently endless mystery for audiences and directors alike. Shakespeare's conventional theatrical pleasures are often achieved by diverting attention from the philosophically fascinating but often difficult or disturbing implications of what goes on in the shadows of the text.

Romeo and Juliet poses similar challenges for the audience. In the discussion of the opening scene of *Romeo and Juliet*, we have seen how an apparently trivial exchange between servants from the Capulet and Montague anticipates the theoretical issues about language that thoroughly infiltrate the love story. Sometimes the hidden theoretical register of a play is sequestered in the shadows of its subplot. The same thing holds for *A Midsummer Night's Dream*. The plot focus in *A Midsummer Night's Dream* is evenly divided between the human lovers' tangled relationships and the conflict between Oberon and Titania, which has disturbed the fairy forest's tranquility. The obvious tension in the play's structure is between the Court of Athens and the fairies' forest world. The Mechanicals' rehearsals of their performance of *Pyramus and Thisbe* are usually considered a minor subplot, providing a degree of comic relief from the lovers' quarrels. And yet, these rehearsals and the final performance of the Mechanicals' play as a wedding masque celebrating the three couples' nuptials at the end of the play are far from marginal aspects of *A Midsummer Night's Dream*. Careful attention by a reader of Shakespeare's text to what had first seemed to be simple comic relief reveals the complex ideas about love, sexuality, and marriage at the center of the play.

Conclusion: the unanticipated pleasures of reading Shakespeare

This final chapter has stressed the hard-won pleasures of approaching Shakespeare through the written text. While there is an intimate relationship between reading and watching a play, they are not the same experience. Watching a great stage or cinematic performance of Shakespeare can bring a play to life in a way that reading the text can rarely do. But I have suggested in these pages that Shakespeare's texts are also home to another kind of life—the life of great ideas. A careful and informed reading of the plays illuminates Shakespeare's grasp of some classic issues in social theory that are not always apparent when the plays are staged. Seeing a great performance of a play whose text we have carefully studied allows for a powerful convergence of the multiple levels at which the play works. It can be a thrilling experience.

Shakespeare confronted the problem of creating a play that was immediately engaging at the level of action and character, but also served as an effective vehicle for an elaborate exploration of social and philosophical questions. In resolving this problem, he had a variety of literary techniques from which to draw. Prose fiction such as novels and short stories use shifts in narrative styles to move the reader closer and further from the action. Because the action of novels is generally narrated rather than directly presented, novelists are free to introduce a reflexive, philosophical voice into their stories in a way that playwrights cannot. Traditionally, playwrights have found ways to inject a narrative voice by using a choric figure, either a character within the play who doubles as the authorial voice or a full-time commentator who stands apart from the play. Shakespeare effectively used all these techniques and added to them the soliloquy, a kind of performed thinking made famous by Hamlet in which the audience is given privileged access to Hamlet's thoughts. In addition to these common techniques for creating theoretical distance in a literary text, Shakespeare apparently adapted for the printed page techniques developed by Renaissance artists for embedding multiple perspectives in their paintings. The best known of these techniques, anamorphosis, allowed for supplementary images to be embedded into conventional scenes such that they could only be seen from oblique angles. In these final two chapters, we have looked carefully, using examples from his plays and poetry, at how Shakespeare adapted sophisticated techniques to open up his plays theoretically.

These techniques do not exhaust how Shakespeare controls and manipulates perspective in his plays, but they represent a set of important literary devices that should help orient readers unfamiliar with Shakespeare's texts to the pleasures of close reading. Not surprisingly, word-play, Shakespeare's "prism-house of language," figures prominently in Shakespeare's art, not merely as window dressing, but as the window itself onto a dazzling world of ideas. Readers need to be alert to Shakespeare's compulsive play with language. Shakespeare's language is often layered with unexpected insight. We have seen how Shakespeare could transform the humble pun into a kind of magical prism where the canny reader can trace unexpected and illuminating connections.

Having explored Shakespeare's play with metaphor, we can see that his use of metaphor ranges from the purely conventional to the thoroughly original. In addition to the seemingly endless flow of metaphor from Shakespeare's pen, we have noted a much more subtle use of buried metaphor. Buried metaphor creates subtle streams of metaphoric imagery that often live in the shadows of the text but emerge periodically to suggest an unexpected commentary on the play's action.

Finally, we looked at numerous places where Shakespeare writes against the grain of expected form. Many of his plays feature strangely dislocated conventions such as

distorted rituals or odd twists on theatrical conventions or apparently minor characters who turn out to be pivotal figures in the play. The effect of these dislocations is
always anamorphic. It is easy enough to overlook Shakespeare's oblique undermining of convention and apprehend the play straight on. But once the ironic twists are
noted, they create a subjunctive space of doubt and question that overtakes the audience's conventional expectations. Shakespeare's fascination with ideas thrives in this
subjunctive space made possible by his many literary elaborations of anamorphic
techniques. We have examined Shakespeare's palette of perspective tricks, which
invite the reader to "look again" at the text. These anamorphic techniques allowed
Shakespeare to enlarge the scope of his scripts, transforming the traditional play of
character and action into a hall of mirrors, shimmering with the play of great ideas.

Notes

1 The English lexicon does not appear to distinguish between the trivial pun, where the
superficial overlap in sound between two words disrupts meaning, and what I call the
"magical pun," where the confluence of sound enhances or extends meaning in surprising ways.
2 Juliet's attempt to dismiss the power of names is very similar to Falstaff's famous attempt
in *Henry IV, Part I*, to dismiss the concept of honor as nothing but air:

What is honour? A word. What is in that word
"honour"? What is that "honour"? Air.

(V, i, 133–134)

3 While their names do not sound alike, it is interesting to note that Goneril and Regan
share four letters, making them weak anagrams of one another.
4 With Rosencrantz and Guildenstern, the alignment is not in the similarity of sound but
that both are three-syllable German names. The impression that the names are transpositions of one another is subtly suggested exploited by Shakespeare in their perfect interchangeability within the poetic frame of iambic pentameter:

CLAUDIUS
Thanks, Rosencrantz and gentle Guildenstern.

GERTRUDE
Thanks, Guildenstern and gentle Rosencrantz:

(II, ii, 35–36)

5 For the definitive identification of the two figures in *The Ambassadors*, see Hervey 1900.
6 For a video clip that shows the anamorphic transformation of the face, see http://lifu.
soup.io/post/396784891/Anamorphosis-Mary-Queen-of-Scots-1542-1587.
7 For other examples of anamorphosis in early modern painting, see Clark 2007: 93–96.
Anamorphosis reappeared in work by modern artists and appears in paintings by Salvador
Dali and Marcel Duchamp and in the lithographs of M.C. Escher. Numerous contemporary artists use various forms of anamorphic projection in their work.
8 Kuchar, Gary, "Andrew Marvell's Anamorphic Tears," *Studies in Philology*, Vol. 103, No. 3,
Summer 2006, pp. 345–381.

BIBLIOGRAPHY

Aamot, Agnar and Enric Plaza. 1994. Case-based reasoning: Foundational issues, method-ological variations, and system approaches. *Artificial Intelligence Communications* 7(1): 39–52.

Ainsworth, Mary D. S. 1967. *Infancy in Uganda: Infant Care and the Growth of Love.* Baltimore, MD: Johns Hopkins University Press.

Ainsworth, Mary D. S. 1968. Object relations, dependency, and attachment: A theoretical review of the infant- mother relationship. *Child Development* 40: 969–1025.

Allen, Steve. 1989. *Meeting of Minds: The Complete Scripts* (Third Series). Buffalo, NY: Prometheus Books.

Altman, Joel B. 1978. *The Tudor Play of Mind: Rhetorical Inquiry and the Development of Elizabethan Drama.* Berkeley, CA: The University of California Press.

Alpers, Paul. 1996. *What is Pastoral?* Chicago, IL: University of Chicago Press.

Argan, Giulio Carlo and Nesca A. Robb. 1946. The architecture of Brunelleschi and the origins of perspective theory in the fifteenth century. *Journal of Warburg and Courtauld Institutes* 9: 96–121.

Aristotle. 1952. *The Politics.* Oxford: The Clarendon Press.

Atkin, Albert. Winter 2010. Peirce's theory of signs. *The Stanford Encyclopedia of Philosophy.* http://plato.stanford.edu/archives/win2010/entries/peirce-semiotics/.

Auden, W. H. 1962. *The Dyer's Hand and Other Essays.* New York: Random House.

Babcock, Barbara, ed. 1978. *The Reversible World: Symbolic Inversion in Art and Society.* Ithaca, NY: Cornell University Press.

Bakhtin, Mikhail. 1981. Discourses of the novel. In Caryl Emerson and Michael Holquist, trans. *The Dialogic Imagination: Four Essays.* Austin, TX: The University of Texas Press.

Baldwin, T. W. 1949. *Shakespeare's Small Latine and Lesse Greek.* Urbana, IL: University of Illinois Press.

Baltrušaitis, Jurgis. 1977. *Anamorphic Art.* New York: Harry Abrams.

Barish, Jonas. 1981. *The Anti-Theatrical Prejudice.* Berkeley, CA: University of California Press.

Barker, Peter and Bernard R. Goldstein. 2001. Theological foundations of Kepler's astronomy. *Osiris*, 16: 88–113. In *Science in Theistic Contexts.* Chicago, IL: University of Chicago Press.

Bateson, Gregory. 1972. A theory of play and fantasy. In *Steps to an Ecology of Mind.* Northvale, NJ: Jason Aranson, pp. 183–198.

Beidelman, Thomas. 1966. Swazi royal ritual. *Africa* 36: 373–405.

Belsey, Catherine. 1993. The name of the rose. In Andrew Gurr and Phillipa Hardman, ed., *Romeo and Juliet. The Yearbook of English Studies* 23. Early Shakespeare special number.

Bentley, Paul. 2020. Why an arranged marriage 'is more likely to develop into lasting love'. *The Daily Mail (Mail Online)*, September 2, 2020. https://www.dailymail.co.uk/news/article-1363176/Why-arranged-marriage-likely-develop-lasting-love.html.

Bergen, Benjamin K. 2004. The psychological reality of phonaesthemes. *Language* 80(2): 290–311.

Berry, Phillipa. 2002. On Hamlet's ear. chap. 11. In Catherine Alexander, ed., *Shakespeare and Language*. Cambridge: Cambridge University Press.

Black, Max. 1962. *Models and Metaphors: Studies in Language and Philosophy*. Ithaca, NY: Cornell University Press.

Blair, Ann. 1990. Tycho Brahe's critique of Copernicus and the Copernican system. *Journal of the History of Ideas*, 5: 355–377.

Bloom, Gina. 2010. Boy eternal: Aging, games, and masculinity. *The Winter's Tale. English Literary Renaissance* 40(3): 329–356.

Blumenberg, Hans. 1987. *The Genesis of the Copernican World*, R. M. Wallace, trans. Cambridge, MA: MIT Press.

Booth, Stephen. 1983. *King Lear, Macbeth, Interpretation and Tragedy*. New Haven, CT: Yale University Press.

Booth, Stephen. 2004. Shakespeare's language and the language of his time. In Catherine Alexander, ed., *Shakespeare and Language*. Cambridge: Cambridge University Press

Bowlby, John. 1969. *Attached*. New York: Basic Books

Bowlby, John. 1988. *A Secure Base: Parent-Child Attachment and Healthy Human Development*. New York: Basic Books.

Boyd, Robert and Peter Richerson. 1988. *Culture and the Evolutionary Process*. Chicago, IL: University of Chicago Press.

Bradshaw, Graham. 2000. Shakespeare in the age of cognitive science. *Shakespeare Studies* (Shakespeare Society of Japan), 38: 17–36.

Bradshaw, G., T. Bishop and M. Turner. 2004. *The Shakespeare International Handbook* 4. Aldershot: Ashgate.

Bray, Alan. 1990. Homosexuality and the signs of male friendship in Elizabethan England. *History Workshop* 29, Spring: 1–19.

Brooke, Arthur. 1957. The tragicall history of romeus and juliet written first in Italian by Bandell, and now in English by Ar. Br. In Geoffrey Bullough, ed., *Narrative and Dramatic Sources of Shakespeare* 1. London and New York.

Brooks, Cleanth. 1947. The language of paradox. In *The Well Wrought Urn: Essays on Poetry*. London: Methuen & Co Ltd, pp. 1–16.

Bruner, Jerome. 1986. *Actual Minds, Possible Worlds*. Cambridge: Harvard University Press.

Bruner, Jerome. 1991. The narrative construction of reality. *Critical Inquiry* 18(1), Autumn: 1–21.

Bruner, Jerome. 1996. *The Culture of Education*. Cambridge, MA: Harvard University Press.

Bryan, Michael. 2009. Early English court reporting. *University of Melbourne Collections*, Issue 4(June): 45–50.

Bryant, J. A. 1955. Shakespeare's allegory: 'The Winter's tale'. *The Sewanee Review*, 63(2): 202–222.

Burke, Kenneth. 1945. *A Grammar of Motives*. New York: Prentice Hall.

Burke, Kenneth. 1950. *A Rhetoric of Motives*. New York: Prentice Hall.

Butler, Judith. 1990. *Gender Trouble: Feminism and the Subversion of Identity*. New York: Routledge.

Calderwood, James. 1983. *To Be and Not To Be: Negation and Metadrama in Hamlet*. New York: Columbia University Press.

Camden, Carroll. 1933. Astrology in Shakespeare's day." *Isis* 19(1).

Carleton, George. 1624. *The Madness of Astrologers*. Oxford: W. Turner.

Clark, Stuart. 2007. *Vanities of the Eyes: Vision in Early Modern European Culture*. Oxford: Oxford University Press.

Clarke, Martin Lowther. 1981. *The Noblest Roman: Marcus Brutus and His Reputation*. Ithaca, NY: Cornell University Press.

Cohen, I. B. 1960. *The Birth of a New Physics*. Garden City: Anchor Books.

Colie, Rosalie L. 1966. *Paradoxia Epidemica, The Renaissance Tradition of Paradox*. Princeton, NJ: Princeton University Press.

Connerton, Paul. 1989. *How Societies Remember*. Cambridge, UK: Cambridge University Press.

Cook, Amy. 2010. *Shakespearean Neuroplay*. New York: Palgrave Macmillan.

Crane, Mary Thomas. 2001. *Shakespeare's Brain: Reading with Cognitive Theory*. Princeton, NJ: Princeton University Press.

Crockett, Bryan. 1995. *The Play of Paradox: Stage and Sermon in Renaissance England*. Philadelphia, PA: University of Pennsylvania Press.

Crowe, M. J. 1990. *Theories of the World from Antiquity to the Copernican Revolution*. New York: Dover Publications.

Culpepper, Nicholas. 1652/2009. *An Astrologo-Physical Discourse of the Human Virtues in the Body of Man*, Deborah Houlding, ed. Skyscript, 2009. Originally published in Culpeper's Complete Herbal (English Physician). London: Peter Cole.

Daniel, David. 1998. *Introduction to the Arden Edition of Julius Caesar*. London: Thomas Nelson and Sons, Ltd.

Davis, Philip. 2007. *Shakespeare Thinking*. London and New York: Continuum.

De Grazia, Magreta. 1978. Shakespeare's view of language: An historical perspective. *Shakespeare Quarterly* 29(3): 374–388.

Devereux, George. 1978. Reflections on the notion of kinship. In *Ethnopsychoanalysis: Psychoanalysis and Anthropology as Complementary Frames of Reference*. Berkeley, CA: University of California Press

Dickens, Charles. 2000. *The Mystery of Edwin Drood*. Penguin Classics Edition. London: Penguin Books, pp. 24–26.

Dollimore, Jonathan. 1984. *Radical Tragedy: Religion, Ideology and Power in the Drama of Shakespeare and His Contemporaries*. New York: Palgrave Macmillan.

Donawerth, Jane. 1984. *Shakespeare and the Sixteenth Century Study of Language*. Urbana and Chicago, IL: University of Illinois Press.

Donne, John. 1959. *Devotions Upon Emergent Occasions*. Ann Arbor, MI: The University of Michigan Press.

Douglas, Mary. 2002. *Purity and Danger: An Analysis of Concepts of Pollution and Taboo*. New York: Routledge.

Dumont, Louis. 1970. *Homo Hierarchicus*, Mark Sainsbury, trans. Chicago, IL: University of Chicago Press.

Dumont, Louis. 1986. *Essays on Individualism: Modern Ideology in an Anthropological Perspective*. Chicago, IL: University of Chicago Press.

Durkheim, Emile. 1893/1997. *The Division of Labor in Society*, W. D. Halls, trans. New York: Free Press.

Eck, Werner. 2002. *The Age of Augustus*, D. L. Schneider, trans. New York: Wiley-Blackwell.

Eder, Walter. 2005. *Augustus and the Power of Tradition*. Cambridge: Cambridge University Press.

Edgerton, Samuel Y. 2009. *The Mirror, the Window, and the Telescope: How Renaissance Linear Perspective Changed our Vision of the Universe*. Ithaca, NY: Cornell University Press.

Eliade, Mircea. 1954. *Cosmos and History: The Myth of the Eternal Return*, Willard Trask, trans. New York: Harper and Brothers.

Eliot, Thomas S. 1921. Hamlet and his problems. In *The Sacred Wood: Essays on Poetry and Criticism*. New York: Alfred A. Knopf.

Erasmus, Desiderius. 1999. *On Copia of Words and Ideas (De Utraque Verborum ac Rerum Copia)*, Donald King and H. David Rix, trans. Milwaukee, WI: Marquette University Press.

Fauconnier, Giles. 1997. *Mapping in Thoughts and Language*. Cambridge and New York: Cambridge University Press.

Fauconnier, Giles and Mark Turner. 2008. Rethinking metaphor. In. R. Gibbs, Jr. ed., *The Cambridge Handbook of Metaphor and Thought*, (Cambridge Handbooks in Psychology). Cambridge: Cambridge University Press, pp. 53–66.

Fergusson, Francis. 1949. Hamlet: The analogy of action. In *The Idea of a Theater: A Study of Ten Plays, The Art of Drama in Changing Perspective*. Princeton, NJ, Princeton University Press.

Ferry, Anne. 1988. *The Art of Naming*. Chicago, IL: The University of Chicago Press.

Figges, John Neville. 2012. *Studies of the Political Thought from Gerson to Grotius. The Birbeck Lectures delivered at Trinity College, Cambridge*. Cambridge: Cambridge University Press (Forgotten Books).

Firth, John. 1930. *Speech*. London: Oxford University Press.

Fish, Stanley E. 1971. *Surprised by Sin: The Reader in Paradise Lost*. Berkeley, CA: University of California Press.

Fisher, Will. 2001. The Renaissance beard: Masculinity in early modern England. *Renaissance Quarterly* 54(1), Spring: 155–187.

Foucault, Michel. 1977. *Discipline and Punishment: The Birth of the Prison*, Alan Sheridan, trans. New York: Vintage Books/Random House.

Frazer, James. 1922. *The Golden Bough: A Study in Magic and Religion*. London: Macmillan and Co.

Freud, Sigmund. 1922/1998. Some neurotic mechanisms in jealousy, paranoia and homosexuality. In Nancy Burke, ed. *Gender and Envy*. New York: Routledge, 213–220.

Frey, Charles. 1978. Interpreting *The Winter's Tale. Studies in English Literature, 1500–1900* 18(2). *Elizabethan and Jacobean Drama*, (Spring, 1978): 307–329.

Geertz, Clifford. 1973. The growth of culture and the evolution of mind. In *The Interpretation of Cultures*. New York: Basic Books.

Geertz, Clifford. 1980. *Negara: A Nineteenth Century Balinese Theatre State*. Princeton, NJ: Princeton University Press.

Genette, Gérard. 1995. *Mimologics*, Thaïs E. Morgan, trans. Lincoln, NE and London: The University of Nebraska Press.

Goffman, Erving. 1959. *The Presentation of Self in Everyday Life*. New York, Anchor Books.

Goffman, Erving. 1982. *Interaction Ritual*. New York: Knopf Books.

Gibbs, Raymond. 1994. *The Poetics of Mind: Figurative Thought, Language and Understanding*. Cambridge: Cambridge University Press.

Gilbert, William. 1898/1958. *De Magnete* (facsimile). P. Fleury Mottelay, trans. New York: Dover Publications Inc.

Gingerich, Owen. 2004. *The Book Nobody Read: Chasing the Revolutions of Nicolaus Copernicus*. New York: Walker.

Goethe, Johan Wolfgang von. 2003. *Faust* (Part I). A. S. Kline, trans. Poetry In Translation. www.poetryintranslation.com.

Graveson, R. H. 1941. Movement from status to contract. *Modern Law Review*, April 1941: 261–272.

Greenblatt, Stephen. 1980. *Renaissance Self-Fashioning: From More to Shakespeare*. Chicago, IL: University of Chicago Press.

Greenblatt, Stephen. 1988. Shakespeare and the exorcists. In *Shakespearean Negotiations*. Berkeley, CA: The University of California Press, pp. 94–128.

Harlow, Harry F. 1961. The development of affectional patterns in infant monkeys. In B. M. Foss, ed., *Determinants of Infant Behaviour*. London: Methuen, 75–97.

Harris, Jonathan Gill. 2010. *Shakespeare and Literary Theory*. New York: Oxford University Press.

Hartsock, Mildred E. 1966. The complexity of Julius Caesar. *PMLA* 81(1): 56–62.

Hassel, R. Chris, Jr. 1971. Donne's 'Ignatius His Conclave' and the new astronomy. *Modern Philology* 68(4): 329–337.

Hazen, Cindy and Phillip Shaver. 1987. Romantic love conceptualized as an attachment process. *Journal of Personality and Social Psychology* 52(3): 511–524.

Heath, Thomas. 1913. *Aristarchus of Samos, The Ancient Copernicus ; A History of Greek Astronomy to Aristarchus, Together with Aristarchus's Treatise on the Sizes and Distances of the Sun and Moon*. London: Oxford University Press.

Hervey, Mary F. S. 1900. *Holbein's Ambassadors: The Picture and the Men*. London: George Bell and Sons.

Hertz, Robert. 2004. *Death and the Right Hand*. New York: Routledge.

Hillerman, Tony. 1993. *Sacred Clowns*. New York: HarperCollins Press.

Hobbes, Thomas. 1651/2011. *The Leviathan*. Seattle, WA: Pacific Publishing Studio.

Hollingsworth, T. H. 1964. *The Demography of the British Peerage* (Supplement to *Population Studies*, xviii). London: London School of Economics.

Hunt, M. 1993–4. Modern and postmodern discourses in Shakespeare's *The Winter's Tale*: A response to David Laird. *Connotations* 5(5): 83–94.

Jacobson, Roman. 1965. Quest for the essence of language. *Diogenes* 13(51): 21–37.

James, William. 1890. *Principles of Psychology* 2. New York: Henty Holt & Co.

Jankowiak, William R., ed. 2008. *Intimacies: Love and Sex across Cultures*. New York: Columbia University Press.

Jankowiak, William and Edwin Fischer. 1992 . A cross-cultural perspective on romantic love. *Ethnology* 31(2): 149–155.

Jardine, Nick. 2000. Koyré's Kepler/Kepler's Koyré. *History of Science* 38: 363–376.

Jászi, Oscar and John D. Lewis. 1957. *Against the Tyrant: The Tradition and Theory of Tyrannicide*. Glencoe, IL: The Free Press.

John of Salisbury. 1990. *Polycraticus: Of the Frivolities of Courtiers and the Footprints of Philosophers*, Cary Naderman, ed. and trans. Cambridge, Cambridge University Press.

Johnson, Nora. 1998. Ganymedes and kings: Staging male homosexual desire in *The Winter's Tale*. *Shakespeare Studies* 26: 187–217.

Johnson, Samuel. 1968. Preface to Shakespeare. In Arthur Sherbo, ed., *The Yale Edition of the Works of Samuel Johnson, Volume VII: Johnson on Shakespeare*. New Haven, CT: Yale University Press.

Joseph, John E. 2000. *Limiting the Arbitrary: Linguistic Naturalism and its Opposites in Plato's Cratylus and In Modern Theories of Language. Amsterdam Studies in the Theory and History of Linguistic Science*, 96. Amsterdam/Philadelphia, PA: John Benjamin's Publishing Company

Kang, Gaye E. 1982. *Marry-out or Die-out: A Cross-cultural Examination of Exogamy and Survival Value*, Special studies 148. Amherst: Council on International Studies, State University of New York at Buffalo.

Kant, Immanuel. 2000. *Critique of the Power of Judgement*, Paul Guyer and Eric Matthews, trans. and eds. Cambridge, UK: Cambridge University Press.

Kantorowicz, Ernst. 1957. *The King's Two Bodies: A Study in Medieval Political Theology*. Princeton, NJ: Princeton University Press.

Kapferer, Bruce. 1989. The ritual process and the problem of reflexivity in Sinhalese demon exorcism. In J. MacAloon, ed., *Rite, Spectacle, Theater: Rehearsals Towards a Performance Theory*. Chicago, IL: University of Chicago Press.

Keats, John. 1900. *The Complete Poetical Works and Letters of John Keats*. Cambridge Edition, London: Houghton, Mifflin and Company.

Keil, Frank. 1987. Conceptual development and category structure. In U. Neisser, ed., *Concepts and Conceptual Development: Ecological and Intellectual Factors in Categorization*. Cambridge, UK: Cambridge University Press, pp. 175–200.

Keil, Frank and Michael Kelly. 1987. Categorical perception: The groundwork of cognition. In S. Harnad, ed., *Developmental Changes in Category Structure*. Cambridge, UK: Cambridge University Press, pp. 491–510.

Kermode, Frank, ed. 1963. *The Winter's Tale. The Signet Classic Shakespeare*. New York: New American Library.

Kinney, Arthur F. 2004. Shakespeare's mirrors. In Chap. 1 of *Shakespeare's Webs: Networks of Meaning in Shakespeare's Drama*. New York: Routledge.

Kinney, Arthur F. 2006. *Shakespeare and Cognition: Aristotle's Legacy and Shakespeare's Drama*. London and New York: Routledge.

Kliger, Ilya. 2007. Anamorphic realism: Veridictory plots in Balzac, Dostoevsky, and Henry James. *Comparative Literature* 59, Fall 2007.

Kobe, Donald H. 1998. Copernicus and Martin Luther: An encounter between science and religion. *American Journal of Physics* 66(3): 190–196.

Kocher, Paul H. 1952. The old cosmos: A study in Elizabethan science and religion. *Huntington Library Quarterly*, 15(2): 101–121.

Kökertiz, Helgë. 1966. *Shakespeare's Pronunciation*. New Haven, CT: Yale University Press.

Kollerstrom, Nick. 2004. *Galileo and the new star. Astronomy News*, October.

Kopf, Daniel. 2016. What is Shakespeare's Most Popular Play? *Priceonomics*, https://priceonomics.com/what-is-shakespeares-most-popular-play/.

Kott, Jan. 1969. Kott, Jan, Titania and the asses' head. In Boleslaw Taborski, trans. *Shakespeare our Contemporary*. London: Methuen.

Kott, Jan. 1987. The bottom translation. In *The Bottom Translation*. Evanston, IL: Northwestern University Press.

Kövecses, Zoltan. 1986. *Metaphors of Anger, Pride and Love: A lexical Approach to the Structure of Concepts*. Amsterdam: John Benjamins Publishing Co.

Koyré, Alexandre. 1973. *The Astronomical Revolution: Copernicus-Kepler-Borelli*. Ithaca, NY: Cornell University Press.

Kuchar, Gary. 2006. Andrew Marvell's anamorphic tears. *Studies in Philology* 103(3), Summer: 345–381.

Kuhn, Thomas. 1957. *The Copernican Revolution*. Cambridge: Harvard University Press.

Kuhn, Thomas. 1962. *The Structure of Scientific Revolutions*. Chicago, IL: University of Chicago Press.

Lakoff, George. 1987. *Women, Fire, and Dangerous Things: What Categories Reveal about the Mind*. Chicago, IL: University of Chicago press.

Lakoff, George. 1994. The contemporary theory of metaphor. In A. Ortony, ed., *Metaphor and Thought* (2nd ed). Cambridge, UK: Cambridge University Press.

Lakoff, George. 2008. A neural theory of metaphor. In. R. Gibbs, Jr., ed., *The Cambridge Handbook of Metaphor and Thought* (Cambridge Handbooks in Psychology). Cambridge: Cambridge University Press, pp. 18–38.

Lakoff, George and Mark Johnson. 1980. *Metaphors We Live By*. Chicago, IL: University of Chicago Press.

Lakoff, George and Mark Turner. 1989. *More than Cool Reason: A Field Guide to Poetic Metaphor*. Chicago, IL: University of Chicago Press.

Langacker, Ronald. 1987. *Foundations of Cognitive Grammar I*, Theoretical Prerequisites. Stanford, CA: Stanford University Press.

Langacker, Ronald. 1991. *Foundations of Cognitive Grammar II*, Descriptive Application. Stanford, CA: Stanford University Press.

Langacker, Ronald. 1999. *Grammar and Conceptualization*. Berlin/New York: Mouton de Gruyter.

Langacker, Ronald. 2008. *Cognitive Grammar: A Basic Introduction*. New York: Oxford University Press.

Langer, Susanne. 1957. *Philosophy in a New Key*. Cambridge, MA: Harvard University Press.

Laniac, Timothy S. 2006. *Shepherds After My Own Heart: Pastoral Traditions and Leadership in the Bible (New Studies in Biblical Theology)*. Downers Grove, IL: Intervarsity Press.

Leach, Edmund. 1957. Magical hair. *Journal of the Royal Anthropological Institute* 88(II): 147–164.

Lecky, W. E. H. 1919. *History of the Rise and Influence of the Spirit of Rationalism in Europe*. New York: D. Appleton.

Levenson, Jill. 2004. Shakespeare's *Romeo and Juliet*: The places of invention. In Chap. 7 of Catherine M.S. Alexander, ed., *Shakespeare and Language*. Cambridge: Cambridge University Press.

Lévi-Strauss, Claude. 1966. *The Savage Mind*. Chicago, IL: University of Chicago Press.

Lévi-Strauss, Claude. 1967. Do dual organizations exist? In *Structural Anthropology*. New York: Doubleday Anchor.

Lévi-Strauss, Claude. 1969. *The Elementary Structures of Kinship*, James Harle Bell, John Richard von Sturmer, and Rodney Needham, trans. Boston: Beacon Press.

Lévy-Bruhl, Lucien. 1935. *Primitives and the Supernatural*, L. A. Clare, trans. New York: E.P. Dutton.

Levy-Bruhl, Lucien. 1973. *Primitives and the Supernatural* (Le surnaturel et la nature dans la mentalité primitive). New York, NY: Haskell House Publishers.

Lewin, Kurt. 1952. Field theory in social science. In Dorwin Cartwright, ed., *Selected Theoretical Papers by Kurt Lewin*. London: Tavistock.

Lewis, C. S. 1936. *The Allegory of Love: A Study in Medieval Tradition*. Oxford: Oxford University Press.

Lindberg, David C. 1986. The genesis of Kepler's theory of light: Light metaphysics from Plotinus to Kepler. In E.C. Spary and Anya Zilberstein, ed., *Osiris*, N.S. 2. Chicago, IL: University of Chicago Press.

Lovascio, Domenico. 2016. *All our lives upon ones lippes depend: Caesar as a tyrant in William Alexander's "Julius Caesar"*. *Medieval & Renaissance Drama in England* 29: 68–102.

Luhrman, Tanya. 1989. *Persuasions of the Witches' Craft Ritual Magic in Contemporary England*. Cambridge, MA: Harvard University Press.

MacAloon, John. 1984. *Rite, Drama, Festival, Spectacle : Rehearsals Toward a Theory of Cultural Performance*. Philadelphia, PA: Institute for the Study of Human Issues.

MacFarlane, Alan. 1978. The origins of English individualism: Some surprises. *Theory and Society* 6(2): 255–277.

Mack, Maynard. 1965. Archetype, parable and vision. In *King Lear in Our Time*. Berkeley, CA: University of California Press.

Mahood, M. M. 2004. *Shakespeare's Wordplay*. London: Routledge.

Maine, Henry. 1861. *Ancient Law*. New York: Henry Holt and Co.

Makkreel, Rudolph A. 2015. *Orientation and Judgement in Hermeneutics.* Chicago, IL: University of Chicago Press.

Malinowski, Bronislaw. 1922. *Argonauts of the Western Pacific.* London: George Routledge.

Malloch, A. E. 1956. The techniques and functions of the renaissance paradox. *Studies in Philology* 53: 191–203.

Marks, Lawrence E. and Marc Bornstein. 1987. Sensory similarities, classes, characteristics and cognitive consequences. In R. Haskell, ed., *Cognition and Symbolic Structures, The Psychology of Metaphoric Transformation.* Norwood, NJ: Ablex, pp. 49, 65.

Mauss, Marcel. 1967. *The Gift: Forms and Functions of Exchange in Archaic Societies,* Ian Cunnison, trans. New York: W.W. Norton.

Medin, Douglas and Lawrence Barsalou. 1987. Categorization process and categorical perception. In U. Neisser, ed., *Concepts and Conceptual Development: Ecological and Intellectual Factors in Categorization.* Cambridge, UK: Cambridge University Press, pp. 450–495.

McDonald, Russ. 2001. *Shakespeare and the Arts of Language.* New York: Oxford University Press.

McFarland, Thomas. 1972. *Shakespeare's Pastoral Comedy.* Chicago, IL: University of Chicago Press.

Miller, Jonathan. 1993. King Lear in rehearsal: A talk. In B. J. Sokol, ed., *The Undiscovered Country: New essays in Psychoanalysis and Shakespeare.* London: Free Association Books, pp. 17–38.

Miola, Robert S. 1985. *Julius Caesar* and the tyrannicide debate. *Renaissance Quarterly* 38(2): 271–289.

Montaigne, Michel de. 1966. Appendix J. In H. P. Pafford, ed., *The Winter's Tale.* Arden Shakespeare. London and New York: Methuen.

Moore, Gerald. 2011. *Politics of the Gift: Exchanges in Poststructuralism.* Edinburgh: Edinburgh University Press.

Morgan, Appleton. 1894. *Introduction, The Comedy of Errors, The Bankside Shakespeare.* New York: The Shakespeare Press.

Muir, Kenneth. 1977. The uncomic pun. In *The Singularity of Shakespeare and Other Essays.* New York: Barnes and Noble Books.

Munn, Nancy. 1969. The effectiveness of symbols in Murngin rite and myth. In R. Spencer, ed., *Forms of Symbolic Action, 1969 Proceedings of the American Ethnological Society.* Seattle, WA: University of Washington Press.

Nadeau, Raymond E. 1952. The Progymnasmata of Aphthonius in translation. *Speech Monographs* 19: 281.

Nederman, Gary, Karen Green and Constant Mews. 2005. *The Living Body Politic: The Diversification of Organic Metaphors in Nicole Oresme and Christine de Pizan.* https://www.brepolsonline.net/doi/10.1484/M.DISPUT-EB.3.3267.

Nöth, Winfried. 1990. *Handbook of Semiotics.* Bloomington, IN: Indiana University Press.

Nuttall, Anthony David. 2007. *Shakespeare the Thinker.* New Haven, CT: Yale University Press.

Oates, Joyce Carol. 1966. The ambiguity of *Troilus and Cressida. The Shakespeare Quarterly* 17(2): 141–150.

Obeyesekere, Gananath. 1984. *Medusa's Hair.* Chicago, IL: University of Chicago Press.

Orgel, Stephen. 1996a. Introduction. In *The Winter's Tale.* New York: Oxford University Press.

Orgel, Stephen. 1996b. *Impersonations: The Performance of Gender in Shakespeare's England.* Cambridge: Cambridge University Press,

Ortony, Andrew. 1993. *Metaphor and Thought* (2nd ed). Cambridge: Cambridge University Press.

Overholser, Winfred. 1959. Shakespeare's psychiatry- and after. *Shakespeare Quarterly* 10(3): 463–479.

Padraic, Monaghan, Richard C. Shillcock, Morten H. Christiansen and Simon Kirby. 2014. How arbitrary is language? *Philosophical Transactions: Biological Sciences* 369(1651): 1–12. Language as a Multimodal Phenomenon: Implications for Language Learning, Processing and Evolution.

Panofsky, Erwin. 1991. *Perspective as Symbolic Form*. New York: Zone Books.

Paul, Robert. 2000. *Sons or sonnets: Nature and culture in a Shakespearean anthropology*. *Current Anthropology* 41(1): 1–9.

Paul, Robert. 2016. *Mixed Messages: Cultural and Genetic Inheritance in the Constitution of Human Society*. Chicago, IL: University of Chicago Press, 2016.

Paul, Robert. n.d. *The not-so-tragical history of Fortinbras*, Prince of Norway.

Peirce, Charles S. 1998. *The Essential Peirce*. Volume 2. Peirce edition Project. Bloomington, IN: Indiana University Press.

Plato. 1982. *The Cratylus, The Dialogues of Plato*, Benjamin Jowett, trans. Oxford: Oxford University Press/London: Low and Byrdon.

Platt, Peter. 2009. *Shakespeare and the Culture of Paradox*. Farnham, England: Ashgate Publishing Co.

Puttenham, George. 1904. *The Art of English Poesie*, The Third Book of Ornament, Chapter 1 ("Of Ornament Poetical") In G. Gregory Smith, ed., *Elizabethan Critical Essays*. Oxford: Clarendon Press.

Quiller-Couch, Arthur. 1916. Shakespeare's later workmanship: "The Winter's Tale". *The North American Review* 203(726): 749–760.

Quine, Willard V. O. 1966. The ways of paradox. In *The Ways of Paradox and Other Essays*. New York: Random House.

Quintilian. 1921. *The Institutio Oratoria of Quintilian, with an English Translation by H.E. Butler*, 4 vols. London: William Heinemann.

Rabin, Sheila. 2010. Nicolaus copernicus. In Edward N. Zalta, ed., *The Stanford Encyclopedia of Philosophy* (Fall 2010 Edition). http://plato.stanford.edu/archives/fall2010/entries/copernicus/.

Rabkin, Norman. 1981. *Shakespeare and the Problem of Meaning*. Chicago, IL: The University of Chicago Press.

Ramasubramanian, K. 1994. Modification of the earlier Indian planetary theory by the Kerala astronomers (c. 1500 AD) and the implied heliocentric picture of planetary motion. *Current Science* 66: 784–790.

Rappaport, Roy. 1979. The obvious aspects of ritual. In *Ecology, Meaning and Religion*. Berkeley, CA: University of California Press.

Ridgely, Beverly. 1958. Saint-Amant and the 'New Astronomy'. *The Modern Language Review* 53(1).

Roach, Joseph. 2009. Herbert Blau and the makeup of memory. *The Winter's Tale. Modern Language Quarterly* 70(1): 117–131.

Rosche, E. and B. Lloyd, eds. 1978. *Cognition and Categorization*. Hillsdale, NJ: Lawrence Erlbaum Associates.

Rouse, Alfred L. 1971. *The Elizabethan Renaissance: the Life of Society*. London: Macmillan.

Ruiter, David. 2007. Shakespeare and hospitality: Opening. *The Winter's Tale. Mediterranean Studies*, 16: 157–177.

Sahlins, Marshall D. 1972. *Stone Age Economics*. Chicago, IL/New York: Aldine Atherton.

Sapir, Edward. 1934. Symbolism. In Edwin Seligman, ed., *Encyclopedia of the Social Sciences* 14. New York, pp. 492–495.

Saussure, Ferdinand de. 1983. *Course in General Linguistics*, Charles Bally and Albert Sechehaye, eds., Roy Harris, *La Salle* trans. Illinois, IL: Open Court.

Schanzer, Ernest. 1955. The problem of *Julius Caesar*. *Shakespeare Quarterly* 6(3): 297–308.

Schechner, Richard. 1985. *Between Theatre and Anthropology*. Philadelphia, PA: University of Pennsylvania Press.

Semino, E. and G. Steen. 2008. Metaphor in Literature. In R. Gibbs, Jr., ed., *The Cambridge Handbook of Metaphor and Thought*. (Cambridge Handbooks in Psychology). Cambridge: Cambridge University Press, pp. 232–246.

Serpieri, Alessandro. 1998. Perspectivism and poliphony [sic] in Shakespeare's dramatic language (notes, and difficult notes, on Shakespeare's language). *Hungarian Journal of English and American Studies*, 4(1/2) *Theory and Criticism, Part I*: 61–62.

Shapiro, Steven A. 1964. *Romeo and Juliet*: Reversals, contraries, transformations and ambivalence. *College English* 25(7): 501.

Shea, W. R. and M. Artigas. 2004. *Galileo in Rome: The Rise and Fall of a Troublesome Genius*. New York: Oxford University Press

Shell, Marc. 1988. *The End of Kinship: 'Measure for Measure,' Incest, and the Ideal of Universal Siblinghood*. Stanford, CA: Stanford University Press.

Shickman, Allan. 1977. Turning pictures in Shakespeare's England. *The Art Bulletin*, 59(1): 67–70.

Shickman, Allan. 1978. The 'perspective glass' in Shakespeare's Richard II. *Studies in English Literature, 1500–1900* 18(2). Elizabethan and Jacobean Drama, Spring, 1978: 219.

Shiff, Abraham S. 2012. Mortal coil and stars with a train of fire: Hamlet Q2 metaphors for the Copernican astronomy and Kepler's nova of 1604. http://triggs.djvu.org/global-language.com/ENFOLDED/SHIFF/MortalCoilDraft16.pdf.

Shklovsky, Viktor. 1917. Art as technique. https://web.archive.org/web/20091205211412/http:/ www.vahidnab.com/defam.htm.

Shore, Bradd. 1982. *Sala'ilua: A Samoan Mystery*. New York: Columbia University Press.

Shore, Bradd. 1996. *Culture in Mind: Culture, Cognition and the Problem of Meaning*. New York: Oxford University Press.

Shore, Bradd. 1997. Keeping the conversation going: An interview with Jerome Bruner. *Ethos* 25(1): 7–62.

Siraisi, N. 1990. *Medieval and Early Renaissance Medicine: An Introduction to Knowledge and Practice*. Chicago, IL: University of Chicago Press.

Smith, Warren D. 1958. The Elizabethan rejection of judicial astrology and Shakespeare's practice. *Shakespeare Quarterly* 9(2): 159–176.

Snell, K. D. M. 1989. English historical continuity and the culture of capitalism: the work of alan Macfarlane. *History Workshop* 27: 154–163.

Snider, D. J. 1875. Shakespeare's *Winter's Tale*. *The Journal of Speculative Philosophy* 9(1): 80–98.

Sondheim, Moritz. 1939. Shakespeare and the astrology of his time. *Journal of the Warburg Institute*, 2(3): 243–259.

Stahl, William. 1970. Aristarchus of Samos. In Pierre Abailard, ed., *Dictionary of Scientific Biography* 1, 1970. New York: Charles Scribner's Sons, pp. 246–250.

Stirling, Brents. 1956. Or else were this a savage spectacle. In *Unity in Shakespearian Tragedy: The Interplay of Theme and Character*. New York: Columbia University Press, pp. 40–54.

Stubbes, Philip. 1583/1933. *The Anatomie of Abuses*, 1583. Reprinted by New Shakespeare Society, Series 6, 4, 12, part II, p. 56. London: Richard Jones.

Thomas, Keith. 1971. *Religion and the Decline of Magic: Studies in Popular Beliefs in Sixteenth and Seventeenth Century England*. Rockport, MA: Peter Smith Publisher, Inc.

Tilley, Morris P. 1926. A parody of Euphues in Romeo and Juliet. *Modern Language Notes* 41(1): 1–8.

Tillyard, Eustace M. W. 1955. *The Elizabethan World Picture*. New York: Knopf.

Tönnies, Ferdinand. 1887/1955. *Community and Association (Gemeinschaft und gesellschaft)*. London: Routledge & Kegan Paul.

Trilling, Lionel. 1973. *Sincerity and Authenticity*. Cambridge, MA: Harvard University Press.

Turner, Mark. 1996. *The Literary Mind: The Origins of Thought and Language*. New York: Oxford University Press.

Turner, Victor. 1969. *The Ritual Process: Structure and Anti-Structure*, Livingston, NJ: Transaction Publishers,

Turner, Victor. 1970. *The Forest of Symbols*. Ithaca, NY: Cornell University Press.

Turner, Victor. 1974. *Dramas, Fields and Metaphors: Symbolic Action in Human Society*. Ithaca, NY: Cornell University Press.

Turner, Victor. 2001. *From Ritual to Theatre: The Human Seriousness of Play*. New York: PAJ Publications.

Usher, Peter. 1999. Hamlet's transformation. *Elizabethan Review* 7(1): 48–64.

Usher, Peter. 2005. Hamlet and the new philosophy. *The Oxfordian* 8: 93–109.

Usher, Peter. 2007. *Hamlet's Universe*. (2nd ed). San Diego: Aventine Press.

Usher, Peter. 2010. *Shakespeare and the Dawn of Modern Science*. Amherst, NY: Cambria Press.

Van Doren, Mark. 1939. *Shakespeare*. New York: New York Review Books.

Vives, Juan Luis. 1913. *On Education: A Translation of the De Trandendis Disciplinis*, Foster Watson, ed. Cambridge: Cambridge University Press.

Watson, Fred. 2007. *Stargazer: The Life and Times of the Telescope*. Crow's Nest, NSW: Allen & Unwin.

Weber, Alan. 2012. What did Shakespeare know about the Copernican revolution. *Romanian Journal of English Studies* 9(1): 351–365.

Weinstock, Stefan. 1971. *Divus Julius*. Oxford: Oxford University Press.

Werner, Heinz and Bernard Kaplan. 1984. *Symbol Formation: An Organismic Developmental Approach to the Psychology of Language*. Rahway, NJ: Lawrence Erlbaum Associates.

Whitaker, Virgil K. 1953. *Shakespeare's Use of Learning: An Inquiry into the Growth of His Mind & Art*. San Marino, CA: The Huntington Library.

White, Stephen D. and Richard T. Vann. 1983. The invention of English individualism: Alan Macfarlane and the modernization of premodern England. *Social History* 8(3): 345–363.

Whittier, Gayle. 1989. The sonnet's body and the body sonnetized. *Romeo and Juliet. The Shakespeare Quarterly* 40(1): 27–41, Spring.

Wilder, Lina P. 2014. *Shakespeare's Memory Theatre: Recollection, Properties, and Character*. Cambridge: Cambridge University Press.

Wrigley, E. A. and R. S. Schofield. 1981. *The Population History of England*. London: Edward Arnold Publishers.

Wyllie, Robert. 2018. Reconsidering tyranny and tyrannicide in Aquinas's *De Regno*. *Perspectives on Political Science* 47(3): 154–160.

INDEX

Page numbers in *italic* refer to figures